AF576585

IMAGES OF RELIGION
IN AUSTRALIAN ART

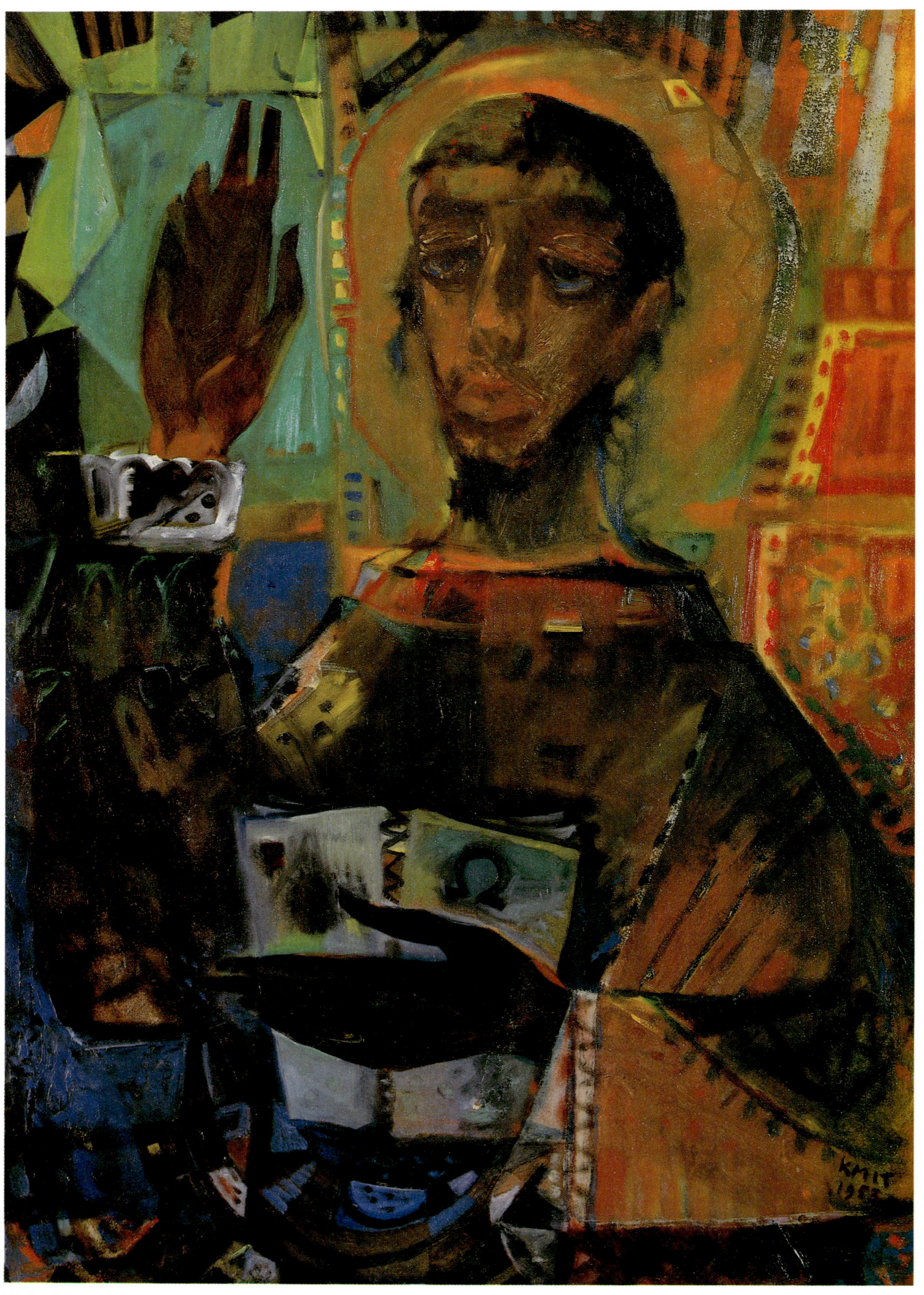

Michael Kmit, *The Evangelist John Mark*, 1953, oil on canvas, 95 x 70 cm

IMAGES OF RELIGION
IN AUSTRALIAN ART

ROSEMARY CRUMLIN

ABORIGINAL ART TEXT BY JUDITH RYAN

BAY BOOKS

Published by Bay Books, 61-69 Anzac Parade, Kensington, NSW 2033
Designed by Susan Kinealy
National Library of Australia card number and
ISBN 1 86256 291 1
Typeset by Savage Type Pty Ltd, Brisbane
Printed in Singapore by Toppan Printing
BB88

CONTENTS

ACKNOWLEDGEMENTS

This book has developed from a long-time concern with the relationship between religion and art, and more specifically, between contemporary religious expression and contemporary painting in Australia. It was written on the occasion of an exhibition, *Images of Religion,* at the National Gallery of Victoria, 30 November 1988–30 January 1989. The decision for the exhibition was taken during the Directorship of Patrick McCaughey, and held with the new Director, Rodney Wilson.

Many people contributed advice and various kinds of assistance over the period of the research and writing of this book. I am grateful to the publishers, Bay Books, and especially to George Barber, Annette Robinson, Elenie Poulos, Tony Barker and Tracy O'Brien.

Jim Briglia, Margaret Woodward, Herman Lombaerts, Jane and John Dillenberger offered valuable theological insights; Jim Briglia and Margaret Woodward read sections of the manuscript. My earlier research thesis on the Blake Prize for Religious Art provided a valuable resource for some of this book, and I recognize the encouragement given me by Patrick McCaughey, John Gregory and Margaret Plant.

My special thanks to those artists represented here who graciously consented to speak about their work, and who also read the relevant section of the manuscript—Davida Allen, Arthur Boyd, John Perceval, Louis Kahan, Albert Tucker, Eric Smith, Elwyn Lynn, Constance Stokes, Mike Kitching, Rodney Milgate, Clifton Pugh, Desiderius Orban, Keith Looby, Alun Leach-Jones, Warren Breninger, Asher Bilu, Brett Whiteley, Leonard French, Lawrence Daws, Jan Murray, John Walker, James Gleeson, Irene Barberis and Alan Oldfield. Pat Counihan spoke for Noel

Counihan, Lyn Williams for Fred Williams and Merle Kemp for Roger Kemp.

I acknowledge the generosity and competence of Judith Ryan, Curator of Aboriginal Art at the National Gallery of Victoria, who wrote the section on Aboriginal painting, and with whom it has been a delight to work.

I thank those colleagues and friends who walked with me along the way, including Ian Brown who also worked with the curating of the exhibition, and Ken Hood at the National Gallery of Victoria; the librarians of the State Library of Victoria and the National Gallery of Victoria; Pauline Smith and Margaret Doyle; the leaders of the Congregations in the Institute of the Sisters of Mercy, Australia. I thank especially Rupert and Anna Murdoch for friendship and encouragement.

Thanks are due to the National Gallery of Victoria; Art Gallery of New South Wales; Australian National Gallery; Art Gallery of South Australia; Warrnambool Art Gallery; Mildura Art Gallery; Penrith Regional Art Gallery; Monash University Gallery; Geelong City Gallery; City of Hamilton Gallery; Museum of Contemporary Art, Brisbane; Wesley Church, Melbourne; St James Church, Sydney; Notre Dame de Toute Grace, Assy, France; Canisius College, Sydney; St Paul's College of the University of Sydney; St Patrick's College, Manly; Griffith University, Brisbane; Brisbane College of Advanced Education; Robert Holmes à Court Collection; Gabrielle Pizzi Gallery; Maurice and Helen Alther and the other private collectors who allowed works from their collections to be used in this book.

FOREWORD

The story of Australian art has entered a rich phase. This country now has a proud record of artistic achievement which has developed its own momentum and is distinguishable from that of other cultures. The serious study and critique of this art has also made significant advances. The pioneering work of scholars such as Bernard Smith, Franz Philipp, Ursula Hoff and Joseph Burke, who devoted their energies over many years to the establishment of a sound intellectual framework for the development of Australian art history, has borne abundant fruit. Today fine collections of Australian art, in public galleries and museums or in private hands, are the object of lively research. Each year sees a growing number of impressive exhibitions which are accompanied by catalogues, splendidly illustrated and meticulously documented. Works are presented in contexts which foster the growing interest of the public and at the same time stimulate further research and sensitive probing by the many able and enthusiastic scholars dedicated to the study of Australian art.

This book and the exhibition which it heralds, focus on a thematic category which is as ancient as art itself. In the great civilizations of antiquity religious imagery held a dominant place. Christianity, after an initial period of uncertainty, strengthened and indeed intensified the links between art and religion. Icons, cult statues, mosaics, cathedral sculptures, fresco sequences, ornamented reliquaries and illuminated manuscripts, all attest to the importance of art for the Church throughout the Middle Ages. The bonds were no less strong in the Renaissance; creative geniuses like Michelangelo and Leonardo never questioned the validity of religious themes as a vehicle for artistic expression. Also, the revival of interest in classical antiquity only served to emphasize religious subject matter, with artists marrying Christian and mythological imagery.

It was not until the eighteenth century that the powerful monopoly of religious imagery over art yielded to the dictates of personal taste. Henceforth the scope of art was increasingly widened so that today it ranges from abstraction to the depiction of every day objects in photographic detail.

As Rosemary Crumlin observes, the Australian art which developed from white settlement never had to make the journey from an all-pervasive religious ambience to one that was predominantly secular, since it took root when explicit reference to religion was already a personal option or the result of an occasional public commission. The paintings assembled here, however, reveal that for a surprisingly large number of gifted Australian artists, the relationship between art and religion has continued to provide a creative challenge. Most of the works, with the exception of the Aboriginal group, draw on the Judaeic or Christian traditions, which allows us to locate them in a context of great antiquity. At the same time we are alerted to much that is new and provocatively challenging in each artist's response.

The inclusion of a group of Aboriginal paintings in this survey does not simply ensure a comprehensive representation of Australian art. The context for these religious images is significantly different. They reflect a culture which is permeated with the power of the sacred, and in which art is not so much a personal comment as a means of presenting to the initiated certain hidden mysteries. But they also express a state of transition from shared celebration to the open market place, where works of art compete for attention on an individual basis. They remind us that in our twentieth-century world, a conscious effort is required to penetrate beneath the surface of material things whether they be the products of the latest technology or creations of the artist.

If we wish to rise beyond the level of responding to works of art as mere furnishings or decorative ensembles, then we must be ready to reflect on the source of their vitality and to taste the joy, hope, anguish or fear which lie behind them. This book's focus on the explicitly religious content of Australian art provides us with the opportunity to contemplate afresh the liberating wisdom of great religious traditions without flinching from the fact that such traditions are always a prey to manipulation for lesser and sometimes quite destructive ends. This book, I hope, will also prompt lovers of Australian art to delve deeper into what is now a rich inheritance.

MARGARET M. MANION,

PROFESSOR OF FINE ARTS,
THE UNIVERSITY OF MELBOURNE,
AUSTRALIA.

21 JUNE, 1988

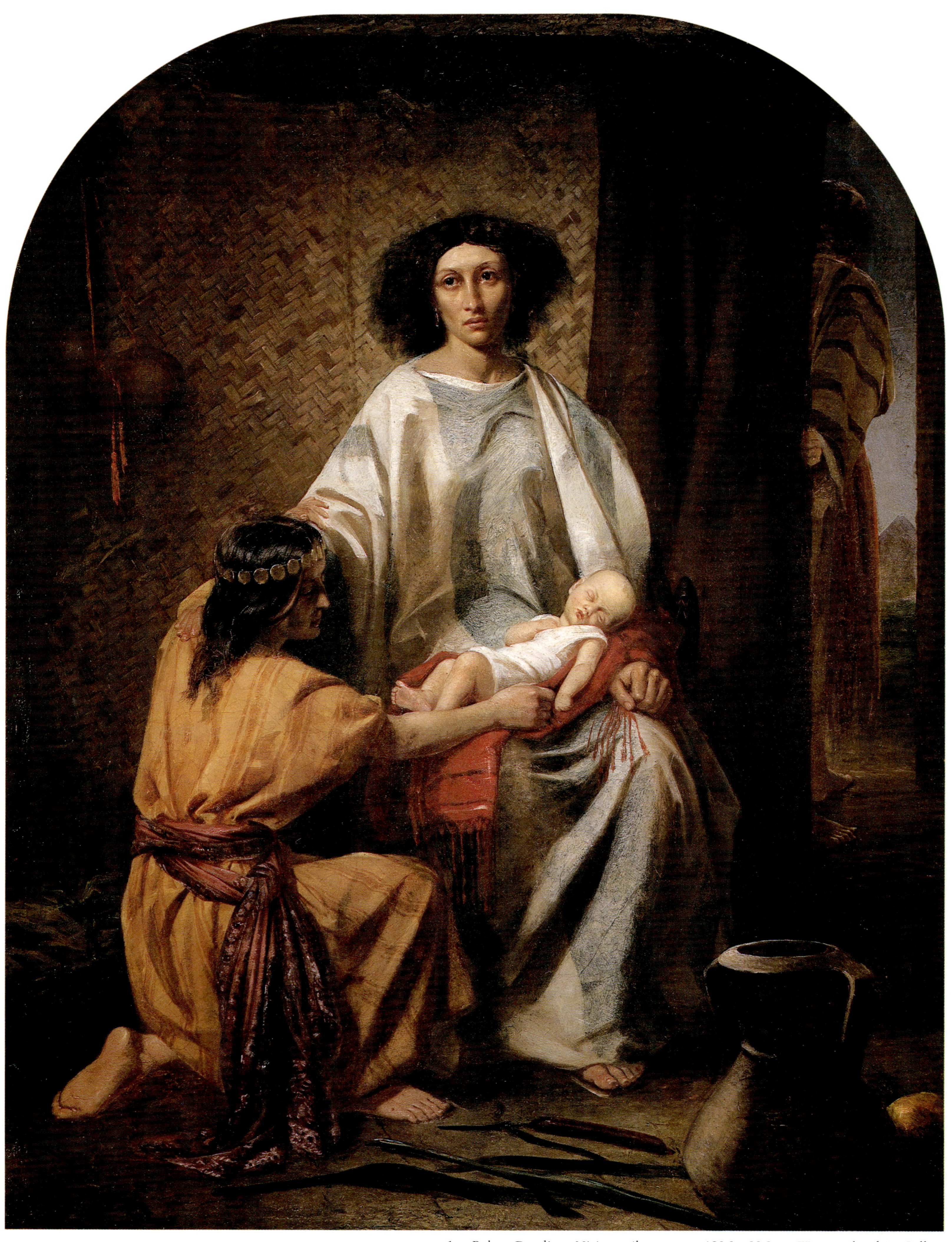

1 Robert Dowling, *Miriam,* oil on canvas, 120.3 x 99.9 cm, Warrnambool Art Gallery.

INTRODUCTION

It is impossible to say when an idea is conceived, for its source is often hidden in the darkness, awaiting a moment of light. But I do remember seeing Arthur Boyd's two *Crucifixions* (Plates 75, 76) when they were first exhibited at the Australian Galleries in Melbourne in 1981. A woman crucified. A man crucified. What does he mean? Why not? To see them there, looking like yet unlike all the crucifixes I had ever seen, was a shock. But right. A woman and a man together; separate, but suffering together in the Australian landscape. I think it was the simplicity and the courage within the act of painting, and then the exhibiting of these two images, which I held close. At the time I wrote to Arthur Boyd and asked that if it were ever possible to have an exhibition of Australian religious art, would he lend these two?

Many of the other paintings in this collection suggested themselves. Simply, it would have been impossible to leave them out, for they are key paintings in the history of Australian art and they make use of some image of religion in a way that bespeaks integrity, often belief, even inspiration.

With these very inexact criteria, Ian Brown and I, who together curated the exhibition Images of Religion at the National Gallery of Victoria, set about making the initial selection. We each bring a lifetime of commitment to both art and religion and were surprised at how easily we arrived at decisions. We agreed that we were not concerned with religious art for worship ('sacred art'), nor were we simply concerned with spirituality in art. An exhibition about the spiritual in Australian painting would have opened floodgates for selection, for it could have included any work—or only abstract art if we had adopted the criteria used in the recent American Spirituality in Art exhibition. We agreed with the suggestion of Patrick McCaughey, then director of the National Gallery of Victoria, that the exhibition should contain paintings with explicit religious reference—images that have their origin in religion, even though the artist may in fact be protesting against institutionalized religion.

As well as a representative range of paintings by many artists, we decided to include three 'islands of reflection', one for Arthur Boyd, one for Leonard French, and one for Aboriginal painters. The decision to include Aboriginal art was inevitable. For Aboriginal people there is no separation between life and religion; everything for them is a unity, a rhythm of the sacred, filled with meaning. Symbolic expression is an integral part of their culture. This, together with their comparatively recent fluency with visual expression in paint on canvas and board, very wide range of paintings. Judith Ryan, curator of Aboriginal Art at the National Gallery of Victoria, was the key person in making this selection and in writing about the paintings.

Writing about the paintings has been for me like going on many journeys of discovery. In selecting biographical details of the artist I tried to respect the sweep of the artist's life while still taking cognizance of the explicit nature of this book, usually giving priority to those aspects of the person's life history which offer the reader and viewer new ways of understanding or experiencing the painting. The writing about the painting aims to be respectful of the open-ended nature of the symbolic experience. Sometimes the text is descriptive of the historical circumstances surrounding the creation of the work; at other times it explores the iconography (subject matter) or the iconology (symbol system).

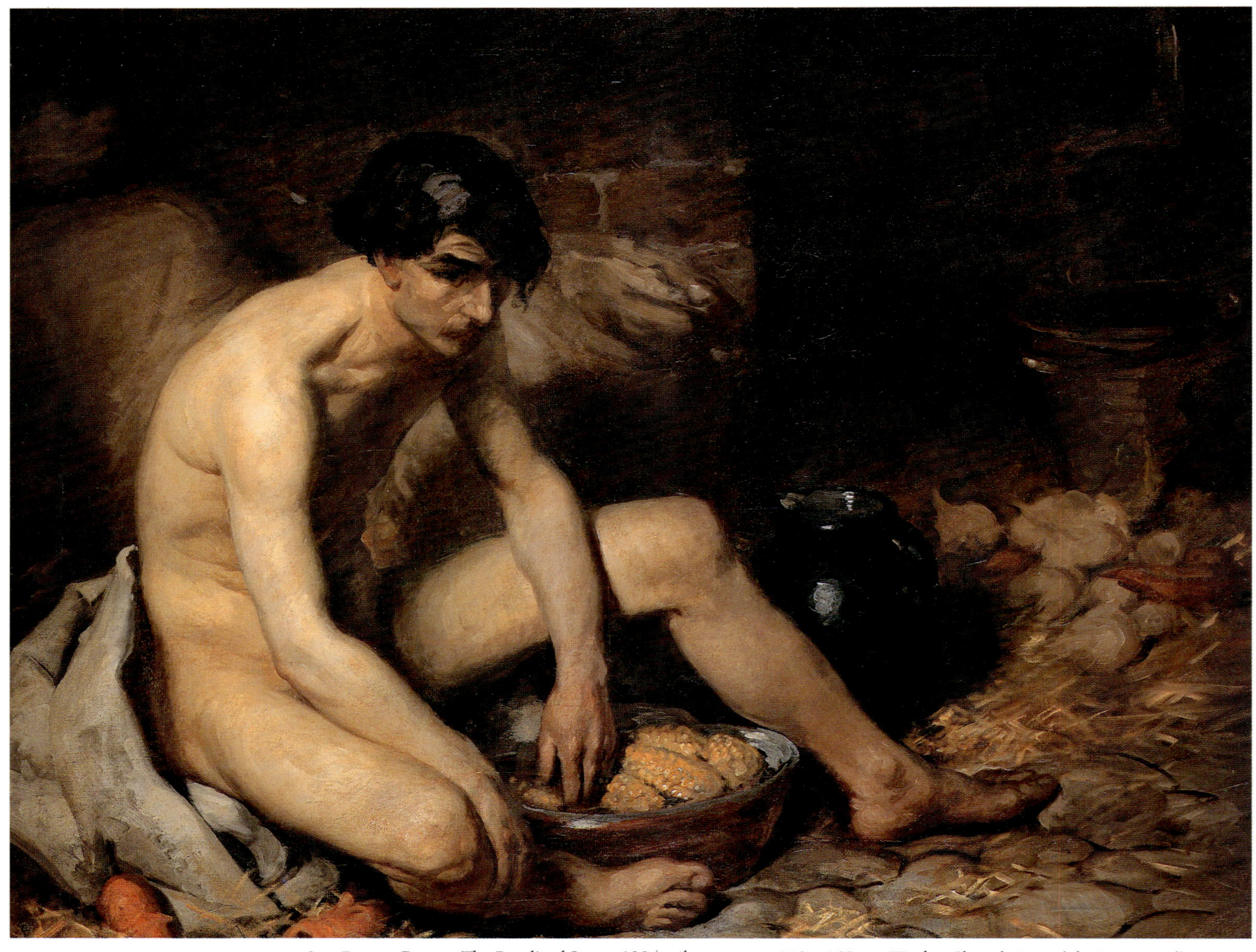

2 Rupert Bunny, *The Prodigal Son,* c.1904, oil on canvas, 119 x 158 cm, Wesley Church, Lonsdale Street, Melbourne.

Usually it also refers to the formal qualities and the methods the artist has used, when these are seen to contribute to the power of the work. My concern has been to work across the various layers that constitute the final work. When parallels are drawn with other paintings, I have tried to refer to works reproduced in this book, although many works also relate very closely to contemporary European and American paintings and movements.

Many of the artists have been consulted about their lives and work and the interrelationship between these two. Some of the interviews took place in the 1970s when I was doing a study on the Blake Prize for Religious Art, but most are more recent. Many artists have checked and responded to the manuscript, and their suggestions have been incorporated where possible.

The most important part of this book is the reproduction of the paintings. No words can substitute for the immediacy of the experience of the painting. Many of these works repay sustained meditation; their mystery unfolds slowly. Because works of art are symbolic, as well as containing identifiable symbols and signs of a religion, each painting will invite response in different ways for different people. Any change of context, whether of geography or time, can radically affect the way a work is understood, even seen. For instance, the paintings of the 1940s look different to those of us who have lived through the threat of nuclear disaster from what they would have looked to those whose understanding of war was edged with the experience of World War II. Similarly, Aboriginal painting will reveal itself to us within the context of our own history and prejudices. The ways we choose to frame our lives, and how tight we make these frames, will influence what we are able to see. Paintings are symbols which reveal and invite; they are not doctrines which define and oblige.

Many of the paintings in this book take the Australian context, even the landscape, as their starting point. Religion is seen as part of everyday life experience. That this is not new in the history of religious art is often forgotten. Byzantine mosaics glitter with the gold and pomp of Christian kings and queens; Renaissance paintings are set in Florence or Siena and peopled with their citizens. Michelangelo's *Last Judgment* is full of portraits of Church dignitaries, many of them in hell. So it should come as no surprise to find Mary and Joseph in the Australian outback or Christ looking like a labourer or Eve a young schoolgirl, or to recognize the Garden of Eden as a local bush reserve or a Queensland cane farm. To find new ways of clothing the myths and symbols at the heart of a belief system is a guarantee against death from a withering familiarity. Religion, like art, must continually find ways that speak out of everyday life experience. Otherwise it dies of irrelevance and boredom.

Before 1940 there was little religious art in Australia. In Europe the divorce between art and the Church had long been declared, and artists, although surrounded by the monuments and expressions of a past religious culture, rarely found in institutional religions either patronage or inspiration. In Australia, there was no such divorce because there had never been a marriage. Colonial Australia was born out of scepticism and pessimism as a penal colony; its earliest settlers were, it might easily be shown, people without strong religious affiliation and certainly without much awareness of or interest in art. The established Churches were more concerned with the nurturing of faith than with the cultivation of beauty. Sacred art, when it could be afforded, tended—at least in Catholic churches—to be imported, mass produced and often saccharine and sentimental. Exceptions to this do exist, but the fact remains that the Churches in Australia rarely took the best artists seriously enough to commission their work.

In spite of this, some nineteenth-century artists occasionally turned to religious subject matter in their painting. Many of them were expatriates, working in London, but often painting for an Australian private market. Robert Dowling's *Miriam* (Plate 1) for example, was painted in London and inspired by Hanna Moor's sacred drama *Moses in the Bulrushes*. Rupert Bunny's *Prodigal Son* (Plate 2), like his many religious paintings, was also completed in London. The wayward son, a surprisingly modern young man, languishes before a bowl of corn cobs. He is the tragic hero of this Pre-Raphaelite morality play–sermon in paint. Another painting that peoples a Gospel narrative with contemporary figures is Blamire Young's *Flight into Egypt* (Plate 3). Again, the space is that of a theatre stage, and Mary and Joseph are its very beautiful players. Years later, the Anglican church of St James, Sydney, commissioned Grace Cossington Smith, Roy de Maistre and Roland Wakelin, all outstanding artists, to paint the walls of the crypt (Plate 4). This commission stands as an exception to generally lukewarm attitudes on the part of the Churches, even over the years covered in this book.

With the founding of the Blake Prize for Religious Art in 1950, many artists turned to the Scriptures for subject matter in their paintings, some of them for the first time. The late thirties and the forties had seen some private religious painting, often in response to the threat and devastation of the war. James Gleeson's *Sower* (1944), based on Millet's interpretation of the parable, was a violent, surrealistic protest against war. Roy de Maistre, reconverted to Catholicism in London, worked often from the

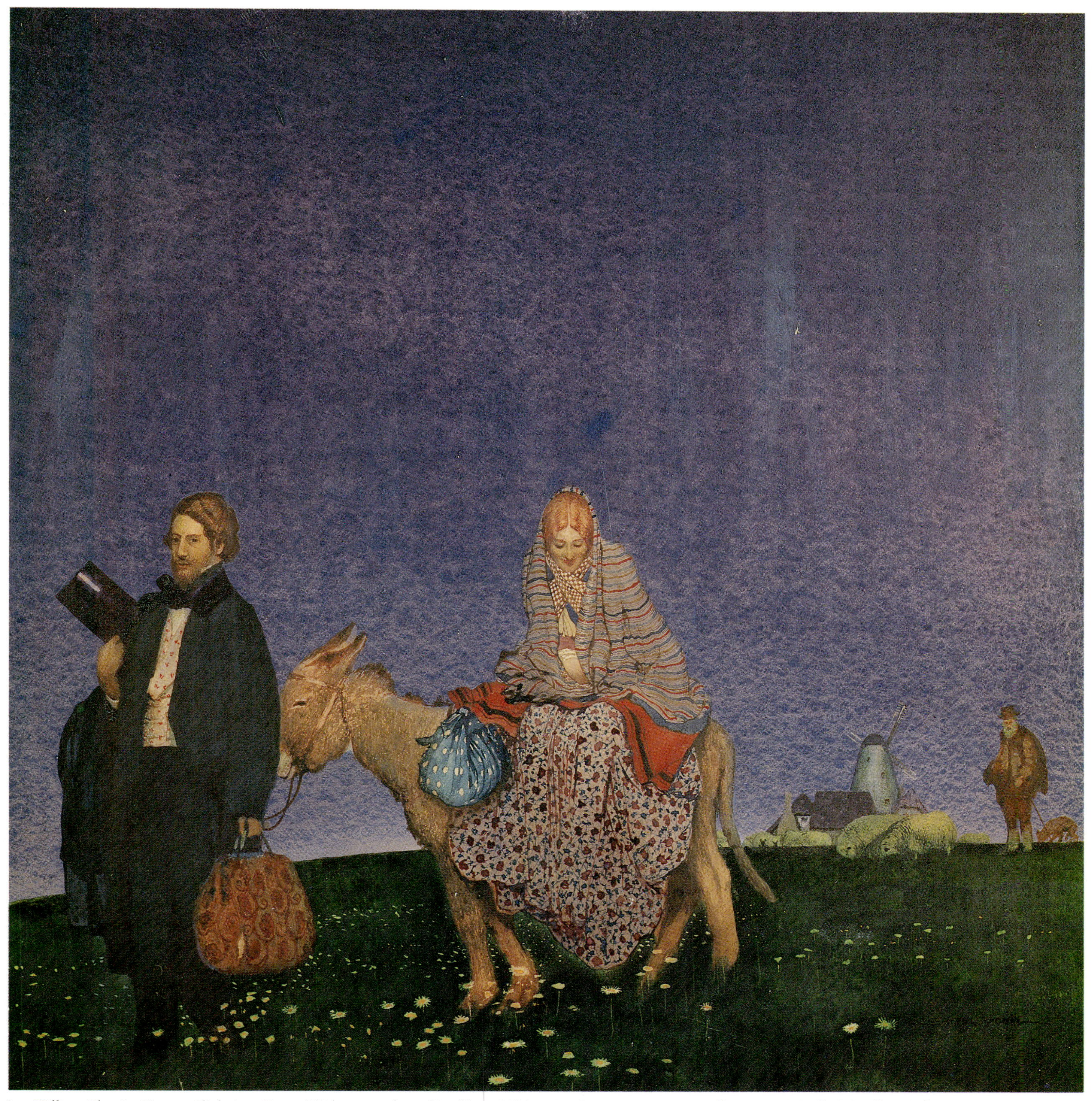

3 William Blamire Young, *Flight into Egypt,* 1924, watercolour, 63 x 64 cm, Mildura Art Centre, permanent collection, originally R.D. Elliot Collection.

Bible and became associated with the Sacred Art Renewal Movement in England. In Melbourne, Russian immigrant Danila Vassilieff used religious subjects, often ironically, sometimes humorously and with zest. In Melbourne also, the Boyd family, always deeply religious, provided its younger generation, including Arthur Boyd and his brother-in-law John Perceval, with an easy familiarity with the Scriptures as texts of faith and guidance for living.

The year 1951 saw the first Blake Prize exhibition in Sydney. The prize was the idea of Michael Scott, a Jesuit priest, and Richard Morley, a Jewish businessman, who saw in it a way of encouraging the Church to become patron of the arts and remedying what they considered the appalling state of the art in churches. They also hoped it would bring artists back not only to religious subject matter but to the Church. The Blake committee looked to the European Sacred Art Renewal Movement centred in France for inspiration. In particular, they admired the small church of Notre Dame de Toute Grâce at Assy in the French Alps. There, within the one building, priest, architect and modern artists had worked together in creative dialogue. At the invitation of the French Dominicans Père Devémy and Marie-Alain Couturier, artists as disparate in style and religious allegiance as Richier, Chagall, Lipchitz, Matisse, Lurçat, Rouault and Léger had created images of great religious power (Plate 5). The founders of the Blake Prize hoped that something similar would happen in Australia.

Many of the paintings in this book were entered in the Blake Prize competition. All but three of the works represented from the fifties and sixties were winners or exhibitors or were rejected from the Blake. In those decades the Blake was one of the most prestigious prizes in the country; hundreds of paintings were submitted each year, and about seventy were exhibited; the prize money of one hundred pounds in the first year was regarded as substantial. The Blake Prize continues today, but after the mid-sixties its importance to artists was mitigated by the changed marketing scene for painters, who joined the 'stables' of art dealers or who later looked to the Australia Council and other organizations for support and patronage. The relationship between the Blake Prize committee with its high-minded goals and the work submitted is complex. Some artists were committed Christians, but many were hardly aware of the goals; most were not church-going, and a large number were without any religious affiliation at all. The competition provided them with an opportunity to exhibit and a stimulus to paint at a time when there were few such opportunities. The works reproduced here from the fifties are a microcosm of Australian painting (and especially Sydney painting) in this important decade. They reveal the penchant of Sydney painters for a neo-Byzantine richness and a preference for the colour rhythms and structures of Cézanne. Clear too is the move, after the 1953 French Painting Today exhibition, towards a linear abstract expressionism based on Europe and not America.

The award of the 1961 Blake Prize to Stanislaus Rapotec's *Meditating on Good Friday* (Plate 38), precipitated a major crisis within the Blake committee. Many of the committee, including two of its founding members, Michael Scott and Peter Kenny, wanted the award disallowed, because they considered the painting too abstract. Religious art, they maintained, must have recognizable subject matter or at least include traditional symbols of religion. Mindful of Sydney art's rush into various forms of abstraction, and the danger of losing the support of many of the best artists, others on the committee moved for compromise. Any art, they came to say, regardless of style, was religious if the artist considered it so. Placing a work in a religious art competition and giving it a religious title was sufficient to make it religious. Another position was taken up by the advocates of total abstraction. As the truths of religion were timeless, other-worldly and transcendent, they said, abstract art was their most appropriate expression. It made possible a depth dimension without the distraction of figuration. For those on the committee who argued from another theological position, such a stance was anti-incarnational. God having become man, his story was already told in the Scriptures, and it was the artist's task and gift to re-present these truths in figurative language of the present day. The purpose of religious art, they said, was to inspire or to teach.

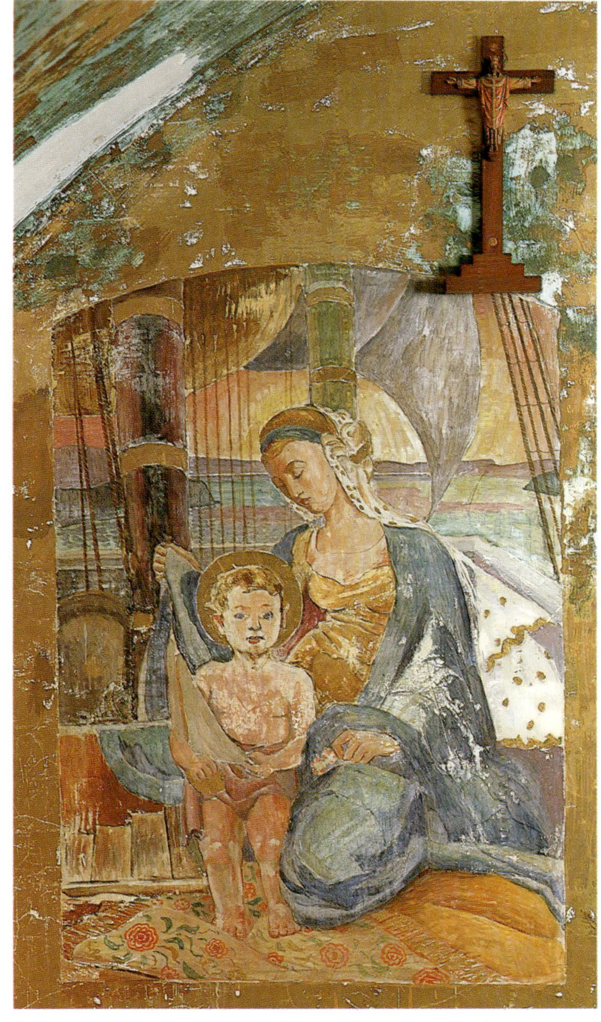

4 Grace Cossington Smith, Roy de Maistre and Roland Wakelin, Crypt of St James Church Sydney (detail).

Fortunately for the history of religious art in this country, those who wanted compromise won through. The Blake Prize exhibition in the sixties and early seventies occasioned some of the best abstract art in the country, much of it reflecting the influence of Eastern philosophies or a residual Theosophy, often mediated through the works of American abstract expressionists or their European counterparts. For artists such as Roger Kemp, Rodney Milgate, Desiderius Orban and Asher Bilu, the act of painting often took on a mystical dimension in which the artist enters into the experience without any clear, predetermined plan. Giving a title is done at the end, after the painting is finished, and thus the title carries less significance than in figurative or narrative art. Abstract art lends itself to myriad interpretations, and titles are clues to experience rather than descriptions of the artist's intention. The same painting often appeared in different exhibitions bearing a different title, which gave the impression that there was no specific content in an abstract painting, nor any objective meaning. Formal qualities and aesthetic satisfaction arising from them were seen to be benchmarks of excellence. With the demise of abstraction—or perhaps its exhaustion—sometime in the 1970s in Australia, art and religious art turned again to expressive figuration. Painters again turned to Europe for direction.

The art of the younger generation of painters in this collection, and of those whose work is dated within the last ten years, has not been motivated by the Blake Prize; nor is it usually the result of a simple exploration of a biblical narrative. Davida Allen, Irene Barberis and Warren Breninger paint out of a personal faith—Allen in a struggle to come to terms with Catholicism, Barberis and Breninger from a more serene, evangelical stance which sees God as always immanent in their lives and so in their work. The paintings of John Walker, Peter Booth and Jan Murray on the other hand are implicitly religious in their exploration of a personal search for meaning and societal alienation and oppression. Walker's painting *Mary* (Plate 64) is a protest against the injustices done to Aborigines within the white legal system as well as a more general statement about the historical oppression of women since biblical times.

Other paintings also express concern with issues of injustice and the attitudes of Christians. Sometimes the artist becomes social and religious critic. In his *Laughing Christ* (Plate 44) for example, Noel Counihan paints Christ as a cynic who leers at a Christian culture which allows people who profess to be Christian or Moslem to kill and maim each other; Albert Tucker's Judas (Plate 24) vomits up the coins of bribery; and Arthur Boyd's Nebuchadnezzar (Plate 74) is filled with gold and burns in agony because of his greed and lust. These are paintings that criticize rather than prop up either the Church or the secular society.

That Arthur Boyd has stood throughout his life on the side of peace over war and justice over various forms of injustice is well known. Much of his subject matter is explicitly religious and has its roots in biblical narratives. But these stories are never simply retold. Boyd enters into a dialogue of meaning with the stories and myths so that his finished paintings are at times celebrations of wonder at creation, but at other times they are critically aware social and moral commentaries. The works shown here are some indication of the breadth of his theological understanding as well as the keenness of his insight. They are 'threshold' paintings, whether or not they use scriptural subject matter. The viewer is enticed to the edge of new awareness and vision. Earthy and sensual, they are paintings that take clear life stances—for openness and against voyeurism in its various forms, against a crass materialism and narcissism, and for a new understanding of the potential of women.

Leonard French has worked throughout his life with themes and techniques that easily evoke religious response. His materials and processes convey the richness of medieval manuscripts, mosaics and stained glass. His base symbols—cross, leaf, vine, fish, turtle—are those of religious iconography, as is his habitual use of thinly glazed layers of rich colour and liberal use of gold leaf, so that even when he declares his intention to be otherwise, and names his paintings differently, they still invoke a sacred, mysterious past. *The Seven Days* (Plates 77–83) began as a simple explanation of the origin of the earth but exists now as a magnificent hymn to the unity of the whole of creation. His later work, typified here by *Shooting Place* (Plate 58) is tougher in its condemnation of racism, violence and war.

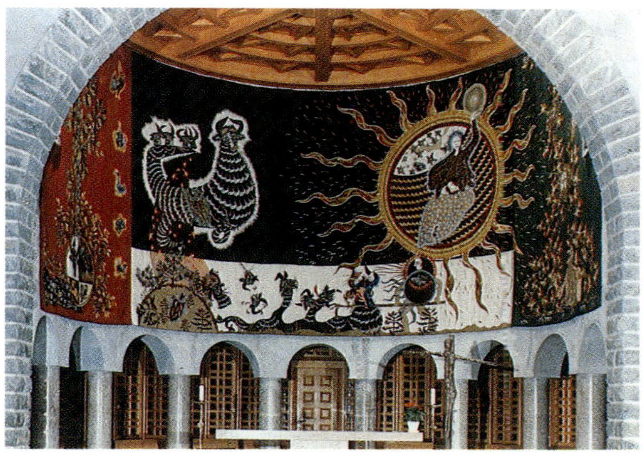

5 Jean Lurçat, *St John's Vision, Apocalypse, Chapter 12*, 1945, Choir Tapestry, Notre Dame de Toute Grace, Assy, France.

The third 'island of reflection' offered in this text is perhaps the only genuinely original Australian art. Aboriginal painting has its origins in the sand designs, the body painting and the ceremonial shields of the corroborees. Painting on canvas and board is a comparatively recent innovation and is, in the minds and intentions of many Aboriginals, including Gary Foley, director of the Aboriginal Arts Board in 1986, always a political act of protest. All the paintings proclaim that, to the Aboriginal people, the land of their group or clan is the land of their Dreaming, is sacred and bound inextricably with their very identity. Because they are a communal people, their paintings as well as the myths and rituals they recall belong to the group. Each painting in this selection carries the name of the group and the location of the land in which the group or clan belongs. To 'read' the paintings as simple designs is not to read at all; it is an act of gross illiteracy born of misunderstanding.

Images of Religion in Australian Art reveals many of the major stylistic trends and the shifting emphases in Australian painting in the years 1940 to 1988; in that sense it presents a history of modern Australian painting through the works of many of its leading artists. But it is more. As religious art, or art that uses images of religion, it also presents a view of religious understanding over the same period and raises serious philosophical and theological questions about the effectiveness of the traditional symbols of religion in an age that openly eschews religion and religious practice and whose art is the product of its secular or profane culture. On the other hand, the paintings do give evidence of the pervasiveness of religious thinking and the power of its myths and symbols. The most successful of these paintings show that the root symbols of religion can still inspire, inform and challenge.

PART I

IMAGES OF RELIGION

PAINTINGS 1940 to 1988

Roy de Maistre
Grace Cossington Smith
Danila Vassilieff
John Perceval
Louis Kahan
Margaret Preston
Justin O'Brien
Sidney Nolan
Weaver Hawkins
John Passmore
Michael Kmit
Albert Tucker
Eric Smith
Elwyn Lynn
Thomas Gleghorn
Roger Kemp
Ian Fairweather
John Coburn
Fred Williams
Godfrey Miller
Constance Stokes
Stanislaus Rapotec
Michael Kitching
Rodney Milgate
Clifton Pugh
George Baldessin
Desiderius Orban
Noel Counihan
Keith Looby
Alun Leach-Jones
Warren Breninger
Peter Booth
Asher Bilu
Brett Whiteley
Leonard French
Davida Allen
Lawrence Daws
John Nixon and Imants Tillers
Jan Murray
John R. Walker
James Gleeson
Irene Barberis
Alan Oldfield

Roy de Maistre

1894–1968

Jacob's Dream, 1940

Oil on composition board
138 × 110 cm
Collection of Helen and Maurice Alther, Melbourne

This picture was completed by Roy de Maistre about 1940. He had been in England for ten years and had been spending about half his time in France, at his beloved Saint-Jean-de-Luz, a fishing village on the Bay of Biscay. *Jacob's Dream* may be set in an idealized version of that harbour.

On a hill in the foreground, framed by trees and enclosed in a womb-like blanket shape, are two figures. One is barefoot, the other wears shoes; one has curly light hair, the other has black and straight hair; one face is turned up in sleep, the other is down. There may be a third figure between them. Directly behind and above is a small boat setting off from the shore. In the distance and high on the canvas are the undulating hills of the far side of the harbour. Everything appears to be alive, yet asleep; all the shapes interlock softly as they weave rhythmic visual patterns throughout the entire picture plane. De Maistre has managed to suggest the twilight time of the dream or vision that takes place between the conscious and the unconscious, between the past and the future, between nature and supernature.

Jacob's Dream is a strange and remarkable painting. Its subject matter does not correspond directly to any particular part of the biblical narrative of Jacob. It does not seem to refer to his vision at Beth-el (Gen. 28: 10–19) or to his struggle of Jabbok (Gen. 32: 22–31). Yet there is within this painting something of the mystery and uncertainty of a profound religious experience, an encounter with God such as Jacob saw his dream to be. De Maistre has chosen to do all this without the use of colour, even though as an artist he was absorbed in colour theory and the creation of paintings where the colour was orchestrated in scales and movements. *Jacob's Dream* is essentially in monochrome, yet it sings—softly.

When Roy de Maistre died in London in 1968, he was better known there than in Australia; most critics thought of him as an English painter. De Maistre was born in New South Wales, the sixth of eleven children in a wealthy pastoralist family. He was christened Leroy de Mestre, but changed his name about 1930. His father was the son of Julie de Mestre, Baroness de Fortisson, and Edward, Duke of Kent, hence the Leroy (or Roi). He was educated at home with tutors and governesses before coming to Sydney to study violin and viola at the State Conservatorium of Music, and art at the Royal Art Society of New South Wales with Dattilo Rubbo. Through Rubbo, he became friendly with Nora Simpson, Roland Wakelin and Grace Cossington Smith. Simpson had recently returned from France with reproductions of the works of the post-impressionists. The four students began to lighten their palettes, shorten their brushstrokes and strive for the underlying structure in their compositions. De Maistre and Wakelin also became interested in modern painting as expounded in the writings of Americans Morgan Russell, MacDonald Wright and Arthur Eddy. Russell and Wright had developed a theory of synchromism, or the generation of pure form using colour; Eddy had written on the relation between colour theory and music.

De Maistre and Wakelin patented a colour wheel based on these theories, for use by artists and interior decorators. In 1919 they held a joint exhibition at Gayfield Shaw's Gallery in Sydney. De Maistre's paintings—for example, *Synchromy in Red Major* and *Caprice in Blue Minor*—were complex intellectual exercises and revolutionary for that time. Howard Ashton, conservative painter and critic, condemned them as 'elaborate and pretentious bosh', and de Maistre turned for a time to the tonal painting of Max Meldrum.

In 1923, George Lambert awarded de Maistre the Society of Artists' Travelling Scholarship and he left for England and France. He returned to Australia in 1926, had a solo exhibition in the Macquarie Galleries in 1927, participated in an important group exhibition of Australian

[*Continued overleaf*]

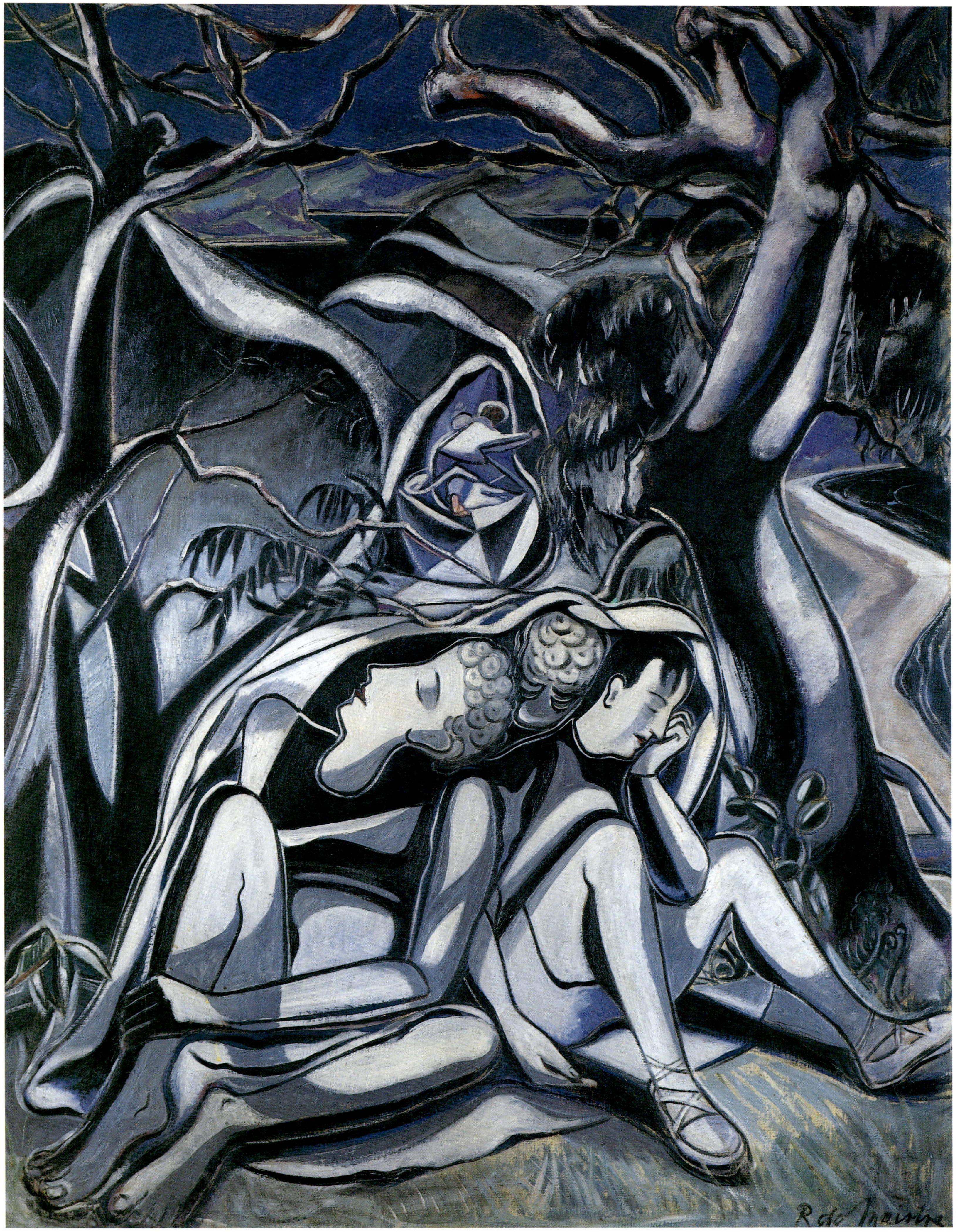

6 *Jacob's Dream*

ROY DE MAISTRE

1894–1968

Jacob and the Angel, 1958

Oil on composition board
61 × 91 cm
Edward and John Ness Barkes, Sydney
Courtesy Bridget McDonnell Gallery, Melbourne

Jacob and the Angel was completed in 1958, when de Maistre was sixty-four, so it is a late work. Sometime in midlife he had experienced a reconversion to the Catholic faith which had affected him so deeply that much of his subsequent painting has religious subject matter. Pictures such as *Crucifixion* (1942–44), *Pieta* (1950) and *Triptych* (1950) are more deeply felt than much of his other work and are better known; *Jacob and the Angel* is less well known.

Like *Jacob's Dream*, this painting draws its inspiration from the Old Testament, but this time the reference is clear. Jacob, fleeing before his brother Esau, sends his family across the ford at Jabbok:

> And Jacob was left alone. And there was one that wrestled with him until daybreak, who, seeing that he could not master him, struck him in the socket of his hip, and Jacob's hip was dislocated as he wrestled with him. He said, 'Let me go, for day is breaking.' But Jacob answered, 'I will not let you go unless you bless me.' He then asked, 'What is your name?' 'Jacob,' he replied. He said, 'Your name shall no longer be Jacob, but Israel; because you have been strong against God, you shall prevail against men. [Gen. 32: 24–28][1]

In *Jacob and the Angel*, tone, colour, shape and direction are involved in a complex and energetic play of thrust and counter-thrust. Jacob is dark and brown, the angel bright with blues and pinks; the left diagonals of the bodies are countered by the right diagonals of the legs. The background shares the turmoil and the essential order: blues and reds balance; tints of colour counterpoint dominant primaries and secondaries. The heroic figure of Jacob is lifted and emphasized with white line which threatens to be, but never quite becomes, a restricting outline.

1. Jerusalem Bible (Darton: Longman and Todd, 1966), p. 54.

'modern' art at the Grosvenor Galleries in 1927, and then returned to England in 1929. At first he shared a studio with Francis Bacon. *Conflict* (1932) reflects de Maistre's brief flirtation with metaphysical imagery, but for the most part his work over the next thirty-five years was set within the boundaries of his studio—flower pieces, still lifes, figure studies and religious subjects. All were approached with seriousness and emotional detachment; de Maistre was absorbed in the formal intricacies of painting, in the rhythmic organization of shapes on the flat surface of the canvas, and in the way colour, if carefully orchestrated, can create a kind of visual music. Only his religious paintings were different; they were often suffused with a serenity born of faith. The Stations of the Cross paintings at Westminster Cathedral were his most important commission.

De Maistre's work was known and admired in art circles in England; however, his choice of subjects, his controlled style and a natural reticence kept him out of the limelight in both Britain and Australia. He had solo exhibitions in London, Leeds and Birmingham and was often represented in important group shows of British painting in the United States. In 1960 a major retrospective of his work was held at the Whitechapel Art Gallery, London.

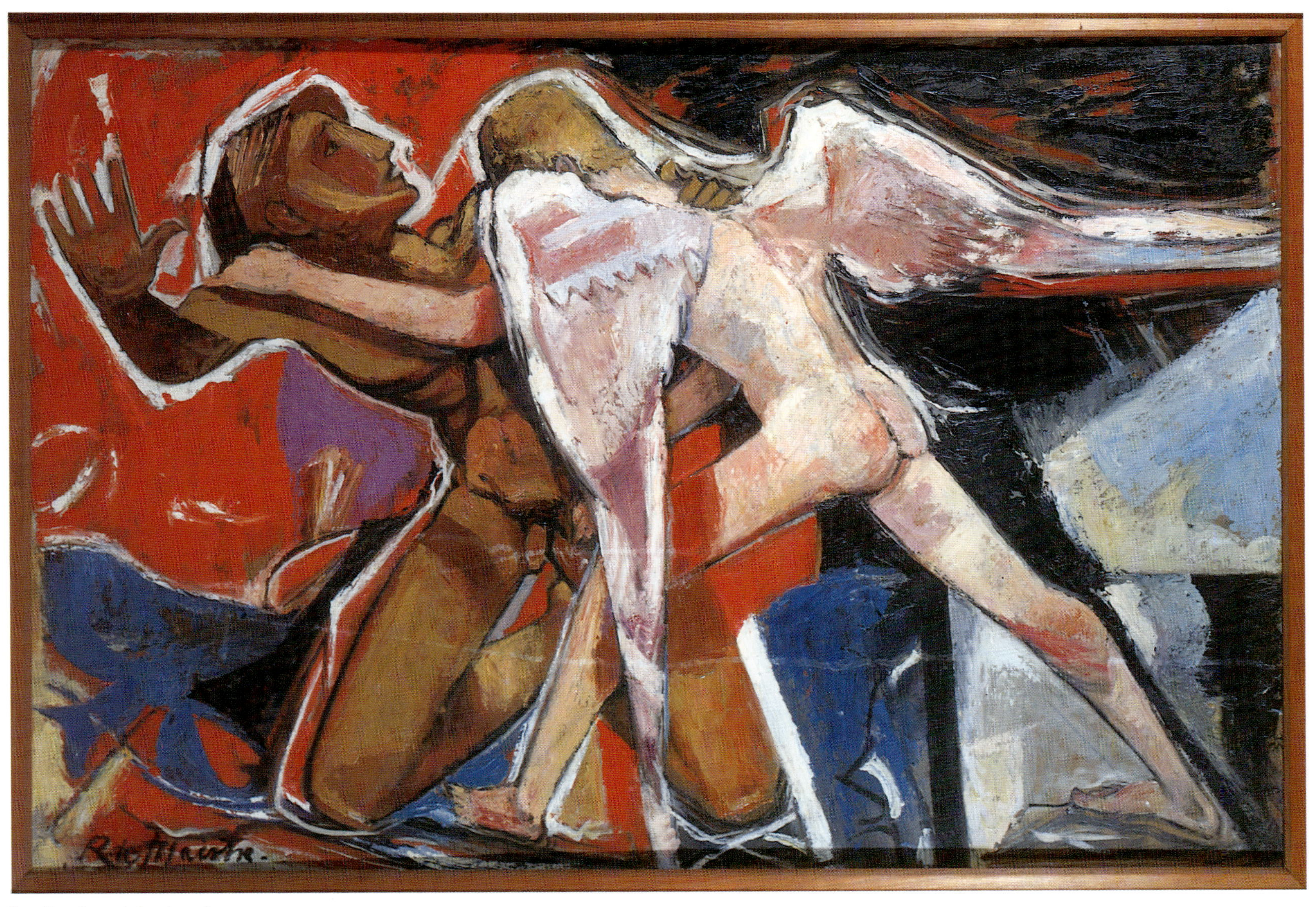

7 *Jacob and the Angel*

Grace Cossington Smith

1892–1984

'I looked, and behold, a door was opened in heaven', 1953

Oil on composition board
86.4 × 59.2 cm
Private collection, Adelaide

'*I looked, and behold, a door was opened in heaven'* is one of the few biblical subjects Grace Cossington Smith ever painted. One other, *'Then one of them, which was a lawyer, asked Him a question'*, was exhibited in the 1953 Blake Prize, from which *'I looked, and behold, a door was opened in heaven'* was rejected. Six other pictures are of wartime services in her local parish church, St James in Turramurra. Yet, in a real sense, all her work can be regarded as religious to the extent that it communicates the serenity, joy and acceptance of life which she experienced. She saw the facets of life as aspects of creation, and colour as its special radiance. 'Art is the expression of whatsoever things are lovely,' she said in 1971, 'at the same time expressing things unseen—the golden thread running through time.'[1]

The subject of this painting is a passage from the Revelation of St John the Divine 4: 1–4. To quote the passage is to identify the content of the painting:

> After this I looked, and, behold, a door was opened in heaven: and the first voice which I heard was as it were of a trumpet talking with me; which said, Come up hither, and I will shew thee things which must be hereafter. And immediately I was in the spirit: and, behold, a throne was set in heaven, and one sat on the throne. And he that sat was to look upon like a jasper and a sardine stone: and there was a rainbow round about the throne, in sight like unto an emerald. And round about the throne were four and twenty seats: and upon the seats I saw four and twenty elders sitting, clothed in white raiment; and they had on their heads crowns of gold.

Grace Cossington Smith has resolved the difficult task of interpreting a vision in a way similar to Alan Oldfield's approach to the revelations of Julian of Norwich (Plate 67), although Smith's intention is less self-consciously theological. Both have taken the text literally, and through composition and colour have indicated some of the symbolism inherent in it. In Smith's painting, John is visible in the right corner, and the door opens on the left to reveal a breathtaking golden vision. But these elements do not make the painting significant, nor alone do they convey the atmosphere of ecstatic devotion. It is the colour and the way the composition is dominated by the concentric circles of light and form which emanate from the central throne that count. The colour has been laid on directly from the tube, each tint a step away from its neighbour and orchestrated like sequences in reflective music. The whole effect is one of serenity and radiance. It is colour that sings. There are few signs of struggle in this painting, only a sense of quiet arrival.

1. Quoted by Daniel Thomas in *Grace Cossington Smith* (Art Gallery of New South Wales, 1973), p. 6.

Grace Cossington Smith was born in 1892 in Sydney, into a middle-class, religious, Anglican family. From 1910 to 1912 she attended the Dattilo Rubbo School; from 1912 to 1914 she toured Europe. Back home again at Rubbo's school in Rowe Street she was introduced to post-impressionism by a fellow student, Nora Simpson, who had recently returned from Europe with prints and reproductions of modern art. With colleagues and friends Roy de Maistre and Roland Wakelin, she led the break away from Australian impressionism; her *Sock Knitter* (1915), is regarded as the first fully post-impressionist painting exhibited in Australia.[1] In 1924 she broke with Rubbo because of his constant criticism of her handling of space, particularly of the way she worked consistently in the frontal plane. Her first solo exhibition at the Grosvenor Galleries, Sydney, in 1928 revealed the depth of Cézanne's influence. In 1932 she exhibited at the Walker Gallery in New Bond Street, London, and thenceforth every few years at the Macquarie Galleries in Sydney. In 1973 Daniel Thomas organized a major retrospective exhibition at the Art Gallery of New South Wales.

Grace Cossington Smith emerges in Australian art history as private, independent and unostentatiously religious. Her home in Turramurra, her day-to-day domestic life and events in Sydney such as the building of the Harbour Bridge provided her with ample subject matter. Although her paintings offer a faithful historical record of the times, her intention was different. Her priority was always with 'form in colour—colour vibrant with light', as she said in 1969, 'but containing this other silent quality which is unconscious, and belongs to all things created.'[2]

1. Daniel Thomas, 'Grace Cossington Smith', *Art and Australia* 4, no. 4 (March 1967), p. 301.
2. Mervyn Horton, *Present Day Art in Australia* (Sydney: Ure Smith, 1969), p. 203.

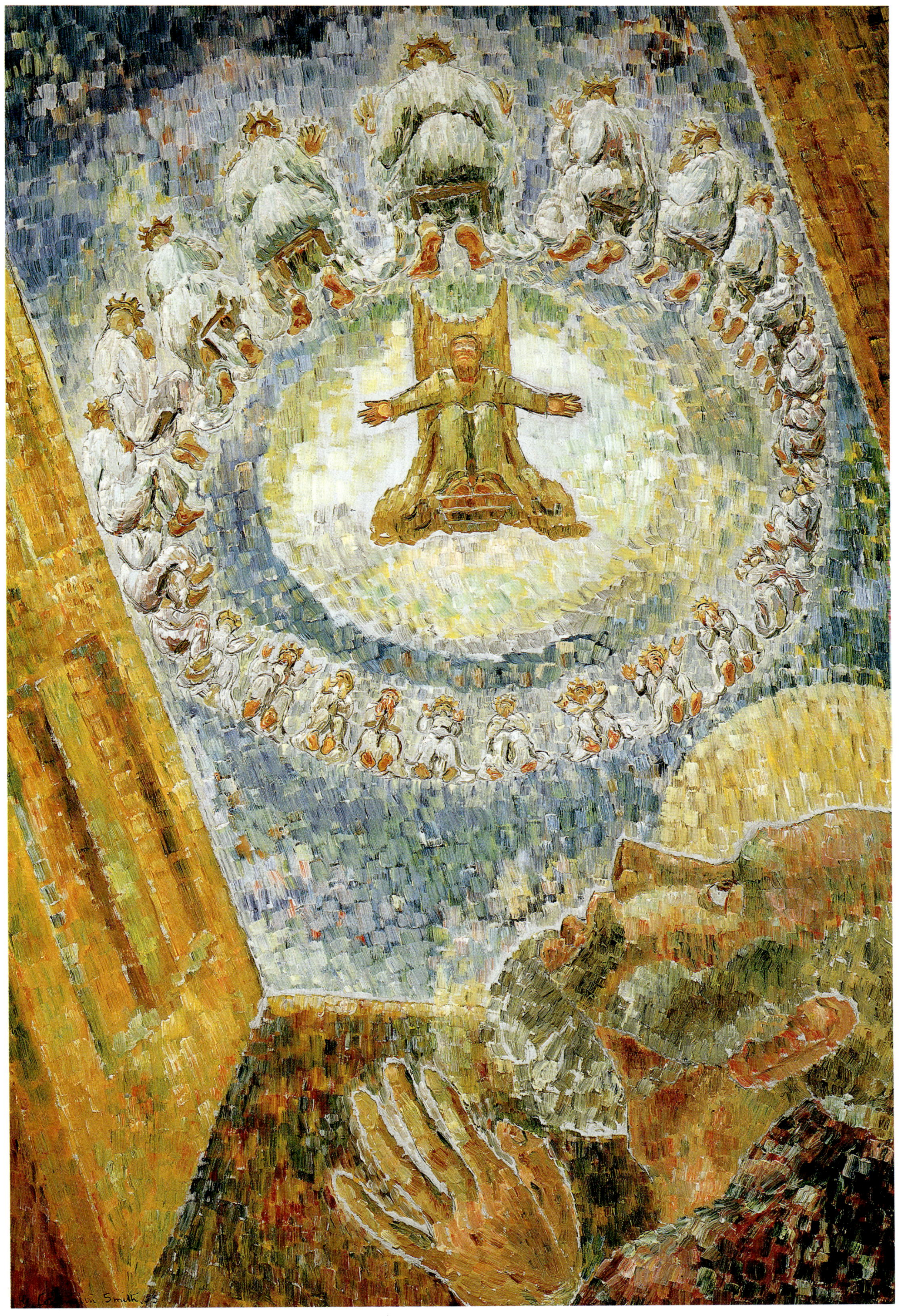

8 *'I looked, and behold, a door was opened in heaven'*

DANILA VASSILIEFF

1899–1958

Expulsion from Paradise, 1940

Gouache on printed fabric
Four panels: 167 × 312 cm overall
Australian National Gallery, Canberra

Vassilieff was commissioned to paint this screen by Connie Smith of Warrandyte. She was an enthusiast for modern art and recognized Vassilieff's talent; she was friendly with Clive and Janet Nield, for whom Vassilieff had painted a bathroom mural, also an *Expulsion*. Both families must have heard Vassilieff tell of his time in Bristol, when, as a parting gift to his hosts, Doris and Lawrence Ogilvie, he had painted another *Explusion*, also in the bathroom. This screen was for Connie Smith's bathroom.

As in *Entry into Jerusalem* (Plate 10), Vassilieff has taken liberties with the scripture narrative, this time to play with the story in a decorative and lighthearted yet mischievous way. A giant serpent wriggles across the four panels, its markings reminiscent of Aboriginal art (which Vassilieff probably knew from his years in the Northern Territory), its huge eye turned knowingly to the viewer. A lascivious Adam and a seductive Eve (both local identities) in the second panel are observed, not only by the snake, but by the crowd behind the palm tree in the first panel, the Cossack-warrior-archangel in the third panel, and a serene and indifferent Buddha-God in the fourth panel. Lush fruit, animals, flowers, plants, insects and a choir of angels proclaim that this is Paradise.

Stylistically, the screen belongs to the long tradition of Russian folklore found in illustrations in children's books and often used in Russian stage sets. Vassilieff may have dredged the images from his childhood memories of Russia, but it is more likely, as Felicity St John Moore has pointed out,[1] that Vassilieff made use of his 1935 experience with Vladimir Polunin, professor of stage painting at the Slade School in London and a former scene painter with Serge Diaghilev in St Petersburg and Paris.

1. Felicity St John Moore, 'Vassilieff's *Expulsion* Screen and Melbourne Expressionism', *Art and Australia* 23 (Autumn 1986), pp. 358–62.

DANILA VASSILIEFF was born in 1899 at Kagalnickaja, near Rostov-on-Don in south Russia. In 1917 he fought with the Cossacks; in 1919, with the Don Cossacks of the counter-revolutionary White Army. In 1920 he was captured at Baku but escaped to Azerbaijan and then to Shanghai, where he married. He subsequently came to Australia and from 1923 to 1929 worked in Queensland and the Northern Territory as a labourer. His decision to become an artist seems to date from 1929, when he met an artist on board a ship between Shanghai and Paris. From Paris he went to Brazil to study under Dimitri Ismalovitch but quickly chafed under classical discipline and struck out on his own. In 1933 he had exhibitions in British Guiana, Trinidad, Jamaica, and Santo Domingo; in 1934 and 1935 at the Albany Gallery, London, and in Somerset, Bristol, Madrid, Lisbon and at Prince Vladimir Galitzine's Gallery, London. These exhibitions set what was to become a pattern for the rest of his life—the paintings were freely executed and expressionist in style; subject matter was usually of people in poor areas and in need; few paintings were ever sold, and those that were went usually to artists; reviews were mixed; and early patrons quickly tired under excessive emotional outbursts often directed at them.

Vassilieff arrived in Sydney in 1934 with an impressive exhibition record and a personal style as expressionist and romantic as his work. At first, patrons and exhibitions were easy to find; Sydney Ure Smith, owner of *Art in Australia*, became friend and patron for a short time; Macquarie Galleries held two one-man shows. Disgruntled and destitute, Vassilieff moved to Melbourne. From 1937, Riddell's Galleries in Collins Street held regular one-man exhibitions, and John Reed stayed a constant admirer. Still little was sold. Vassilieff was so poor that he lived for a time in a packing case.

[*Continued overleaf*]

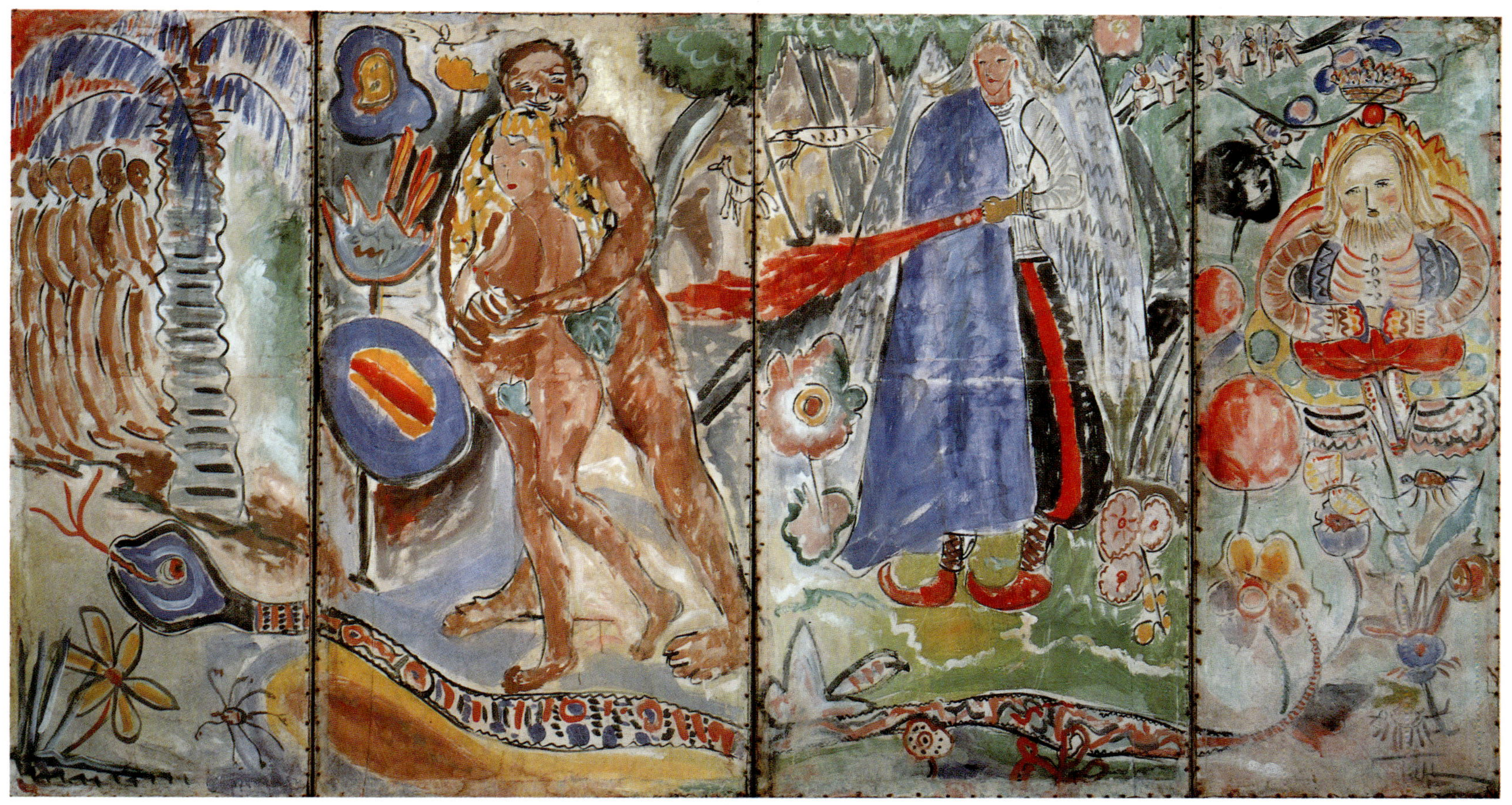

9 *Expulsion from Paradise*

DANILA VASSILIEFF

1899–1958

Entry into Jerusalem, 1947

Oil on canvas
60.8 × 73 cm
Australian National Gallery, Canberra

Entry into Jerusalem was painted by Vassilieff during a period of emotional and financial stability shortly after his marriage to the writer Elizabeth Hamill. With her encouragement he had begun an autobiography and a book on children's art and had started sculpting in the hard Lilydale stone. His painting, perhaps under the influence of the exhilaration of sculpting for the first time, became more direct, expressionist and seemingly unsophisticated. *Entry into Jerusalem* and *White Corroboree* are major works from this time. They share a directness of approach and a clarity and simplicity of colour, and they make critical social comment. In many ways they look to the expressionist tradition in Western art, particularly to the early twentieth-century painters James Ensor and Emil Nolde.

The subject matter of *Entry into Jerusalem* is not what it appears—Christ riding triumphant into Jerusalem on the Sunday before his crucifixion. There is a figure on a donkey, there is a procession and some waving of palm branches, but it is unlikely that Vassilieff intended that this be the Christ of history. This man is wearing a top hat, his face is like a skull, and he is accompanied by soldiers and watched by crowds from behind barricades; children and a dog run alongside. The figure looks more like a caricature of Uncle Sam, the procession like rabble soldiers, and the city, Melbourne. It seems reasonable to assume that Vassilieff, the Cossack and short-term communist, is casting a jaundiced eye on the 'Americanization' of Melbourne during and just after World War II. It may also be that in using this particularly sacred story from the Christian tradition he was intending to ridicule religion, just as his use of white 'king-soldiers' in *White Corroboree* dishonours a sacred Aboriginal ritual.

Both *Entry into Jerusalem* and *Expulsion from Paradise* are unusual when seen in the perspective of the whole range of Vassilieff's work in that they draw on heroic stories from the Christian tradition. Most of Vassilieff's other work takes its subject matter from his everyday existence—streets where he lived, landscapes he visited, portraits of children and his friends or even his landlords. Stylistically, there is great variety in his work, especially after Lowenfeld and Read opened ways for him to vent his emotional distress and anger in his painting, but always his paint quality has spontaneity, energy and confidence.

From this period came the wonderful street scenes and portraits from around Collingwood and Fitzroy. Younger-generation artists—Tucker, Boyd, Nolan—sought him out for advice, and he exhorted them to be free and spontaneous.

In 1939 he moved to Warrandyte, to a shed on the grounds of an experimental school started by Clive and Janet Nield. With Helen McDonald he quarried stone and gradually built a house, Stonygrad. It became a gathering place for Melbourne's art community. Vassilieff's ideas, stories and wild Cossack dances became legend. Yet few paintings sold, although he worked prodigiously and angrily. In 1944, critics such as Adrian Lawlor and Alan McCulloch, who had once admired his work, declared it 'wayward', 'careless' and 'naive' and inferior to the work of the younger generation such as Boyd and Nolan.

In 1946 Vassilieff resolved to return to Russia and put Stonygrad on the market but ended by marrying the buyer, Elizabeth Hamill, and remaining there. Elizabeth persuaded him to sculpt in the local stone and introduced him to the work of Henry Moore. Victor Lowenfeld's *Creative and Mental Growth* and Herbert Read's *Education Through Art* influenced him greatly. Still few works sold, and reviews were bad. In 1954, his marriage at an end, he left Stonygrad to become an assistant art teacher in Mildura; in 1956 he taught at Eltham High School. In 1957 a major retrospective in the Gallery of Contemporary Art failed. He died suddenly in 1958 while having tea with John Reed. The following year John Reed mounted a major memorial exhibition, which, ironically, was a huge critical and financial success. Vassilieff, who never doubted his own genius, was recognized the year after his death.

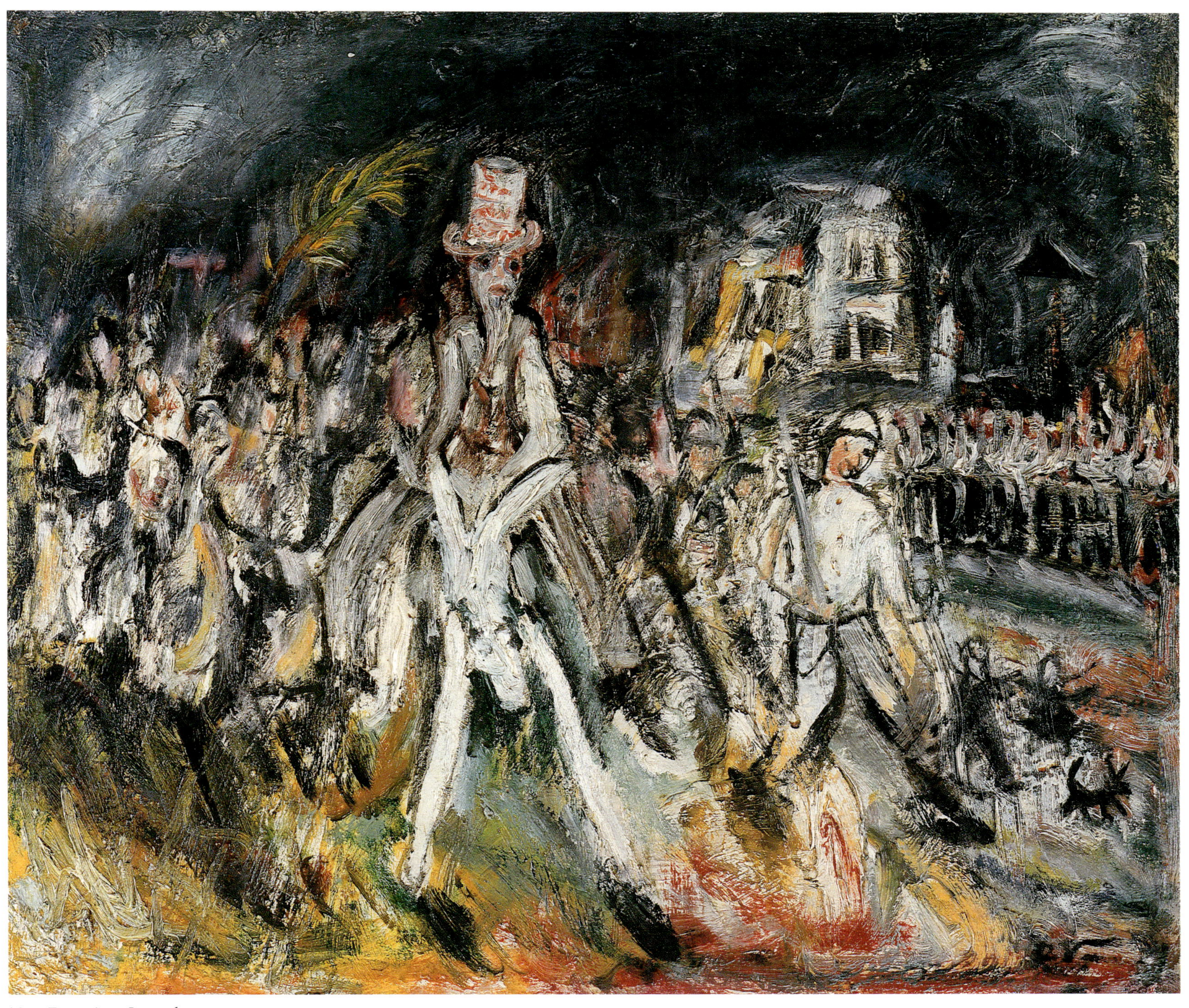

10 *Entry into Jerusalem*

JOHN PERCEVAL

Born 1923

Christ Dining in Young and Jackson's, 1947

Mixed media
73.7 × 78.7 cm
Collection of Helen and Maurice Alther, Melbourne

John Perceval has set his scene in a famous Melbourne hotel, Young and Jackson's in Flinders Street. If it were not for the portrait of the nude on the wall in the background (*Chloe* in the real hotel), the setting could be anywhere. Christ is at first indistinguishable from the other patrons; the composition leads the viewer to a particular table and then recognition occurs. Christ is in the midst of the celebration. Under his table a greyhound, muzzled for safety, searches for crumbs. A woman swings across the room carrying a typical Australian dinner —baked chicken and potatoes. Perceval has managed to create noise as the figures, dishes, barrels and tables tumble against each other in a bustle of movement. It is a painting to enjoy. The presence of Christ in such a raucous gathering raises few theological questions today, although many took offence at such familiarity when it was first exhibited, forgetting that Brueghel and the Renaissance painters did the same kind of thing.

JOHN PERCEVAL was born in Bruce Rock, Western Australia, in 1923. He had no formal art training but met Arthur Boyd while in the army and later married Mary Boyd and settled in the Boyd house, Open Country, at Murrumbeena, near Melbourne. There he became part of a wide circle of artist friends, including Sidney Nolan and Albert Tucker, who, with the Boyds, were leaders in the vital art climate of the forties. In 1945, with Arthur Boyd and Peter Herbst, he founded the Murrumbeena Pottery, which, although set up to make utilitarian ware, led to the creation of a series of pots and ceramic sculptures in the fifites which won him international acclaim.

Perceval's paintings during the war years—for example, *Exodus from a Bombed City* (1942) and *Boy with Cat* (1943)—were often strong protests against the horrors of war, especially as they affected the young. In 1947–48 he painted a number of pictures with explicitly religious subject matter. Arthur Boyd had been working with both Old and New Testament themes for a couple of years, but Perceval came to concentrate more on the New Testament and on its celebratory aspects, particularly the nativity. He and Boyd used similar techniques, experimenting with formulas found in Max Doerner's *Materials of the Artist*, given to them by Tucker. Both were indebted to Brueghel, and both were fascinated by the ordinary life around them. Boyd's absorption with religion was longer lasting. In the 1950s Perceval chose to work with landscape—a series at Williamstown by the docks, another at Gaffey's Creek. The paintings were rollickingly optimistic—celebrations of shimmering colour and swirling paint, akin to impressionism but almost abstracts.

[*Continued overleaf*]

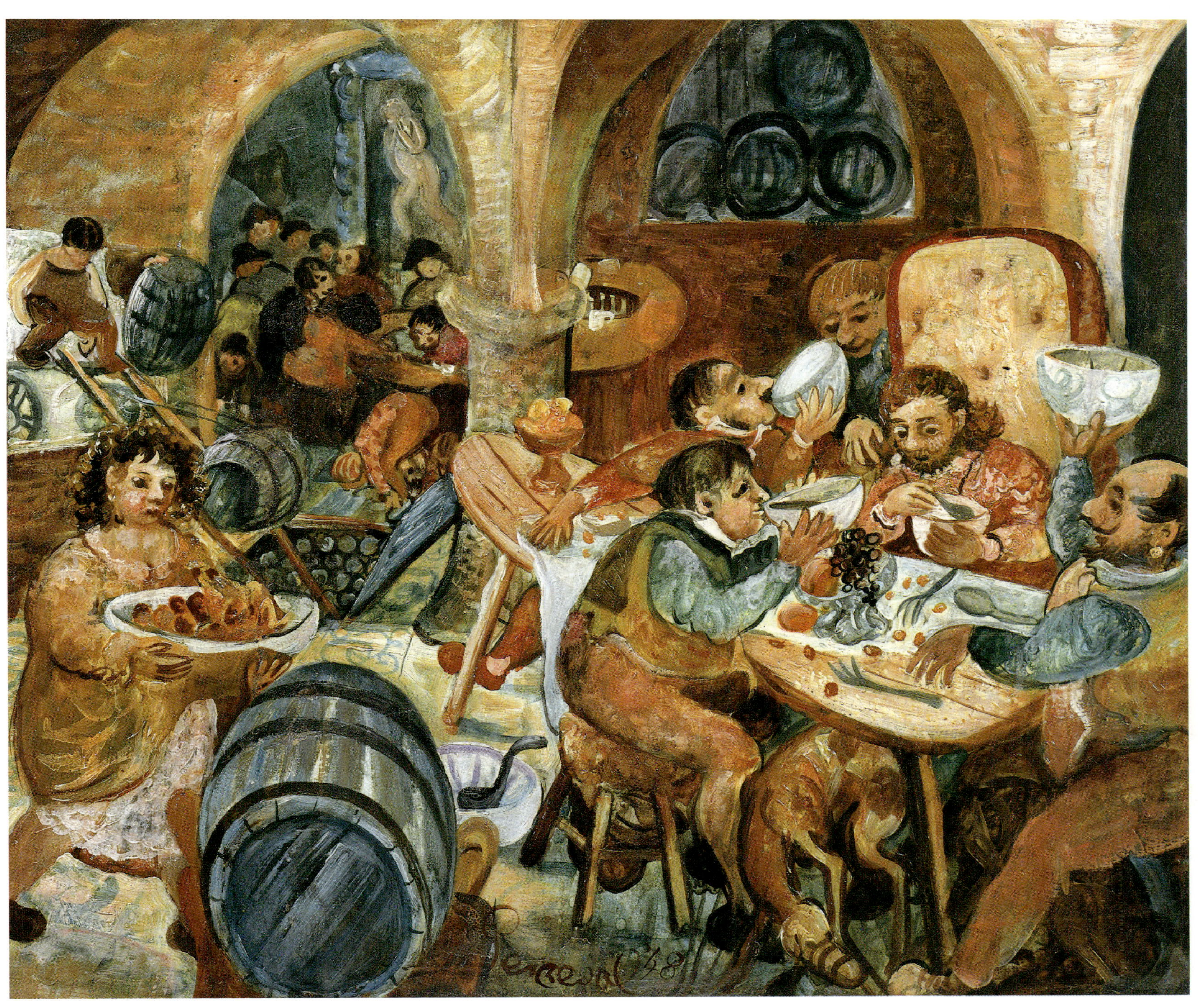

11 *Christ Dining in Young and Jackson's*

JOHN PERCEVAL

Born 1923

Christmas Eve, 1947–48

Mixed media with egg tempera and resin
78.7 × 83.8 cm
Collection of Helen and Maurice Alther, Melbourne

Christmas Eve and other religious paintings done at this time by John Perceval while he was living with the Boyd extended family in Murrumbeena owed much to the general atmosphere in a home where religion was a part of life and discussions about it as lively as other current matters. Merric Boyd, Arthur's father and Perceval's father-in-law, was a prophet-type figure in the house, intensely religious with a reverence for the scriptures. Prayer was a part of the daily routine.

Christmas Eve is a rollicking, bucolic celebration of suburban Melbourne life, a Brueghel-like updating of the nativity story. The stable is a partly constructed house by a bay that is recognizable as Port Phillip. Gum trees straggle near by. A factory and church are in the background; at the right foreground a fowl is being plucked for Christmas dinner while a boy turns his head away from the sight of it. Perceval views this scene from a distance, remaining an observer; he is yet to achieve a familiarity with the Australian light and colour which enables him to step inside and surround himself with it in the same way as he came to do so easily in the landscapes of the sixties.

In 1959 Perceval joined with Boyd, Charles Blackman, John Brack, Clifton Pugh and others in an exhibition affirming the superiority of the image in painting. The Antipodean Exhibition, as it was called, was the summation of years of friendship of the group. From this time also date Perceval's first ceramic sculptures of angels. *Dancing Angel* (1958–59), *Angel Barry in Heaven* (1957–58) and others in the series demonstrate superb mastery of clay and deep red glaze. Like his wartime pictures, these angels have about them a recklessness that defies the fragility of the material. Their inspiration may have come from della Robbia and Donatello in Renaissance Italy, but their mischievous and impish stances are Perceval's genius.

[*Continued overleaf*]

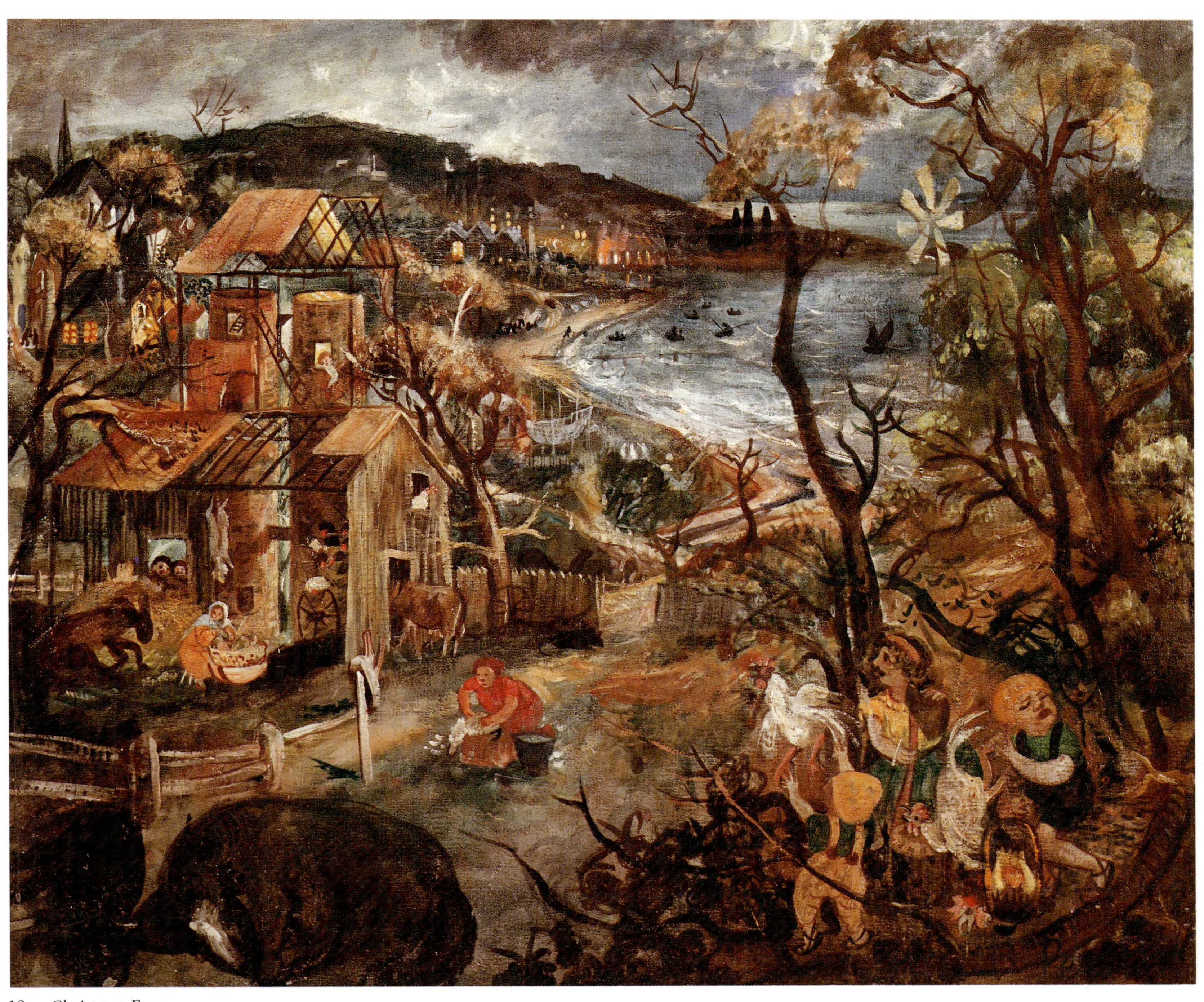

12 *Christmas Eve*

JOHN PERCEVAL

Born 1923

Crossing of the Red Sea, 1947–48

Mixed media
109 × 114 cm
Collection of Helen and Maurice Alther, Melbourne

Crossing of the Red Sea was painted while Perceval and Boyd were partners in the Murrumbeena Pottery. Both men were friends, shared enthusiasms for Bosch and Brueghel as well as for van Gogh. They had also been in the same army unit in South Melbourne, passed the same scenes in the streets, and lived now with young families at Open Country. Like Boyd's *The mining town (Casting the Money Changers from the Temple)* (Plate 68), Perceval's *Crossing of the Red Sea* is a summation of his paintings to this time—a tapestry of familiar figures, colours and moods.

In the foreground is a Christ-like figure wearing a halo. He is Perceval's Moses, not the Old Testament patriarch such as Boyd has painted (Plate 70), but a gentle, caring father-saint figure. The child he holds is Matthew, Perceval's son. One hand blesses the friendly, domesticated lions, a goat, some fish, a lamb and a fox; the other reaches towards the woman who sits at his feet. From the swirling waters a stream of people, some on crutches, are led to him, watched over by a most serious angel. Higher on the canvas, nude figures cavort wildly, suggesting a Goya-like Witches' Sabbath.

Once again Perceval has taken one of the great Scripture narratives and domesticated it, this time by setting it along Port Phillip Bay shoreline. There is no attempt to re-create an event as history. Perceval is content to evoke the mood and the complexity of the biblical event. With him, the crossing of the Red Sea of the Book of Exodus remains both story and myth.

In 1963 Perceval packed up and followed Nolan and Boyd to England, intending to settle there. His English paintings won critical success in London, but he never felt at home in England. He returned to Australia in 1965 to take up the first Creative Fellowship for an Artist at the Australian National University, Canberra. Around 1969 Perceval again turned to religious subjects (e.g., *Veronica and the Conspirators*, 1967; *Moses and the Dragonflies*, 1969), with results even more exuberant and lyrical than his earlier paintings.

John Perceval lives in Melbourne.

> I do not hold any particular attitude to my work or to art in general. I chose early not to work from any aesthetic theory or concept but prefer the results to be governed by developments that occur while the work is in progress . . . my work is primarily a response to the subject, to light and trees, air, people, etc.[1]

1. John Reed, *New Painting* (Melbourne: Longmans, 1963), p. 28.

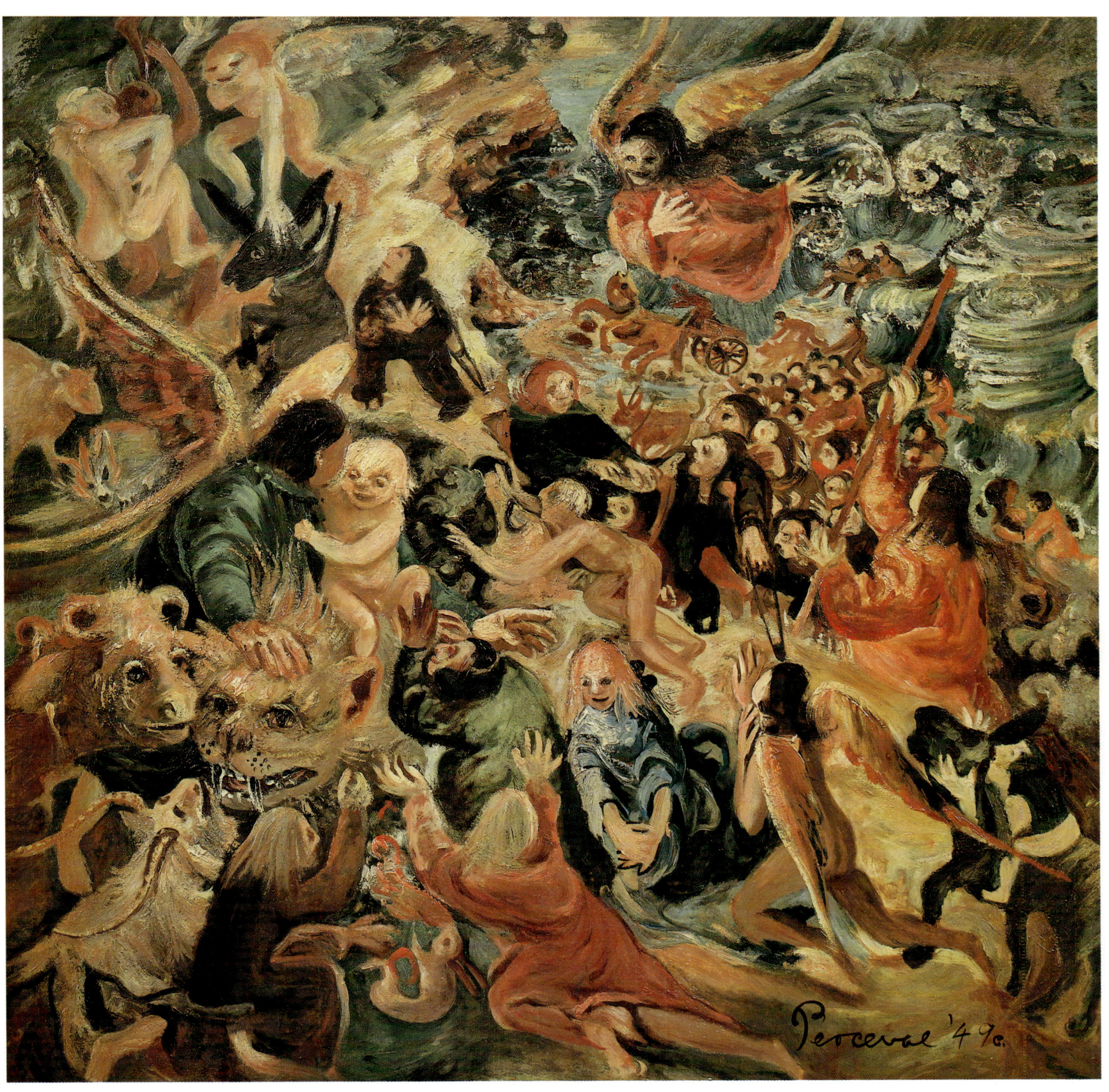

13 *Crossing of the Red Sea*

LOUIS KAHAN

Born 1905

The Wedding Feast at Cana, 1949

Oil on canvas
48 × 73 cm
Collection of the artist

Louis Kahan has always been fascinated by Bible events, from both the Old and New Testaments, not so much as history but rather because he believes they have significance for our lives. In 1952 he won third prize in the Blake competition with the painting *Flight into Egypt*, in which the Holy Family are in a utility truck driving through barbed wire away from a large city. They are guided by a star, and their destination is signalled by a map of Australia reflected in the headlight.

The Wedding Feast at Cana, likewise updates the Gospel narrative. The place is Australia, the characters are local people, the setting is a dinner table in a shallow pictorial space. Jesus remains close to the traditional figure of piety—a young man, haloed (by a street light), serene; his hands encompass the sacramental cup. The guests, men and women from different walks of life, are meant to symbolize stages of belief and unbelief: a young couple gaze in wonder at Jesus, a woman feeds dogs while children go hungry, a well-fed businessman is watched over by the allegorical maiden of fecundity. Stylistically, the painting with its soft edges of clean colour, looks to the French impressionists more than it does to painters such as the German group Die Brücke, who were also concerned with allegory and social message.

LOUIS KAHAN was born in Vienna in 1905. In 1925 he left for Paris, where he worked mainly as a designer and illustrator. In 1939 he joined the French Foreign Legion and was a war artist in North Africa from 1942 to 1945. On his return to Paris he worked as a staff artist for *Le Figaro*, started painting, and studied print-making and stained-glass painting. In 1947 he migrated to Australia. Since then he has worked as a painter, print-maker, stained-glass artist and stage designer in Australia and England. He won the Archibald Prize in 1962. His early work was influenced by Brueghel, Dürer and Cézanne. Later he came to admire Egon Schiele greatly. Albert Marquet first encouraged him to paint.

Louis Kahan lives in Melbourne.

> I have always considered each work an accomplishment at the time when I did it. However, when seen in retrospect, it is nothing more than a lesson learned for the next time.[1]

1. Louis Kahan, interview with author, 21 November 1987.

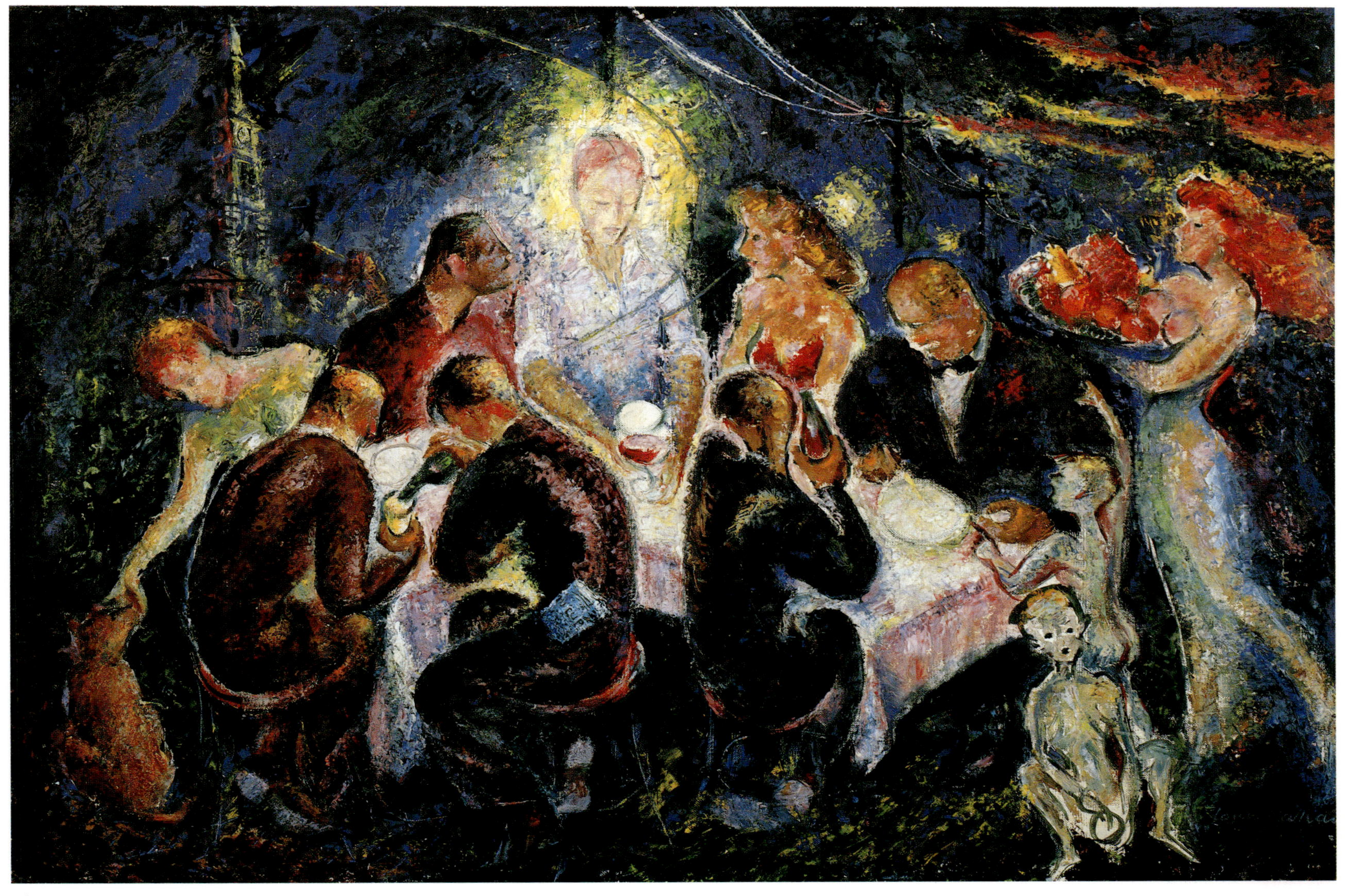

14 *The Wedding Feast at Cana*

MARGARET PRESTON
(1875–1963)

Adam and Eve in the Garden of Eden, 1950

Stencil and gouache
50.1 × 49.5 cm
Art Gallery of New South Wales, Sydney
Purchased 1950

Taken together, *Adam and Eve in the Garden of Eden, The Expulsion* and *Christ Turning the Water into Wine* represent a body of work that Margaret Preston completed early in 1953. All are gouache stencils on black paper and have biblical subject matter. Until this time, almost all her work had been of everyday subjects—still lifes, landscapes, flowers—without polemic, unlike her speeches and writings, which were usually passionately involved with some cause, often nationalistic. The reason for the switch to scriptural subjects is not known, but it may be that the Blake Prize for Religious Art, founded in Sydney at this time, motivated her. Many of her artist friends entered the competition in the first years; others were on the organizing committee. The prize itself seemed to canonize a neo-Byzantinism as the most appropriate form of religious art in churches. So these prints may have been her response, perhaps her protest, about the way many of the committee and artists were looking to European art and the Church at Assy for inspiration.

All three works use obvious Australian motifs and settings and an approach that emphasizes simplicity and naivety. The images have strength, but their overriding mood is of charm and mild protest. In 1950 she was seventy-five and most of her rage was burnt out. In 1963 she told Hal Missingham, the director of the Art Gallery of New South Wales, that her intention with *Adam and Eve in the Garden* was for it to have 'real Australian incident and feeling. The Garden of Eden, obviously here in Australia, the oldest land of all. Equally obviously, Adam and Eve would be black, *our* Aborigines, with a history stretching back to the dreamtime. And our unique and wonderful wildflowers must go in, Sturt's Desert Pea, flannel flowers, and the koala, kangaroo, emu and echidna; birds and fish.'[1]

1. Hal Missingham, 'Margaret Preston', *Art and Australia* 1, no. 2 (August 1963), p. 99.

MARGARET PRESTON was born in 1875 in Port Adelaide, South Australia. She studied briefly with William Lister Lister in Sydney in 1888, at the Design School at the National Gallery of Victoria with Frederick McCubbin in 1893 and with Bernard Hall in 1896, and at the Adelaide Gallery School with H. P. Gill and Hans Heysen in 1898. By 1904, when she left for Europe, she had established herself as a teacher, a draughtswoman and an accomplished painter of still lifes. In Paris from 1904 to 1906, she studied Japanese art at the Guimet Musée and revised her way of organizing pictorial space to be flatter, more 'decorative', as she described it. Such paintings as *Blue and Pink* (1908) and *An Australian Portrait* (1911) painted after her return to Australia, reveal the impact of Japanese art, mediated through Manet and the impressionists.

The years 1912 to 1919 were spent in England studying painting and sometime teaching pottery and craft in Seale-Hayne Neurological Military Hospital. In 1919, aged forty-four, she married a former AIF second lieutenant, William Preston. The marriage lasted until her death at eighty-eight in 1963 and brought her happiness, loving encouragement and financial security. They settled in Sydney, she to full-time painting, print-making and promoting her work and her ideas through lectures and writing. *Art in Australia, The Home* and *Australian Home Journal* frequently featured her paintings, prints and articles as she came to be one of Sydney's best-known artists. She was articulate, energetic, restless and avaricious for new visual experiences. With William Preston she visited New Caledonia in 1923, Bali, Singapore, Siam, Angkor, Macao and Hong Kong in 1924–25, China in 1926, north Queensland in 1927, New Zealand in 1930, Tahiti in the steps of Gauguin in 1932, North and South America in 1937 and London in 1938.

[*Continued overleaf*]

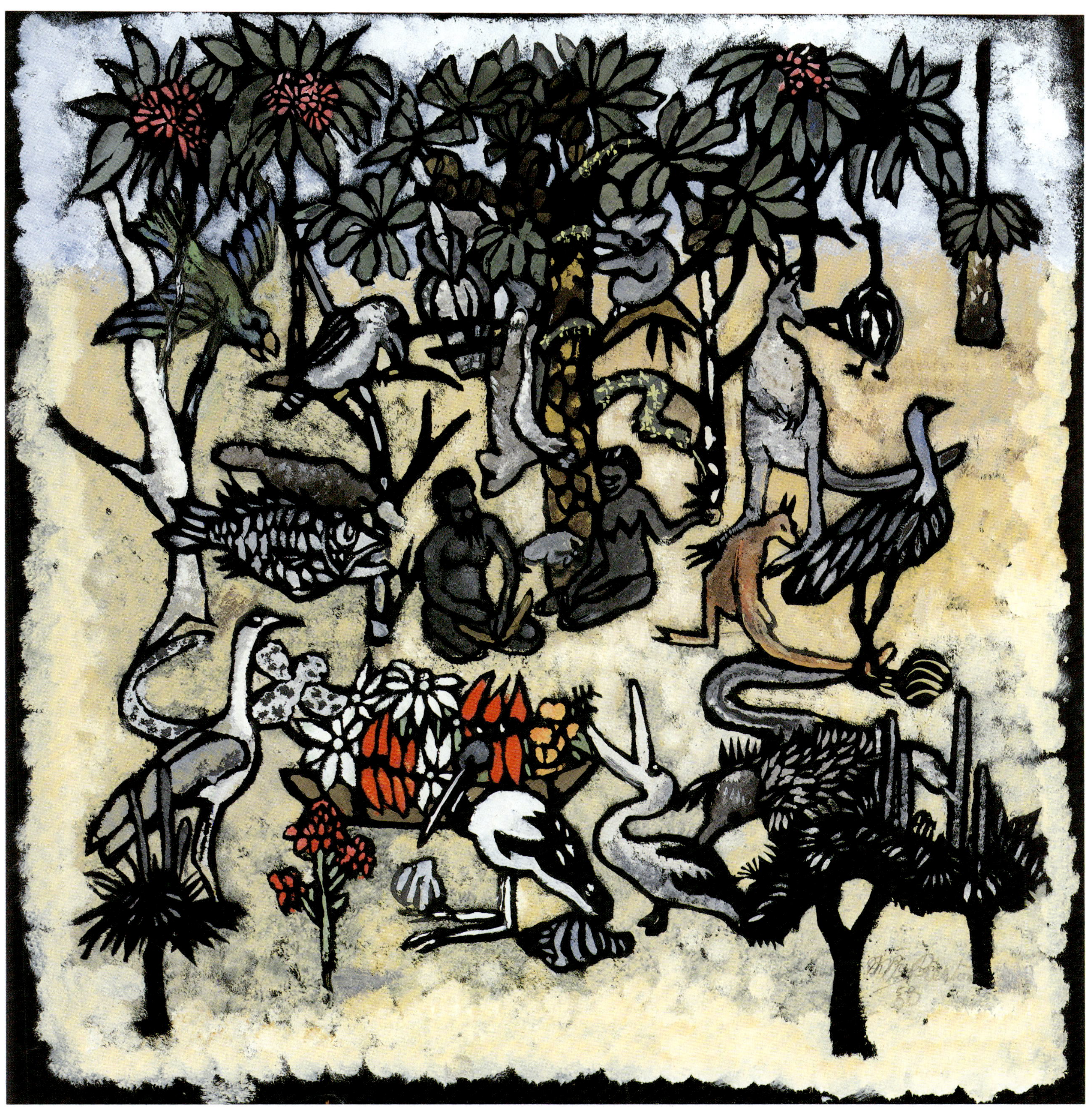

15 *Adam and Eve in the Garden of Eden*

MARGARET PRESTON

(1875–1963)

The Expulsion, 1952

Gouache, stencil and overpainting on black paper
64.1 × 50.9 cm
Art Gallery of New South Wales, Sydney
Gift of W. G. Preston 1967

Adam and Eve leave the Australian Garden of Eden, with its koalas, kangaroos, gum trees and flannel flowers; the wire gate is locked behind them, the lock on the outside; behind the gate the white angel of wrath, whip in hand, casts them out. Outside, among the thistles, thorns and threatening shadows, black Adam and Eve begin their journey. Adam raises one arm in anguish, but Eve smiles at the newborn child at her breast. Not all will be bad outside the garden.

Preston's treatment of this theme may have been political, as suggested by Roger Butler in *The Prints of Margaret Preston.*[1] She may have been speaking in polemical terms about the dispossession of Aborigines by white Australians, but there is little evidence in her writings of such a prophetic stance. Rather, her interest in Aboriginal art was part of her search for a genuinely Australian motif; her image of the Aborigine has much in common with the romantic view shared by many writers and artists—they are 'noble savages', European in shape but with black skins.

1. Roger Butler, *The Prints of Margaret Preston* (Australian National Gallery, 1986), p. 27.

Her paintings moved in the direction of simplified form, shallow picture space with a very limited palette. Some of her best work—for example, *Implement Blue* (1927), *Western Australian Gum Blossom* (1928), *Self Portrait* (1930), *Monstera* (1934) and *Brown Pot* (1940)—demonstrate this development. From 1920 she worked increasingly at etching, woodcuts and monotypes, believing that they provided the opportunity for inexpensive originals for people who would never be able to afford a painting. Her hand-coloured woodblocks from these years, such as *Bird of Paradise* (*c.*1923), *Lorikeets* (1925), *Wheel Flower* (1928), and *Aeroplane* (*c.*1936), reveal her masterly handling of the woodcut and her respect for the flatness of the picture surface.

Margaret Preston was a woman of enthusiasms, and one of her enduring quests was to find a distinctively Australian visual and symbolic vocabulary which did not derive from European art. To do this she turned to Aboriginal art. By 1930 she had limited her own palette to ochre, black and white and was advocating that others also study Aboriginal designs and colours to rid themselves of Western influences. By 1945 she knew that this was an impossible dream, that the creation of a national style would not come about simply by denying European ancestry; she then advocated a purification of traditional European standards in favour of a study of modern art.

[*Continued overleaf*]

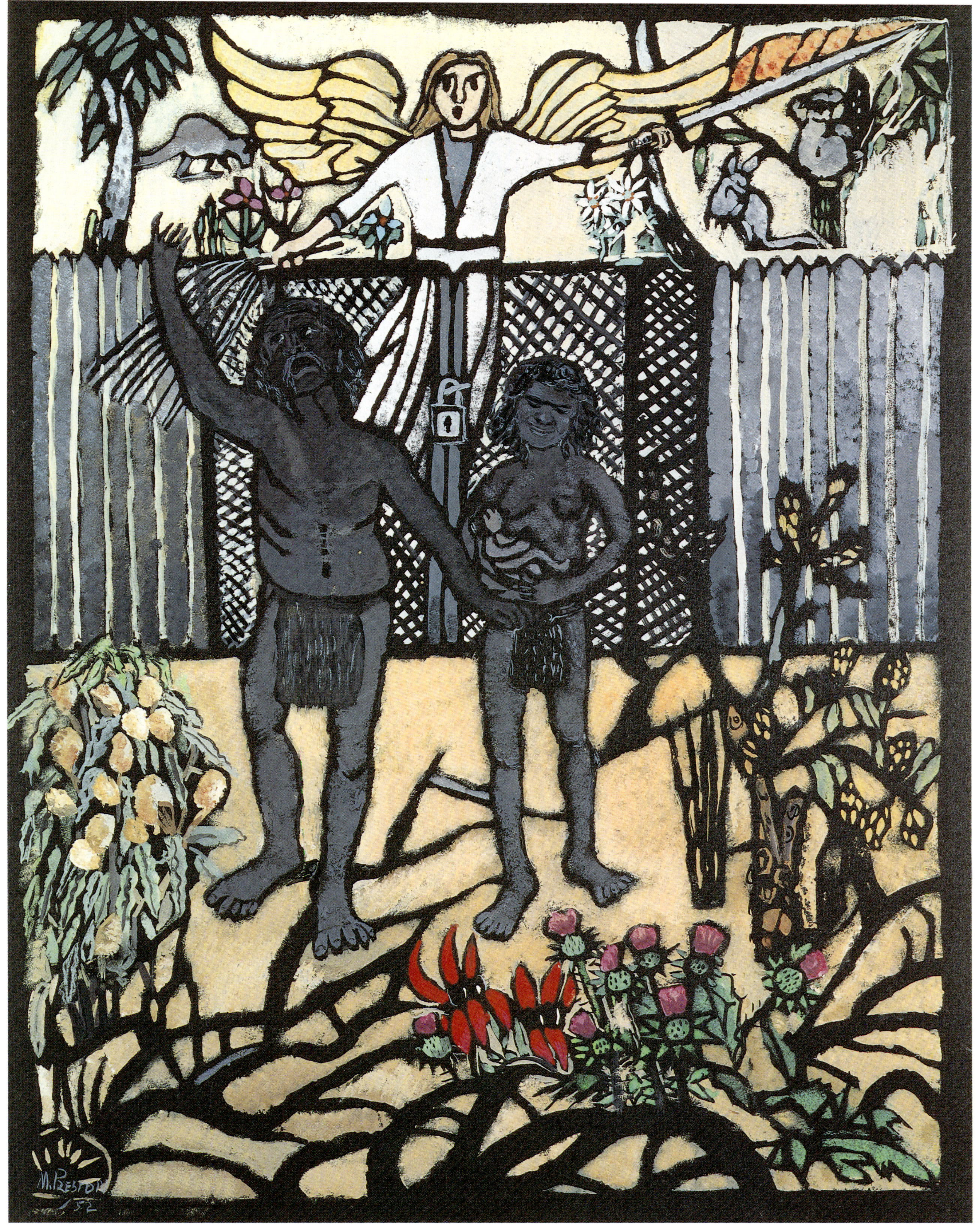

16 *The Expulsion*

MARGARET PRESTON

(1875–1963)

Christ Turning the Water into Wine, 1951

Gouache stencil on black card, (coloured)
47.6 × 40.2 cm
Art Gallery of New South Wales, Sydney
Gift of W. G. Preston

Again in a most unsophisticated way, and with naive and charming vision, Margaret Preston locates the Gospel miracle story of the wedding at Cana in a recognizably Australian landscape. Guests crowd the veranda under the corrugated-iron roof, a pair of kangaroos stop playing near the gum tree and the water tank to witness the miracle. A picture-book Christ lifts his hands over giant water jars while a haloed Mary watches from the door of the house. An Italianate fountain spurts water in the parched yard.

There are strong echoes here of past works. The shallow space organized in horizontal strips recalls earlier woodcuts—for example, *Rocks and Waves, Balmoral* (1929), the patterning of the gum trees in *Gums* (1925) and *Grey Day at the Ranges* (1942). The kangaroos are from *Adam and Eve in the Garden of Eden.* The lick of colour on the water jars is a relic from early times when her concern was to master the illusion of three dimensions on a flat surface.

The war with Japan angered and depressed her. She admired and respected Japanese art, while being herself intensely nationalistic and, at this time, obsessively committed to all things Australian. Between 1940 and 1944 she travelled throughout Australia, lecturing in schools and to women's groups. After the war she moved to Mosman; already seventy years old, she now repeated in her work many of the motifs of earlier years—flowers, plants, landscapes on small canvases or in monoprints and stencil. Her religious prints may be the most innovative of her output in her last years.

A major retrospective of her work was organized by the Art Gallery of South Australia in 1980.

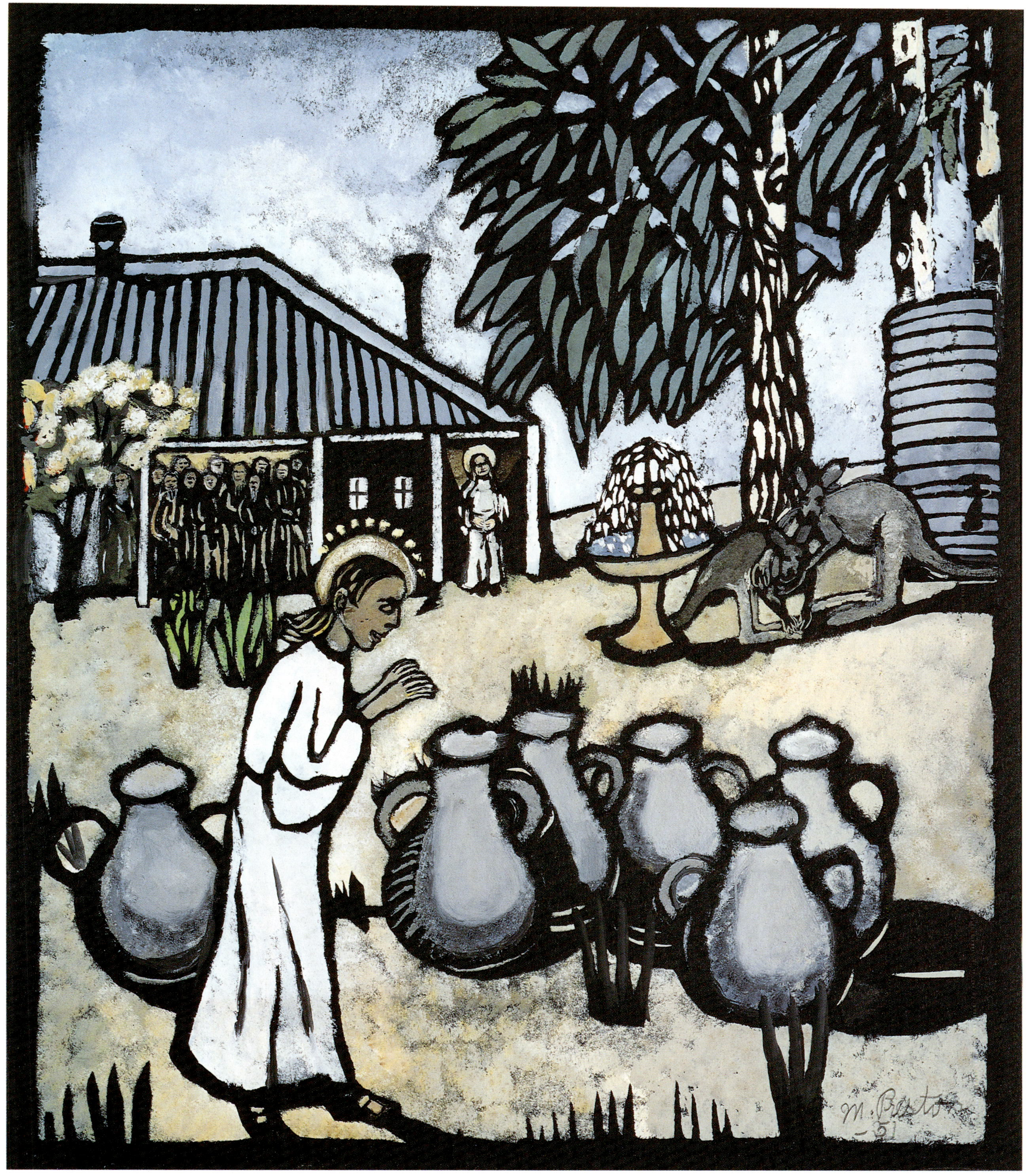

17 *Christ Turning the Water into Wine*

JUSTIN O'BRIEN

Born 1917

The Virgin Enthroned, 1951

Oil on canvas
Three panels: 113 × 49.2, 113 × 81.2, 113 × 49.2 cm
National Gallery of Victoria, Melbourne
Felton Bequest 1951

Justin O'Brien's *The Virgin Enthroned* won the first Blake Prize for Religious Art in 1951. The founders of the prize, Michael Scott, SJ, and Richard Morley, hoped to bring about a revival of interest among artists in religious art and to involve the Churches as patrons of the arts after a lapse of centuries. Both men deplored the type of religious art common in Australian churches by the late forties. Justin O'Brien's entry in the first year was greeted with delight; it more than fulfilled the hopes of the founders. The artist was young, sincere, religious; the work was traditional, yet modern, and superbly executed.

The Virgin Enthroned looks firmly to the Western European tradition of religious art and is indebted particularly to Giovanni de Paolo and Sassetta in technique, landscape and composition. The subject matter, explicitly religious and Christian, reflects the theology and devotional emphases of the 1950s, when personal piety was highly valued, Mary was seen as the mediatrix of redemption, the saints as intermediaries with God. The left panel portrays Adam and Eve at the moment of the Fall. They are in an opulent garden from which an ultramarine angel flees, face covered. In the centre panel a serene Madonna, the new Eve, reigns over apostles and saints. The right panel shows Christ, the new Adam, being baptized by John in the Jordan and watched by angels and men.

Technically, the painting is meticulously executed with a finished surface which glows translucently through layers of thin oil glazes, each chromatically adjusted as it touches its neighbouring colour. No brush mark shows except where delicate patterns have been drawn on garments and trees with a fine sable brush. The composition, which was drawn out first and then transferred to the canvas panels, is equally traditional. Figures and landscape are carefully modelled with lighting from the left. The rhythms and shapes build to a crescendo of colour and form around the centre of the middle panel in a wide double arc which holds the enthroned figure of the mother and child. Colour is decorative rather than descriptive, with occasional use of liturgical colour symbolism; as O'Brien said in a letter to Michael Scott in 1962, 'The use of red in the figure of Christ is a symbol of his passion.'

JUSTIN O'BRIEN was born in Sydney in 1917. From the age of thirteen until he was nineteen he studied art privately with Edward Smith, a conservative religious painter and disciple of Julian Ashton. During World War II he served as a surgical nurse in Palestine and in Greece and then was a prisoner of war in Poland. In 1945 he held a joint exhibition with fellow ex-POW Jesse Martin at the Macquarie Galleries in Sydney. The exhibition was a critical success, and O'Brien later came to exhibit regularly with Jean Bellette, Paul Haefliger and others of the Sydney Group. In 1946 he began teaching art at the Sydney private school Cranbrook, where he stayed until he moved permanently to Rome in 1967.

In 1948–49 O'Brien visited Italy and studied at first hand the Florentine and Sienese trecento painters whom he loved. While he acknowledges the influence of Byzantine art, he readily admits his admiration for the Italians and especially for the richness of surface and the control of line of Duccio.

Much of his work uses explicitly Christian iconography. Those paintings completed before he renounced Catholicism in 1954 he saw as expressions of a deeply held faith; those after that time were less so and more about his concern to anchor his style firmly to an already established tradition of art, the Italian Renaissance.

Justin O'Brien lives and works in Rome, but continues to exhibit regularly in Australia.

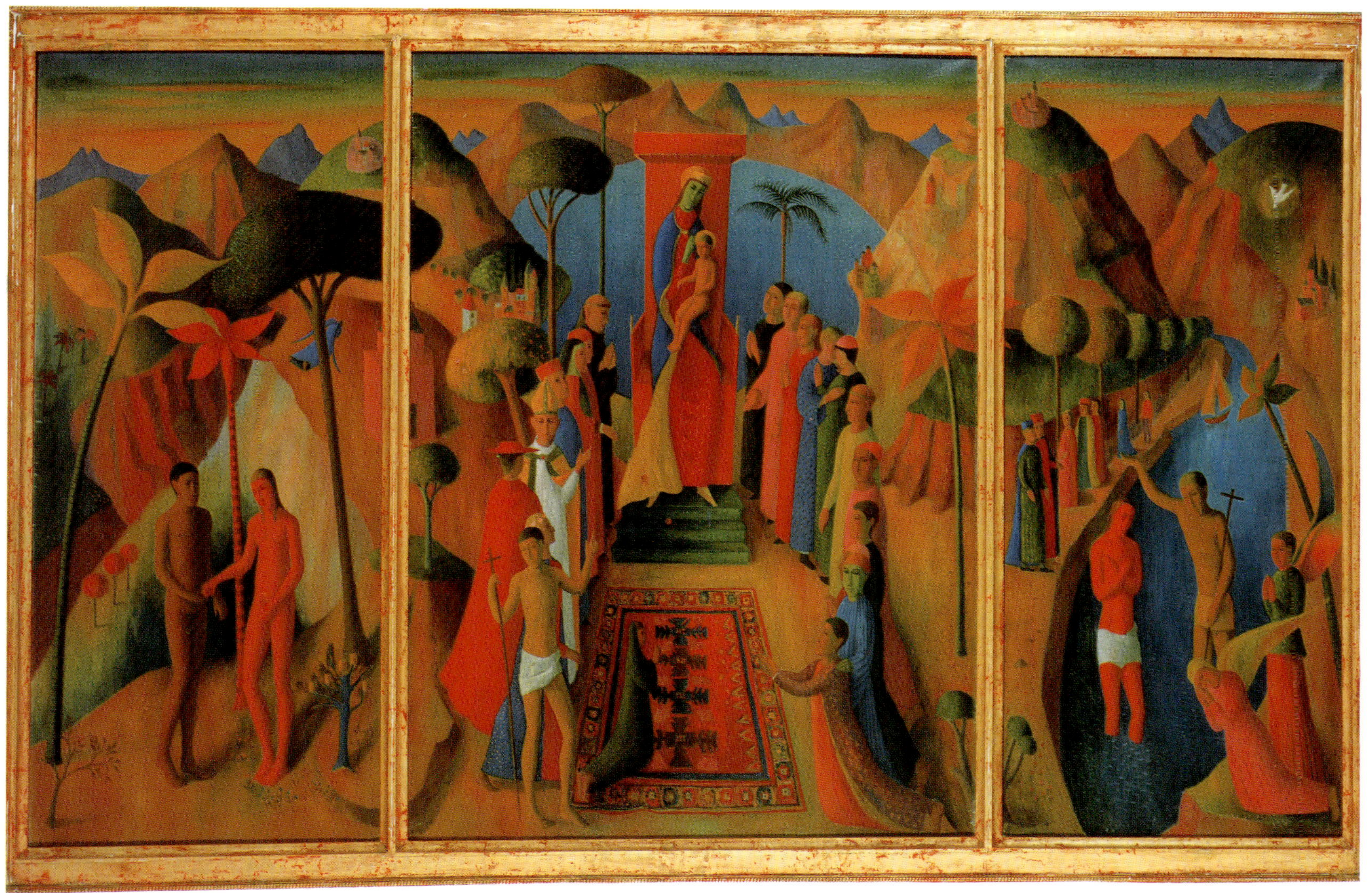

18 *The Virgin Enthroned*

SIDNEY NOLAN

Born 1917

Flight into Egypt, 1951

Ripolin on composition board
91.4 × 121.9 cm
Collection of Sir Keith and Lady Shann, Canberra

Nolan exhibited *Flight into Egypt* in the Blake Prize of 1952. He had travelled extensively through central Australia and was bewitched by its Genesis-type landscape and with the colours when viewed from the air, 'like a rainbow beginning with bright cobalt blue at the horizon and changing from purple to the most brilliant pink, and last to orange . . . there are whites of every kind . . . here is a world of deep space, yet of two dimensional forms . . . light is everywhere, reflecting from one shape to another, so that the European ideas of solidity expressed in light and shade, no longer hold good.'[1] From his desert journeying had come his Burke and Wills (1949) and the Inland Australia paintings (1950). In late 1951 Nolan visited Europe for the first time and took the opportunity to study Renaissance religious art at first hand.

Flight into Egypt owes much to both experiences. The landscape is obsessively Australian and outback, close to the aerial realism of the Inland Australia series, but Nolan has added trees on the horizon, a tent and the exotic plant behind the figure of Joseph. Mary, the Child and the donkey are delicately modelled and reminiscent of the paintings of Fra Angelico and other early Florentine and Sienese painters. The angel that hovers is delightfully idiosyncratic and recalls 'pretty polly' from the 1948 painting *Pretty Polly Mine* and foreshadows the floating devil in Nolan's 1952 *Temptation of St Anthony* (Plate 20). In *Flight into Egypt* Nolan makes no attempt at a historical recreation of a particular Gospel event. His interpretation is lyric and poetic. To enter into the painting demands a leap into the unknown, a forsaking of the familiar territory so often traversed by other painters, a suspension of credibility that is beyond the kind of rationality so valued by traditional theology. It is a painting both witty and serious.

1. Mary Cecil Allen, 'Notes on Central Australia', *Meanjin*, Spring 1950, p. 191.

SIDNEY NOLAN was born in Melbourne in 1917. He studied design and craft at Prahran Technical College and painting intermittently at the National Gallery School between 1934 and 1936, and engraving and lithography at Atelier 17, Paris, between 1947 and 1949. Despite this, he regards himself as self-taught. He acknowledges the influence of Blake, Rousseau, Picasso, van Gogh and Matisse among painters and was also influenced by the writings of Rimbaud, Nietzsche, Kierkegaard, Marx and the Bible. His early years in Melbourne saw deep friendships with John and Sunday Reed, the *Angry Penguins* circle, and stimulus from the diverse artistic circles in Melbourne, which included Arthur Boyd, John Perceval, Albert Tucker, Joy Hester and Danila Vassilieff.

Nolan has always been fascinated with myth and story on the one hand and the underlying mood of what he observed on the other. 'I must get steamed up with what I'm thinking about as content before I start to find forms,' he said in 1964. 'The message, if that is not too pompous a word, is the necessary trigger for me, with nothing really worked out.'[1] Thus it is not surprising that much of his prodigious output has been concerned with series of paintings inspired by myths which reveal some critical aspect of the human story. His Ned Kelly, in the series painted in 1947–48, is at once bushranger, criminal and hero. But Nolan goes beyond narration; in his hands the drama becomes an epic account of each person's struggle to survive in a society that has become highly institutionalized. The series can become for the viewer a time of revelation and identification. Other series include Inland Australia (*c.*1950), Leda and the Swan (*c.*1958), Gallipoli (1959), Rimbaud in Africa (*c.*1963), Antarctica (*c.*1964), Oedipus and the Sphinx (1975). The last major retrospective of Nolan's work was in Australia in 1987–88.

Sidney Nolan lives in England.

1. Noel Barber, *Conversations with Painters* (London: Collins, 1964), p. 94.

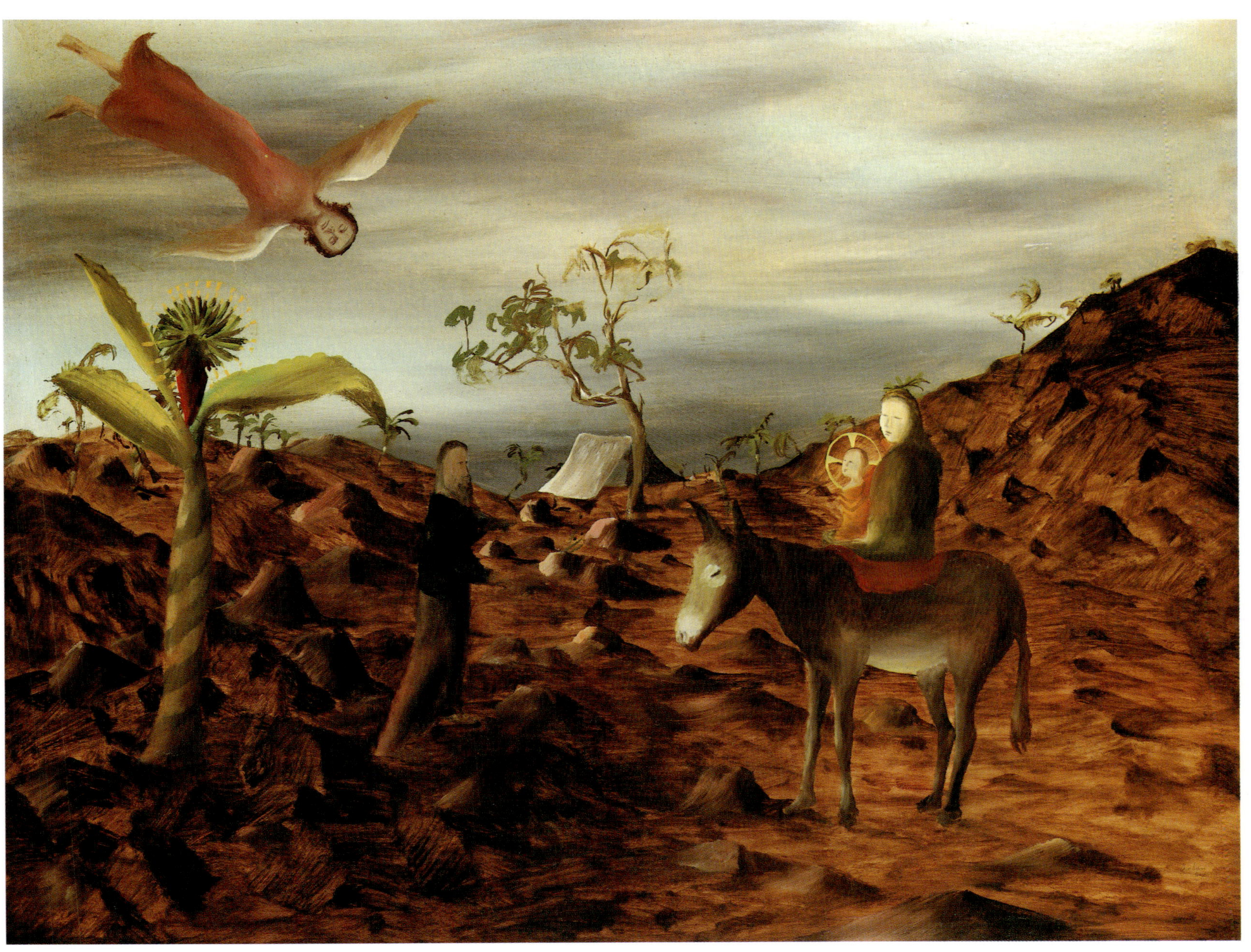

19 *Flight into Egypt*

SIDNEY NOLAN

Born 1917

Temptation of St Anthony, 1952

Synthetic polymer on composition board
122 × 96.5 cm
Art Gallery of South Australia, Adelaide
On loan from private collection

Sidney Nolan entered the Blake Prize for the third and last time in 1953 with *Temptation of St Anthony.* The prize went to Michael Kmit's *The Evangelist John Mark* (Plate 23), the Sydney judges preferring Kmit's soft neo-Byzantine colour and handling of space to Nolan's more complex iconography.

Nolan's Blake entries, *Temptation of St Anthony, St Francis Receiving the Stigmata* and *Flight into Egypt,* are among the religious paintings that Nolan completed on his return from Italy. The immediate encounter with Italian, Flemish and German Renaissance art seems to have aroused his interest in religious subject matter in an extended way for the first time. Like Arthur Boyd and John Perceval he set his narrative within an Australian landscape; unlike them, he was fascinated at this time with outback Australia and, with Ripolin enamel, had developed ways of creating the breadth of space and the peculiar light that is distinctive of the central Australian desert.

Saint Anthony, the fourth-century Egyptian abbot-hermit and patron saint of the sick, was a popular subject with Renaissance painters. Hieronymus Bosch and Matthias Grünewald had both painted pictures of the temptation of Saint Anthony in which the saint is seen at prayer resisting the allure of ultimate religious betrayal. With Bosch the temptation is to take part in a black mass; Grünewald places his Anthony in the allure of sexual licence. Arthur Boyd, a great admirer of both artists, had completed in 1951 two ceramic paintings of the temptation of Saint Anthony in one of which a nude temptress swings upside down from a branch of a tree while the saint bathes in a pool in the Australian countryside; a ram, serpent and blackbird look on.

Nolan has sent his Anthony back into the desert, not the Egyptian desert but to the Northern Territory, which Nolan knew well and which he had flown over in 1951. The saint is not at prayer but dancing with a female spirit, possibly his guardian angel. A huge dragonfly and a giant lizard or goanna join in the dance. The hand of God thrusts in from outside the picture space to protect and bless him, and a male spirit, complete with horns, wings and webbed feet, hangs upside down. The nature of Anthony's temptation is not clear. Nolan has set his scene in the surreal world between reality and dream; like the flower that blooms in the sky, Nolan's vision tilts at reality.

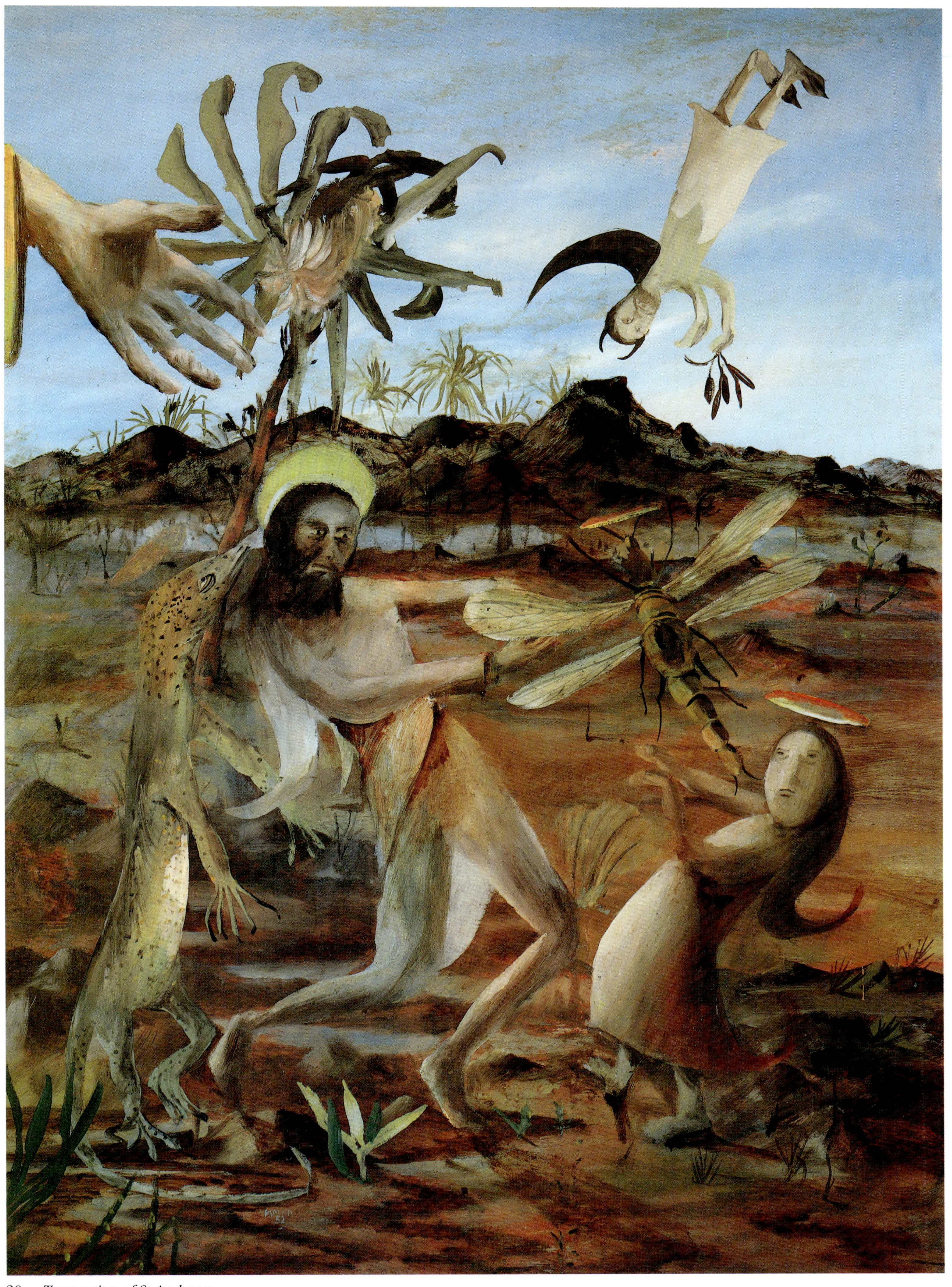

20 *Temptation of St Anthony*

WEAVER HAWKINS
1893–1977

Persecution, 1951

Oil on composition board
121.9 × 182.9 cm
St Paul's College, University of Sydney

Between 1951 and 1972 Weaver Hawkins exhibited thirty-two paintings in the Blake Prize. They are usually regarded by art historians as the most important group of works in his artistic output. They document, over twenty-one years, Hawkins's concern with tightly controlled colour and form and carefully planned structure as well as his interest in using biblical subject matter as a way of addressing some issue of wide social concern.

Persecution is typical of his religious paintings. The composition is tight, the space shallow and dominated by large rhythmic figures, the most important outlined in white. Each figure is more stereotype than portrait, an overstatement of emotion—the Christ who drags himself over such sharp and mechanical stones, the huge arm which points in accusation, the young man who reaches out in compassion, the men who scream in the background. Although the Christ figure is the Christ of history, Hawkins's intention is, as always, to explore a major current issue; persecution in war and its horrible aftermath was often discussed in 1951 as thousands of refugees came to try a new life. It is a painting of men and about men.

In 1962 Hawkins wrote the following description of the work in a letter to Michael Scott: 'It incorporates the symbols of its title. It is as much a depiction, in my own personal way, of the scriptural subject as of the modern world. Apart from the matter, the forms and colours throughout are by aesthetic intent designed and adapted to fit together in a cohesive, harmonious unity, but at the same time to convey the feeling of poignancy.'

WEAVER HAWKINS was born in London in 1893. He studied painting at the Camberwell School of Arts and Crafts, the Westminster School of Art, the Royal Academy and the Royal College of Art. Between 1923 and 1927 he lived in Paris and Siena; in 1927 he moved to Malta and began to sign his work 'Raokin' to avoid the attention he often received because of a crippling war injury to his hands. In 1935 he settled in Australia but did not exhibit paintings until about 1948. It is often suggested that this was because he was critical of Sydney painting with its classical formats and muted colours.

In 1948 he became actively involved with the New South Wales Contemporary Art Society and was president from 1954 to 1963, a period that saw Sydney avant-garde art move relentlessly towards a painterly abstract expressionism. Hawkins remained committed to a peculiar kind of realism which met with criticism from fellow artists, who labelled his work 'hard', 'insensitive' and 'simple'. It took the Hard Edge abstraction movement to cause his work to be reassessed, and a major retrospective exhibition, Project 11, Weaver Hawkins, at the Art Gallery of New South Wales in 1976 to affirm his place in these decades.

Yet it seems that Hawkins remained confident of himself, as his private notebooks testify. 'I am as logical in my art as was Cézanne,' he wrote, 'though less subtle and complex, of course, but too stark for many . . . I am primarily a classic artist, an intellectual artist, an architectonic worker . . . People say [my work] is too intellectual and cold.'[1] This pursuit of the intellectual, the logical, is not always apparent in Hawkins's work, which often appears distorted and harsh and the bearer of deep emotion.

1. Daniel Thomas, Introduction, Exhibition Catalogue, *Weaver Hawkins, 1893–1977* (Ballarat Fine Art Gallery).

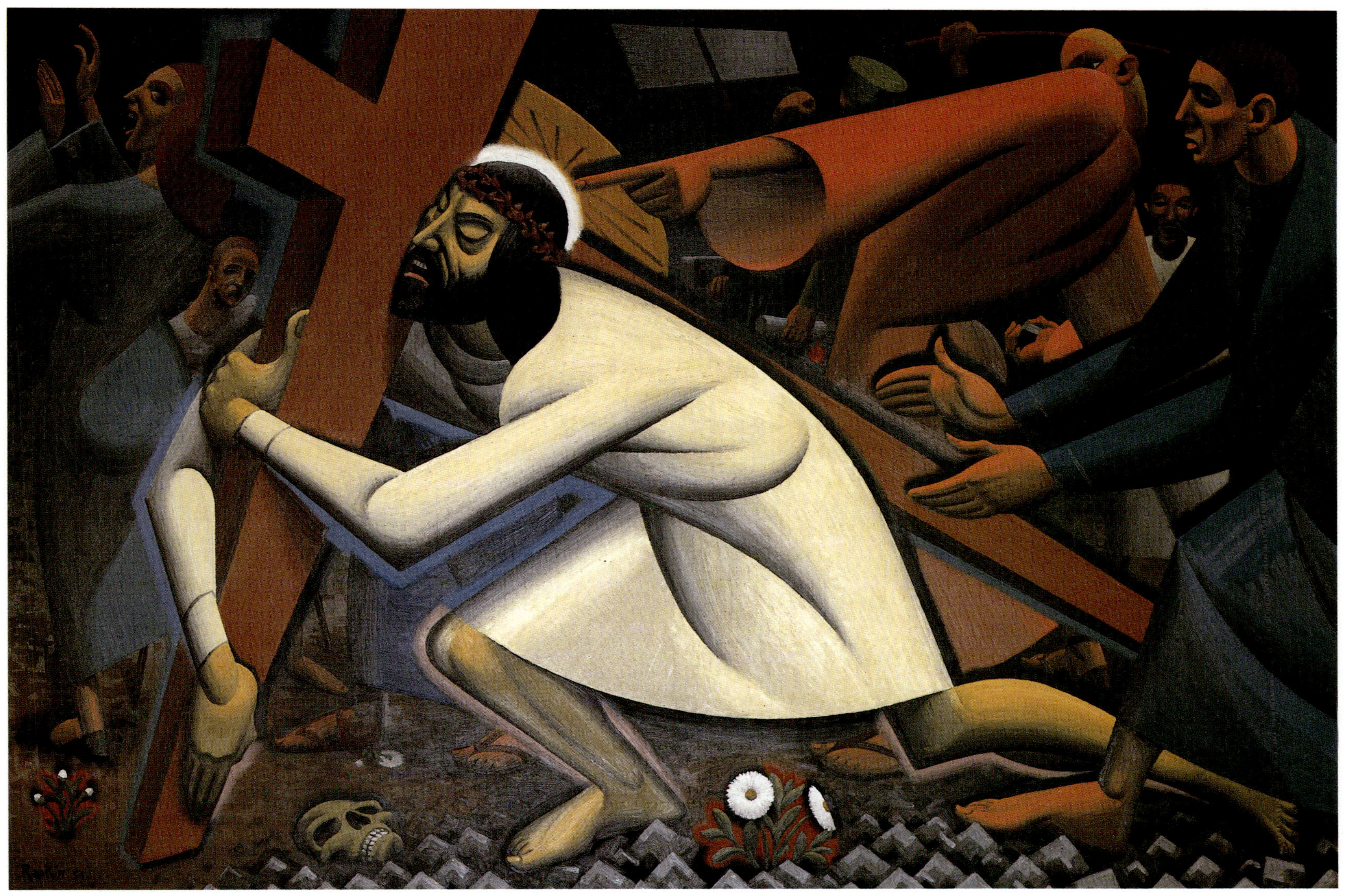

21 *Persecution*

JOHN PASSMORE

1904–84

Miraculous Draught of Fishes, 1952

Oil on composition board
119.4 × 182.9 cm
Private collection
Courtesy Lauraine Diggins Fine Art Pty Ltd, Melbourne

It is probable that John Passmore painted *Miraculous Draught of Fishes* for the 1952 Blake Prize competition at the suggestion of Jean Bellette and Paul Haefliger. As members of the Blake committee, they often contacted their friends to submit paintings, and they were staunch supporters of Passmore. However, the real genesis of this major work may well have been two paintings in a 1948 London exhibition of Passmore's friend, Keith Vaughan. One of these, *Raft of the Medusa* (after Géricault's nineteenth-century masterpiece), also had a group of figures crouched on a platform against a wide expanse of sky. But Passmore's shifting planes of transparent blues and greens pay homage to Cézanne, even though in scale and mood the two are different. The religious subject matter of this painting—as of Passmore's 1953 Blake entry, *The Baptism*[1]—is unusual in the whole range of Passmore's work, and *Miraculous Draught of Fishes* belongs more easily with other studies of the sea and fishermen from this time. It is a romantic painting which made few concessions to the ideals of the Blake committee, who looked for art for worshippers and a conversion of heart for the artist. *Miraculous Draught of Fishes* is not a narrative painting, nor is it about doctrine, nor does it comment on society. If it can be called religious, it is because it speaks so powerfully of the surface complexity yet underlying unity of the whole of life; it is a hymn to nature and an intellectual homage to art.

1. Now in the University of Texas at Austin collection, but originally owned by Bellette and Haefliger.

Within the history of Sydney painting of the post-war years, JOHN PASSMORE's stature among artists is unique. Although his life was a progressive withdrawal from people, he is revered as a great teacher, a guru, a genius of a painter.

Born in Sydney in 1904, Passmore studied part-time at the Julian Ashton Art School in 1918–19, and then at the East Sydney Technical College until 1933, when he left for England. There he studied, as did many Australians, at the Westminster School of Art under Mark Gertler and Bernard Meninsky, who became his mentors. He was also greatly influenced by his friend and colleague Keith Vaughan. In 1937–38 he travelled through France and Italy with Jean Bellette and Paul Haefliger. Always an admirer of Cézanne, this trip gave him the opportunity to study the master at first hand. It put an indelible mark upon his future.

In 1951 he returned to Australia to teach, first at Julian Ashton's, then at Newcastle Technical College and finally at the National Art School. These teaching years greatly influenced the course of Sydney painting. His pupils often became like disciples. John Olsen, Peter Upward, John Henshaw and William Rose were among them. As a teacher, Passmore was clear about his priorities: art before all else; painting must be coupled with thinking and solitude; nature is clothed in mystery; Cézanne is the great master of our time.

The year he returned to Australia he had a small and very successful exhibition at the Macquarie Galleries. The next years were very productive, with drawings, small and large seascapes and landscapes filled with patterns of light and with structures never quite resolved. In 1956 he began exhibiting abstracts and participated in Olsen's important Direction 1 at the Macquarie Galleries.

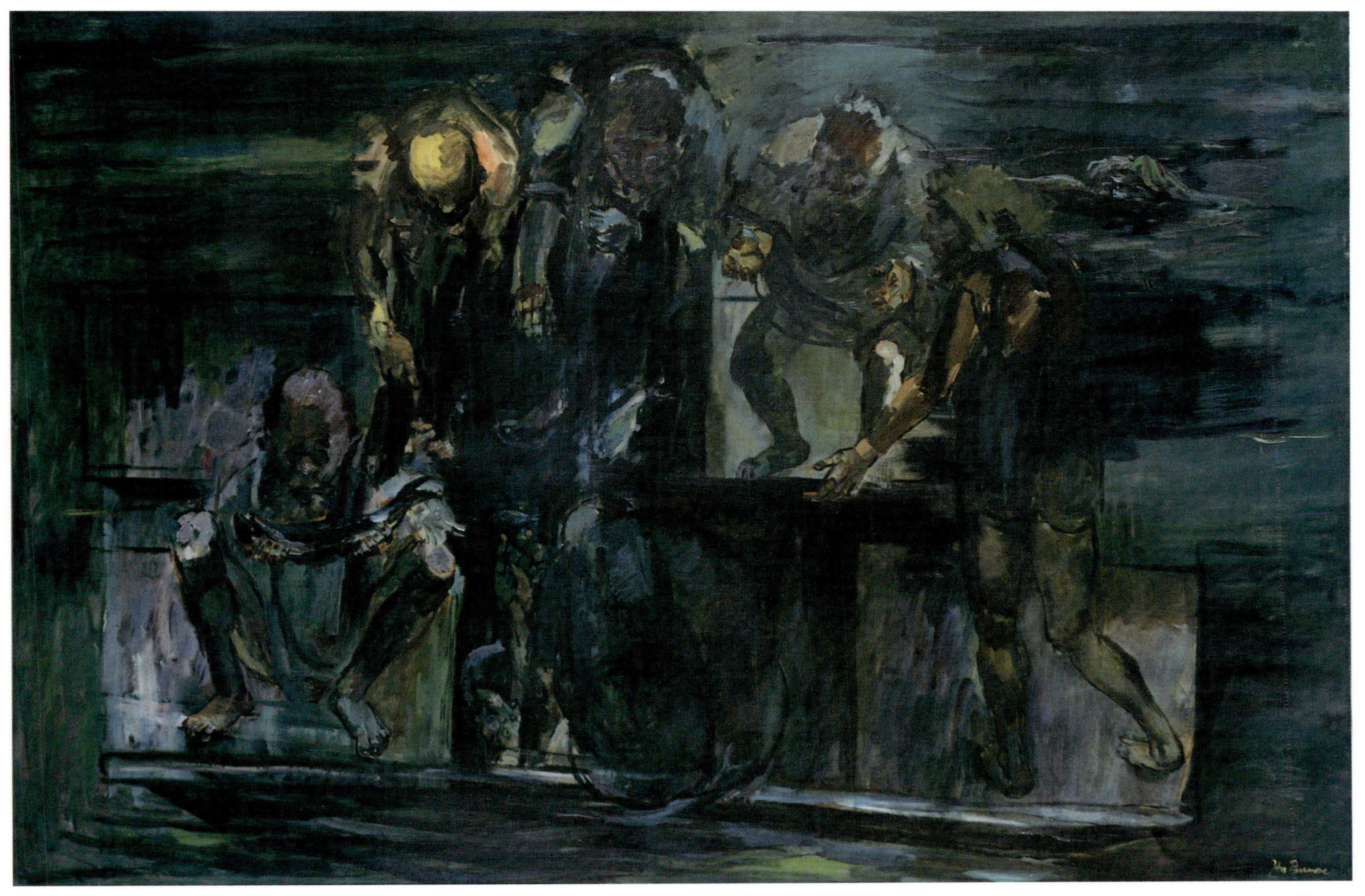

22 *Miraculous Draught of Fishes*

MICHAEL KMIT

1910–81

The Evangelist John Mark, 1953

Oil on canvas
95 × 70 cm
Art Gallery of New South Wales, Sydney
Purchased 1961

The Evangelist John Mark was awarded third Blake Prize for Religious Art in 1953. Kmit was well known to the Blake committee and to the judges through his association with Jean Bellette and Paul Haefliger. Moreover, he was manifestly and deeply religious with a cultural heritage which allowed him to move unselfconsciously with religious symbolism, particularly that of Eastern Orthodox Christianity. In 1952, his *Ascension* was given second prize over Sidney Nolan's *Flight into Egypt*, and critics had been quick to praise its icon-like character as being particularly suitable for religious art for churches.

The Evangelist John Mark is indebted to both the Russian tradition of illustration and the soft colour orchestration of the French impressionists, particularly Pierre Bonnard. The evangelist is portrayed iconically, gazing through and beyond the viewer. His right hand is raised in blessing while his left protects the holy book of the Bible, bearing the symbols Alpha and Omega, 'the Beginning and the Ending'. In his earlier religious paintings, Kmit had been criticized for the way he failed to handle background areas. In this painting he has almost filled the space with the figure, so that the small amount of background can be easily organized with soft, shallow rectangles of colour. Although more successful than his earlier works, he has sacrificed a sense of excitement and risk.

Michael Kmit was born in the Ukraine in 1910 and arrived in Sydney in 1950. He had studied art in the Academy of Fine Arts in Cracow, Poland, and taught painting in Lvov, Ukraine, and Landeck, Austria; he had also worked in Italy, Paris and Vienna. From 1950 he exhibited with the Sydney Group. His particular brand of neo-Byzantinism, with its flat shapes and soft, chalky yet rich colour, appealed to Sydney artists and critics, who were familiar with the heavy browns, greys and red ochres of painters like Jean Bellette, Francis Lymburner and Russell Drysdale in the late forties.

In 1958, at the peak of his popularity in Australia, Kmit left for America. By the time he returned in 1965, the leadership in the art world had passed to a younger generation who looked firmly to the American abstractionists as models and who expressed scant enthusiasm for Kmit's icon-like figuration. The older generation, though—both critics like James Gleeson and Bernard Smith and the remainder of the Sydney Group—continued to speak of the substantial contribution he was making to Australian painting, particularly in his use of clean tesserae of bright colour.

Michael Kmit died in 1981.

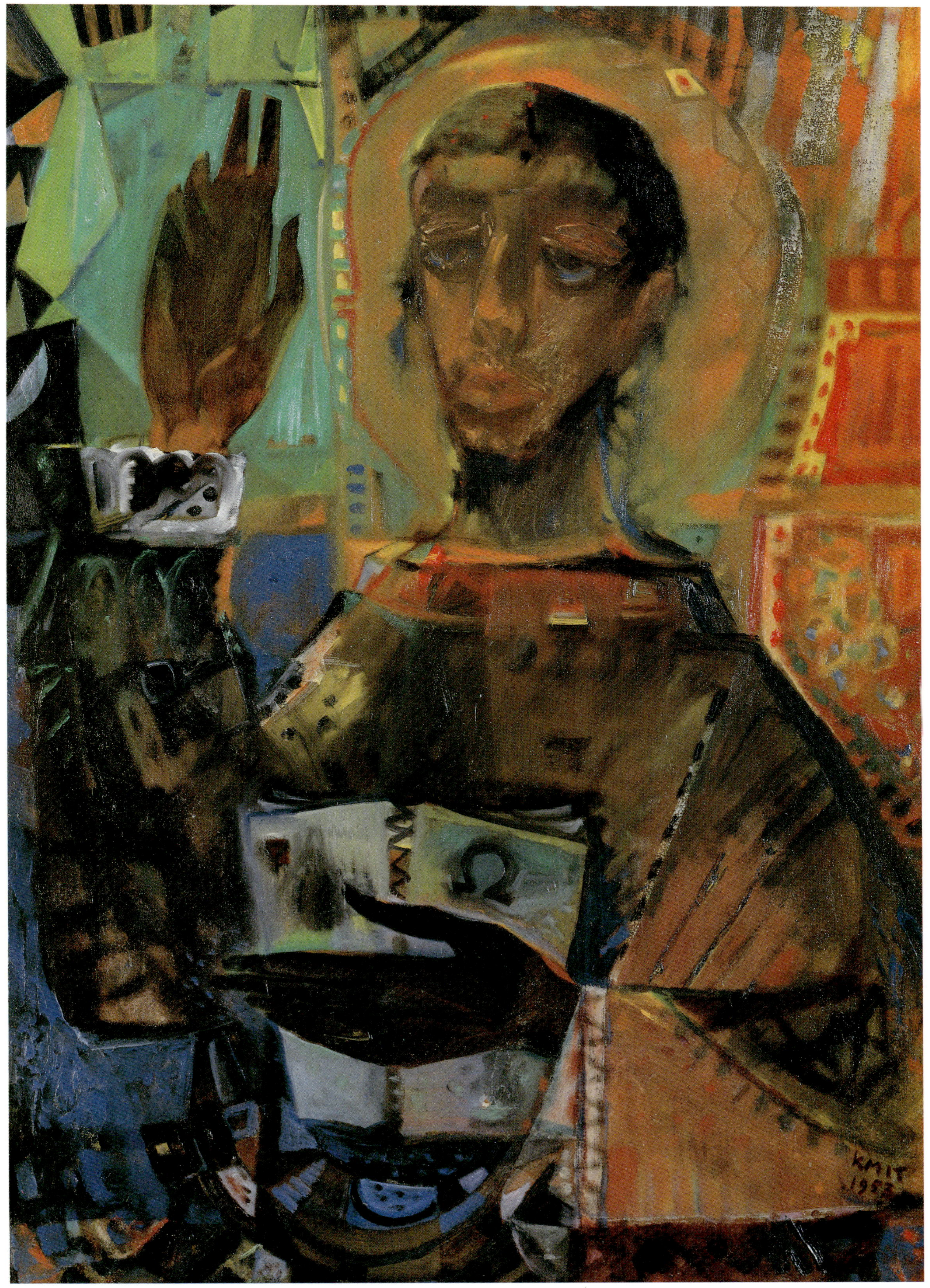

23 *The Evangelist John Mark*

ALBERT TUCKER

Born 1914

Judas, 1955

Oil on hardboard
96.5 × 129.5 cm
National Gallery of Victoria, Melbourne

Although Albert Tucker painted *Judas* in 1955 in Rome, the painting more properly belongs with the long series of explicitly religious works from the months spent in Noli. Tucker had become fascinated with Jungian symbolic theory, and biblical narratives had become an avenue to explore a problem that had always fascinated him—the battle between the forces of good and evil and the way this is acted out in history and in myth. But it is with the incarnation of evil that most of his religious work is concerned. At its best, as in *Betrayal* (1952), *Pilate* (1952), *Job* (1954) and this *Judas*, his paintings become revelations of violence, anger and despair—in his own words, 'portraits of the Devil himself'.

Here the huge figure of Judas almost fills the entire picture space as it squats over the earth, vomiting up the price of such horrendous betrayal. The rope with which he is about to hang himself lies limply around his neck, reminiscent of that other archetypal symbol of evil, the snake of the Garden of Eden. Tucker's man is dominating the earth in a gesture of profound disrespect, yet at the same time he is at one with it: the head with its matted red hair and craggy face and the skirt stretched tight between the knees suggest some primordial landscape, some great outcrop in a green and brown desert.

ALBERT TUCKER was born in Melbourne in 1914. He attended art classes part-time from 1933 to 1939 at the Victorian Artists' Society and at George Bell's school briefly in 1936. He was a foundation member of the Victorian Contemporary Art Society, and, like Nolan and to a lesser extent Boyd and Perceval, found friends and patrons in John and Sunday Reed, of Heide, at Bulleen. His work between 1939 and 1947 established him as an intense, literate advocate of the poor and the derelict. From the streets of Fitzroy and St Kilda he wove a basic expressionist set of symbols which he has continued to use. His affinities even at this time lay with the German expressionists, especially with Max Beckmann, Otto Dix and George Grosz. Fellow Melbourne artists Danila Vassilieff and Josl Bergner became exemplars, with their immediacy of expressionism and freedom from inhibition. From this period come the Images of Evil series (later called Night Images), powerful meditations on the nature of modern evil.

In 1947 Tucker left for Europe, a refugee, he said, from Australian culture. But he was so dogged by poverty and lack of affirmation that he produced few works of substance until 1952. Then, in a single year, in the small Italian fishing village of Noli, he produced at least seventeen major works, most of them with religious themes. They reflect the influence of Italy—not the Renaissance, so beloved by Justin O'Brien and Sidney Nolan, but the brutal shapes of Etruscan sculpture and the stern emotionalism of Gothic wood carving. These religious paintings, like his social realist Melbourne paintings, show Tucker to be obsessed with the dark side of life. Religion for him was suffering, passion and death; hardly ever is it about Resurrection.

[*Continued overleaf*]

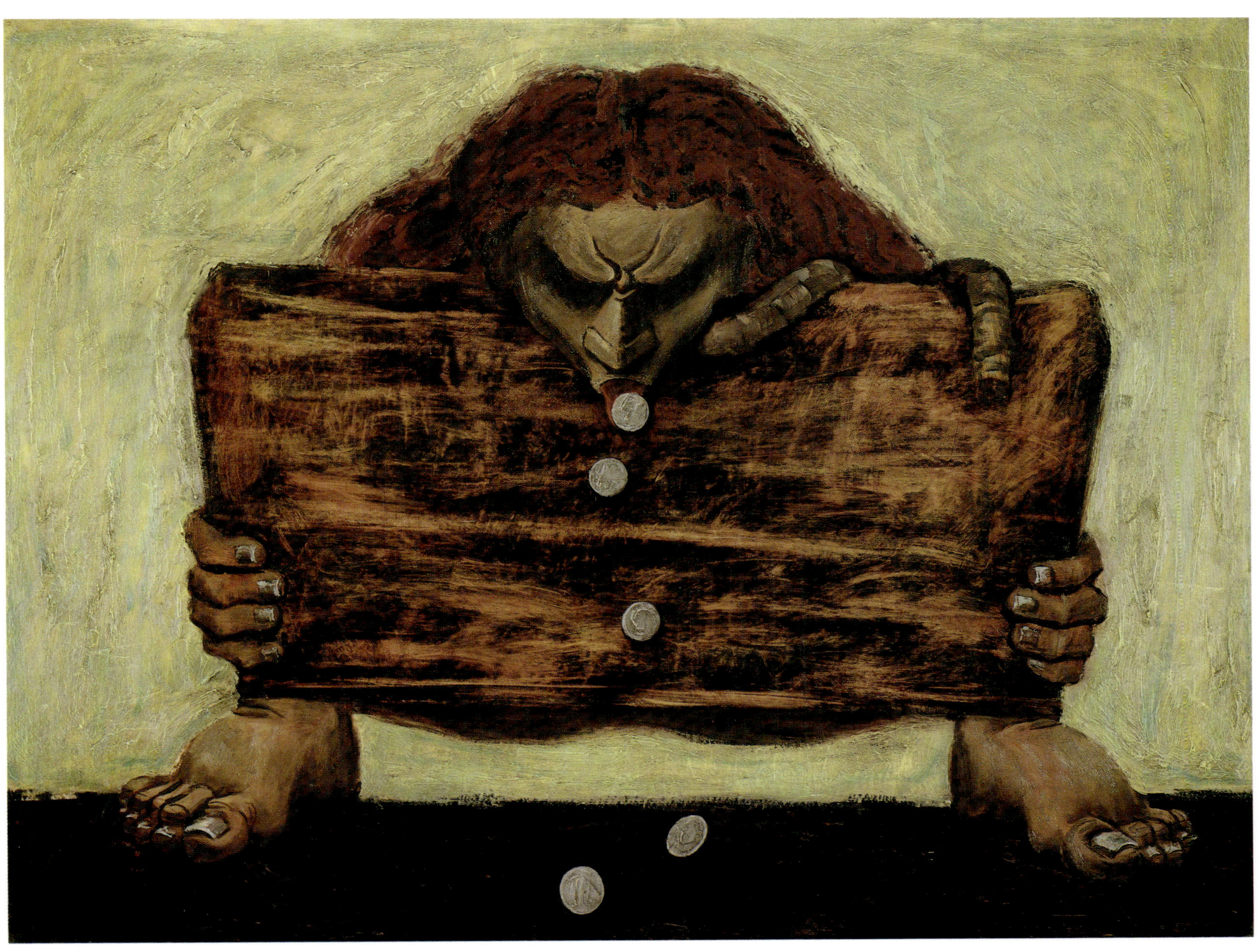

24 *Judas*

ALBERT TUCKER

Born 1914

Ascension, 1962

Acrylic on hardboard
130.2 × 96.2 cm
National Gallery of Victoria, Melbourne

Tucker began *Ascension* in London in 1958 and completed it in Melbourne in 1962. By this time he had won acceptance internationally and then in Australian art circles, and his paintings reflect a rather less pessimistic view of life. Unlike *Judas*, *Ascension* is a painting not of ultimate despair and rejection but of redemption and the promise of a life after death; thus its title. Again Tucker fills the space with a single figure; this time with a Christ hanging crucified. The raised arms, the subtlety of the shifting colour against the vivid green and the crescent red wound suggest hope; the head bears its thorns like a crown, with fortitude and compassion.

As with *Judas*, Tucker again evokes a relationship with the earth and the Australian landscape. This time he does so with a profound sympathy; his Christ is in unity with the land, the body a landscape of low hills and craters worn almost flat with the passage of time, but sharing in the act of redemption. *Ascension* is Tucker's finest religious work.

In 1954 Tucker and Nolan exhibited together in the Foreign Press Club in Rome. The exhibition was well received. Tucker got another surge of creative energy, sparked off in part by photographs that Nolan had taken in outback Queensland during the great drought of the previous years. Carcasses of starved cattle, eroded and denuded desert landscapes, drovers of the outback, skeletal trees and brightly coloured parrots became a new vocabulary. Australia came to be 'home' in a way it had never been for him before.

By the time he reached London in 1958 he had found acceptance among a prestigious circle of modern painters, including David Smith and Eduardo Paolozzi. Exhibitions of his European paintings aroused favourable critical review. Later that year he set out for Australia on a thousand-dollar *Woman's Weekly* Art Prize, stopping on the way in New York, the mecca of abstract expressionism. Again fortune smiled—this time by way of an exhibition at the Hirschel and Adler Galleries and the purchase of his paintings by the Museum of Modern Art and the Guggenheim Museum.

In 1960 he returned to Australia to exhibit at John Reed's Museum of Modern Art in Melbourne. Though confident of his importance and recognized elsewhere, he was still virtually unknown in Australia, one of many artist expatriates to return to revitalize the next decade. Recognition came quickly this time and, with it, financial security.

Albert Tucker lives and works in Melbourne. His images and vocabulary are those evolved early, his overriding concern the same. As he said to John and Sunday Reed in 1950, 'To sing of death and disaster does not make for popularity, but it's my song and I've got to sing it.'[1]

1. Quoted by Richard Haese in *Albert Tucker* (Tolarno Galleries, Melbourne, 1982).

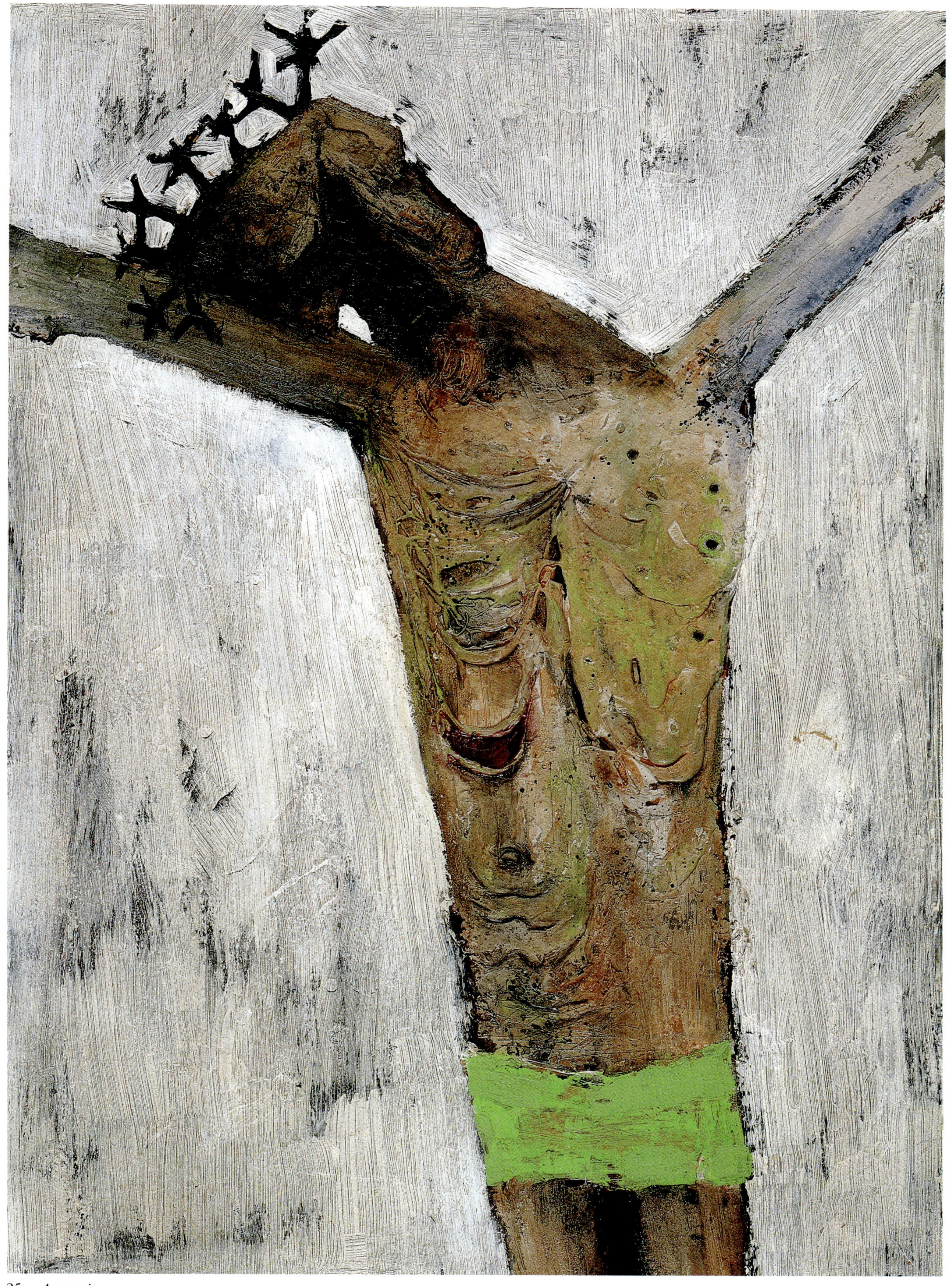

25 *Ascension*

ERIC SMITH

Born 1919

The Scourged Christ, 1956

Oil on composition board
116 × 85 cm
Penrith Regional Art Gallery, NSW
Lewers Bequest

The Scourged Christ marks a climax in Eric Smith's early religious paintings. With it he won his first Blake Prize. As he said of it in an ABC interview in 1975, 'I think that painting was the culmination of a series of Christs I'd been painting for the previous two or three years; it was also a turning point. It preceded my moving into more abstract form. The distortion in that painting was about as far as I was prepared to go at that time, and I had started to think about the possibilities of abstract form.' The single figure of Christ with head bowed, crowned with thorns, standing meek but strong, his hands manacled, is the Biblical 'man of sorrows', as it is reminiscent of a Rouault stained-glass window. The extraordinarily serene mood of the painting owes much to the large, rectangular blocks of soft tertiary colour which Smith created by building layer upon layer of rough impasto primary colours and soft tints of mauves. Behind the head a glowing halo of gold sings discordantly. In its colour orchestration it is already abstract.

The Scourged Christ is a religious painting in so far as it is a statement of Smith's personal faith. It communicates what it portrays—a suffering Redeemer who triumphs. Yet it was, as Smith came later to say, an image from the past translated rather than rethought into the present: 'You felt you were being modern, but basically you were painting stained-glass windows . . . with an affinity with the art of that time. But when it was all boiled down, it had little more to say than had been said in the past, and I thought the development of myself as a painter had to move away from that.'[1]

1. Interview with the author, 19 July 1977.

ERIC SMITH was born in Melbourne in 1919. Between 1936 and 1937 he studied commercial art at Brunswick Technical School. After demobilization from the army in 1946 he completed a diploma of art at the Royal Melbourne Institute of Technology. In 1951 he moved to Sydney and joined the group of artist friends who became known as The Sydney Group, led by Jean Bellette and Paul Haefliger. Through them, Smith came into contact with the newly formed Blake Society for Religious Art and with the Jesuits Michael Scott and Peter Kenny. A recent convert to Roman Catholicism, Smith found in the Blake Prize and in the friendships within the committee an outlet for his own deeply felt faith and hope in the message of Christianity and particularly in the person of the historical Christ as Risen Lord. Between 1952 and 1975 he exhibited forty-four paintings in the Blake Prize; all of them, regardless of title, were really resurrections. In all, he won the Blake Prize six times.

Smith's place in the history of Australian art has yet to be seriously assessed. He is highly respected among Sydney painters and has won many prestigious awards, including the Archibald Prize for portraiture three times and the Wynne Prize for landscape twice. Yet no monograph on him has been written. It may be that to write so closely of a man whose faith stance is so closely linked with so much of his work has been too daunting a task in a secularized Sydney art world.

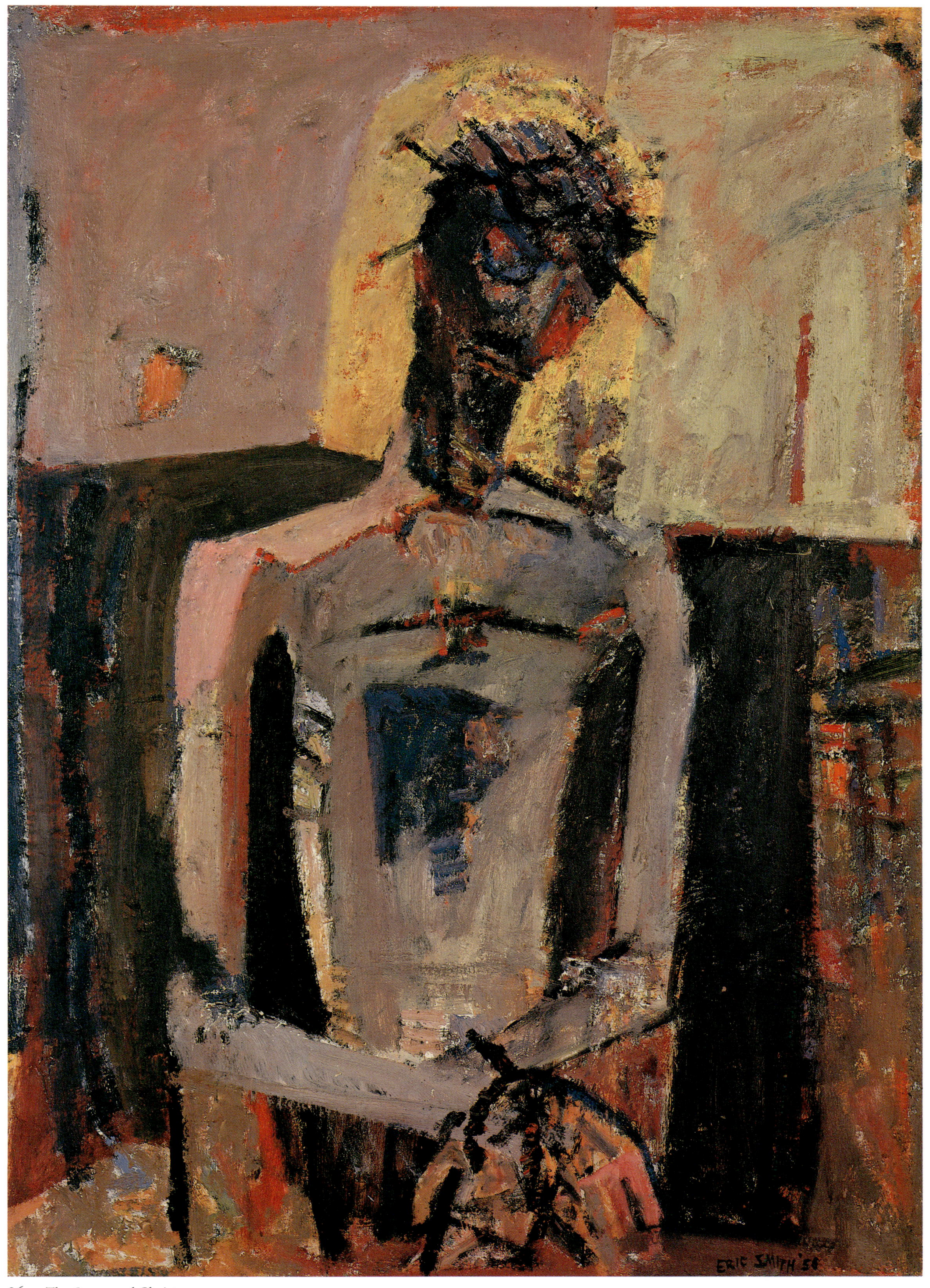

26 *The Scourged Christ*

Eric Smith

Born 1919

Christ Is Risen, 1959

Oil on composition board
220 × 115 cm
Canisius College, Pymble, NSW

Late in 1956 Eric Smith exhibited at the Macquarie Galleries with a group of Sydney painters that included John Olsen, William Rose and Robert Klippel. That exhibition, Direction 1, was to label avant-garde painting in Sydney as abstract expressionist, even though most of the work was then, and continued to be for the next ten years, only semi-abstract. So when Smith won the Blake Prize for the third time (having won previously in 1956 and 1958) with this painting *Christ Is Risen*, many on the committee and elsewhere protested that it could not possibly be religious because it was without intelligible subject matter. Yet clearly it is as much a portrait of Christ as is *The Scourged Christ*, and its theological message is the same. What is different, apart from the level of abstraction, is that whereas the earlier figure is still, frozen endlessly in a timeless space, *Christ Is Risen* moves across the surface until it sweeps upwards out of the picture surface in fractured shafts of colour. In *The Scourged Christ* the figure is personalized, human and emotive; the Christ in this painting is the cosmic Christ. But they are both the crowned and slender figures of the Judaeo-Christian tradition and have antecedents in art history.

Despite the difference in the styles of the two paintings, Smith remained dissatisfied; neither, he felt, was addressing the question that had become his own—how to portray a Christ that makes sense in a modern, secularized world? The next years were to see him struggle to find an iconography adequate to his own changing understanding of both Christianity and his art. In 1969 he again won the Blake Prize, this time with a series of commissioned posters, The Apostles Creed, which contained collages of photographs from the Vietnam War. In 1975, however, he decided to abandon religious subject matter. 'Of recent years I can no longer see the face of Christ,' he told the author.

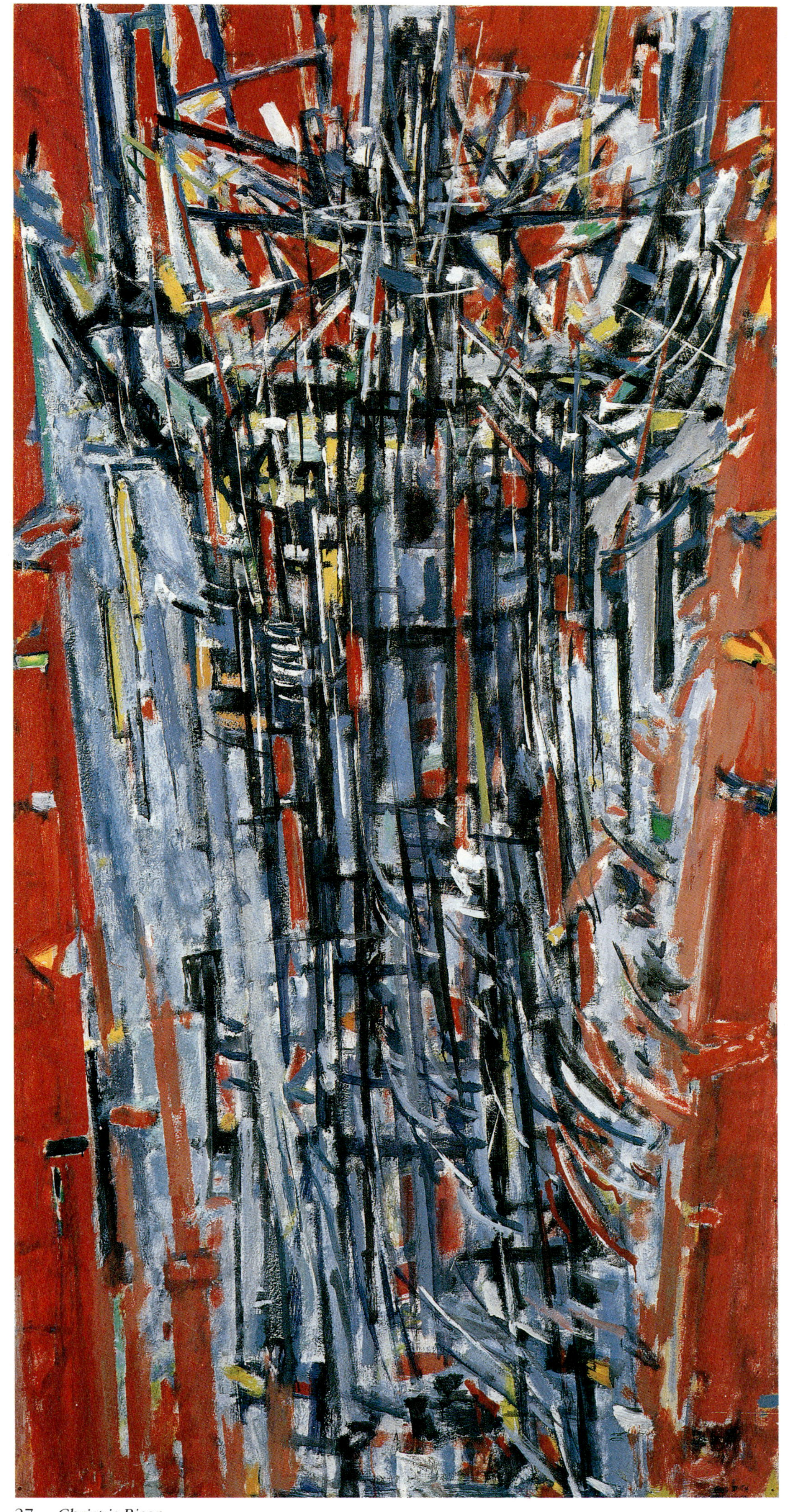

27 *Christ is Risen*

ELWYN LYNN

Born 1917

Betrayal, 1957

Oil on composition board
90.8 × 121.3 cm
National Gallery of Victoria, Melbourne
Purchased 1957

Elwyn Lynn's *Betrayal* was awarded the 1957 Blake Prize for Religious Art. The judges' decision was unanimous and almost certainly was in part a response to a demand by those responsible for the prize that the award should be given only to a painting with intelligible religious content. The year before, the Direction 1 exhibition had sent shock waves through the committee and raised questions about the place, if any, of abstraction in the art of the churches. Somewhat reluctantly they made conditions for the 1957 award.[1]

Betrayal, although the work of a relatively unknown painter, fulfilled the criteria laid down by the Blake committee. It was a figurative, symbolic representation of a scripture narrative, yet with some reference into the present time. On the right a garish, crowing cock, exultant symbol of evil, refers to Peter's threefold denial of Christ; brilliantly hued in reds, greens, crimsons and yellows against a giant flaming ball, it looks to Jean Lurçat's choir tapestry at Assy. On the left the distorted hands of a crucified and crowned Christ, expressive of degradation and suffering, pay direct homage to Grünewald. *Betrayal* was intended by Lynn to be a meditation and comment on what loyalty to country and friends can involve, and to express abhorence about betrayal and disloyalty. As he said in a letter to Michael Scott in 1962, 'Though it refers specifically to Peter's denial, I had in mind Judas' betrayal, and indeed the whole question [of loyalties and betrayals], which has become once again a great moral issue, especially since the thirties.'[2]

1. Minutes of the Blake Committee, 1956–61.
2. Elwyn Lynn, letter to Michael Scott, 17 September 1962.

ELWYN LYNN was born in Canowindra, New South Wales, in 1917 and studied history and philosophy for an arts degree at Sydney University. Between 1941 and 1968 he taught English and history in secondary schools in Sydney, while retaining an active involvement in the arts. From 1955 he was secretary of the Contemporary Art Society and editor of its broadsheet; he followed Weaver Hawkins as president from 1963 to 1965. As long-time editor of the society's broadsheet, he entered into lively correspondence with the Blake Society over the issue of abstraction in religious art, and over the standard of the judging of the Blake Prize in general.[1] Since that time he has written constantly as a critic and historian about Australian painters and paintings. His stature in Australian art has been acknowledged in a series of important appointments, including chairman of the Visual Arts Board, senior editor of *Art International*, 1982, and curator of the Power Gallery of Contemporary Art.

Lynn began painting and exhibiting in the mid 1940s, but the Blake Prize of 1957 was his first major award and happened at a time when he was ready to move from figurative painting. In 1958–59 he visited Europe and the United States and returned an enthusiast for the work of the Spanish tachist Antoni Tapies, with its use of thick paint and collage to create a lyric affinity with the earth. His 1960 exhibition at the Macquarie Galleries in Sydney contributed to a wave of 'texture' painting in Sydney. Lynn's art criticism at this time, informed by first-hand understanding of American abstract expressionism and modern European French and German art, was one of the formative factors in directing younger Sydney artists to look to the United States rather than to Europe for further experience. Although Lynn's more recent painting occasionally uses the symbols of traditional religion, his prime concern remains with the spirit of the country evoked symbolically through texture as well as form.

Elwyn Lynn lives and works in Sydney.

1. See *Contemporary Art Society Broadsheet*, May 1959, pp. 3–4.

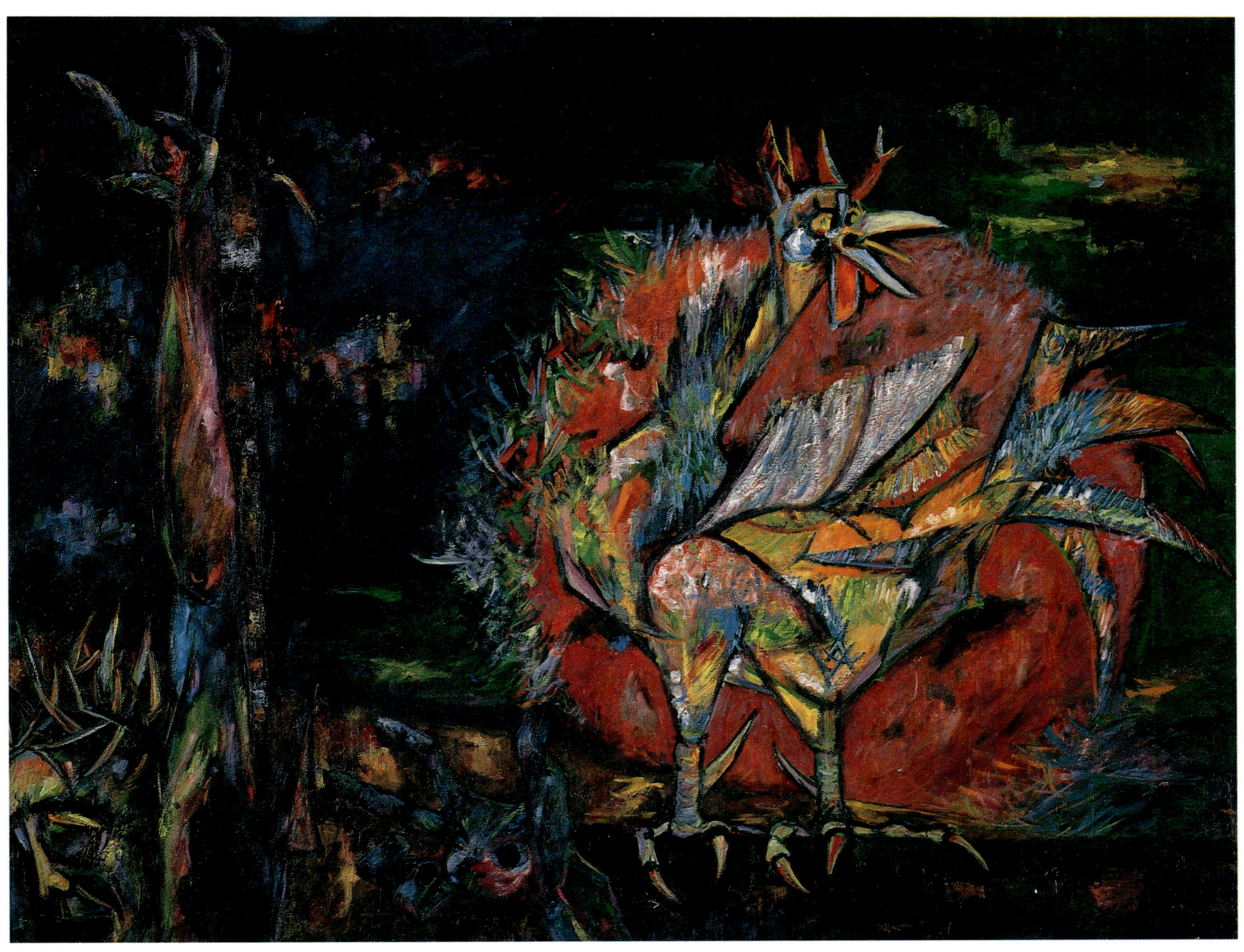

28 *Betrayal*

THOMAS GLEGHORN

Born 1925

Head of Christ, 1958

Oil on composition board
88 × 60 cm
Blake Society for Religious Art, Sydney

Head of Christ was awarded the special Christus Prize in the Blake competition in 1958. The prize had been introduced as a way of ensuring that some recognizable religious images came into the competition and thus to the attention of those responsible for purchasing or commissioning art for churches. It was hoped that the Christus would succeed where the Blake had failed.

In Tom Gleghorn's winning *Head of Christ,* many of the more conservative committee members felt that at last the Blake had produced a work that more than fulfilled their early dreams. It was popular and clearly modern, yet it was recognizably an image of Christ, deeply humane and suffering. Peter Kenny, one of the judges, wrote: 'Gleghorn outshone all competitors. His work was a semi-abstract, yet perfectly intelligible "Christus" painting conveying an impression of immense and dynamic personality. It made most of the other entries, even the good ones, look insipid and unoriginal. It alone, I felt, really suggested the *mystery* of Christ, the mystery of the Godhead.'[1]

Gleghorn began the painting with an image on the canvas which he then broke down with grids of black lines. In spite of the subsequent faceting, and the way the colour flows across the areas behind the grids, the huge face of Christ crowned with thorns gazes down sorrowfully yet serenely on the viewer. The face and expression recur frequently in nineteenth-century Nazarene art and in its successors, the sweet and pious holy cards of the twentieth century. In spite of its drama and mystery, Gleghorn's Christ remains a comforting and intimate image.

1. J. P. Kenny, 'The Blake Prize Exhibition 1958', *Twentieth Century,* winter 1958.

TOM GLEGHORN was born in Newcastle, England, in 1925 and migrated to Newcastle, New South Wales, in 1928. With encouragement from William Dobell, but without formal art study, he came to painting while an engineering apprentice at BHP in Newcastle. He brought to his painting a curiosity about surface structure and spatial relationships which has permeated his works ever since. These emphases were highly acceptable in Sydney in 1957, and the award of the Rockdale Prize that year and the Christus Prize soon after won him recognition and acceptance. He found in Hal Missingham, director of the Art Gallery of New South Wales, a mentor of substance. Awarded the Helena Rubinstein Travelling Scholarship in 1961, he travelled to Europe in 1962–63. Like Elwyn Lynn and other Sydney painters of his generation, his allegiance has been more to the European abstractionists than to the Americans. By 1969 his earlier habit of breaking down a surface image by faceting it with grids of line had been replaced by more lyrical and spontaneous use of colour and form. He lives and works in South Australia.

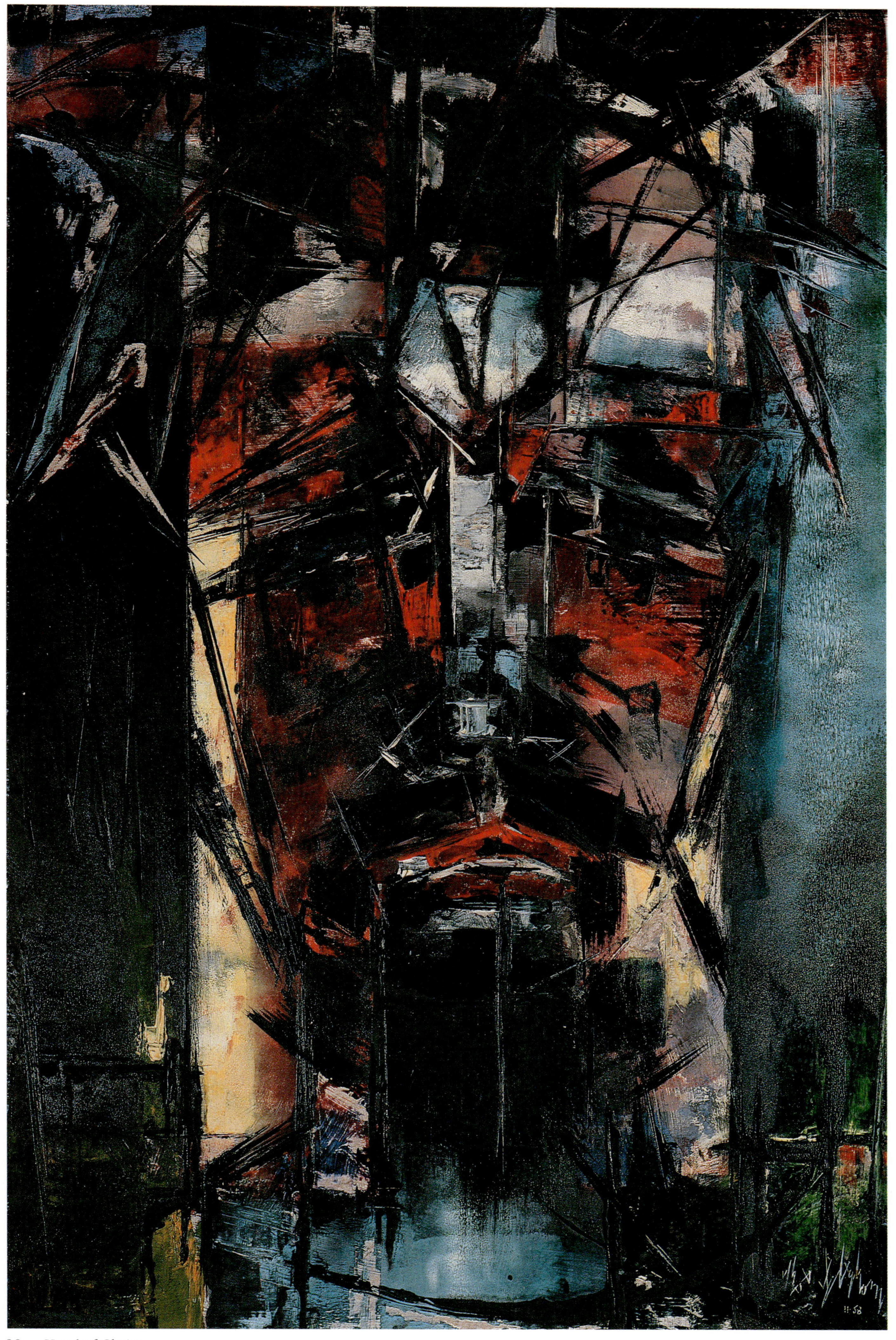

29 *Head of Christ*

ROGER KEMP

1908–87

*Ascension, c.*1960

Acrylic on board
120 × 183 cm
National Gallery of Victoria, Melbourne
Purchased 1983

Roger Kemp was finishing this painting, *Ascension*, at about the time another Melbourne artist, Albert Tucker, was completing his *Ascension* (Plate 25). Both artists were concerned with a vision of man as ultimately redeemable, that is, as being able to transcend the daily grind and experience a more noble destiny. Both had a firm belief in the relationship between person and environment; both were concerned with the idea of Jesus Christ, crucified, but resurrected. To both, the surface structure of the painting was of great importance. But where Tucker turned to the German expressionists for inspiration, Kemp dealt with the pictorial problems as primary and then with the symbolic content. For Kemp, the theme emerged in the process of bringing the painting to resolution, and only then was the picture named.

Kemp's starting point was here, as always, a basic unit, a *thematic fragment*. The figure on the cross wearing a circle of light is the unit that Kemp moves through the pictorial space, setting up visual rhythms which are perceptively demanding but satisfying. The whole picture surface is in movement, like the steps of some obscure and exotic dance, inviting and coercing participation. Line, colour and the stained-glass effect enhance the sense that this is a sacred dance, a holy ritual.

At its essential symbolic level, *Ascension* allows multiple interpretation. It is the measure of the greatness of Kemp that he so easily creates symbols which open up meaning and allow those who view the painting to discover for themselves a meaning that touches their own experience. For Christians, his painting is clearly about Christ crucified and risen, the circle of light a symbol of the endless perfection of the Godhead; but for others the meaning may be more metaphysical, closer to Kemp's expressed intention. 'I am following out a big idea which is motivated by a big order of things, a cosmic sort of thing,' he said in a newspaper interview in 1978. 'All the crosses in my paintings are actually like figures, like ballet choreography starting to move with the music. They break, then come together again.'[1]

1. *Australian*, 12 September 1978.

ROGER KEMP was born in Bendigo in Victoria in 1908 and died in Melbourne in 1987. In the 1930s he studied at the National Gallery School and at Melbourne Technical College. His first solo exhibition was in 1945, at the age of thirty-seven, but it was not until the 1960s that his work began to be widely recognized. He won the McCaughey Prize in 1961, the Georges and Transfield prizes in 1965, the Blake Prize in 1968 and 1970. A major retrospective organized across four Melbourne galleries to celebrate his seventieth birthday in 1978 confirmed his status as a major Australian artist of this century.

Kemp's stature was slow to be acknowledged, partly because his work came slowly to maturity. As early as the 1930s his reading of Rudolf Steiner and the Theosophists had helped form his vision of painting as abstract and metaphysical; like these writers, he believed that art, science and religion are a unity, and that truth is within. But the formal language and the artistic structures to express these concerns were not available to him. His 'art language' was limited to what was around him in Melbourne —the talk and work of his teachers and fellow artists and reproductions in the limited number of books and periodicals available in libraries and shops. So from the thirties until the middle fifties he struggled, with uneven success, to express himself through the language of figurative, expressionist painters. The modern movement that was most akin to his concerns, cubism, was simply not available to him.

[*Continued overleaf*]

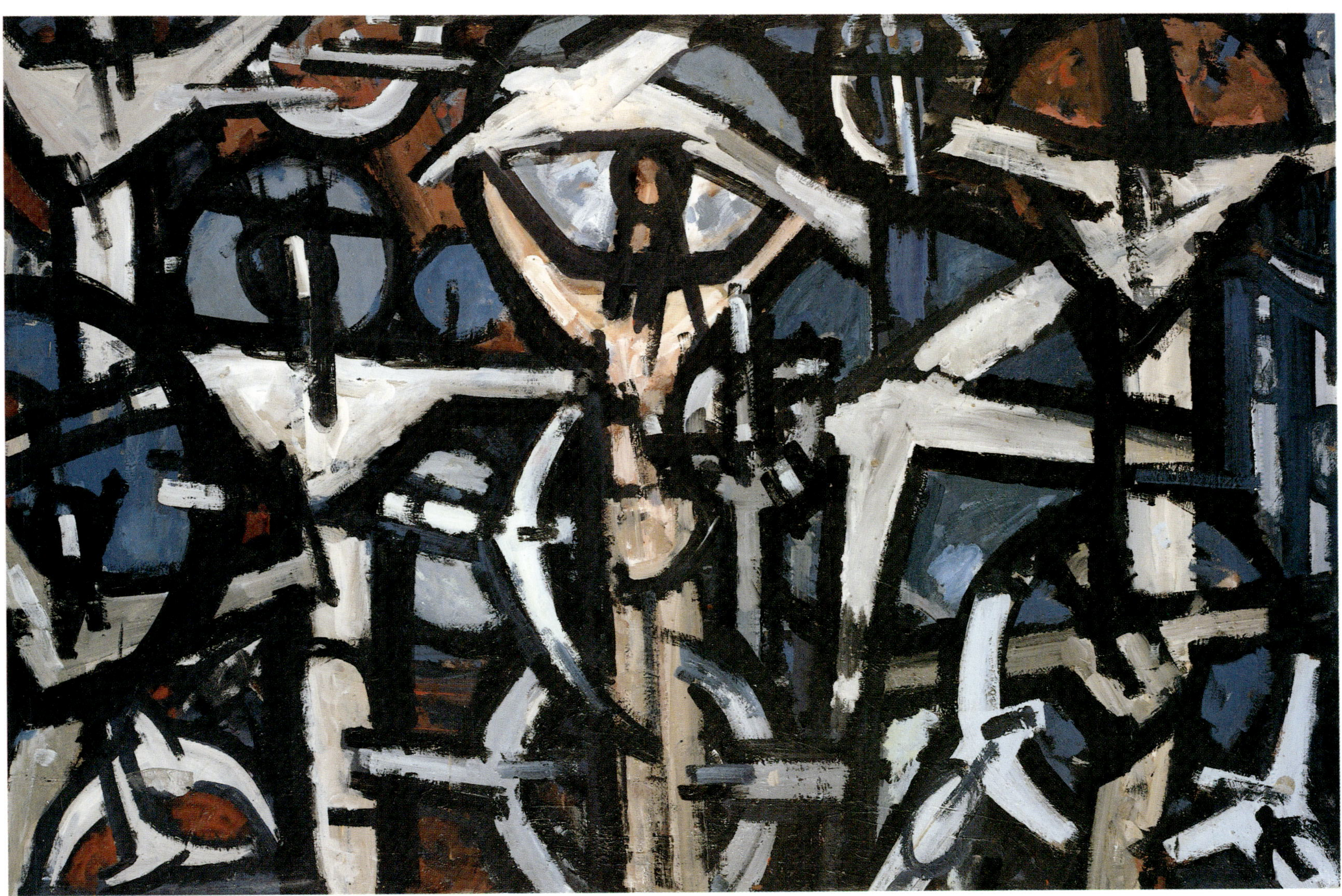

30 *Ascension*

Roger Kemp

1908–87

The Cross, 1968

Oil on composition board
181.5 × 116.5 cm
Monash University, Melbourne

By 1968, the year Roger Kemp won the Blake Prize for the first time with this painting, *The Cross*, his system of signs and his style had become so familiar to those who followed the competition that they were seen to be explicitly religious in their reference. Since 1954 he had exhibited eighteen paintings in the competition, and his persistent use of the circle-and-cross motif together with the brooding, stained-glass–like colour rhythms easily evoked biblical narratives, especially those of the Passion.

The cross in this painting is both a formal device and a symbol. It is the key formal element in the painting, acting both as thematic fragment and as a repetitive, dynamic, structural grid which allows the spaces to be related vertically and horizontally as well as backwards and forwards. Each cruciform shape pivots around the centre and around the muted blue cross that dominates the central area of the painting. The use of black line, although reminiscent of leading in stained glass, is actually closer to the painterly way Jean Bazaine and Alfred Manessier had reflected Romanesque art in their paintings of the early 1950s.

While the cross motif is the theme, its meaning is not restricted to the cross on which Jesus Christ was crucified or to the historical event of the crucifixion. As Kemp said when he spoke about the painting in a television interview in 1975, 'The central cross represented a kind of magnet which is drawing each person back to his own centre. Modern life has got away from what spirituality is all about. We tear down structures but we do not replace them. We are without direction. We have lost our centre. The cross is to bring us back. People are alienated today. The central cross is a point of balance, of reference. The cross stands for rebirth.'[1] *The Cross* thus becomes, for those who understand Kemp's symbolism, a painting that comments powerfully on contemporary society's alienation from nature and from transcendence, and the cross itself functions as a symbol of the relevance of the historical crucifixion for the present day.

1. ABC interview, 23 August 1975.

Whereas artists in Europe and America who shared Kemp's obsessive concern with pictorial space and surface structure had before them the discoveries and means of analytical and synthetic cubism, Kemp had to rediscover them for himself, slowly over more than twenty years. His works on paper in the thirties, the Heidelberg landscapes, even the polemical war paintings of the forties, reveal his struggle to discover for himself what the cubists had arrived at in the first two decades of the century.

Kemp's paintings are more than exciting and complex visual abstract adventuring; through the use of a powerful but limited symbolic language composed largely of the circle and cross and the colours red, blue and black, his best works open up meanings to the viewer. They evoke reflection on the ultimate meaning in life, on self-understanding and the need to keep returning to the centre, and on the relationship between individuals and between people and the environment.

The three paintings reproduced here are major paintings from Roger Kemp's artistic maturity; they mark different moments within its journey.

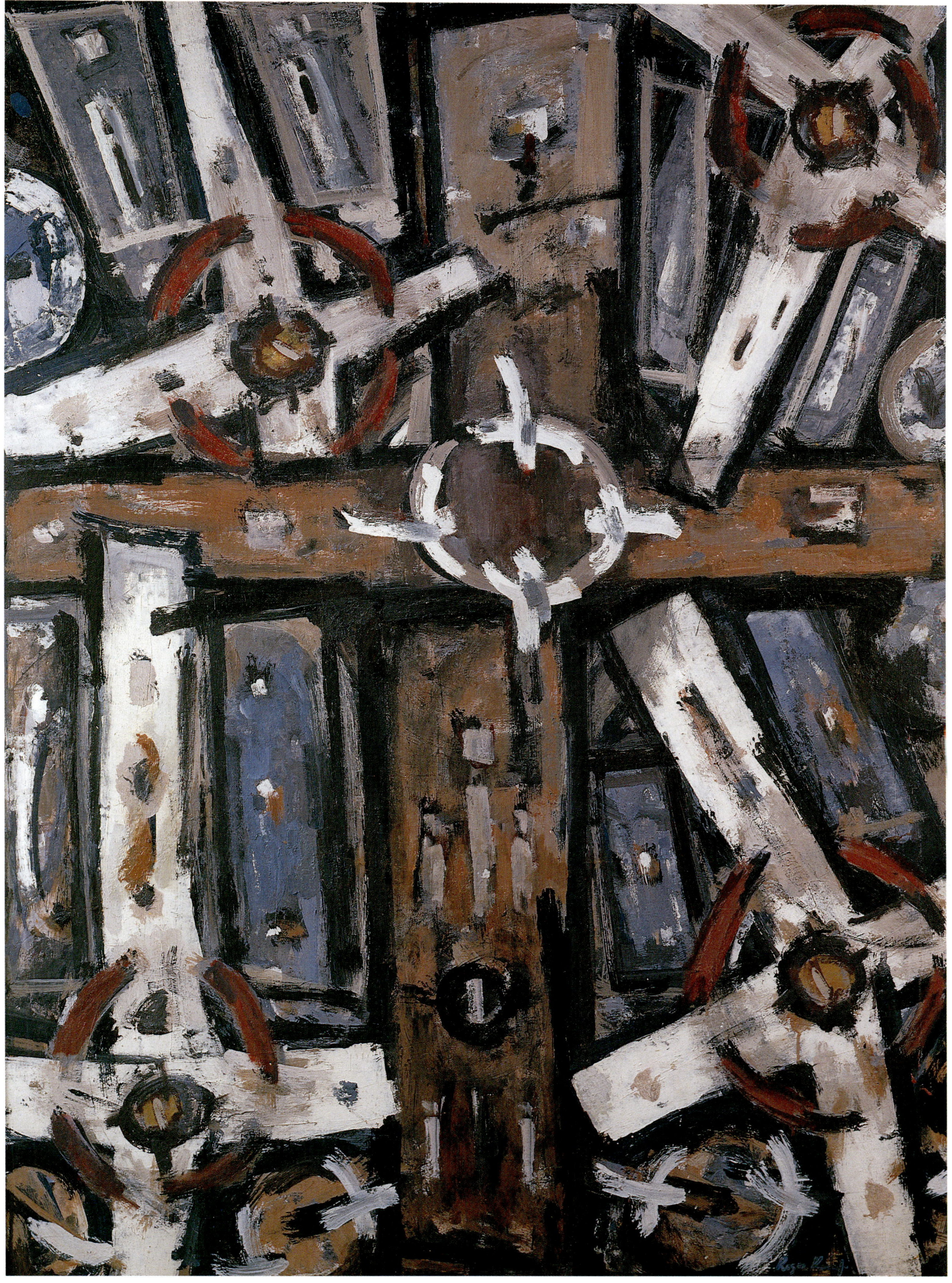

31 *The Cross*

Roger Kemp

1908–87

Movement 5, 1980–81

Acrylic on canvas
204 × 272 cm
National Gallery of Victoria, Melbourne

Movement 5 is a late painting by Roger Kemp. It dates from the time in his life when he knew that his significance had been recognized through prizes, awards and especially the major retrospective. By 1981 he had spoken often publicly and enough had been written about him to assure that his metaphysical intention and his philosophy were known, if not understood. The painting is one of quiet confidence, almost of serenity. It is as structurally complex as *Ascension* or *The Cross,* but it is without their assertiveness and drama. The thematic fragment is again the cross, this time smaller and with only the slightest suggestion of a figure. Again the units move around each other and backwards and forwards through the space like movements in an orchestral composition; again Kemp restricts his use of colour to a minimum—blues, blacks and a touch of pink. But the handling of the paint is different. In *Ascension* and *The Cross,* Kemp worked on composition board; his method was brutal and direct as he attacked the surface with strength and energy. *Movement 5* is on canvas, a softer and more sympathetic surface which encourages greater subtlety in colour and line.

Movement 5 is a painting to delight in. What Kemp said in an ABC television interview in 1978 about his other works is exemplified here in an extraordinary way: 'It's not a thing you look at visually, but it's something you move into; you experience the movements of it by your perception [and] by thinking about it. You pick up a movement and it goes from one to another . . . The unit becomes the group and then the group metamorphoses itself into another group, just like music . . . one note catching the other becomes a reality and the reality finally [becomes] a big concept.'[1]

1. ABC interview, 7 February 1978.

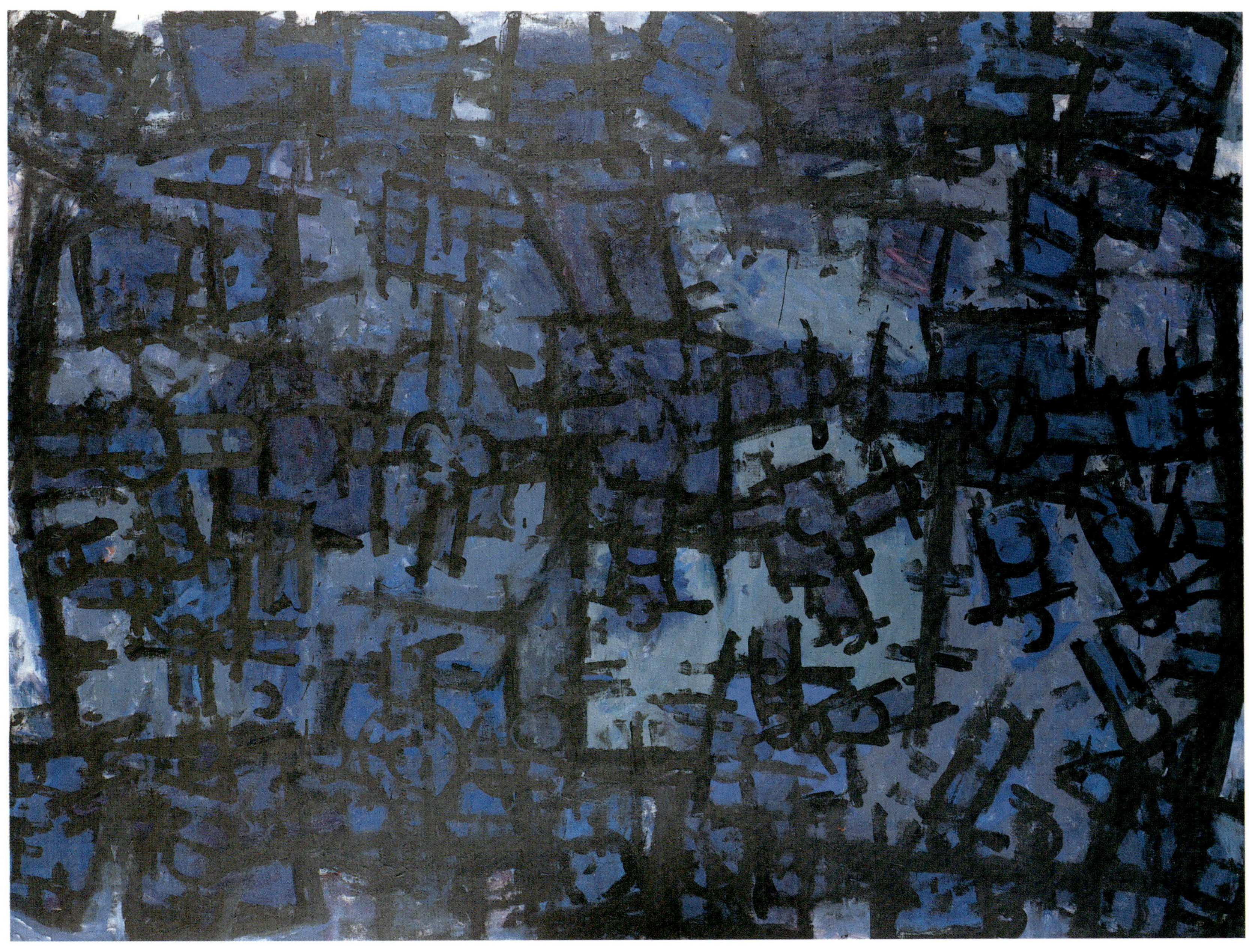

32 *Movement 5*

IAN FAIRWEATHER
1891–1974

Hallelujah, 1959

PVC on paper on board
146.8 × 157.5 cm
National Gallery of Victoria, Melbourne
Purchased 1983

Hallelujah is one of the first in a series of religious works which Fairweather painted between 1958 and 1963 on Bribie Island. The others include *Last Supper* (1958), *Gethsemane* (1958), *Annunciation* (*c.*1958), *Flight into Egypt* (1961), *Monastery* (1961), *Epiphany* (1962) and *Marriage at Cana* (1963). It is probable that the impetus for these came from the Blake Prize competition which he entered at the suggestion of Treannia Smith of the Macquarie Galleries, where he was exhibiting annually. Only *Gethsemane* and *Annunciation* were entered in the competition.

While not the greatest of Fairweather's religious works, *Hallelujah* is a painting typical of his maturity. He had come to Bribie to settle. Already sixty-eight years of age, he had absorbed diverse influences through his study, travels and personal preference for an Eastern philosophy and way of life. He was as much at ease with Chinese calligraphy as he was with Aboriginal decorative art, as skilled at classical representation as he was at the flat, linear manipulation of surface areas without depending on colour to create volume.

Hallelujah has the solemnity of an Ajanta cave mural or an Aboriginal bark painting. The figures stand frontally but in procession, arms raised; the colours—earth ochres and russets with hints of grey—emphasize the ritual of the occasion. *Hallelujah* is not so much 'a shout of hosannahs', as Murray Bail has suggested,[1] as the solemn intoning that signals the beginning of the procession.

1. Murray Bail, *Ian Fairweather* (Sydney: Bay Books, 1981), p. 154.

IAN FAIRWEATHER was born in Scotland in 1891. After private education with a tutor in Switzerland, he spent 1912–14 at officer-training school in Belfast. He spent almost the entire war years as a prisoner-of-war, mainly in Germany, under a regime benign enough for him to study Chinese and Japanese and to illustrate local prison journals. He studied art at The Hague in 1918, and then in 1920–24 at the Slade School, London, as favourite pupil of the director, Henry Tonks. Diffident and restless but sure of his calling to be an artist, he left England in 1927 in search of visual satisfaction and spent much of the next twenty-seven years in Canada, Shanghai, Bali (1933), Melbourne (1934), Peking (1935), Brisbane (1938), Alligator Creek, Cairns (1939), India (1940–44), Melbourne, Brisbane, Cairns, Darwin (1944–52) and Indonesia (1952–53). In 1954, aged sixty-three, he built a thatched, Malay-type hut on Bribie Island, in Moreton Bay, north of Brisbane, his first real 'home', his first time of financial sufficiency and the first time he had allowed others to acknowledge him personally and as an important artist.

Tracing Fairweather's journeying is to understand the influences in his mature painting—classical drawing and composition, Cézanne, Chinese landscape and calligraphy, Aboriginal art, cubism and futurism (forty years after their advent in Europe). Naming the journeys is also to indicate subject matter, for he painted what was at hand. He painted with whatever and on whatever he could afford—often only newspaper. For Fairweather, it was the involvement in the act of painting which was of first importance; communication came second, and posterity could see to itself.

Fairweather died in Queensland in 1974.

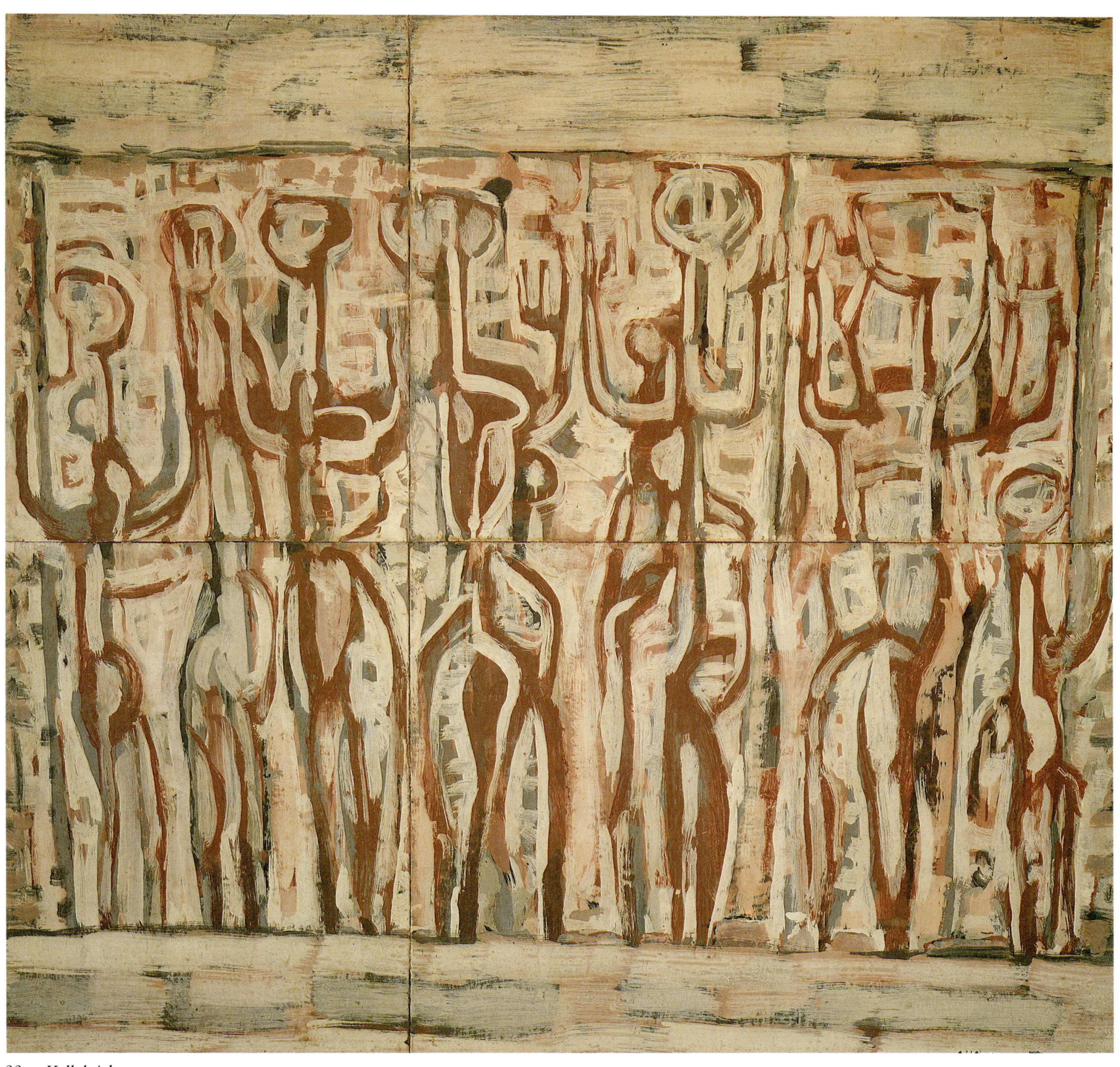

33 *Hallelujah*

JOHN COBURN

Born 1925

Triptych of the Passion, 1960

Enamel on composition board
Three panels: 106 × 182 cm overall
Courtesy St Patrick's College, Manly, NSW

Triptych of the Passion was John Coburn's eighth and most successful entry in the Blake Prize and dates from a period when he was intensely interested in religious art as a means of expressing faith symbolically, but with discipline. His own faith was secure and nurtured by strong friendships within his new Church, although his acceptance within the avant-garde Sydney artists was less so at this time.[1] *Triptych* was painted in two days, while Coburn was on holiday in Queensland. It is painted in ordinary house enamels of red, white, blue and black on masonite bought at the local hardware store. There is little spontaneity in any of Coburn's work, but the Passion triptych reflects his obvious concern that the finished work should be able to be 'read' as a symbolic portrayal of the scourging, crucifixion and crowning of Christ, even though it is without representational figures. This is clear from Coburn's description of the painting written in 1963, and also from the way the symbols of the cross, crown and thorns are overstated against a background which lacks the subtlety of his later works:

> The Triptych is an abstract painting which attempts to evoke through colour and form certain aspects of Our Lord's Passion. The centre panel, 'The Crucifixion', is dominated by the symbol of the Cross, while in the right hand panel, 'The Crowning with Thorns', the crown of thorns is suggested at the top. In the left hand panel, 'The Scourging', the sharp spiky black forms burst in from the sides to a central column, suggesting the action of whipping. The colours are partly symbolic and partly emotional, red representing blood and violence, blue expressing sadness. The harsh texture and sharp angular forms throughout the painting suggest Christ's agony and suffering, yet it was my intention to create in the overall effect a feeling that this was a triumph, a glorious event.[2]

1. Coburn was excluded from the Sydney 9 group in 1960 on the grounds that his work was shape, not linear, abstractionist.
2. Letter to Michael Scott, 15 February 1963.

JOHN COBURN was born in Ingham, Queensland, in 1925. After naval war service he studied art full time at the East Sydney Technical College under the Commonwealth Post-War Reconstruction Scheme. He taught there in 1959 and was head of the National Art School from 1972 to 1974. Formative influences on his work he acknowledges as his wife, print-maker Barbara Woodward, his teacher and friend Wallace Thornton and the painters he first encountered in the French Painting Today exhibition in 1953. Matisse, Lurçat, Manessier and de Stael have been especially important to Coburn, as were his three years in France (1969–72) with a tapestry firm in the Aubusson area.

Coburn is a convert to Roman Catholicism from High Church Anglicanism. He has always seen his art as a vehicle for his religious sensibilities and beliefs. To examine his work closely is to trace his religious development from an intense, deeply felt faith to the struggle of his mature years to find relevant ways to express symbolically the spiritual dimension of life. His vocabulary of form, shape and colour has remained very limited: simplification of forms from nature; lush, often tropical, or heraldic colour; and the elemental symbols —circles, crosses, thorns, squares. 'Appearances are distracting,' he has said. 'What you feel about a thing is important, not what it looks like. I don't want to teach people to see, I want them to feel.'[1]

Among Coburn's finest works are his entries in the Blake Prize, the tapestries in the Sydney Opera House, and the Creation series in the John F. Kennedy Center for the Performing Arts in Washington.

John Coburn lives in Sydney.

1. *Observer*, 15 March 1959.

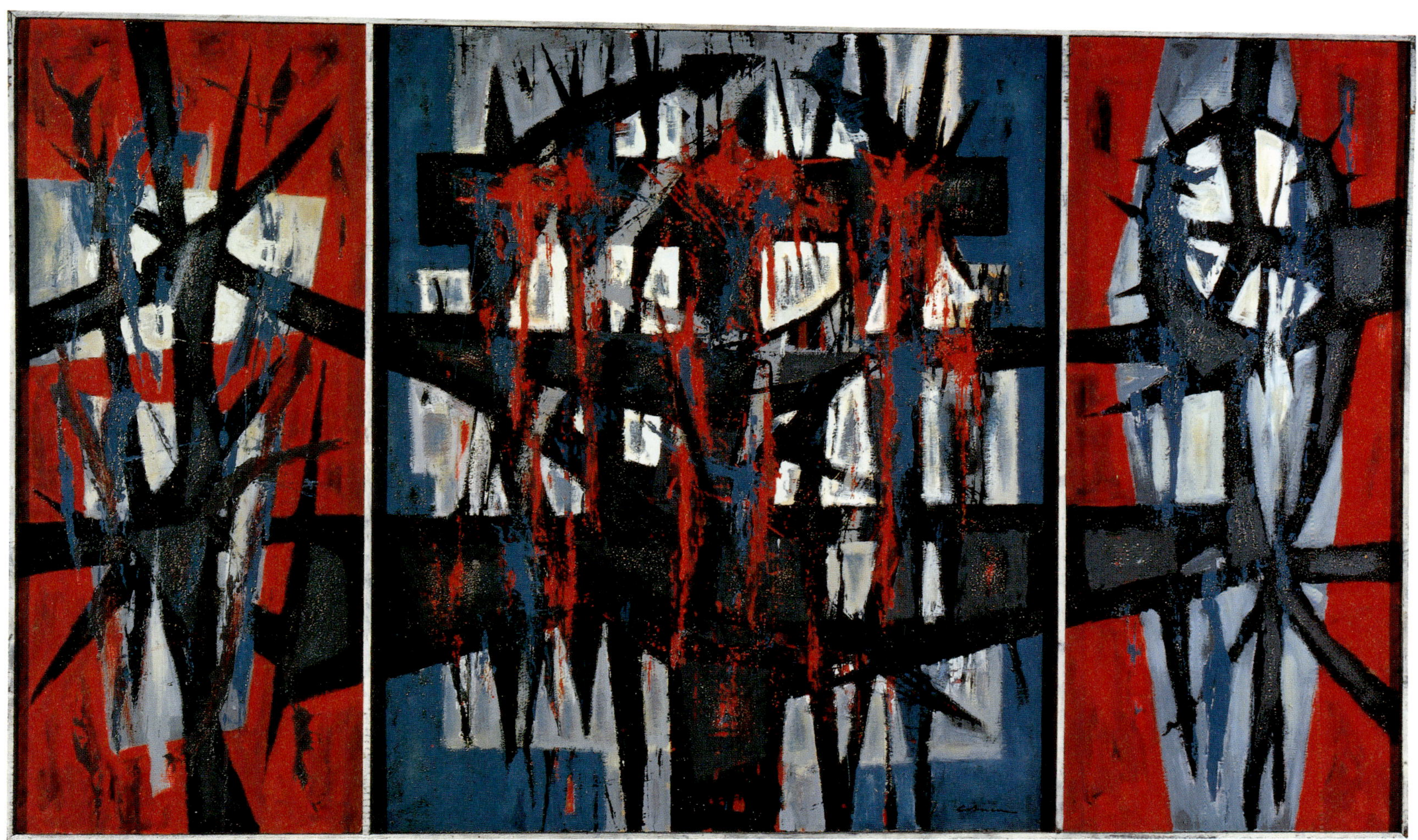

34 *Triptych of the Passion*

FRED WILLIAMS

1927–82

Adam and Eve, 1960–61

Oil and tempera on composition board
122 × 70.5 cm
Private collection, Melbourne

Fred Williams completed *Adam and Eve* during a critical period in his life. Since returning from England in 1957 he had exhibited four times with the Australian Galleries in Melbourne with moderately favourable reviews but without selling many works; his 1961 exhibition at Kim Bonython's Adelaide gallery was a critical disaster. Consequently, although more than thirty years of age, he could not afford to live away from home and painted in a tiny room above his stepfather's plumber's shop in Exhibition Street, Melbourne. Moreover, he was still smarting from being excluded from the important 1959 Antipodean Exhibition, which brought critical attention to many of his friends and contemporaries. His own work, as he saw it, was equally good and could also be seen as a protest against Sydney's headlong rush to complete abstraction. By the end of 1961, things were better: his future commitment to landscape was clearer; Rudy Komon, the Sydney dealer, was interested to have him join his stable, which would bring some financial stability; and he met and married Lyn Watson.

Adam and Eve is an important painting within Williams's *oeuvre.* The two figures stand starkly against a flat reddish-brown background, their feet planted firmly on the earth. (Williams was to use this compositional device later in his portraits *Sir Louis Matheson* [1976], *J. Davis McCaughey* [1976], and *Rudy Komon* [1978].) There is no attempt to create atmospheric depth; the figures are solidly built with planes of flat washes of viridian, ochres and mauve. The paint quality is easy and confident, even though the stance, and particularly the interrelationship of the two heads, is extremely complex. The painting is indebted to Manet and Cézanne, but Williams has understood the ways these artists worked with space and colour and incorporated this understanding into his own pictorial language.

Adam and Eve is probably Fred Williams's only biblical painting. Usually he avoids myth and symbol. Adam and Eve stand solemnly together in a gesture of easy intimacy; they look out of the picture into some uncertain future. For once Williams has allowed a painting to hold something of his own inner life. Adam and Eve are not simply the first man and the first woman; they are each man and each woman who choose to face life decisions together. The impact is all the more poignant because Williams, always restrained and unromantic, seems to have made the figure of Adam a self-portrait.

Born in Richmond, Victoria, in 1927, FRED WILLIAMS attended the National Gallery School between 1947 and 1950, classes at George Bell's school at the same time, and the Chelsea Art School, London, from 1951 to 1956, with four months in etching classes at the Central School of Arts and Crafts. He was a brilliant student, excelling in classical drawing, figure composition and portraiture; as he said, he was in no hurry to develop his own style but was dogged in his pursuit of understanding the way artists as diverse as Hugh Ramsay, William Dargie, Cézanne, the cubists, Matisse and even Sickert had solved the structural problems of picture-making. From the London years his Music Hall etchings reveal Williams as the outsider, the onlooker, the gazer who seeks to understand not the psychological dimensions or the symbolism of his subject matter but its potential for picture construction. His gift was simply this—to create without bias, to record without succumbing to the tyranny of past ways of seeing. On his return to Australia in 1957 he chose to concentrate on the Australian landscape, deliberately breaking with both the romantic and expressionist traditions.

By the time of his death in 1982, Fred Williams had changed the way we are able to see our own landscape with series such as the You Yangs (1962–64), Upwey (1965–66), Hillside and Hummock (1965–67), Tibooburra (1967–68), Yarra River (1970–74), Gorge (1975–78), and Waterfall (1979–80). His stature within the history of Australian art was further assured through the very important Fred Williams Retrospective Exhibition organized by James Mollison, director of the Australian National Gallery, which toured the country in 1987–88.

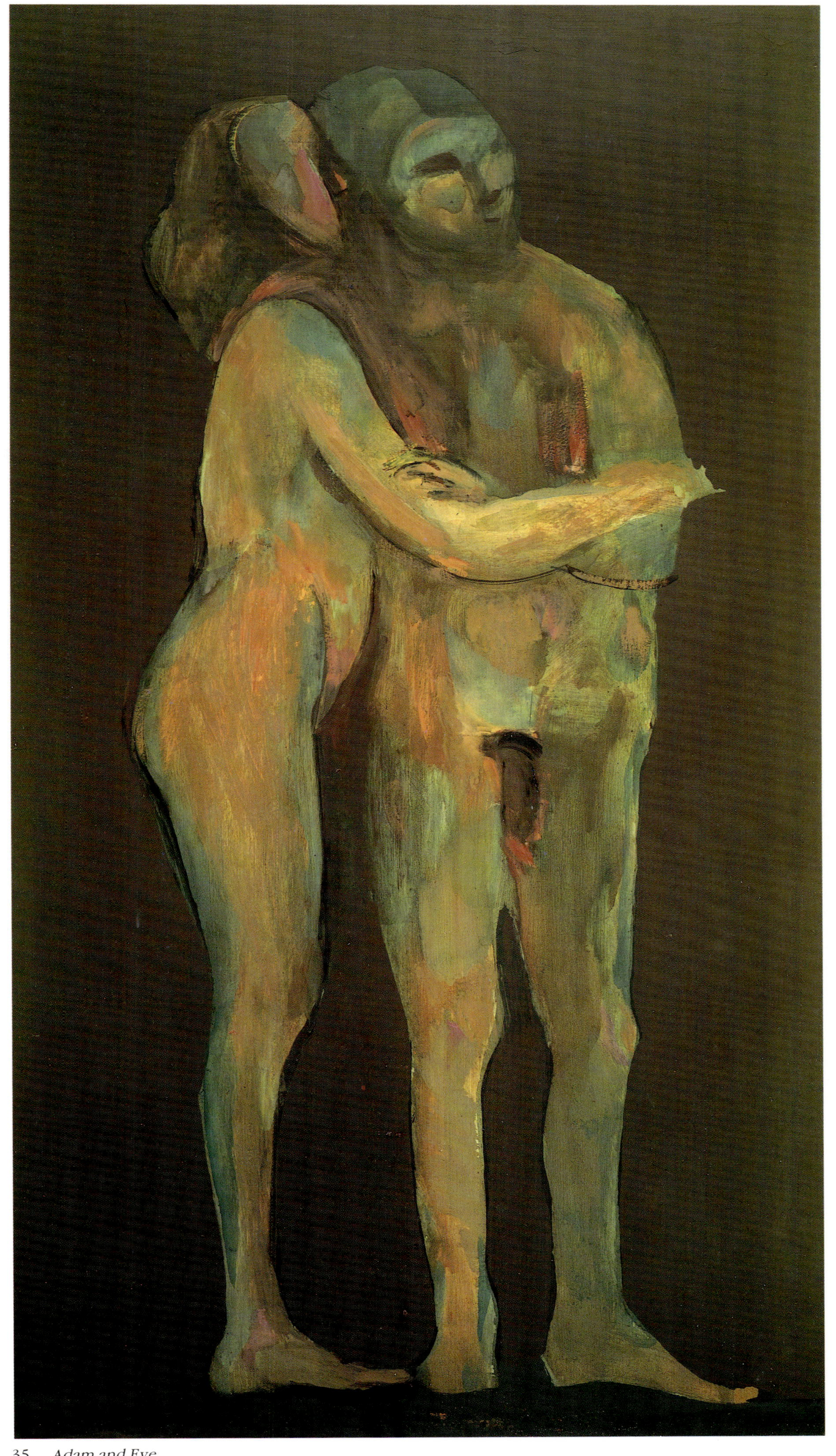

35 *Adam and Eve*

GODFREY MILLER

1893–1964

Madonna No. 1, 1960–64

Oil on canvas
33 × 22 cm
Private collection, Melbourne

Godfrey Miller was still working on *Madonna No. 1* up to the time of his death. It is one of seven paintings of madonna images that he began after 1948; all of them give evidence of his preoccupation with structure and mathematical precision in brushwork and in colour orchestration.

The structure of the composition in *Madonna No. 1* is simple yet strong. The positioning of the mother and child is central and traditional; the mother holds the child as do many Renaissance madonnas. A cross, slightly angled, has been drawn or ruled over the surface, counterbalancing the soft curves of the figure. Then the myriad colour rhythms have been created by flooding the tiny shapes with thin oil washes of greys, prussian blues, viridian, and lemon and cadmium yellow. The total effect is of a tessellated glass surface of great subtlety. The mood is reticent and lyrically devotional.

But Godfrey Miller is here also pursuing his lifelong quest for understanding the philosophical and painting problems raised by Cézanne, Seurat and the post-impressionists. The subject matter may be of little consequence; Miller's attention to detail, his ordering of the colour spectrum and his way of building form to a crescendo of unity are identical with that in his other mature paintings. His concern is with the universal, not with a particular place, person or incident. The reverence he communicates is not so much with religious belief as with an underlying, universal order which he perceived in the whole of nature and sought to translate in painting and drawing.

GODFREY MILLER was, during his lifetime, along with John Passmore, one of the most revered of Sydney artists. He was an artist's artist, immensely influential in directing Sydney painting towards the post-impressionism of Cézanne. While he was never non-figurative in his work, those who followed him usually became so. Miller was a recluse when he chose to be, and his life and works encouraged the popular image of the artist as impoverished because of his ideals, specially chosen, immensely gifted and slightly eccentric.

Born in New Zealand in 1893, Miller was a graduate in architecture from Wellington University, a soldier at Gallipoli and a student of sculpture at the Slade School in London before he settled in Australia for the first time in 1922. Between 1929 and 1939 he studied part time at the Slade under Tonks and Mitchell, before Douglas Dundas, impressed by his superb draughtsmanship, offered him a position at the East Sydney Technical College. Miller worked slowly and meditatively, sometimes for up to seventeen years on a single small painting, and then never regarded it as finished, refining and perfecting the surface in the pursuit of, as he said, 'the elusive, underlying principle'. *Nude and Moon* (1954–58), *Trees in a Quarry* (1952–56) and *Summer* (1960–64) are among his most important paintings. In 1955, aged sixty-two, Miller had his first solo exhibition, and in 1959 the Art Gallery of New South Wales honoured him with a major retrospective.

Miller had a great belief in his own artistic integrity and importance. His will requested that his paintings go only to major galleries and important private collections. Only about seventy of his paintings are known to exist.

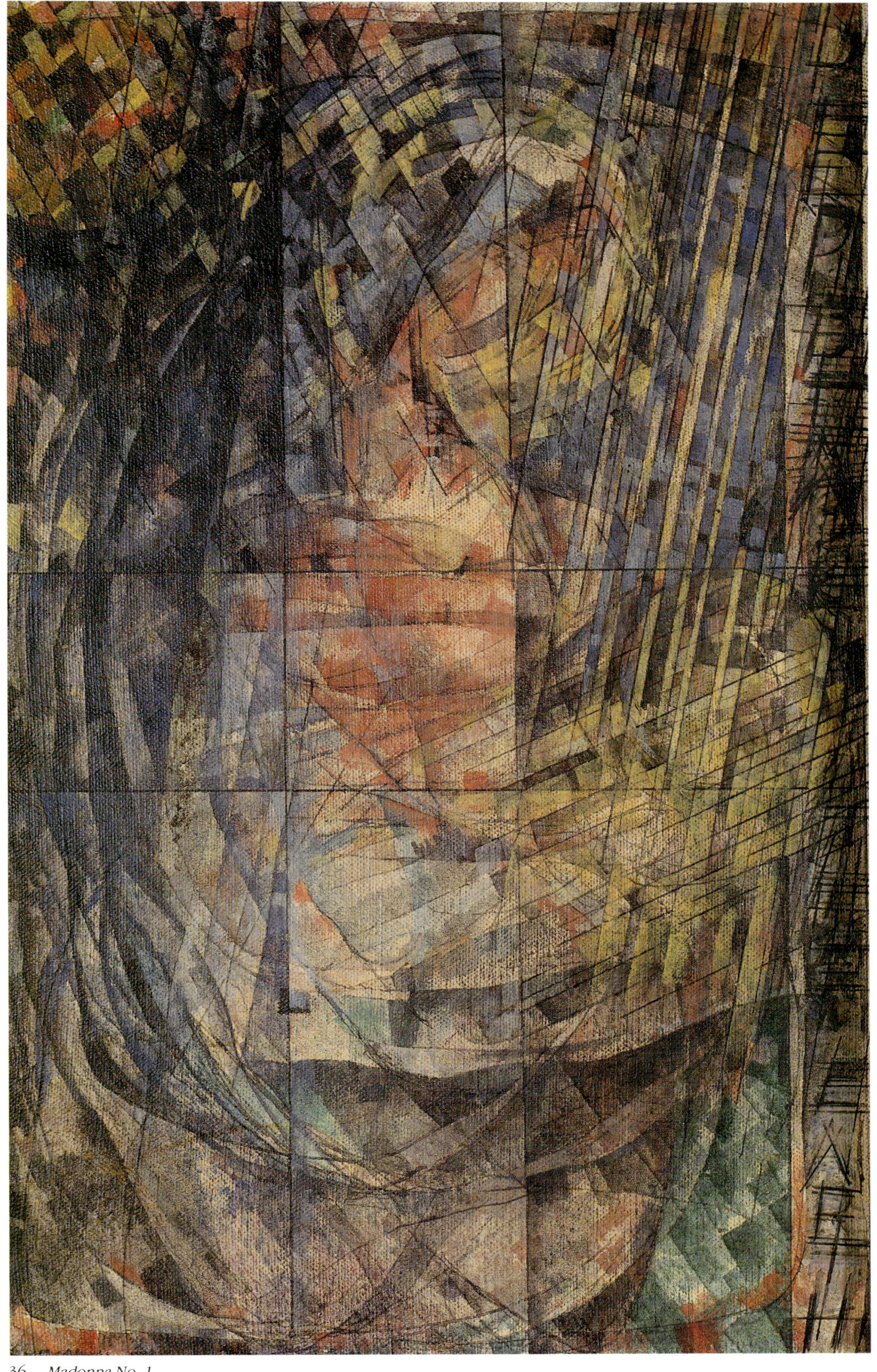

36 *Madonna No. 1*

CONSTANCE STOKES

Born 1906

Sorrowing Mother, 1960

Oil on composition board
61 × 50.5 cm
Geelong Art Gallery
Gift of Ford Motor Company Australia Pty Ltd 1963

Constance Stokes painted *Sorrowing Mother* around the time when she was grieving over the death of her own mother. The woman portrayed here may be the Virgin Mother of Sorrows of the Catholic tradition, or it may be the image of all women who mourn deeply or simply the image that grew slowly as Stokes reflected at that time. Probably it is all three.

Over a ground of burnt siena and indian red, the figure has been brushed in freely and completed by working back and forth across the whole picture plane in line and colour, much as Constance Stokes had observed Lhote to do when she was a student in Paris. Sometimes, as in the face and hands, the colour is laid on quite flatly, with contrasts suggesting depth as the fauves and Matisse had done; elsewhere, as in the cloak and the bottle, the colour is more summary, reminiscent of Cézanne. Behind the apparent ease and grace of *Sorrowing Mother* is Stokes's superb grasp of the anatomy of the human figure and her much-admired draughtsmanship.

Constance Stokes regards *Sorrowing Mother* as her most satisfying religious painting. Few of her other religious works exist. Her Blake Prize entries *Christ with Simon Peter and Andrew* (1953) and *The Crowd Has Passed* (1964) she has destroyed, but a fine figure composition, *The Baptism* (1952), is owned by the National Gallery of Victoria.

CONSTANCE STOKES was born Constance Parkin in 1906 in Miram Piram, in the Wimmera district of Victoria. She became an outstanding student at the National Gallery School under Bernard Hall between 1925 and 1929 and was awarded the Gallery Travelling Scholarship in 1929. Between 1930 and 1933 she studied under William Monnington at the Royal Academy School, where she again excelled in anatomy and life drawing. A 1933 summer school with cubist painter André Lhote in Paris caused her to question classical methods of building tone, but it was not until the 1960s that she actually began building depth in her own paintings with juxtaposed colour as Lhote and the fauves had done.

In 1932 she married Eric Wyborn Stokes and returned to Australia briefly in 1933 to hold her first solo exhibition at the Joshua McClelland Gallery in Melbourne. Her next solo exhibition was to be thirty years later, at the Leveson Street Gallery in Melbourne in 1964. She did continue to draw, paint and exhibit in a limited way in the years between, but most of her creative energy went into being a parent. In 1939 she was represented in the first Contemporary Art Society Exhibition, in 1941 at the Carnegie Institute exhibition of Australian Art in the United States and in 1953 at the Venice Biennale, as well as regular exhibitions of the Victorian Artists' Society. In 1974 and in 1985 major retrospective exhibitions were held in Victoria.

Constance Stokes is an important representative of the Melbourne figurative painting movement of the forties and fifties. She is closer in temperament and style to George Bell, Russell Drysdale and William Dobell than she is to Tucker, Boyd or Perceval. She refused to flirt with abstraction or landscape but remained constant to her commitment to the human figure in line and paint.

Constance Stokes lives in Melbourne.

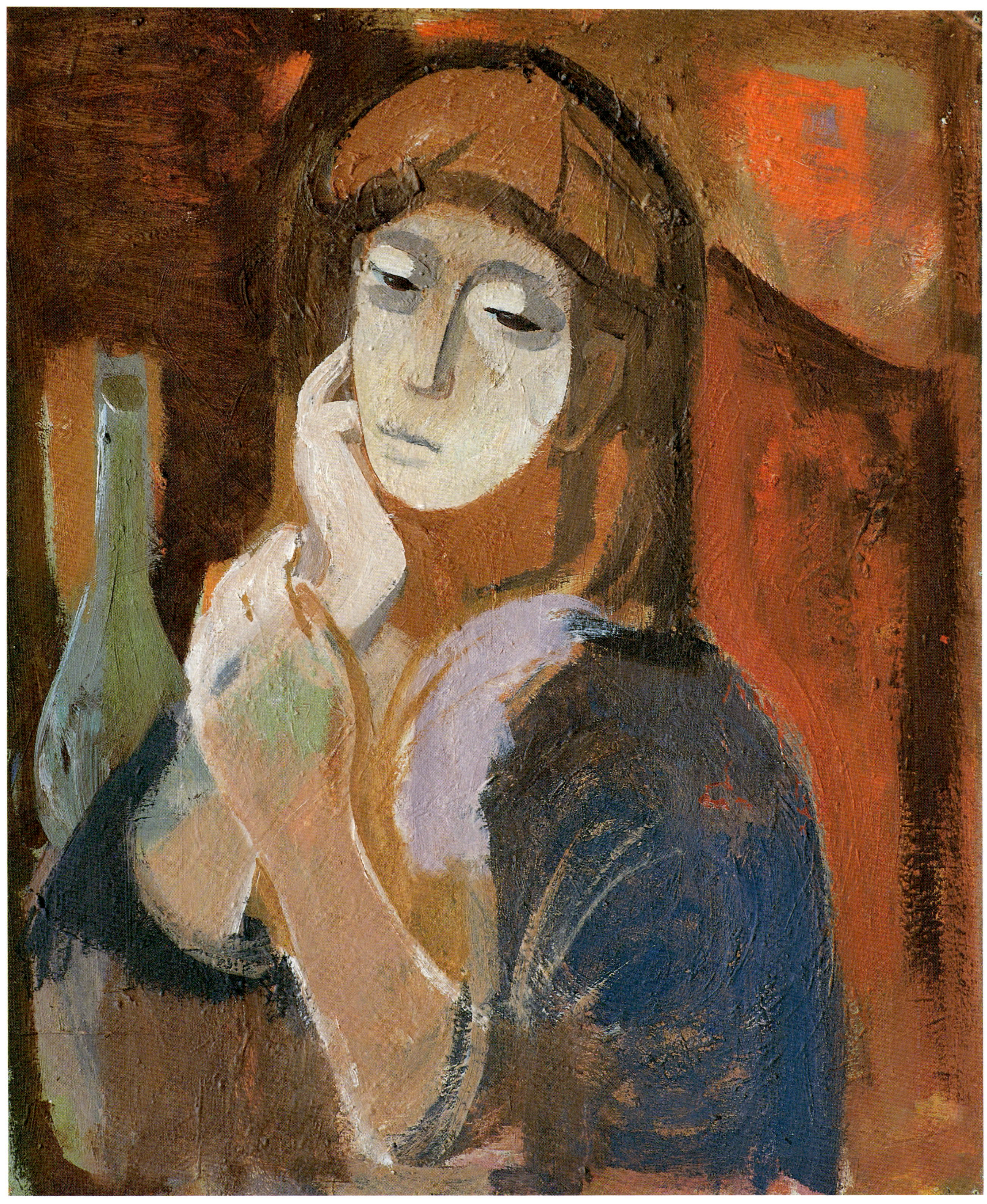

37 *Sorrowing Mother*

STANISLAUS RAPOTEC

Born 1913

Meditating on Good Friday, 1961

Oil on composition board
164.1 × 411.5 cm
Collection of P. J. Pacquola, Melbourne

Meditating on Good Friday, awarded the 1961 Blake Prize for Religious Art, was Rapotec's most violent and defiant assertion of the power of immediate gesture over premeditated narrative. In the words of Elwyn Lynn, its thick blue-black and brown lines 'flowed, sank, whipped, became embedded, struggled across grey brown and black swamp lands inhabited by Kafkaesque monsters and beetles.'[1] But *Meditating on Good Friday* is not without direct religious reference, for Rapotec has spat out crosses among the verticals of his front plane and a golden light to penetrate the darkness behind in a way that evokes the Easter vigil.

Robert Hughes, then art critic on *Nation* and a competitor in the Blake Prize, defended Rapotec in the controversy that followed the award.[2] He argued that abstract art had the capacity to communicate directly with the viewer and to elicit deep, emotional responses. Moreover, he said, religious art is not so because it sets out to teach, but 'because it draws its sustenance from religion. To think of art primarily as a means of communicating a conceptual idea debases both art and the idea. It transmits a state of being, which is a different matter.'[3]

Meditating on Good Friday remains Rapotec's most important work, not simply because of the way it foscused public discussion; the work remains a grand gesture, a perceptual experience, a challenge to forsake the limits of the frame, enter into its huge size and be swept along in the turmoil of its energy.

1. Elwyn Lynn, 'Avant Garde Painting in Sydney', *Meanjin*, September 1961.
2. Robert Hughes, *Nation*, 11 and 25 March 1961.
3. *Nation*, 25 March 1961, p. 18.

STANISLAUS RAPOTEC was born in Yugoslavia in 1913 and studied economics and history of art at Zagreb University from 1933 to 1939; he had no formal art studies. He served as a commando in the Yugoslav army during World War II and migrated to Australia in 1948. In 1955 he moved from Adelaide to Sydney and settled in Victoria Street, Kings Cross, home to many of Sydney's avant-garde painters, including John Olsen, William Rose, Russell Drysdale, John Passmore and Sali Herman. In the new environment, Rapotec's emphasis shifted from Byzantine-type figuration and outback landscapes to the immediacy of direct gestural painting on large surfaces. Between 1955 and 1962 he was in the forefront of a drive to complete abstraction which centred in Sydney. As well as being identified with the Victoria Street group, he was a member of the Sydney 9 group with Olsen, Rose, Clem Meadmore, Eric Smith, Peter Upward, Hector Gilliland and Carl Plate. They all looked to the European abstractionists, and especially to the Spanish, for inspiration, although by 1960 the work of the American abstract expressionists was also becoming known in Sydney.

Between 1955 and 1961 Rapotec entered the Blake Prize each year, always with big, lumbering abstractions in which heavy black brushstrokes and weighted colour struggled dramatically on the surface. These paintings enraged those on the Blake committee, who considered that to be religious a painting had to have recognizable, figurative subject matter; as Peter Kenny said of Rapotec's 1958 *Via Crucis*, it 'might just as easily be entitled "neon signs", "squabbling cats", "harbour at night".'[1] Rapotec's entries precipitated a major crisis in the history of the Blake Prize, which eventually resulted in a general broadening of understanding of the limits of religious art, and—at least on the part of many—a welcoming of abstract art as peculiarly suitable for religious expression. After 1963, Rapotec's art became more lyric and less concerned with religious expression.

Stanislaus Rapotec lives and paints in Sydney.

1. J. P. Kenny, 'The Blake Prize Exhibition 1958', *Twentieth Century*, winter 1958, p. 300.

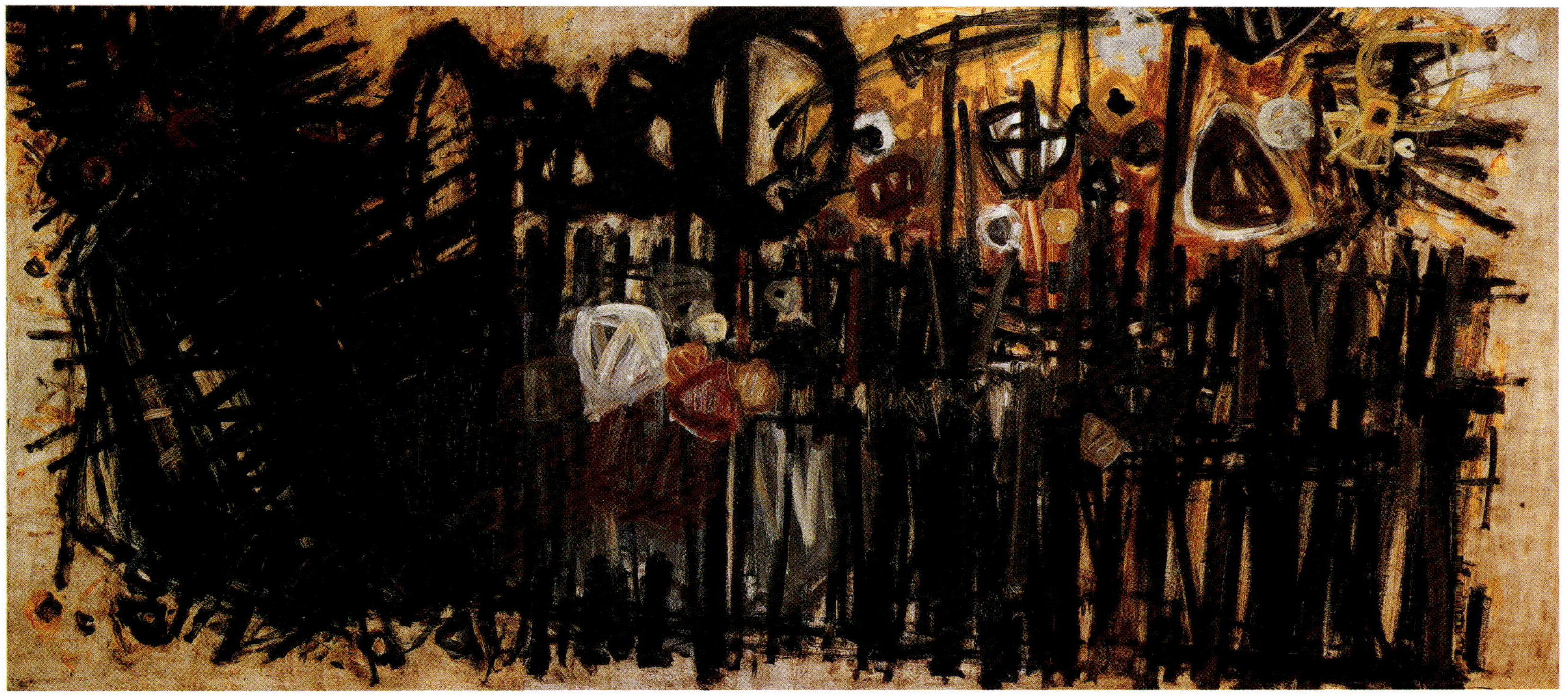

38 *Meditating on Good Friday*

Detail from centre panel of *Meditating on Good Friday*

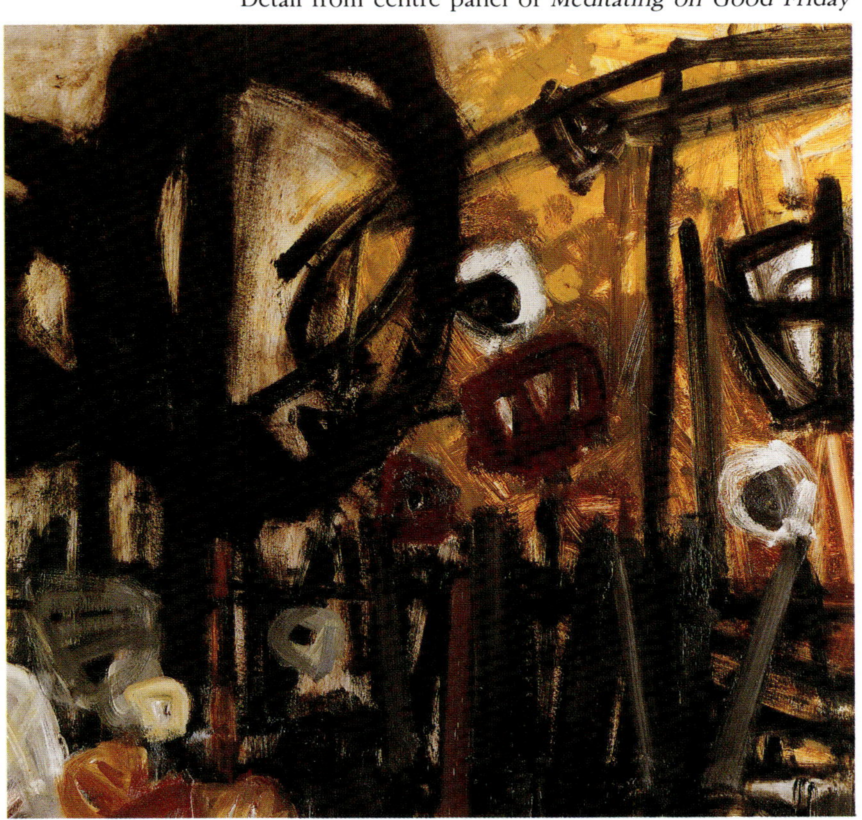

Michael Kitching

Born 1940

Last Supper—Premonition, 1964

Wood, metal, plastic paint on board
188.5 × 223 cm overall
Private collection, Sydney

Mike Kitching won the Blake Prize in 1964, the year that John Olsen was a judge; Kitching was only twenty-four at the time and virtually unknown in Sydney. Olsen found the work among the rejects from the submissions and he brought it to the attention of the other judges. In Olsen's view, it was clearly the best work, the most innovative and, in its use of ready-made parts, the equal of the work of the young avant-garde Sydney painters such as Colin Lanceley.[1]

At the time of working on *Last Supper—Premonition,* Kitching was a great admirer of Leonard French's work. He admired the way French, in his *Seven Days* (Plates 77–83), created finished works with the quality of medieval icons. The task of the religious artist, as Kitching understood it at that time, was to create sacred objects which looked precious and beautiful. *In Last Supper—Premonition,* Kitching's intention was to translate into the different materials the scriptural elements of the Last Supper in such a way that the finished work resembled a sacred, medieval object, gold and crusty, as he said, and three or four hundred years old.

Thus it is possible to 'read' the various segments of the work as if it were the narrative. The large red disc is the symbol of Christ suffering for all people; the smaller white ones are the Apostles at the Supper and the wafers at the communion table; the three nails in the centre panel are the Trinity; the chalice in halves signals the impending departure of Jesus in death; the right panel stands for Easter, and so on. All this Kitching intended.[2]

In spite of this quite literal use of sign and symbol, and the overall goal of recreating a medieval precious object, *Last Supper—Premonition* remains one of the most innovative religious works produced in the sixties in Australia.

1. Mike Kitching interview with the author, 8 February 1983.
2. Ibid.

Michael Kitching was born in Hull, England, in 1940 and arrived in Sydney in 1952. He studied manual arts and taught the subject in 1959. In 1960, without formal art studies, he turned to painting full-time. The award of the Blake Prize in 1964 and the subsequent recognition enabled him to be taken seriously in the Sydney art scene while allowing him freedom to pursue his fascination with technology in art. Since then he has exhibited as a painter, sculptor and designer and has received many Australian and overseas commissions.

Since 1967, Kitching has worked almost exclusively in three dimensions, using acrylic plastics and polished aluminium. The major influence in his work he acknowledges to be Eduardo Paolozzi. This is most true of his work in his formative years, when many of his Sydney contemporaries, including Colin Lanceley, Mike Brown and Ross Crothall, also found in the assemblages of the English sculptor witty and imaginative alternatives to simple carving or modelling techniques. Kitching's work is often linked with that of Lanceley and the other Imitation Realists, but, unlike them, he usually avoids satire and overt social comment. His remarks about a recent work, *Cathedral,* reveal his concern with the meaning of life and of the presence of God within it. The work, a four-metre-high sculpture completed after the Apollo ascent to the moon, is of two rocket-like shapes in polished metal and perspex, arched by a red and gold metal plate. The inscription on this plate reads:

IN
THE TIME
THAT WE LIVED
BELIEVING THAT GOD
IS THE CONSISTENT UNIVERSE
WE DESIGNED AMAZING ARCHITECTURE
AND WITH CHEMISTRY SENT IT INTO THE SKY
IN THESE SANCTUARIES MAN VOYAGED TO THE MOON
SUCH WERE OUR CATHEDRALS SUCH WERE OUR
CATHEDRALS

Mike Kitching lives and works in Sydney.

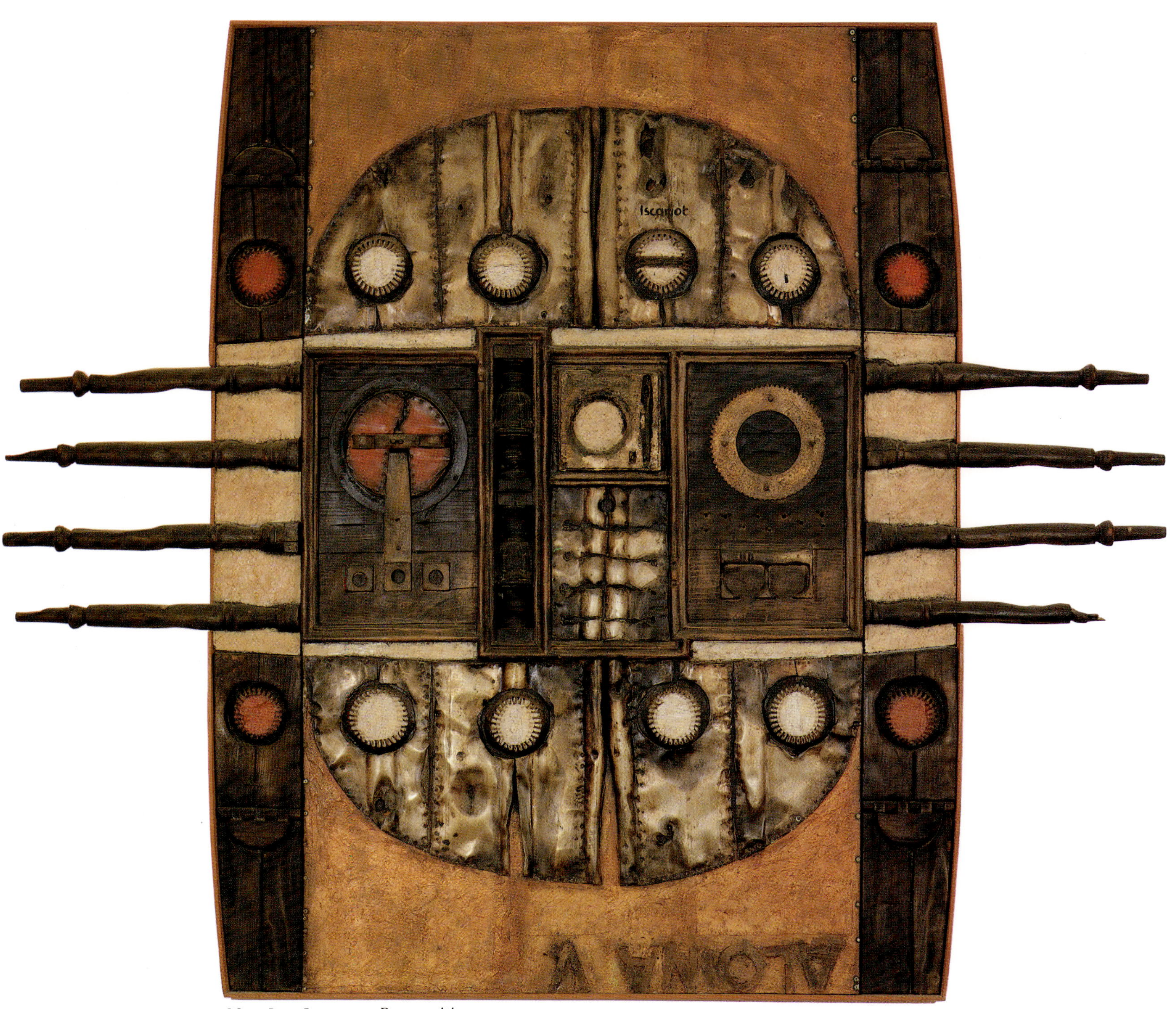

39 *Last Supper — Premonition*

Rodney Milgate

Born 1934

Ascension, 1966

Encaustic, oil on composition board
Two panels: 243.8 × 182.9 cm overall
City of Hamilton Art Gallery, Victoria

Ascension is made up of two large panels. The subject matter is not the ascension of Christ as portrayed in scripture, but rather the result of Milgate's meditation on the possibility of life outside the earth on another planet. It was only as he worked across the surface in an unpremeditated way that Milgate became aware of the possibilities of the painting as suitable for a religious competition. But *Ascension* remains for him, like his other paintings, about his own internal questioning, and more particularly, as he said in 1975, 'whether man can one day rise from the earth and evolve into a completely different form'.[1]

However, given the title and the nature of the exhibition, the judges in the Blake Prize, where *Ascension* was first exhibited, were quick to identify explicitly religious subject matter. James Gleeson, a judge that year and an admirer of Milgate's work, wrote in description and enthusiasm: 'In the lower section the ideogram representing the dead Christ is enclosed in an ideogram representing the earth . . . the upper panel is the inverted image of the lower panel except that the colour tells us that the ideogram is now enclosed in the ideogram for air . . . surely Milgate is telling us . . . that the spirit of Christ remains on earth even though the physical body ascended into heaven.'[2]

Milgate denied Gleeson's interpretation, and the controversy was argued out in the media. Gleeson asserted that it was valid for the viewer to bring an interpretation to painting. 'Between the intention and the fact stands the making of the picture,' he wrote in his own defence, 'and who knows what elements may have slipped into the unconscious levels of the artist's mind?'[3]

Milgate's method of working backwards and forwards across the surface with ribbons of paint, his use of fire and water in the process of discovering what is waiting there for release, and above all his meditative approach to the very task of painting, link him not only with Ian Fairweather, Godfrey Miller and Roger Kemp but also to the approach to painting of many present-day Aboriginal artists. Old Mick Tjakamara's *Old Man's Dreaming on Death or Destiny* (Plate 86) has a remarkable affinity with Milgate's *Ascension.*

1. ABC interview, 5 October 1975.
2. *Sun-Herald,* 2 October 1966.
3. James Gleeson, *Sun-Herald,* 9 October 1966.

Rodney Milgate was born in Kyogle, New South Wales, in 1934. He studied art at the East Sydney Technical College from 1953 to 1955 and at Sydney Teachers College from 1981 to 1983, and drama at Sydney Teachers College in 1980–81. Since 1981 he has published plays and poetry and worked as art teacher, art critic and actor. He has held a number of important administrative positions in art education but has always given sustained and priority time to his painting.

Much of Milgate's work has a religious dimension, although he rarely sets out to paint subject matter associated with traditional religion. His approach is to work meditatively with the surface of the painting, allowing images or moods to emerge as the work comes to completion. Yet his overriding concern is religious in the broad sense. As he has said, 'Painting for me provides a constant reminder of our interrelationship with past and future, and with one another: never an ability, always a fierce, demanding, disciplined search-activity for inner survival. The main aim of all my pictures is to discover reality, the truth of myself and my relevance in the world.'[1]

Milgate has been a keen supporter of the Blake Prize almost since its inception in 1951. He has exhibited more than twenty times, has been a member of the committee and a judge. He won the prize in 1966, 1975 and 1977 (jointly). In 1970 he won the Darcy Morris Memorial Award for a Scriptural Subject.

1. Quoted by Daniel Thomas in *Hemisphere,* March 1968, p. 13.

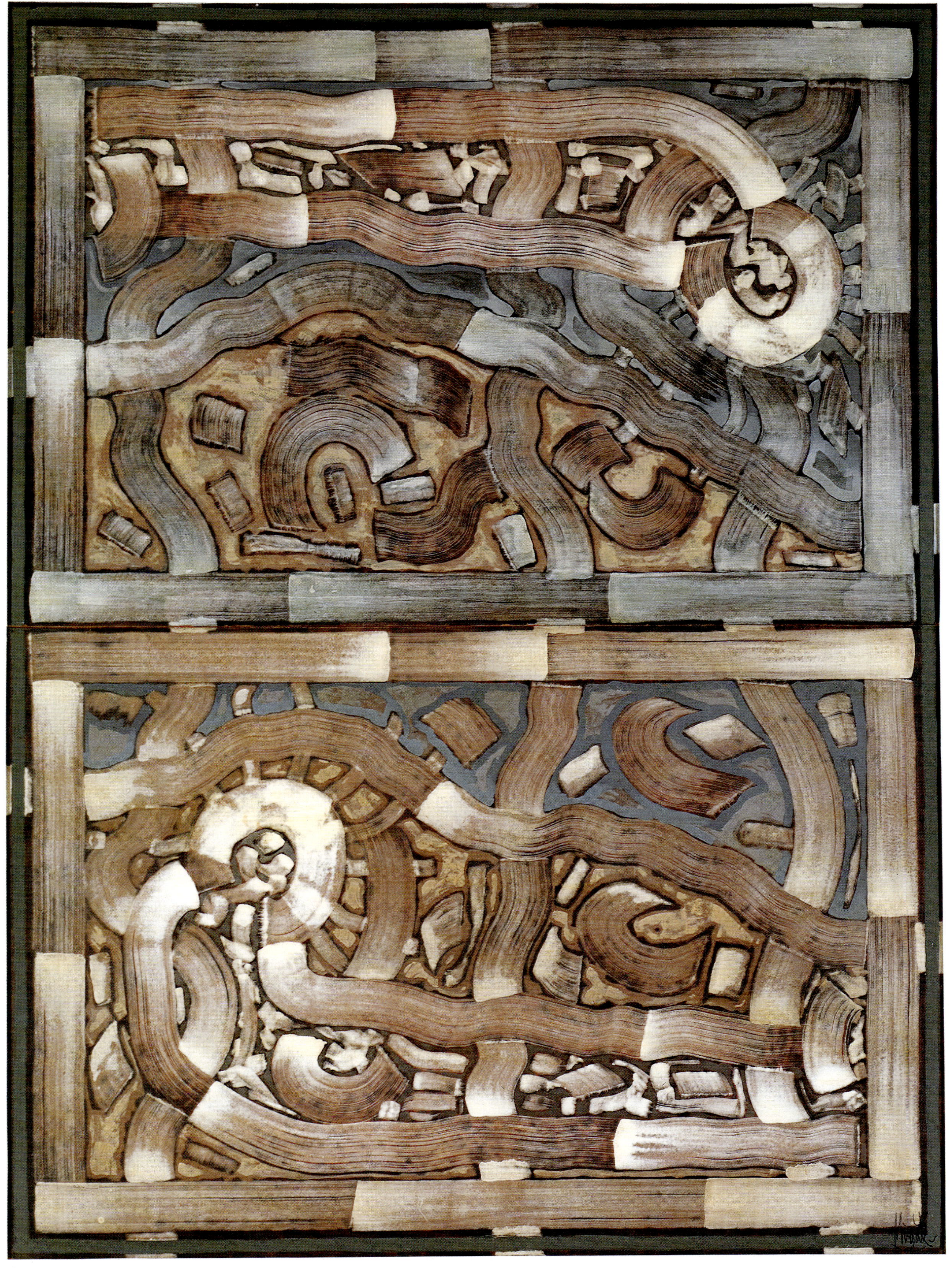

40 *Ascension*

CLIFTON PUGH

Born 1924

The Penitents, No. 9, 1967

Oil on composition board
121.9 × 91.4 cm
Collection of the artist

The Penitents, No. 9 is one of the series The Penitents, which Clifton Pugh completed during 1965–66. Much of that time he had spent in Mexico, in northern villages which were centres of religious pilgrimage by Indians as well as Latin Americans. One town, Guanajuato, was the site of a macabre church containing chained, mummified standing figures of dead villagers; another, near San Miguel de Allende, was the whitewashed church-home of the scourged, blood-spattered *Christ at the Pillar*. Pugh, who had never before been outside Australia, was horrified as well as fascinated by such extreme expressions of religious fervour as carnival-like processions of atonement, self-flagellation by women as well as men, and the deliberate spilling of blood.

The Penitents, No. 9 is Pugh's response to this essentially alien context. The male penitent who dominates this painting has rent his clothes and cries out in anger and angst. A highly realistic statue of the crucified Christ looks on, impassive, in the background. There are no other paintings in Pugh's *oeuvre* to match the raw emotion which his Penitents conjures up. Even his St Francis paintings and his earlier Crucifixions of 1959, where savagery and threat lie just beneath the surface of the Australian outback, have a calm born of understanding. But in Mexico he was, as he has said, confronted with an experience for which, as a young Australian without any religious affiliation, he was totally unprepared. The resulting paintings, including *Penitents, No. 9,* communicate a Goya-like horror and bewilderment, not so much at religion itself, but rather at this cultural expression of it.

CLIFTON PUGH was born in Melbourne in 1924 and educated at Ivanhoe Grammar School. After service with the AIF in World War II he studied art at the National Gallery School from 1948 to 1950 under William Dargie. Dargie was an eminent portraitist, a classical draughtsman and a strong teacher. Pugh became highly skilled in portraiture, winning the Archibald Prize in 1965 (*R. A. Henderson*), 1971 (*Sir John McEwen*) and 1972 (*The Hon. E. G. Whitlam*). In 1955 Pugh began exhibiting with the Group of Four, the others being Lawrence Daws, Donald Laycock and John Howley. In 1969 he was one of eight signatories to the famous Antipodean Manifesto, which upheld the supremacy of the figurative over the abstract and called on artists to build their work from their lives and surroundings so as to begin to create a distinctive Australian myth. Pugh's commitment to this ideal is evident in more than forty solo exhibitions in Australia, England, the United States, Canada, Mexico and New Zealand as well as in the films he has made—for example, *Painting People* (Commonwealth Film Unit) and *Bird and Animal* (Eltham Films)—and in his stage designs for *Mumba, Jumba and Bunyip* (1959) and, with John Olsen, *Waiting for Godot* (1961).

Much of Pugh's work is the outcome of a deeply held belief in the interdependence of life—plant, animal and human. He has been inspired throughout by a spiritual affinity with the Australian desert landscape; at times he has used the battle for survival there in metaphorical ways, as in his 1965 St Francis series, where the saint (alias Pugh), is witness to both brutality and beauty (e.g., *St Francis Receiving the Stigmata* and *Crucifixion*).

Clifton Pugh lives at Cottlesbridge, Victoria, in a house he has built in the bush.

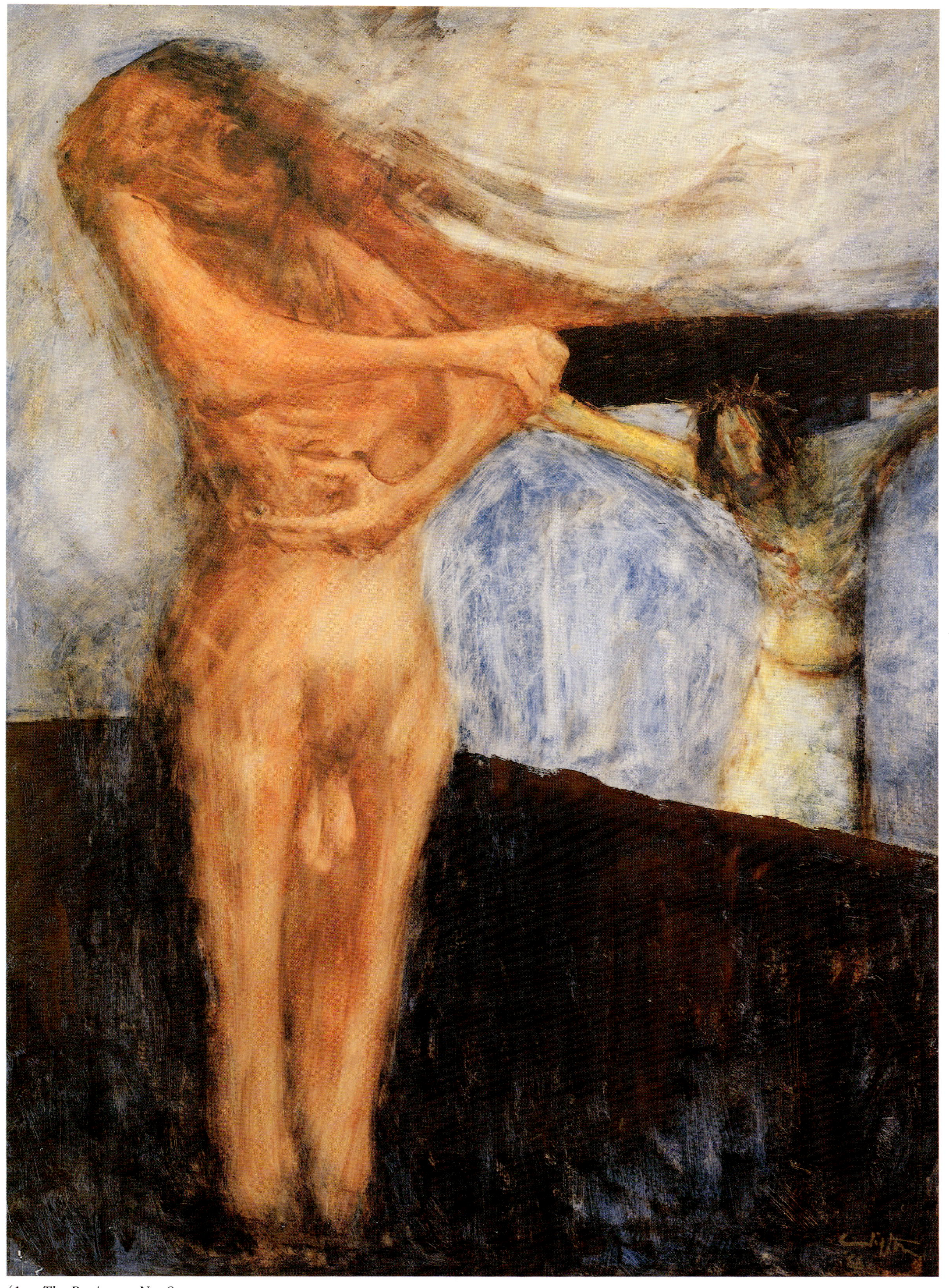

41 *The Penitents, No. 9*

George Baldessin

1939–78

First View over the City, 1967

Mixed media on composition board
380 × 430 cm
Private collection, Melbourne

George Baldessin completed *First View over the City* in 1967, at a time when he was riding the crest of success with etchings and sculptures which distorted and mutilated the human figure and took enormous liberties in the use of scale and space. Critics were writing of the paradoxes in his work—its beautiful yet sinister quality, its images of innocence and corruption, its 'asexual nakedness and frigid sensuality'. *First View over the City*, however, does little to confront or alarm the viewer. Without sustained attention it can appear of little consequence.

As Baldessin explained to the painting's present owner, he intended the painting to be religious and its subject matter to be scriptural: 'When he [Jesus] came within sight of the city [Jerusalem], he wept over it and said, "If only you had known, on this great day, the way that leads to peace! But no, it is hidden from your sight." ' (Luke 19: 41–42). The narrative goes on to prophesy the destruction of Jerusalem.

Baldessin's Jerusalem is contemporary Western life. The scene is set within a box-like room which he has created with coloured shapes framed to give the convention of depth. In the close space of the room are three figures, all women. They are superbly drawn and have the elegance but none of the sexual ambiguity of his printed images. Like the characters in hell in Sartre's play, *No Exit*, they do not communicate; each is alone. In the centre of the picture Baldessin has stuck on a drawing of the framework or skeleton of a church. It is a gothic cathedral, symbol of the most religious age in the Church. Now it is empty, a shell. In front of it, in another picture plane and using another artistic convention, life goes on.

When George Baldessin died in a car crash in 1978, the Australian art world mourned. He was thirty-nine years of age. Baldessin was born in Italy in 1939 and came to Melbourne as a child; from the age of thirteen he worked as a waiter at the Menzies Hotel, entering RMIT to study painting from 1958 to 1961. In 1962 he left for London and the Chelsea Art School and managed to spend a seminal eight months in the Academy of Fine Arts of Brera, Milan, under Alik Cavaliere, assistant to Marino Marini.

Back in Melbourne, his first solo exhibition at the Argus Gallery in 1964 and subsequent exhibitions revealed his prodigious talent. He was obsessively fascinated by the human body, not as classical beauty, but as vulnerable, disjointed, and often mutilated and desexed. He appeared as the natural heir to the Antipodean tradition, although his stylistic ancestry was in erotic surrealism, Goya and Japanese art. He frequently used his etchings as beginning points for his sculptures, creating in three dimensions the objects, figures and perspectival space of his prints. His prints, drawings and sculpture usually had an aloofness and elegance that was more European than Australian but an ambiguity of scale that is not so easily ascribed. In 1967 he won the Alcorso-Sekers Sculpture Prize, in 1970 the drawing prize at the Second International Biennale in Yugoslavia, in 1971 the Comalco Invitation award for sculpture. In 1975, with Imants Tillers, he represented Australia at the Biennale Sao Paolo in Brazil. In 1976 he worked in the Lacourie Etching Studio in Paris.

Baldessin gave Melbourne print-making a tremendous impetus when he shared his giant workshop in the Olderfield Buildings in Collins Street with other artists, including Roger Kemp, Fred Williams, Tate Adams, Jan Senbergs and Les Kossatz.

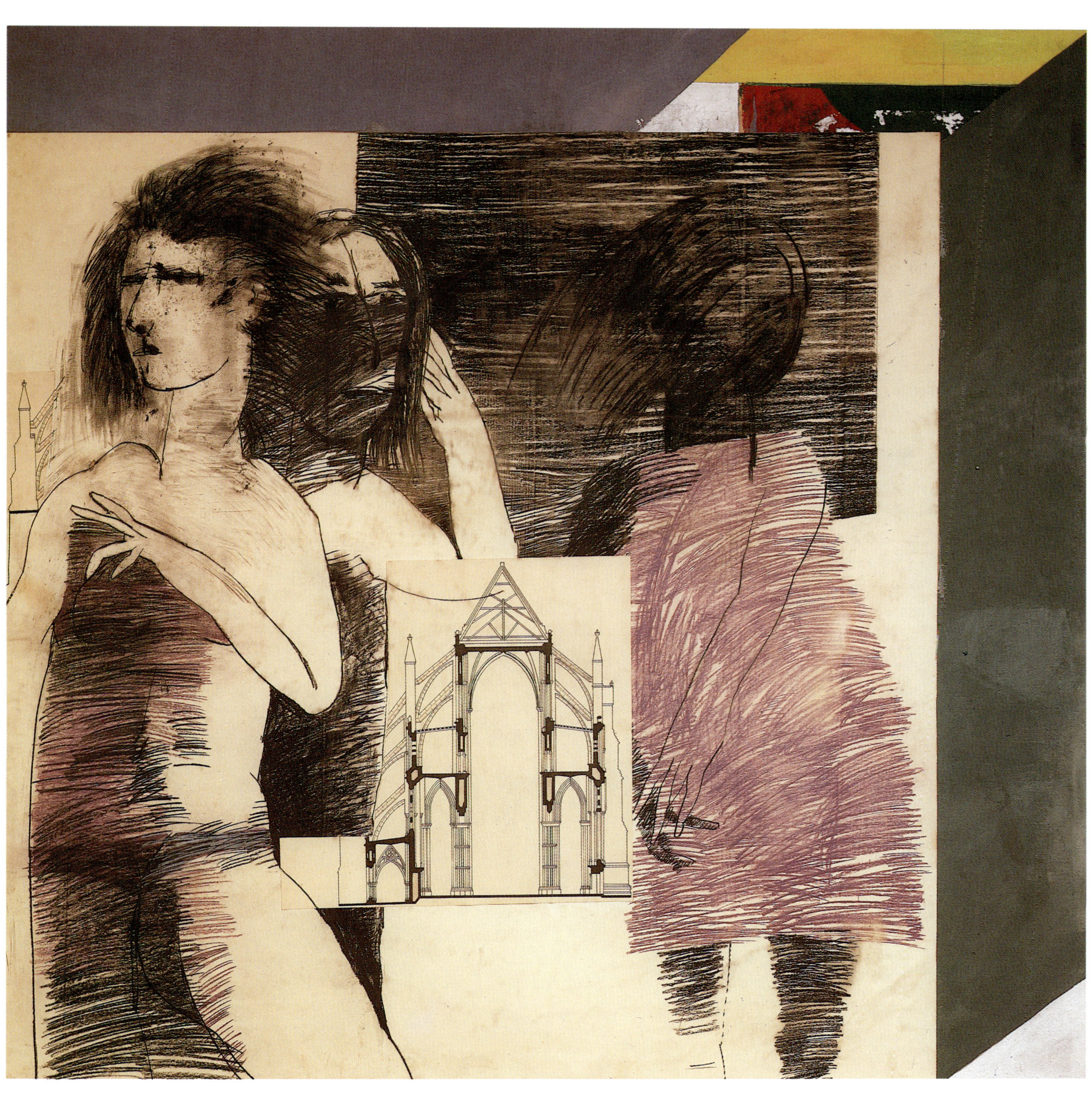

42 *First View over the City*

Desiderius Orban

1884–1986

Transition to Christianity, 1971

Oil and felt-tipped pen on pineboard
Two panels: 153.7 × 276.8 cm overall
Art Gallery of New South Wales, Sydney
Gift of the artist 1972

Transition to Christianity won the Blake Prize for Religious Art in 1971. Orban had won the prize once before, in 1967, with his *Hosannah.* Both paintings stand somewhat outside his declared philosophy of painting in so far as they have some premeditated subject matter. However, in speaking about *Transition to Christianity,* Orban said that it was completed long before it was named, and that it might just as easily have been named differently and entered into an entirely different exhibition.

But the experience of looking at this painting does not support Orban's words, either as to his intention or to the generalized nature of the subject matter. Clearly Orban is working with surface effects which evoke specific religious traditions. The two panels are like doors into a Jewish temple or a Christian church. The gold paint creates a precious quality, and the markings on the surface, drawn in with a felt-tipped pen, are gathered from ancient traditions, again mainly Hebrew and Christian.

Even though Orban has not sought to tell a story in this painting but to create a unity, a 'spirituality', *Transition to Christianity* is representational and narrative in a way similar to his 1967 *Hosannah,* where he also used richly gilded and carved surfaces which recall the long tradition of Byzantine and Orthodox iconography. The work is without strong tonal contrasts or dramatic patterning. It does not command visual engagement but rather asserts its presence serenely, like an ancient relic or a statue of Buddha.[1]

1. At this time, Orban became very enthusiastic about Zen Buddhism, recognizing in its tenets a philosophy close to his own.

Desiderius Orban was born in Györ, Hungary, in 1884. He studied mathematics at Budapest University, but most of his art education, both philosophy and practice, was acquired informally. In Paris he was greatly influenced by the Hungarian community who often met in the studio of Gertrude Stein. There he encountered Picasso and Matisse. Their ideas as well as the radical colour of their works challenged him to move away from the sombre browns and blacks of his own palette. Back in Budapest, he established a considerable reputation with the Eight Group, and founded the Atelier Art and Craft Academy in 1931.

In 1939, aged 55, he migrated to Australia to find friends and support among the small circle of Sydney artists, including Jean Bellette, Paul Haefliger, William Dobell and Elaine Haxton. His philosophy of art, derived in part from Theosophy and Surrealism, greatly influenced Michael Scott and Richard Morley, the founders of the Blake Prize. A true work of art, he maintained, was distinguished by a quality that could be recognized, but not described. This quality he called 'spirituality'. Art should never simply tell a story, nor should it stoop to propaganda. The call to be an artist was a vocation which was to be followed; the act of painting was a meditative act where the artist stood humbly before his canvas, and allowed the subject matter to emerge. The moment of completion was a moment of recognition.

Orban exercised great influence as director of his own art school, the Orban School of Art at Circular Quay, Sydney, and during his presidency of the New South Wales Contemporary Art Society from 1945–1954.

In 1985 the Art Gallery of New South Wales honoured him with a major retrospective exhibition.

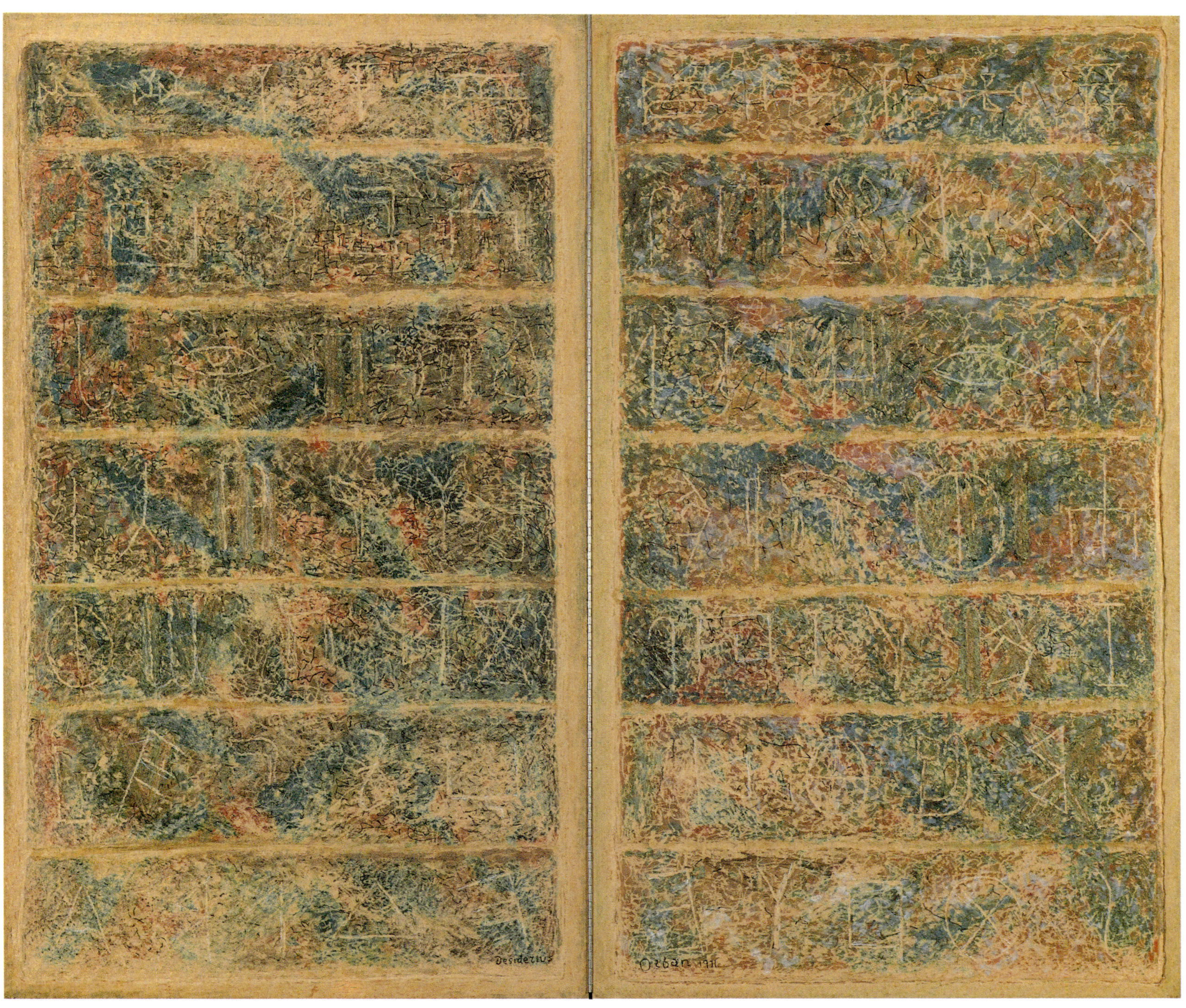

43 *Transition to Christianity*

NOEL COUNIHAN
1913–86

Laughing Christ, No. 10, 1972

Oil on canvas
122 × 106.5 cm
National Gallery of Victoria, Melbourne
Purchased 1985

This painting is the tenth in a series completed by Noel Counihan in the 1970s, each work having the same title: *Laughing Christ*. They are all meant to be strong anti-war statements, directed against Australian and American involvement in Vietnam. His earlier, 1967, series, Boy in a Helmet, had drawn attention to the tragic loss of adolescent boys as soldiers in a war that was not of their making. In the Laughing Christ series, Counihan took the traditional sacred image of religion, the figure of the Christian saviour, the Man of Peace crowned with thorns, and distorted it in a quite shocking way. The Christ laughs or grimaces or shows rows of teeth in a skull-like grin.

Although at first sight these paintings appear to attack and ridicule Christianity, Counihan has denied that this is so. What angered him was what he saw to be institutionalized religion's support of the war. Chaplains accompanied the army, even on killing missions against other Christians and Buddhists. This, to Counihan as to many Christians, was a denial of the heart of Christianity. Thus Counihan's Christ laughs in derision at the charade of Vietnam.

Many of the other paintings in the series were strongly influenced by the wooden village Christs which had so impressed Counihan in 1969 in Poland, Russia and Mexico. The Christ here is different. He is Australian. He sits upon the cross, arms folded across his body, like a wharf-labourer at a union meeting. He wears the crown of thorns indifferently, even jauntily. The bulky figure exudes apathy and indifference, the mouth wide with cynicism and condemnation.

NOEL COUNIHAN was born in Melbourne in 1913. Throughout his life he spoke out and used his art as a weapon for justice. Even as a child he was prepared to act on the side of those he considered unjustly treated, siding with his mother in family arguments, defending fellow students in his five years at St Paul's Choir School. He left school aged fifteen after a year at Caulfield Grammar School. His 'university', he said, was involvement in the struggles of the unemployed in the Depression. He read Marx, Engels, Dostoevsky, Schopenhauer and Nietzsche. In 1931 he helped found the Workers' Art Club and in 1939 the Contemporary Art Society. He started to paint only during World War II and worked closely with Vic O'Connor and Josl Bergner. The three became known as social realists. His paintings in the forties were anti-Fascist (*The New Order,* 1942), anti-poverty (*At the Corner of Nightingale Street,* 1944) and for fair working conditions (*In the Eighteen Inch Seam, Wonthaggi,* 1944). Artistically, his enthusiams were for Rembrandt, Daumier, Goya and George Grosz and the German expressionists. From 1949 until 1952 he was in Europe working as a caricaturist-cartoonist on Fleet Street and elsewhere. His works there and until the end of the Vietnam War were sometimes satirical. (*They Think that Freedom Can Be Jailed,* 1950), occasionally allegorical (*Strontium 90,* 1959), aggressively anti-war (Boy in a Helmet series, 1967; The Good Life series, *c.*1967; Laughing Christ series, *c.*1972) and sometimes tender, especially when they concern women (*Aboriginal Mother and Child,* 1960). As well as painting portraits and themes of day-to-day life, towards the end of his life Counihan did paintings and prints that looked at personal fear (*Image of Lear I,* 1977), isolation (*Old Woman,* 1981), terrorism (*Beirut,* 1983) and death (*Confrontation,* 1983).

[*Continued overleaf*]

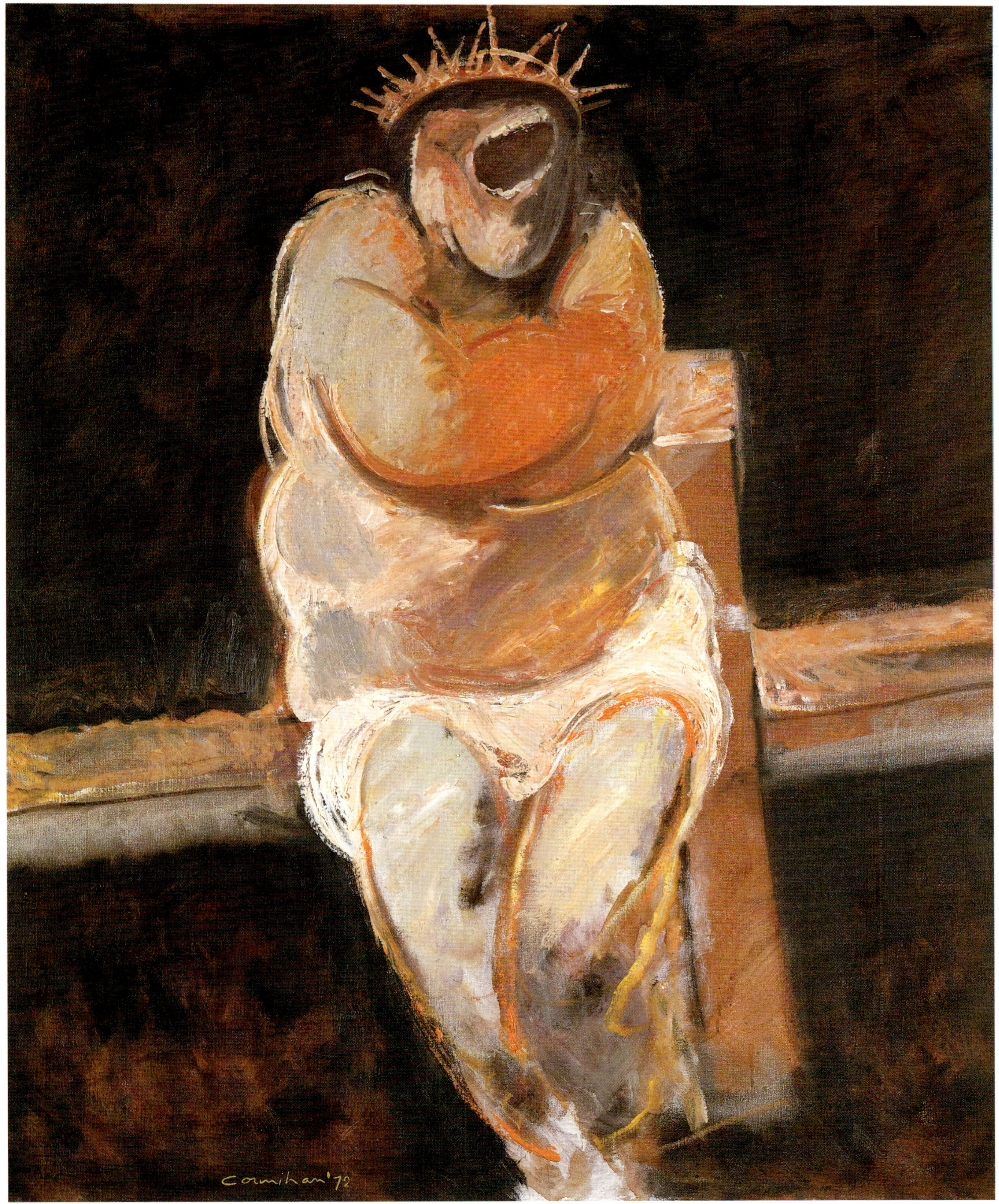

44 *Laughing Christ, No. 10*

NOEL COUNIHAN

1913–86

Homage to Goya (Requiem for El Salvador), 1985

Oil and tempera on canvas
97 × 122 cm
Private collection, Melbourne

Homage to Goya was painted by Noel Counihan towards the end of his life. It was meant to be a tribute to the people engaged in the political struggles of Latin America, in particular to those in El Salvador. But it is more than that. It is like Counihan's last hurrah, his last protest at yet another massive injustice. This image of a man with his arms outstretched is the embodiment of fear and horror in the face of impending disaster and personal death. Counihan's man stands in white with his ribcage echoed in the rising sun behind him; his body, like his eyes, gaping out of his clothes.

Counihan's involvement with the plight of the oppressed ripples throughout his entire work. It wells up in recurring themes and images, particularly images reminiscent of crucifixion—for example, *Albert Namatjira* (1950), *Boy in a Helmet 4* (1967), *Rape* (1968), as well as many of his Laughing Christ series. This is not to suggest that Counihan's use of this most powerful of religious symbols was always intentional—often his declared intentions expressed anger and alienation from established religion—but some of the power in his most poignant work comes out of a sensitivity and compassion akin to a deep religious sense and finds outlet in images that can easily be called religious.

The title *Homage to Goya* refers first to Counihan's long-standing admiration for Goya as a painter and print-maker who comments powerfully on the human condition through his documentation of the decay of his own society. More specifically, the title refers to Goya's *The Third of May, 1808* (1814), in which the central figure faces the French firing squad, also with his arms raised and his face alight with fear.

'I am concerned with the theme of the Prisoner,' Counihan wrote in 1969. 'The barbarous gaols of Spain, Mexico, Greece, South Africa and other lands are filled with political prisoners, isolated for their principles. Many of the rest of us carry our gaols around with us—our individuality so restricted and confined by modern life . . . The resultant apathy and indifference to the spiritual needs of man and to such urgent issues as the Vietnam War and its loss of life on both sides, its corruption of youth, are direct expressions of the affluent society.'[1]

1. Quoted by Max Dimmack in his *Noel Counihan* (Carlton, Vic.: Melbourne University Press, 1974), p. 70.

Counihan exhibited widely, both inside and outside Australia, including London and Warsaw in 1951, Moscow and Leningrad in 1960 and 1969, and Perpignan, France, in 1982. He was also a consummate print-maker. As early as 1930 he was able to use the lino cut as a quick means of sharp and sometimes brutal comment (*The Tycoon,* 1931; *Albert Namatjira,* 1959). Later, partly through the encouragement of Arthur Boyd, he worked with drypoint (*The Good Life,* 1969), etching and lithography (*Old Woman,* 1981).

Noel Counihan is unique in the history of Australian art because of his constant political involvment with the cause of justice. 'My politics are simply my outlook on life,' he said, 'and my work is an integral part of that.' But he was not aggressively polemical: 'I don't paint political pictures. I paint pictures about life, about the exploited, the dispossessed and the unemployed trying to cope with their own problems . . . my images are largely ones of compassion.'[1]

1. Quoted by Rosslyn Beeby, The *Age*, 8 July 1986.

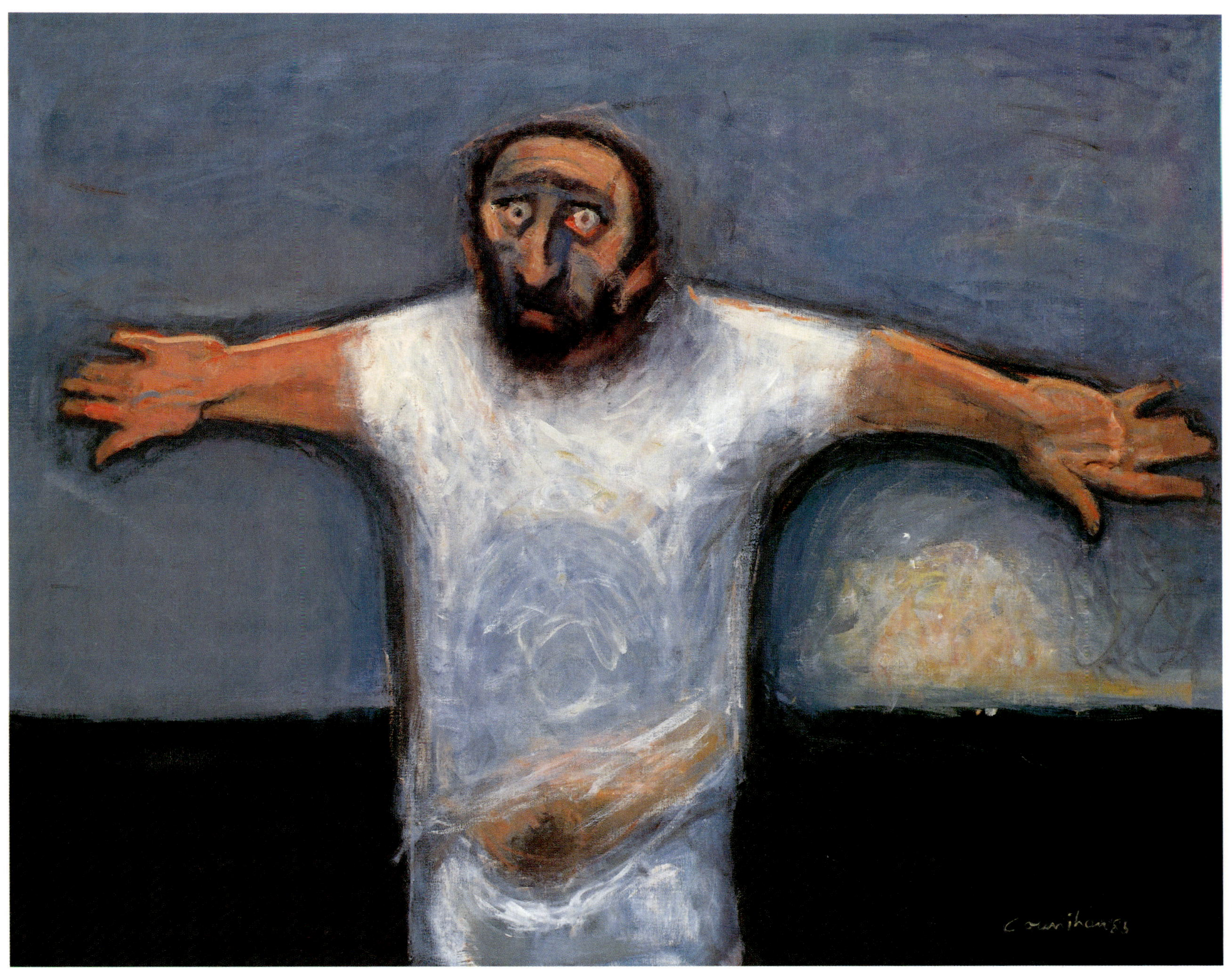

45 *Homage to Goya (Requiem for El Salvador)*

KEITH LOOBY

Born 1940

Knock, Knock, Is God Home?, 1972

Oil and pencil on composition board
Six panels: 275.4 × 367.5 cm overall
Australian National Gallery, Canberra

Knock, Knock, Is God Home? won the Darcy Morris Memorial Award for a non-abstract religious painting in the 1972 Blake Prize. Looby had won the award twice before with paintings that were crowded with Bosch-like figures cavorting against religion. Many, including the donors, considered these paintings were against the spirit of the award. Rather than promote religion, they were seen to criticize and satirize the hierarchical structures of the Church. When *Knock, Knock, Is God Home?* received the 1972 award, the donors withdrew the money for the award and the Darcy Morris Memorial prize was discontinued.

Knock, Knock, Is God Home? is one of the last works in which Looby combines drawing with painting on this scale. After this, his paintings become an exploration of the act of painting and rarely a vehicle for him to explore social and religious questions. But here the title *Knock, Knock, Is God Home?* seems to invite a specifically religious interpretation: Is it possible to believe in a God when what we experience in society seems to be His absence? Who can sit in these big, soft chairs, wrapped as parcels and bursting their strings? What are the floating shapes? Are they rocks, Looby's personal symbol for power? What is the meaning of the intestine-like figures in the smaller panels? Like religion itself, Keith Looby's *Knock, Knock, Is God Home?* raises questions rather than provides answers, challenges rather than comforts. It is a painting more about doubt than belief, and much of its power lies in the mood it creates.

Named upon completion, the title *Knock, Knock, Is God Home?* is both Looby's question to the finished work and his comment on a way of life and a religion with which he is disillusioned.

KEITH LOOBY was born in Sydney in 1940. He studied at the East Sydney Technical College from 1955 to 1960 and then moved to Italy, where he studied the Italian and Flemish Renaissance painters. He was also, he has said, pursuing his own religious quest;[1] since the death of his mother, a strict Catholic, when he was twelve, he had been cut off from the Church. Much of his work in those years, and on his return to Australia in 1967, was the direct outcome of his struggle to understand hierarchical religion, coupled with his fascination with the way Brueghel, Bosch and the English artist Stanley Spencer had observed and recorded the odd, the eccentric and the detail of everyday life around them. From these years date a number of strongly linear, satirical paintings. Some, like *The Rejection of the Wholly One* (1968), and *Those Days We Murdered Jesus* (1969), attacked the anachronisms of religious institutions and reveal Looby as moralist, thinker and commentator.

[*Continued overleaf*]

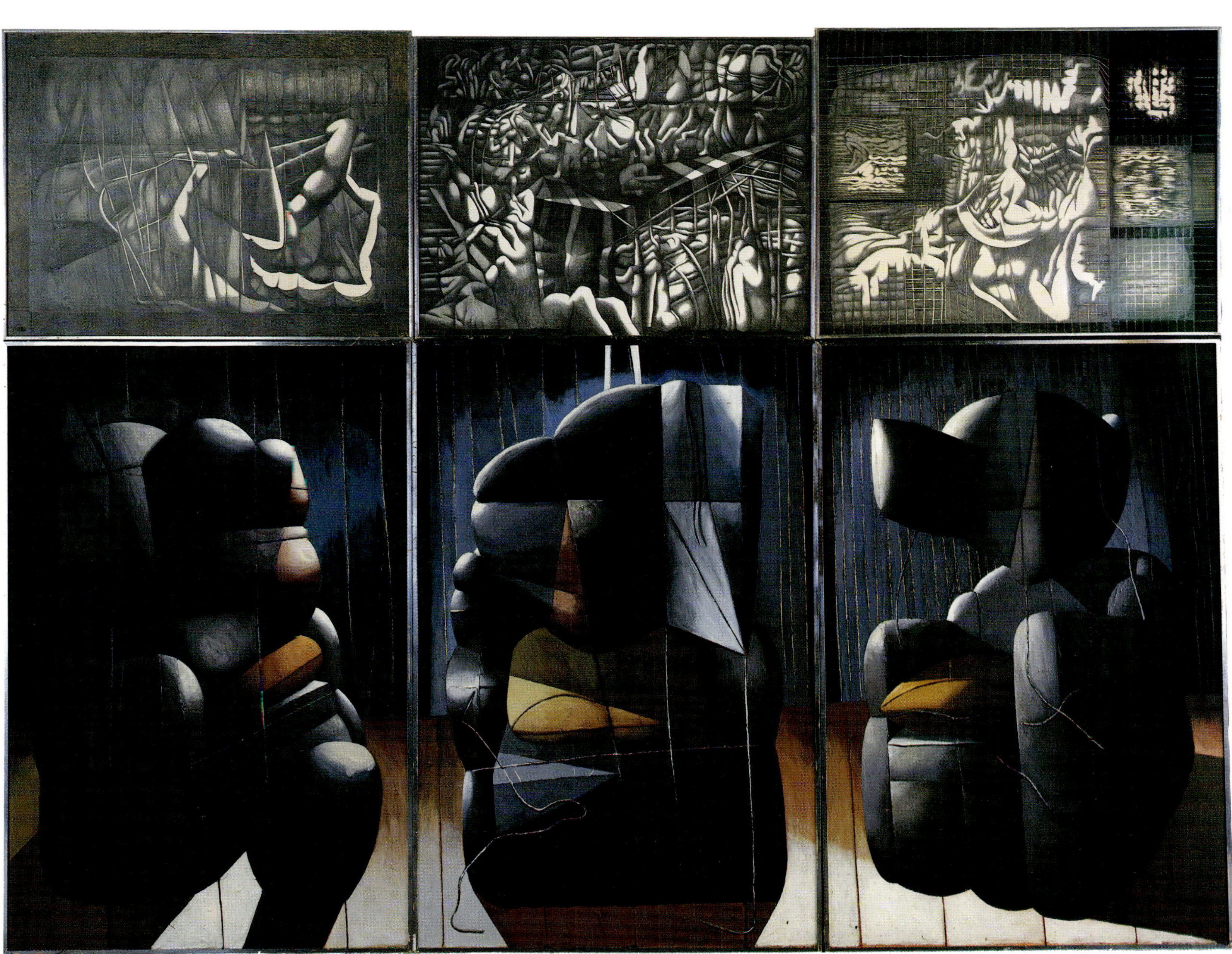

46 *Knock, Knock, Is God Home?*

KEITH LOOBY

Born 1940

Your Motel Calvary Still Life Flowers, 1973

Oil on canvas with mirrored glass
Two panels: 259.1 × 289.6 cm overall
Griffith University, Brisbane

Your Motel Calvary Still Life Flowers won the 1973 Blake Prize. It was Keith Looby's sixth and last entry in a series of paintings with religious subject matter which he began on his return from Italy in 1967. Taken together, Looby's religious paintings can be seen to document his break with an electicism built out of his European enthusiasms and the establishment of a style that is more personal and idiosyncratic. They also reflect a gradual freeing of his religious orientation.

Like *Knock, Knock, Is God Home?* (Plate 46), *Your Motel Calvary Still Life Flowers* was named by Looby after he had completed the work when he discerned that the finished painting had religious overtones.[1] Its title is ironical; unlike many of his earlier paintings, which were about the intervention of a biblical God, this is about the absence of a God, or even the impossibility of a God in a society which is nationalistic (the flag), materialistic (the soft chairs), aesthetic (the tree) and power hungry (the stones). This interpretation is made backwards, as it were. It depends not on Looby's premeditated intention but on the finished painting and the way it contains elements such as the flag, tree, chairs and stone, which are a part of his symbolic vocabulary and about which he has often spoken.[2]

Technically, the painting is masterly. Looby is as much in deliberate control of his formal qualities as is Ken Reinhard, Peter Powditch or any Pop painter in Australia at the time. His paint is smooth, without sign of brushstroke, but with volume meticulously built up through carefully controlled use of tints and tones of primary and secondary colours, and lighting from above and to the right, outside the picture frame. Space, as in most of his work, is restricted but is relieved somewhat by the device of the open window which looks on to a landscape with another chair. The light that suffuses the work is the bright, clear sunlight of Australia.

1. Interview with the author, 28 January 1978.
2. John Hopkins, 'Ideas and Ideals', *Hemisphere* 19, no. 10 (1975).

By about 1973 he had exhausted his anger with religion and his consuming concern to make his paintings include political or social comment. He had come to believe that his paintings should, as he has said, have a life of their own; their subject matter should not be predetermined but should emerge as the painting progressed because the act of creation is more a discovery and identification than a premeditated gesture.[2] This shift in attitude placed him more within the mainstream of Sydney avant-garde painting. Alongside the Central Street Gallery 'colour field' abstract painters, or even the abstractions of the older generation artists such as Stanislaus Rapotec, Eric Smith and John Coburn, his early work with its satire and meticulous line drawing looked old-fashioned and out-of-tune. Not so his paintings after 1970. They are more abstract, hard-edged and emotionally neutral even when they retain figures and still-life objects.

Looby is a master draughtsman. By 1980 he had completed three volumes of his *History of Australia*—the first volume its prehistory, the second its history after white settlement, and the third a personal history. The many hundreds of meticulous drawings testify to his wit and imagination and the sharpness of his mind as he explores injustice against people and the devastation of the land.

Keith Looby lives in Sydney.

1. Interview with author, 28 January, 1978.
2. Mervyn Horton, *Australian Painters of the 70s* (Sydney: Ure Smith, 1975), p. 37.

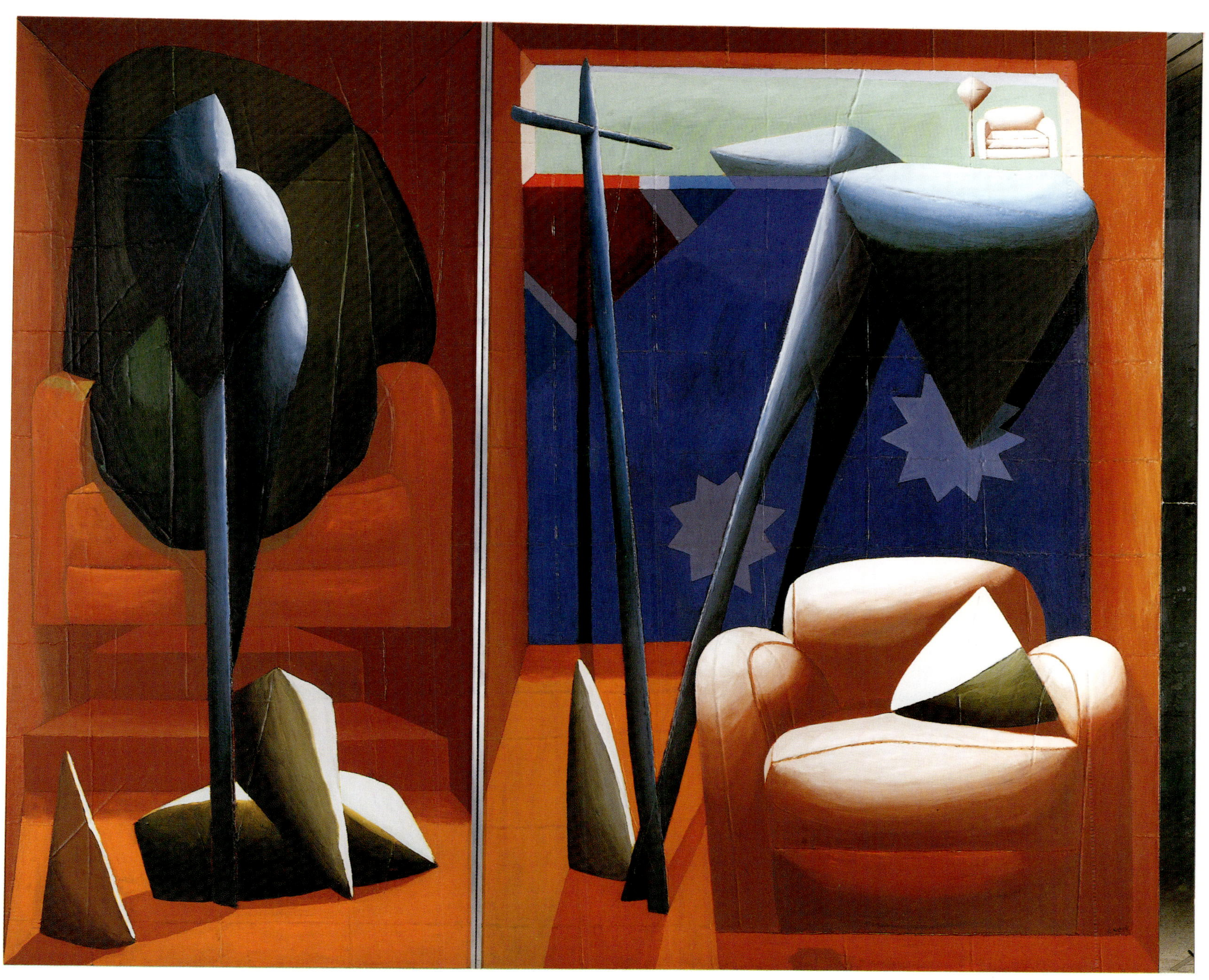

47 *Your Motel Calvary Still Life Flowers*

ALUN LEACH-JONES
Born 1937

Time and Silence, 1972

Synthetic polymer on canvas
244 × 198.3 cm
Brisbane College of Advanced Education
Purchased 1979

Alun Leach-Jones painted *Time and Silence* as a summation of his belief that a perfect world is possible for those who are prepared to enter through the doors into a world beyond the physical. The original shape of the painting was that of a retable, the flat panel at the back of an altar. Leach-Jones removed the outer panels from the finished painting. What remains is the flat centre panel containing the central door or gate, the steps leading up to the altar and the surrounds filled with tightly interwoven interlocking shapes. Suspended in front of the door is a huge green egg, a deliberate reference to Piero della Francesca's *Sacred Conversation with Kneeling Donor* in Milan, where the egg is symbolic both of virgin birth and of new life and resurrection. In Leach-Jones's painting the egg summons the viewer to enter into a more perfect existence.

The style of *Time and Silence* is meant to be a metaphor for perfection. The surface is smooth, the line consummately controlled, the colour graded exactly to create both harmony and dissonance. Every element is orchestrated to affect and beguile the eye and the mind. The individual shapes, although apparently random and abstract, reward sustained meditation and become recognizable —crosses, triangles, squares, trees, flowers, body forms. For the initiated, the ground plan of Angelsea Cathedral and other elements of Leach-Jones's private vocabulary of sign and symbol are there.

Leach-Jones's notebook reveals his process. As carefully as any architect or master craftsman, he plans every detail—page after page of drawings, notes about placement, poems about meaning, graded strips of colour—little is left to chance. Once he starts on the canvas, though, he draws freely and surely with fine sable brushes loaded with carefully modulated colour.

To see first the colour
Then to see next the individual stripe of colour
then next to become aware of the shape/image
that carries the colour and the stripe of colour
Then to see next the architectonic structure—
my hidden drawn forms on which
pivots the movement of the picture . . .[1]

In *Time and Silence*, as in most of his other paintings, Leach-Jones is never far from history. This painting is a particular homage to medieval manuscripts and to the painters of the fifteenth century whom he so admires—Fra Angelico, Piero della Francesca, van der Weyden and van Eyck. Like them, he has worked with patience and skill so that the viewer may be enticed into a calm meditation on the meaning and possibility of a more perfect world that is just out of reach.

1. From Alun Leach-Jones's notebook.

ALUN LEACH-JONES was born in Wales in 1937. Some of his earliest memories are of Welsh singers around his grandfather's piano, his father reading poetry aloud and going water-colour painting with an uncle through the snow. In 1949 he attended evening art classes in Liverpool College of Art and became apprenticed to a law writer. These formative influences have marked his whole life in visible ways. He loves music and harmony, he is a voracious reader of poetry and history, he is preoccupied with literary symbolism in his painting, and his three years as a law writer have given him mastery of line and graded colour laid effortlessly with fine sable brushes.

In 1959 he emigrated to Australia and studied part-time at the South Australian Art School under print-maker Udo Sellback. The years 1964 to 1966 were spent in Europe, studying at first hand the fifteenth-century Sienese and Florentine masters; 1973–74 saw him in New York and India; in 1980 he was artist-in-residence at the Bethanien Artists' Studios in West Berlin, and in 1981 at New York State University.

Leach-Jones sees his work since 1964 as a series of personal explorations into the meaning of life. Four major series date from this time: the Noumenon paintings (1964–72) are private reflections on the search for 'otherness' in life; the Gesangkunstwerk paintings (1970–78) are explorations into multiple life systems; the Romance of Death paintings (1980–86) are his attempt to confront the inevitability of death; since 1986 he has been working on a series, Gardens of the Voice.

Leach-Jones denies that his paintings are abstract in the sense that they are without subject matter. Pure decoration is abhorrent and empty to him. He has a consuming fascination with meaning, both as signified and symbolic. His is a highly developed personal iconography, often obscure and esoteric but fascinating to the initiated. Thus his paintings have more than formal excellence; they are visual equivalents of the kind of poetry that is rich in literary allusion and complex, layered imagery.

Alun Leach-Jones lives in Sydney.

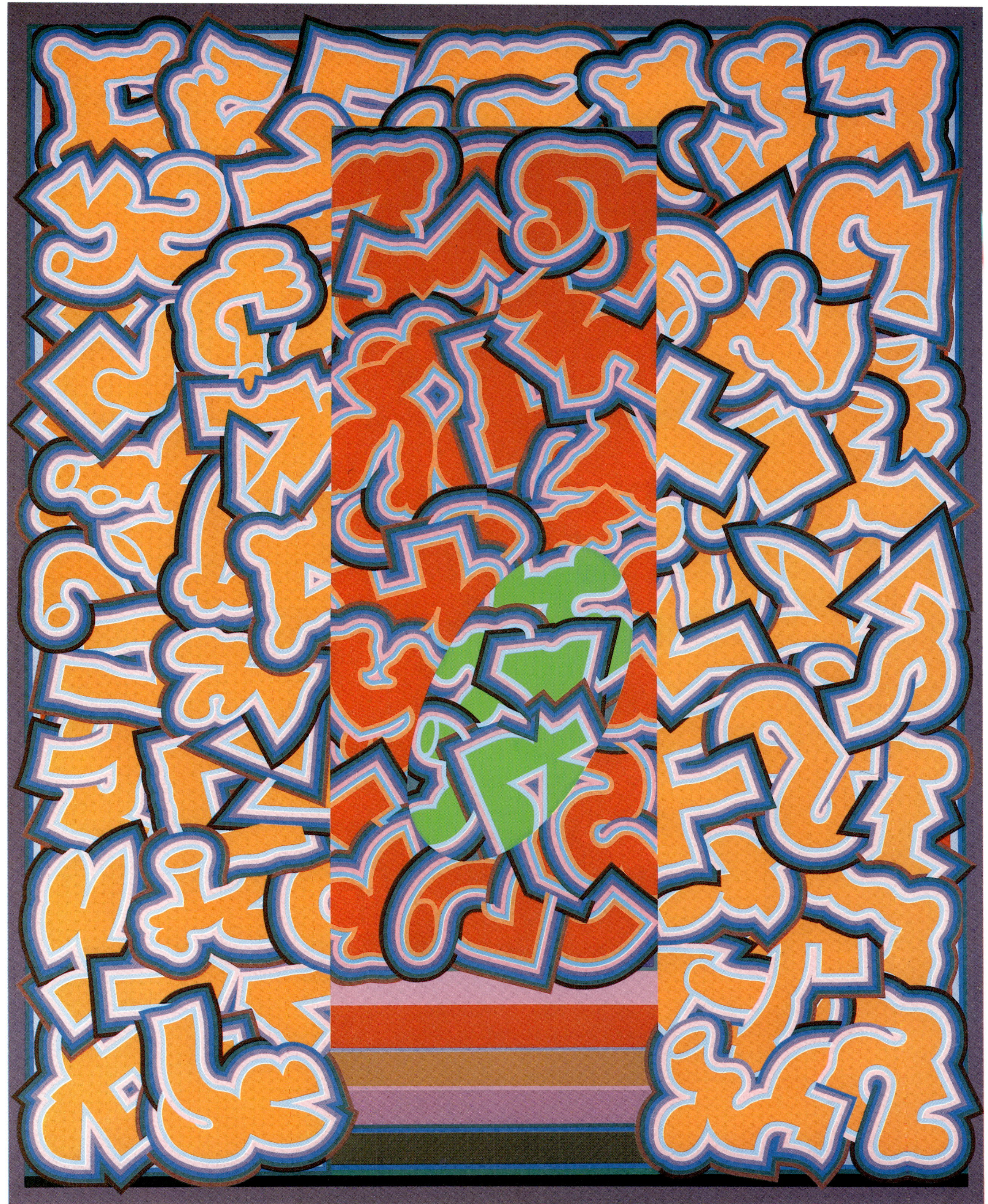

48 *Time and Silence*

WARREN BRENINGER

Born 1948

Tomb of Eve Opened, 1978–79

Mixed media (silver bromide etching, gum arabic prints and photo silk-screen drawing and painting media)
Three panels: 215.9 × 299.7 cm overall
Collection of the artist

Warren Breninger completed the *Tomb of Eve Opened* in 1979. He had been working on the image of the biblical Eve since the early seventies, exploring ways in which an original photograph could be shaped and reshaped to reflect the passage of life, of good and evil, consent and denial in each of us. Each person's life, to Breninger, carries the visible revelation, or 'opening', of God.

The sixteen images of Eve's face here represent a single instant in the Genesis account of the Fall. Eve hovers on the edge of expulsion from Paradise, 'passing under the angel's flaming sword'; in a moment of time she experiences the whole gamut of human emotion, from ecstasy to despair. Breninger's Eve reflects intense beauty, innocence, even serenity, but she also portrays ugliness, pride and the pain of birth. All will be possible in this new world—evil, passion, hope, redemption. The side panels hold a young, pubescent female in a gesture suggestive of crucifixion, her body map-like. She is one of those faithful female martyrs at the end of the twentieth century about whom Breninger has written:

The lifeboat leaves full of men,
Women stay aboard,
daring to die[1]

Viewed in this way, Breninger's *Tomb of Eve Opened* rewards sustained reflection; it easily becomes a moment of revelation and invitation.

Without this 'insider' understanding, *Tomb of Eve Opened* can remain an enigma. Breninger has placed himself outside the mainstream of current Australian painting in many ways: he has ignored the established boundaries between photography, drawing and painting; his nudes are drawn with renaissance-type accuracy and idealism; his view of the female figure and the whole picture as symbolic of God's creative word is out of tune not only with a world sceptical and apathetic about religion but with a Judaeo-Christian tradition which has always regarded the nude human figure, and especially the female nude in art, with some suspicion. Because of all of this, Breninger is likely to have a continuous struggle for the recognition that his work rightly deserves.

1. Warren Breninger, 'Borrowed Light', a poem, 1987.

WARREN BRENINGER was born in Melbourne in 1948. He studied art for higher diploma in secondary arts and crafts at Melbourne Teachers College from 1968 to 1971 and diploma of art and design at Caulfield Institute of Technology in 1975, where he became fascinated with the expressive possibilities of photography and quickly won critical acclaim. Breninger's more recent work, which emphasizes the accurate portrayal of the female form, lies outside the more easily recognizable trends in contemporary Australian art but has been influenced by post-war European humanist schools through the work of Francis Bacon, Jean Ipousteguy and Ernest Trova. These artists have rejected pure abstraction to concentrate on the human figure as purveyor of a moral stance; they have chosen to emphasize the male person. Breninger's attention, to this time, has been with the female (I'm artistically bored with the male image,' he said in 1987)[1] in a series of vertical or aerially viewed nudes, or as portrait heads, either frontal or viewed from above and developed from a single photographic image.

Breninger sees religion and his personal fidelity to God as the core of his life and art. Religion, life and art are inseparable. At the pivot of his religious stance is the belief that, as creatures, we are also—since the fall from grace—deeply flawed. The human face—'the point of vulnerability, the exposed place of transparency'—reveals 'the remains of paradise, our lordship of creation and the image of our maker.' But it also, for Breninger, 'reveals death—the consequences of sin and rebellion, originally declared through our mortality, frailty, depravity and tragedy. Our spiritual history is built into our image. My work,' he said, 'tries not to lie about what we are.'[2]

Breninger's works often contain clear references to paintings by Mantegna, van Eyck, Michelangelo and Munch. Breninger means this to be a mark of respect and affection; it is never done cynically or from high-mindedness.

Warren Breninger lives in Melbourne.

1. Interview with author, 3 December 1987.
2. Interview with author, 1 February 1988.

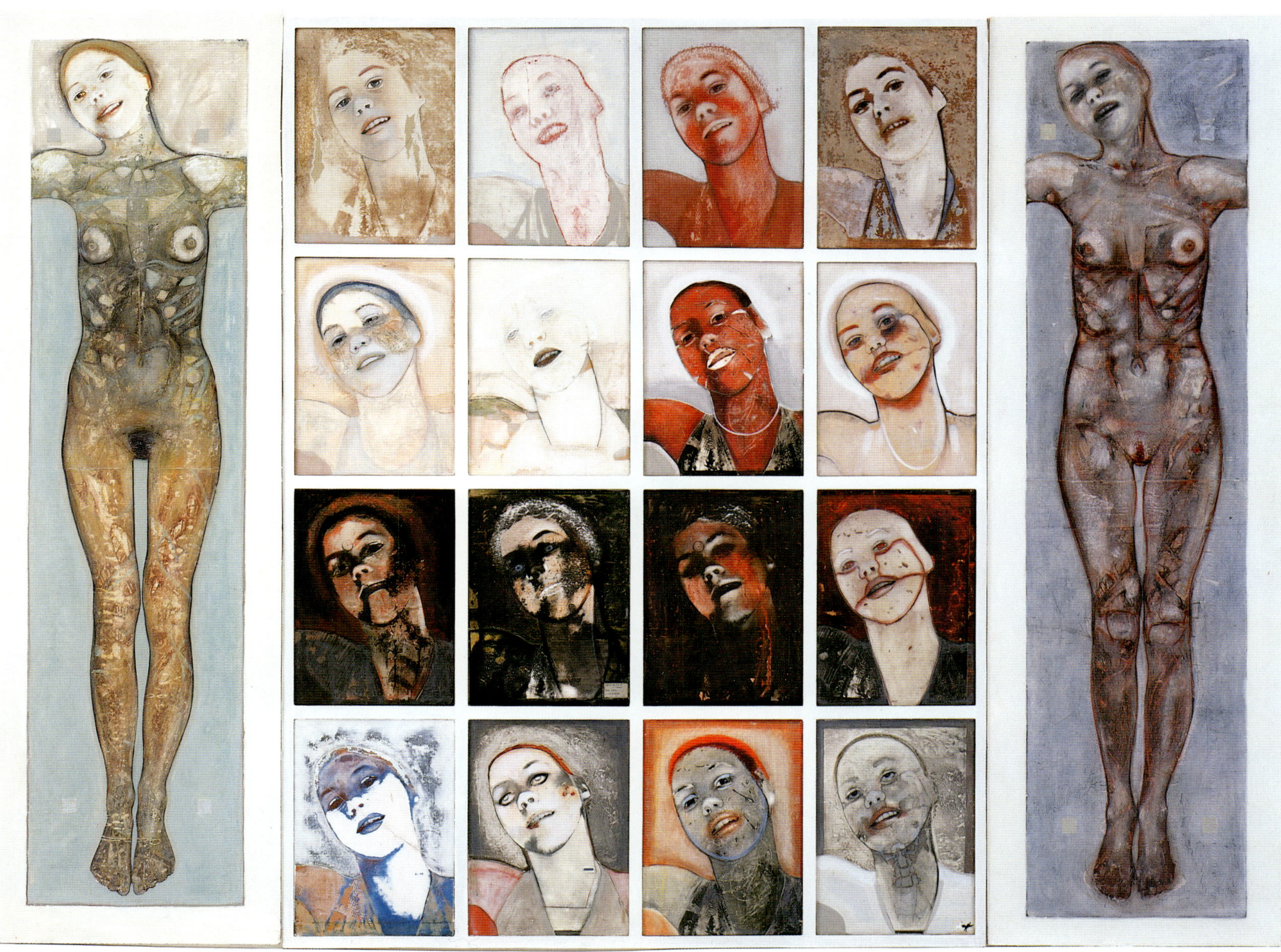

49 *Tomb of Eve Opened*

WARREN BRENINGER

Born 1948

Expulsion of Eve, Series III, No. 4, 1980–87

Mixed media on C-type colour paper
75 × 50 cm
Collection of the artist

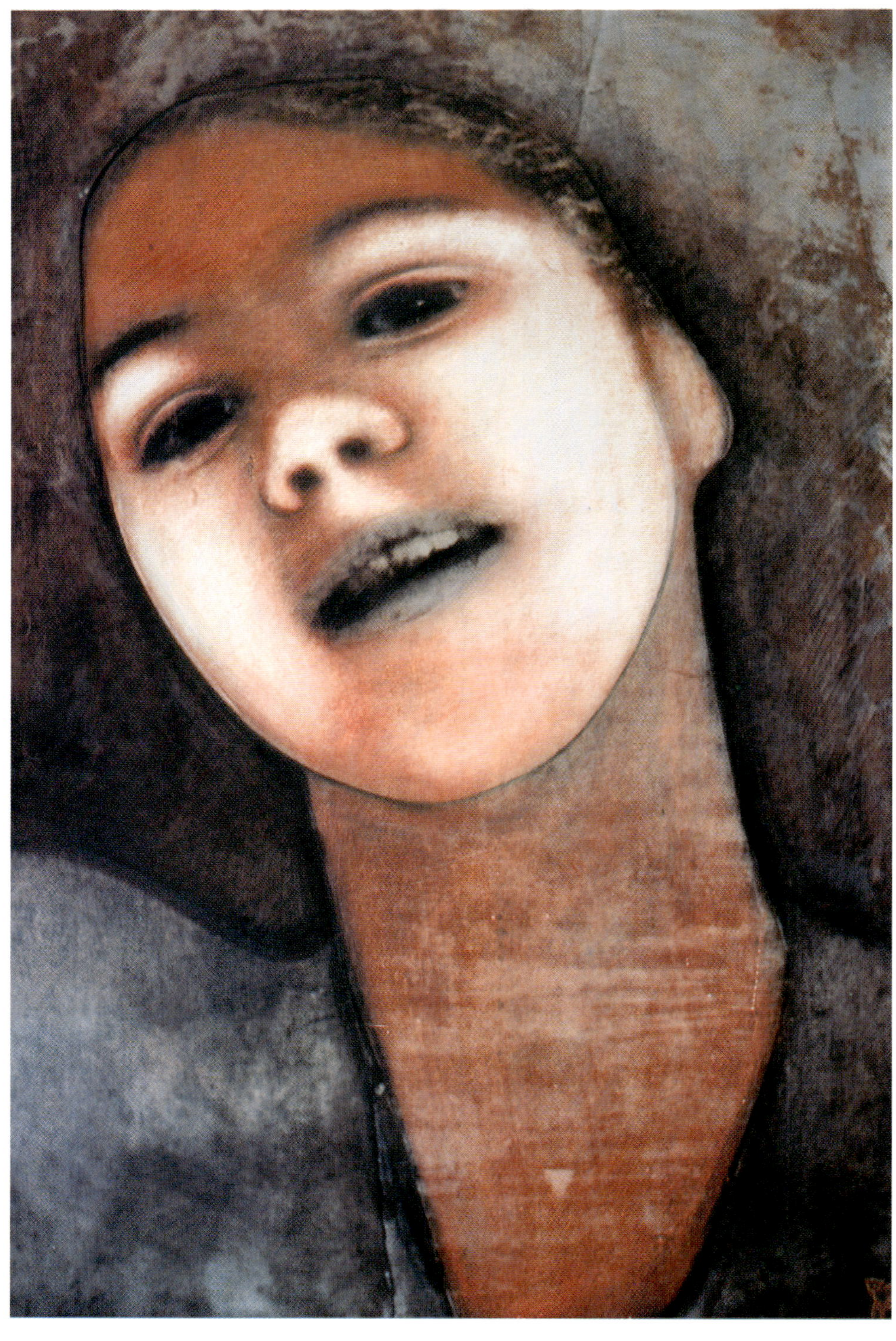

50 *Expulsion of Eve, Series III, No. 4*

WARREN BRENINGER
Born 1948

Expulsion of Eve, Series III, No. 22, 1980–87

Mixed media on C-type colour paper
75 × 50 cm
Collection of the artist

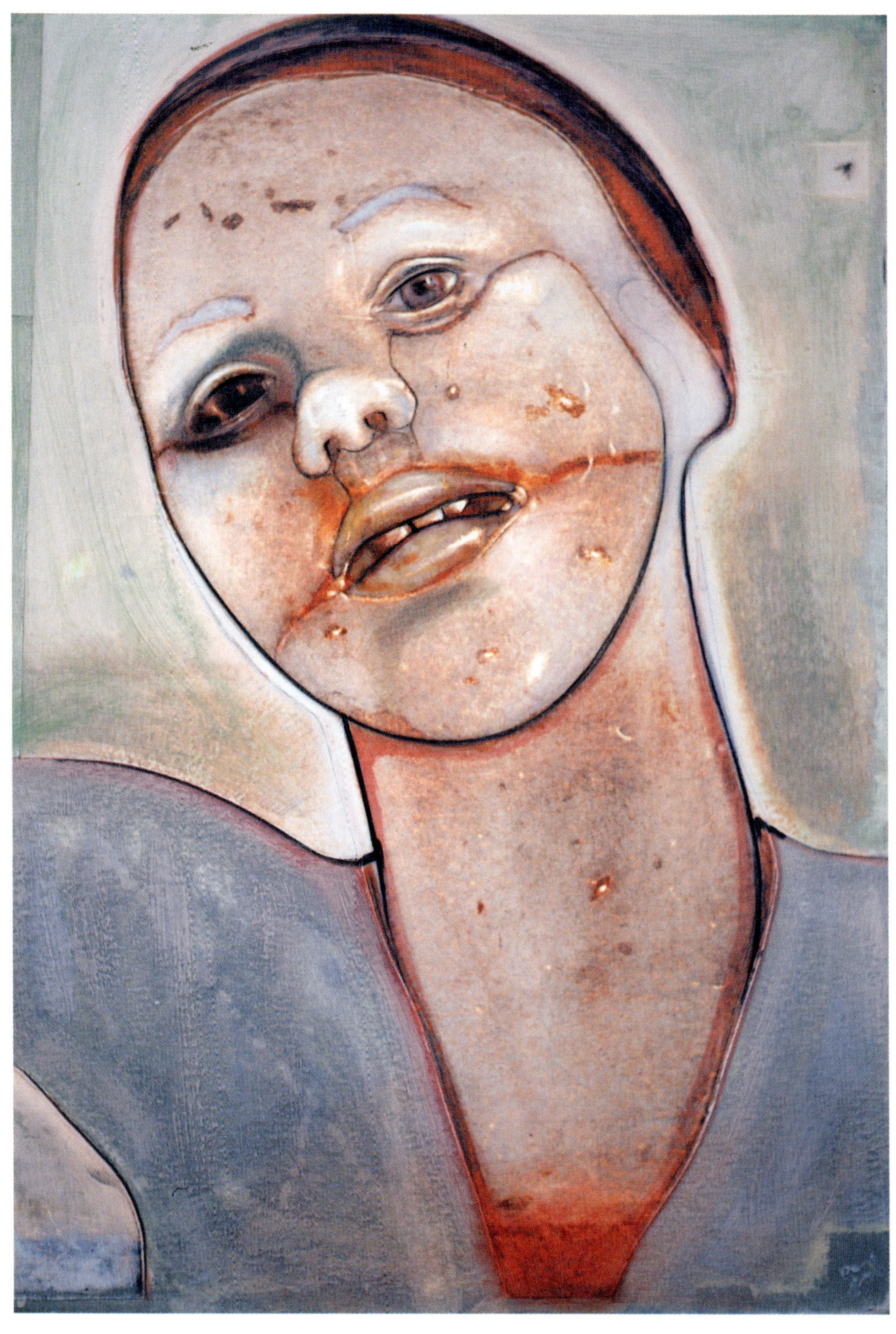

51 *Expulsion of Eve, Series III, No. 22*

Peter Booth

Born 1940

Painting 1977, 1977

Oil on canvas
182.5 × 304.5 cm
National Gallery of Victoria, Melbourne
Presented by the artist in memory of Les Hawkins 1978

Painting 1977 is generally acknowledged to mark Peter Booth's initiation of a return to figuration among younger painters in Australia at the end of the 1970s. They often copied but never matched the power of Booth's imagination to conjure up images of fear, alienation and positive threat or his command over paint as a tool of his urgency. Reds, yellows and blacks, with a touch of blue, reinforced an economy of statement which shocked an art world resigned to flat or amorphous shapes on a sea of canvas. The antecedents of *Painting 1977* lie clearly with the German expressionist Emil Nolde, the German group Die Brücke and the later European surrealists, but the scale of this painting, the deliberate neutrality and anonymity of its subject matter and Booth's awareness of the disciplines of minimal painting are new in Australia.

The single figure of the man in the overcoat, red-eyed like the sun, moves down the road. Near him is a white bull terrier dog. All around is a barren landscape of Kafka-like fatalism. Booth's symbols are those of a religious apocalypse—fire, blood, sun and moon. The road alone suggests life, but the man who is on it is ominously still and passive. It is a vision without hope.

Booth has spoken recently in much more modest terms about this painting:

> About the time I painted this picture, a very close friend of mine was killed in the city. He was hit by a bus. I was standing just next to him and survived it. I remember that just before the accident happened, maybe a month earlier, I'd had a dream that I was sitting on the edge of a kerb on a street and there was someone lying down, near me. I don't know who that someone was. And up in the sky was a big kind of orange form. I don't know what the form was, it was just a shape.
>
> And then a month later we were hit by this bus, on a street corner. My friend was lying in the gutter, where the bus had hit him, and the bus was orange. But it wasn't in the sky. It was on the bloody road.[1]

1. Quoted by Heather Kennedy in the *Age*, 16 March 1985.

Peter Booth was born in Sheffield, England, in 1940. He attended drawing classes at Sheffield College of Art in 1956–57 before coming to Melbourne in 1958. Between 1962 and 1964 he studied at the National Gallery School, Melbourne; in 1964 he won the Bernard Hall Prize for Figure Painting. From 1966 to 1969 he taught at Prahran Technical College and from 1967 to 1986 at the National Gallery School, where he influenced a generation of younger painters, including Irene Barberis and Jan Murray. Since 1969 Booth has had regular solo exhibitions in Sydney and Melbourne and has participated in important group and invitation shows, including Recent Australian Art, at the Art Gallery of New South Wales in 1973; Minimal Art, at the National Gallery of Victoria in 1976; the Biennale of Sydney in 1979; Australian Perspecta, at the Art Gallery of New South Wales in 1981; Eureka! Artists from Australia, at the Serpentine Gallery, London, in 1982; Venice Biennale in 1982; Recent Australian Painting, at the Art Gallery of South Australia, Vox Pop into the Eighties, at the National Gallery of Victoria, and From Another Continent, at the Museum of Modern Art, Paris, all in 1983; and Australian Visions, at the Guggenheim Museum, New York, in 1984.

Booth sees his work as being concerned with art as a way of understanding and probing the mysterious levels of the subconscious. As he said in 1985, 'The place called the Id, because of its mystery, its strangeness, its influence and its power, is essentially what interests me, and the path I have taken is to find the landscape inside the brain.'[1] Only since 1977 has Booth pursued this journey through figurative paintings which explore his memories, fantasies and dreams. His arrival at this figurative expressionism has been slow, for his early training was quite classical and his Gallery School experience took place at a time when minimal art was fashionable and critically rewarded. His paintings from the late 1960s are non-figurative. For example, *Painting, 1971* derived some of its inspiration from Ad Reinhardt and is the best known of his many 'doorway' paintings, where

[*Continued overleaf*]

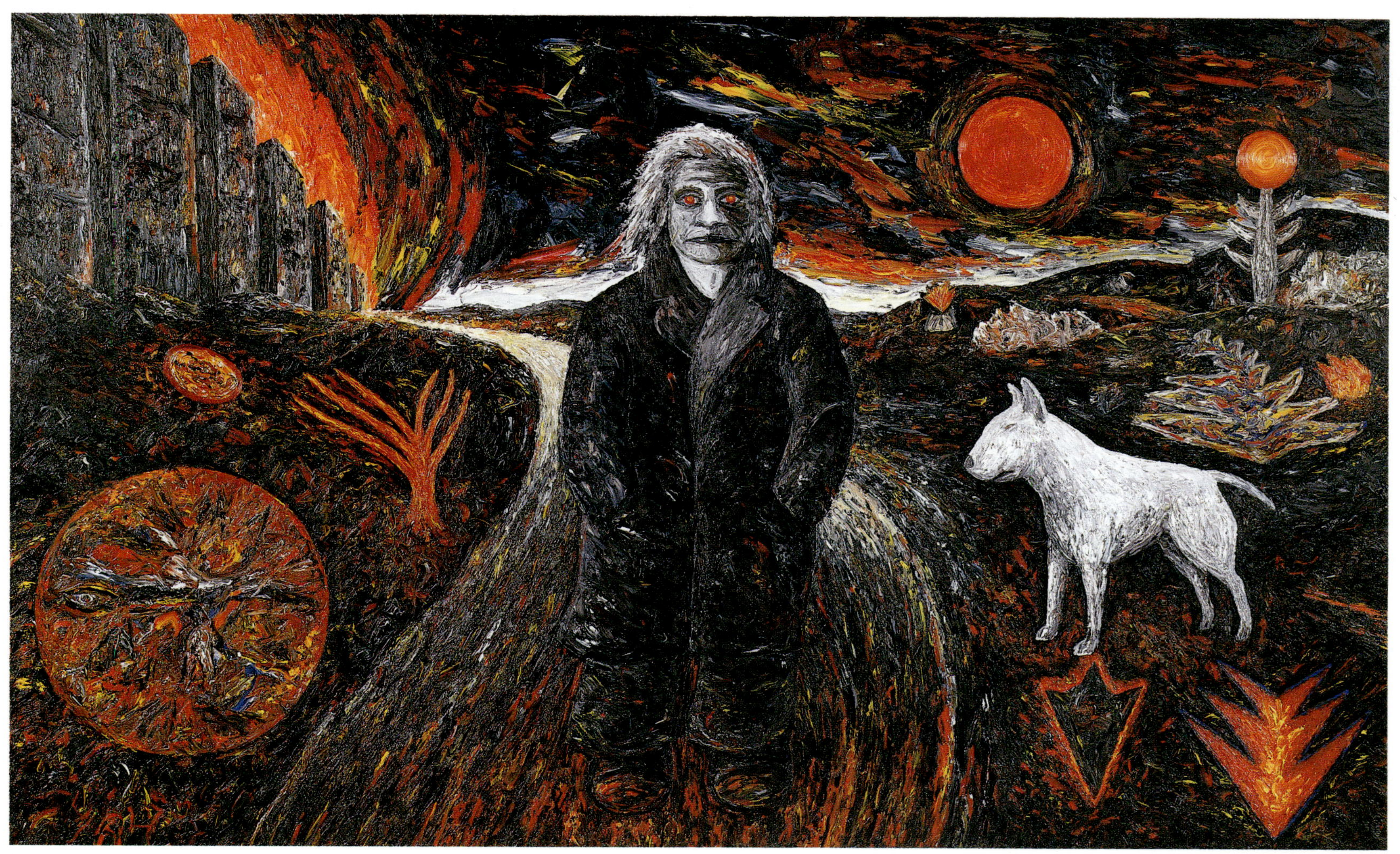

52 *Painting 1977*

PETER BOOTH

Born 1940

Painting 1982, 1982

Oil on canvas
197.7 × 274 cm
Art Gallery of South Australia, Adelaide
A. M. Ragless Bequest Fund 1983

In *Painting 1982,* Peter Booth again makes use of religious imagery and symbolism, some of it familiar through the works of Bosch, Goya and the twentieth-century surrealists. The painting suggests that the fate threatened in *Painting 1977* has arrived. The apocalypse or ultimate disaster has happened, and those living devour the human dead in frenzied orgy. Symbols of evil, like the figures, crowd each other out—dismembered bodies, gruesome, bleeding heads, piles of bones and human limbs. In the background, the black spectre of Death flaps his arms in satanic glee, while the eagle, sacred to Jupiter, pecks at a new Prometheus. The snake, serpent of old, the evil one, the biblical devil, winds his way through this new, man-made hell. *Painting 1982* is a drama of ultimate evil, and Peter Booth has made all the players male.

most of the canvas is covered with layers of black paint which dribble occasionally over an edge of colour, frequently a pink or red. The effect is one of visual ambiguity and submerged violence. These sixties paintings challenge the notion that a painting must have a focal point to hold interest, for here it is the huge void that is inescapable.

By 1974 the doorway device had given way to a separation of the canvas by a stripe of closely toned paint. In 1976 Booth exhibited a series of intensely coloured abstracts often on a dark ground. His 1977 exhibition at Pinacotheca Gallery took Melbourne art circles by surprise—the large figurative paintings foreshadowed and probably influenced the shift to a new wave of expressionist paintings that characterize much present avant-garde painting in Australia. Not since the 1940s when Boyd, Nolan and Tucker followed Vassilieff and Bergner into expressionism, has Australia witnessed such a strong shift. Booth's subsequent exhibitions likewise contained large figurative and symbolic paintings born of his psychological necessity to exorcise his fantasies and pain.

Like Davida Allen and Brett Whiteley, Booth is extremely interested in inspiration, or the creative moment when the work of art seems to take on its own life and the painter's task is not to inhibit with his self-consciousness. 'There are times when my work is a mystery to me,' he has said, 'in as much as that the images and establishing the colour and the mood of the picture are not thought out . . . the picture forms itself to a certain extent as I go.'[2]

Peter Booth lives in Melbourne.

1. Quoted by Heather Kennedy in the *Age*, 16 March 1985.
2. ibid.

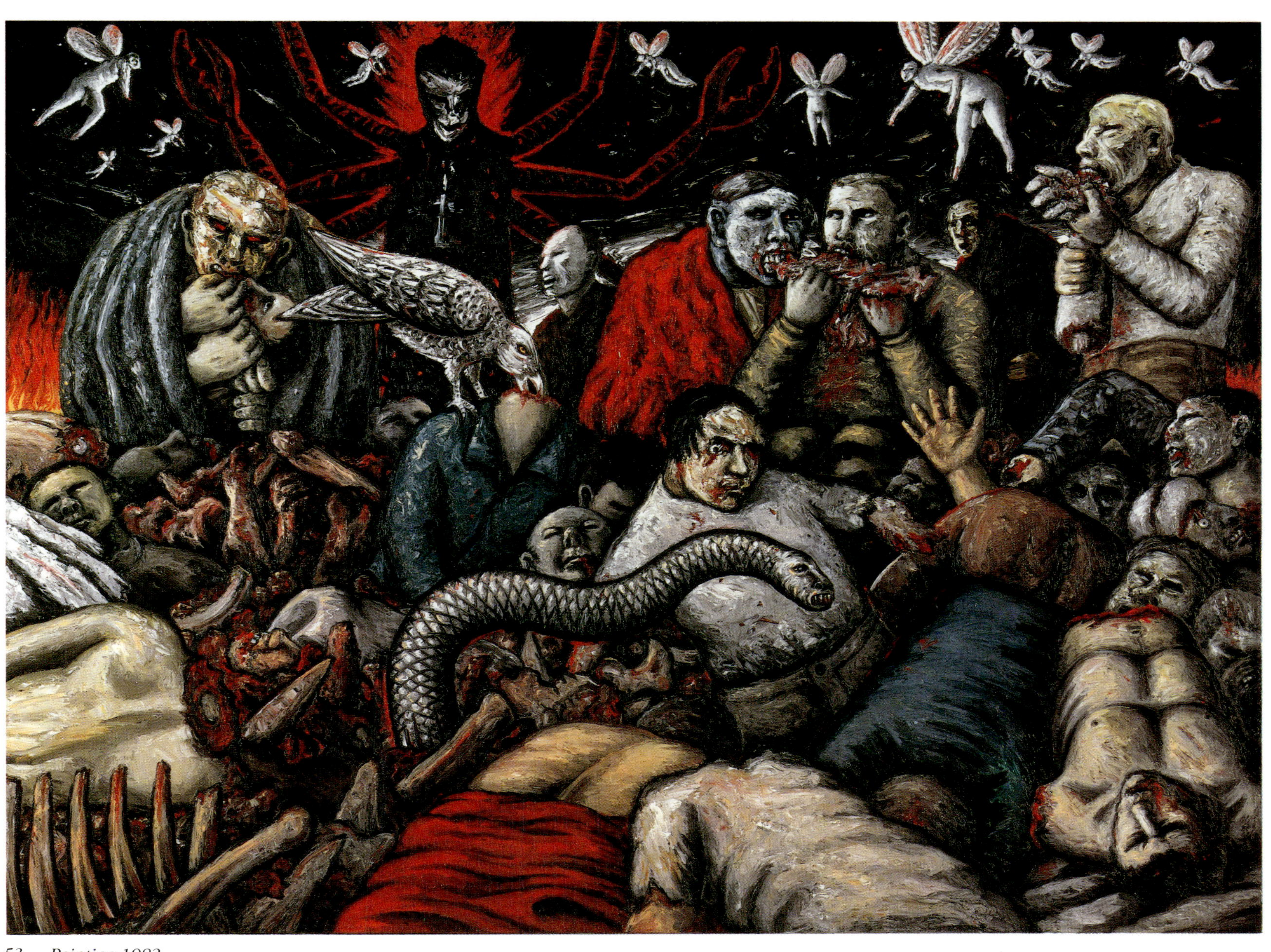

53 *Painting 1982*

ASHER BILU

Born 1936

Spill-out, 1979

Mixed media on plywood
274(H) × 488(W) × 122(D) cm
Collection of the artist

Spill-out is a symphony, and Asher Bilu both composer and conductor. Using hundreds of painted, cut-out wooden shapes, Bilu has created a three-dimensional surface so complex and so filled with ambiguities that it almost defies analysis. To stand quietly in front of it is to enter into a visual adventure: light traps shapes, and the boundary between the world of reality and illusion disappears; colour, which from a distance can appear covered with a blue-grey haze, becomes blue, yellow, red, pink and seems organized in sequences and movements across and within the picture planes; movement, as the title suggests, does seem often to spill out from top to bottom and roll across the floor, but at other times the illusion is of the sucking back of a giant wave. Although there is no real sound, the work suggests whispering and winnowing breezes.

Spill-out is meant to be a metaphor of life. So much of it remains hidden beneath the surface, yet the effect is dependent on the layers and shapes beneath the surface. It is a metaphor of the human body. It lives because of its complexity; behind its skin are the organs of life and growth. 'Whatever I put into a painting is seen, even if it is not seen,' Bilu said in speaking of this painting.

Formally, the painting is built around the circle, purveyor to Bilu of spirituality, mystery and mathematical satisfaction. Individual segments are parts of circles, and the whole structure is a segment of a huge circle where the levels of the shapes are organized three-dimensionally to conform within the sweep of the sphere.

This work has no clear antecedent in Australian painting. In it Bilu has challenged, without abandoning, the established boundaries of what has been regarded as the limits of pictorial expression. 'I tried to put all my experience into this one work—everything in it,' he said in November 1987. 'It is a painting which evokes the past and the future and leaves you in awe. Its presence is so enormous that when it was assembled for the first time I looked at it and said, My God, did I do that?'

ASHER BILU was born in Israel in 1936 and came to Australia in 1957. He spent his childhood in a kibbutz, his young manhood in the Israeli army in Suez, and arrived in Australia without any formal art training but with skill and facility as a musician, a great love of poetry and a mystic's fascination with the cosmic symbols of light, fire and water. By 1965 Bilu had a well-established reputation among artists and critics in Australia; he had had one-man exhibitions in Melbourne (1960, 1961 and 1962), Sydney (1962), Adelaide (1962), London (1963) and Rotterdam (1964). Since then he has exhibited regularly in Melbourne and Sydney.

In 1965 Asher Bilu won the Blake Prize for Religious Art with the painting *I Form Light and Create Darkness—Isaiah 45: 7*, which is dominated by a large meteor-like shape suggesting a dramatic moment in the birth of life out of chaos. Bilu used water and fire to manipulate the resin into crusty, mysterious surfaces. At the time, Bilu, like Donald Laycock and Alun Leach-Jones, was fascinated by Eastern mysticism, with its emphasis on cosmic reality. Bilu remains fascinated by the act of picture-making, which he sees as an extension of a meditative stance towards the whole of life. The artist participates in the creative act; his role is to enter into new creation, to make through physical involvement.

This stance led him in 1982 to create a three-dimensional painting, *Maze*, three metres high and nearly forty-nine metres long. The viewer enters the painting physically and walks between layers of colour and light. Watcher becomes actor, outsider becomes insider, and the traditional ways of visual experience are challenged and stretched. 'It is like being inside a van Gogh painting, surrounded by light,' Bilu said recently. 'To me it is very Aboriginal with its concentric circles of life journey.'

Asher Bilu lives in Melbourne.

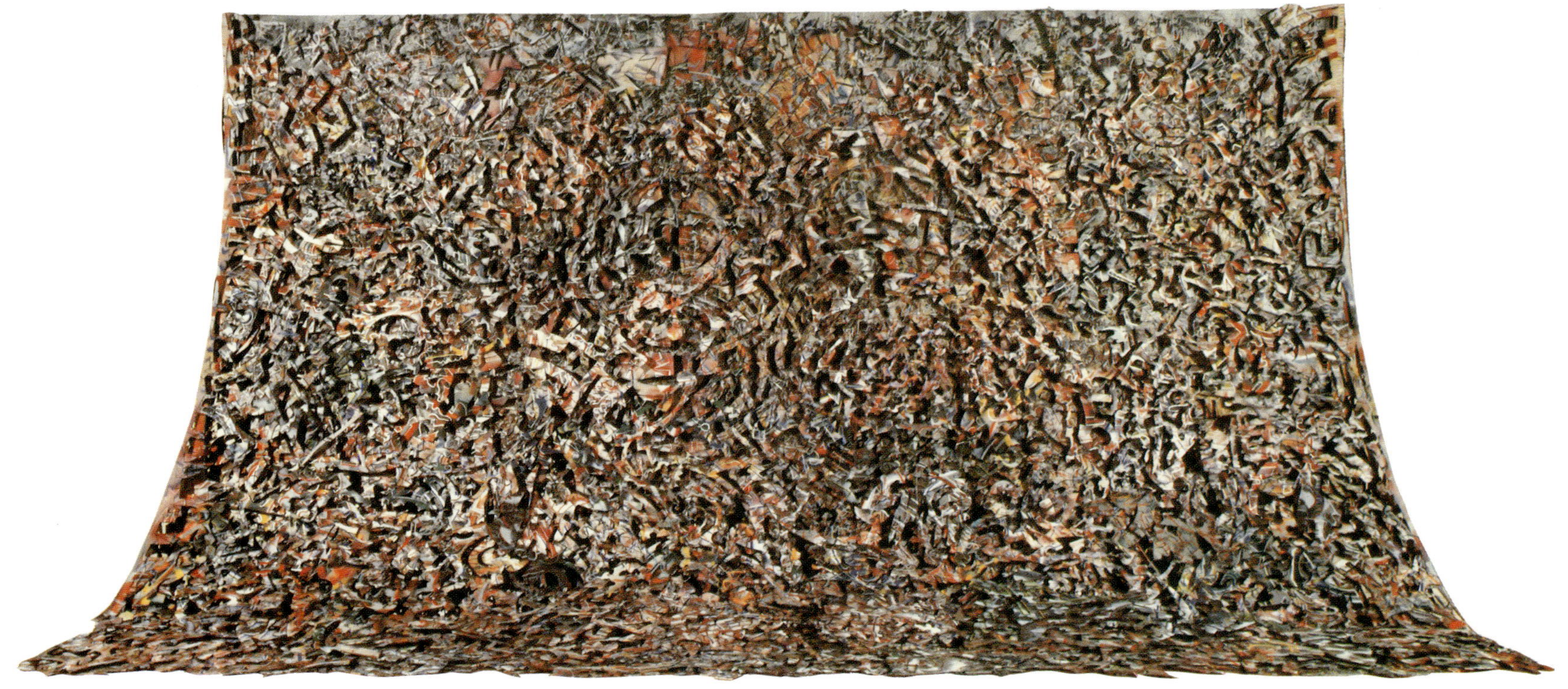

54 *Spill-out*

Brett Whiteley

Born 1939

'My God, my God . . . why . . .', 1979–80

Oil, gold leaf and steel on composition board
259 × 134 cm
Collection of the artist

In 1980 the young Australian sculptor Joel Elenberg died of lymphoma. During the months of his dying he lived in the Whiteley household. These paintings are Whiteley's memorial, reflection, meditation, as well as his cry of anger and anguish for his friend. It is Elenberg who hangs on the cross in *'Father forgive them . . .'* and in *'My God, my God . . . why . . .'* and after death in *The Giving Up*.

The crucifixions represent different moments in the act of dying/living of a single person. They draw some inspiration from the great images of Christ's crucifixion in Christian art history, particularly from those of the artists whom Whiteley esteems—Grünewald, Cimabue, Sassetta and Duccio. But Whiteley has not copied: the hands may recall Grünewald's from his great Isenheim altarpiece, but Whiteley has distorted his until they become carriers of pain so great that they cannot be contained within the boundary of the painting; the gold leaf may be the same as that used by the Sienese, but in Whiteley's hands it has become like a mirror in which the viewer can almost see who it is that looks on.

The crucifixion is one of the most powerful images in Western art. Each age has found a particular way to embody its expression of the mystery of God-made-man who gives up his life—is put to death—so that others might live. The crucifix is always a sign of contradiction and radical confrontation. Brett Whiteley's crucifixions were wrung from him in a time of crisis. He had never before been able to paint a crucifixion; these ones, he says, came to him in a moment of inspiration, and he responded.

Born in Sydney in 1939, Brett Whiteley is mainly self-taught. From an early age he was sure he would be a painter, and the family climate encouraged it. The life of van Gogh and Herbert Read's *Art Since 1945* affected him profoundly. At the age of nineteen, and already known to William Dobell and Russell Drysdale, he won the Italian Government Art Scholarship over such established artists as Robert Dickerson, Margot Lewers and John Coburn. In Siena, Duccio's *Maesta* (1308–11) bewitched him with its warmth of colour, its expressive line and its Byzantine use of abstraction. By 1962, the time of his first solo exhibition at the Matthiesen Gallery in London, Whiteley was a critical and financial success; the purchase by the Tate Gallery of *Untitled Red* from the 1961 Recent Australian Art exhibition at the Whitechapel Gallery had assured that.

Whiteley married Wendy Julius in 1962, and since then he has celebrated their love constantly in paintings (*Summer at Sigean*, 1962–63; The Bathroom series, 1963; *Weet*, 1968), drawings (*The Chair*, 1975; *Nude*, 1976) and sculpture (*Four Studies for Her*, 1975–76). In 1965 he was catapulted further into fame and controversy with his Christie paintings, which personified evil and the debasement of female sexuality through explicit portrayal of the Christie murders.

Whiteley's relationship to Francis Bacon is clear but ambiguous. The paintings in no way imitate Bacon; they are emotionally more direct and explicit and are based, as is all of Whiteley's work, on his close personal identification with his subject. The same is true of his later flirtation with surrealism (e.g., *Fidgeting with Infinity*, 1966–67; *The American Dream*, 1969; *Alchemy*, 1972). Whiteley battles previous art history rather than succumbs to it, but his relationship to romantic poetry, especially to Baudelaire and Rimbaud, is more intimate (e.g. *Portrait of Baudelaire*, 1970; *Portrait of Arthur Rimbaud*, 1971).

[*Continued overleaf*]

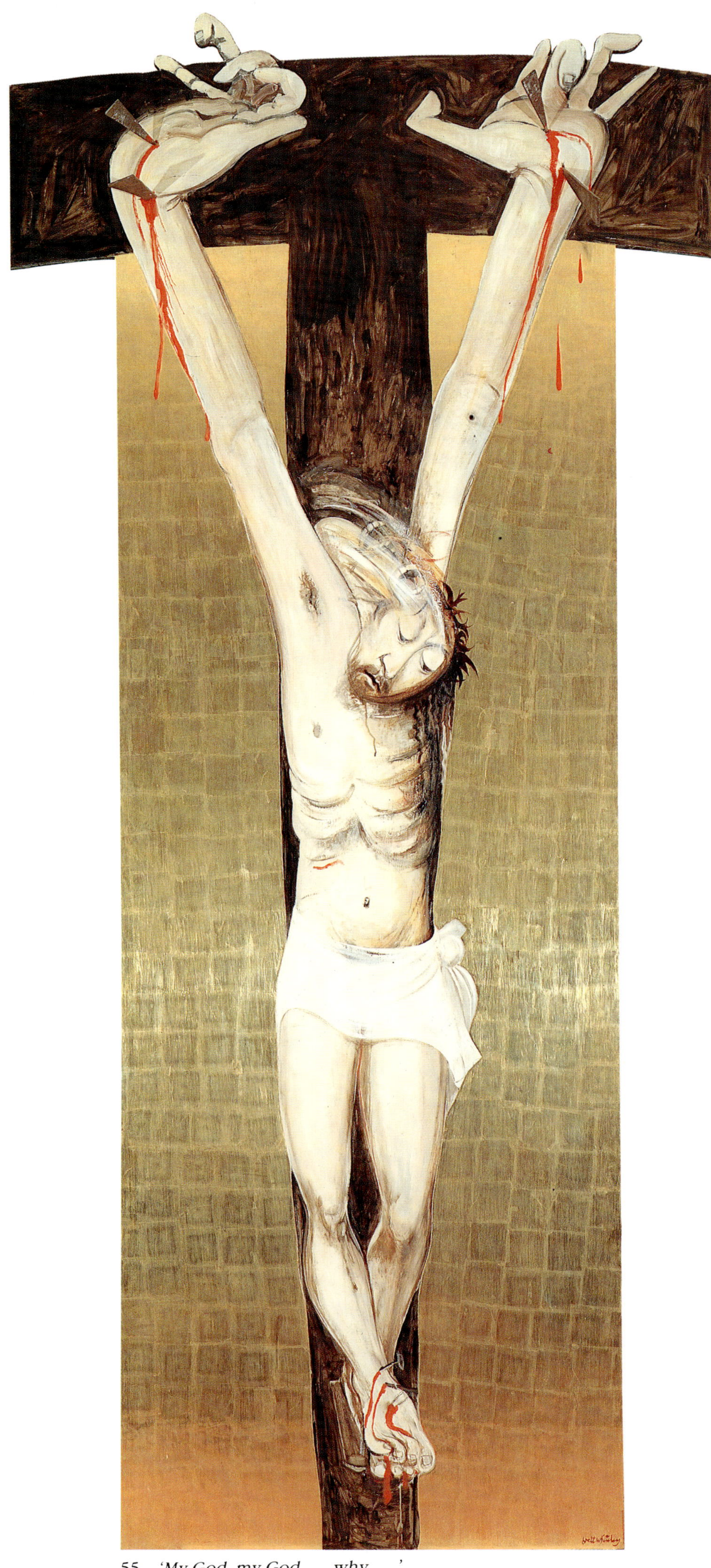

55 *'My God, my God . . . why . . .'*

BRETT WHITELEY

Born 1939

The Giving Up, 1979–80

Oil on steel
256 × 114 cm
Collection of the artist

One of the hardest things is to discipline oneself to keep looking until one sees to the point of almost insistent madness, to concentrate on one vision until it discloses its third and fourth veil, to keep seeing past what you have just seen requires feeling and ambition, and the more open, the more unexpected and extraordinary the intervention—that's surrealism, but eventually a natural, uncomplicated real glimpse appears and that's what one is after. Heightened ordinariness, just like being supernaturally sober just after sleep.[1]

1. Brett Whiteley, from the catalogue of his 1976 exhibition at the Australian Galleries, Melbourne.

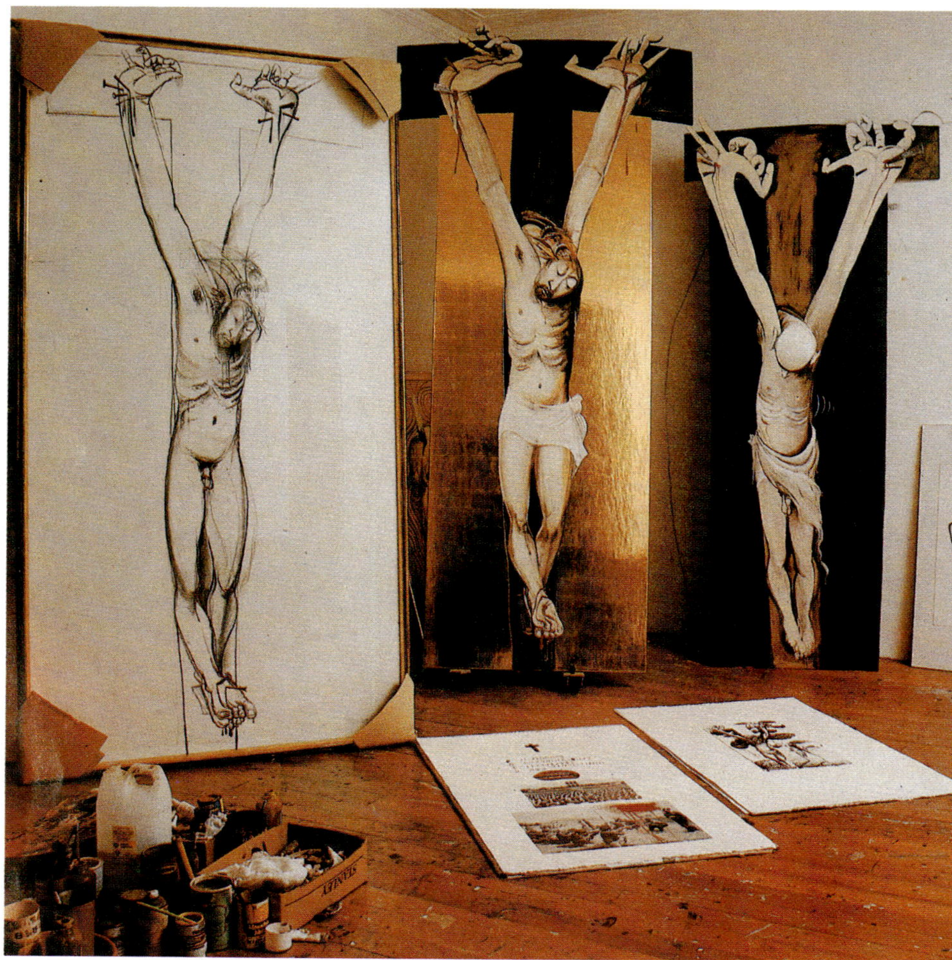

56 *The crucifixions (photograph taken in Brett Whiteley's studio)*

Whiteley returned to Australia in 1969 after a personally destructive year in New York trying to paint out his fantasy of the American dream-gone-wrong. For a time around 1974 his paintings, as he has said, 'were records of optical ecstasy, where romanticism and optimism overshadow any form of menace or foreboding' (e.g., *Henri's Armchair,* 1974–75; *Lavender Bay in the Rain,* 1974). It seemed that the revolutionary in him had been tamed. In 1977 he won the Archibald, the Wynne and the Sulman prizes in Sydney, an unprecedent achievement and a sign in some way of the esteem of the whole art community.

Whiteley's stature is international, his vision extraordinary and his self-understanding profound. In his diary he has written: 'I possess a violated and tender spirit' (1973). 'The curve is the most beautiful of all forces. Art should astonish, transmute, transfix. One must work at the tissue between truth and paranoia' (1972).

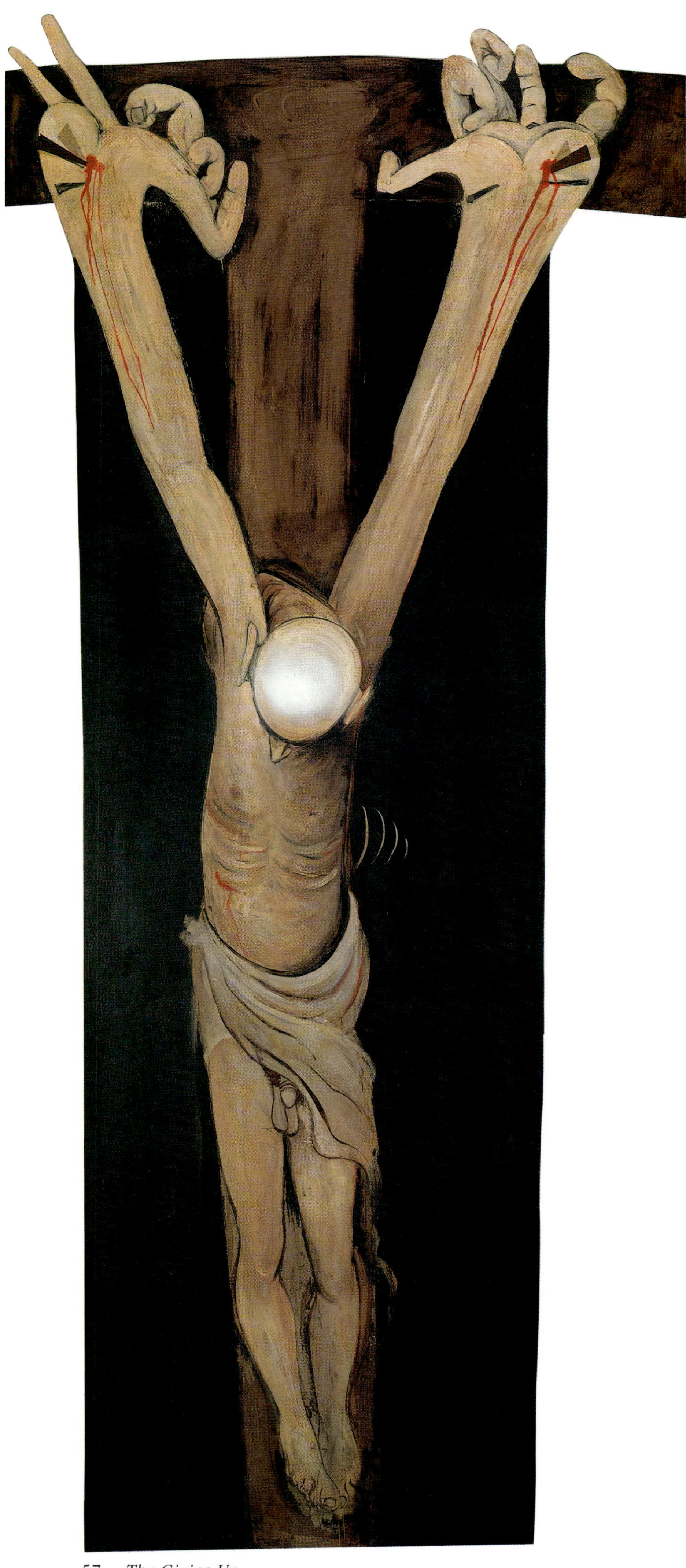

57 *The Giving Up*

LEONARD FRENCH

Born 1928

*Shooting Place, c.*1980

Enamel, oil and gold leaf on hardboard
122 × 137 cm
Collection of the artist

Shooting Place was first exhibited in Sydney in 1981 as part of a series called A Dark Circus. Among other titles in this series are *Broken Horse, The Grand Carousel, The Performers,* and *Cage and Furnace.* Like *Shooting Place,* they contain images of a circus as well as images from French's own childhood. But they are not simply narrative paintings. Although more figurative and realistic than his earlier work, they reflect a seriousness bordering on pessimism that was usually absent before French responded to his North American experience with the Journey paintings (1970) and to the Latin American situation in the Death of a Revolution paintings (*c.*1977).

Shooting Place memorializes the death of Camilo Torres, the Colombian priest-guerilla killed in action in 1966. A Brazilian priest friend had sent French a photograph of the bullet-ridden body 'with arms outstretched and bearded face lolling to one side'. French has the priest lying spent and empty—a shell, a clown, a medieval crusader, a child's cut-out—on the ground in an alleyway. The body is full of holes. On the left is the red wall of the Brunswick brickworks of French's childhood, on the right a galvanized-iron fence. In the opening are circus animals from a broken-down carousel at the carnival. They too are full of holes.

The holes in all the paintings of this series have special significance for French. As early as in *Death of a Hero* (1958) and *Death of a Martyr* (1960), French used punched-out holes to signal violent death, but here he has gone further. 'I painted one black shape like a hole in the sky,' he said in 1981. 'Totally black . . . it seems I have to punch black holes in what I'm doing. Underneath all the brightness, there's not a dead thing, but a frightening sort of thing.'[1]

French does not see himself as a religious person in the sense of belonging to any established religious system; nor does he readily admit to religious belief. Yet most of his work is associated with the symbol systems and the questions of religion. His *Seven Days* (Plates 77–83) draw on the biblical account of Creation and manage to evoke the poetic rhythms of Genesis 1; his Campion paintings have as hero a Catholic martyr; his Death of a Revolution, Journey and Bridge paintings all raise questions that are at least implicitly religious in their probing of the meaning of suffering, oppression and death. *Shooting Place* again takes up the theme of a priest-victim but has little of the monumental optimism and sense of transcendent meaning that are evident in The Seven Days and the Campion series. The pervading mood of *Shooting Place* is altogether more ominous.

1. Quoted in *Weekend Australian*, 8–9 August 1981.

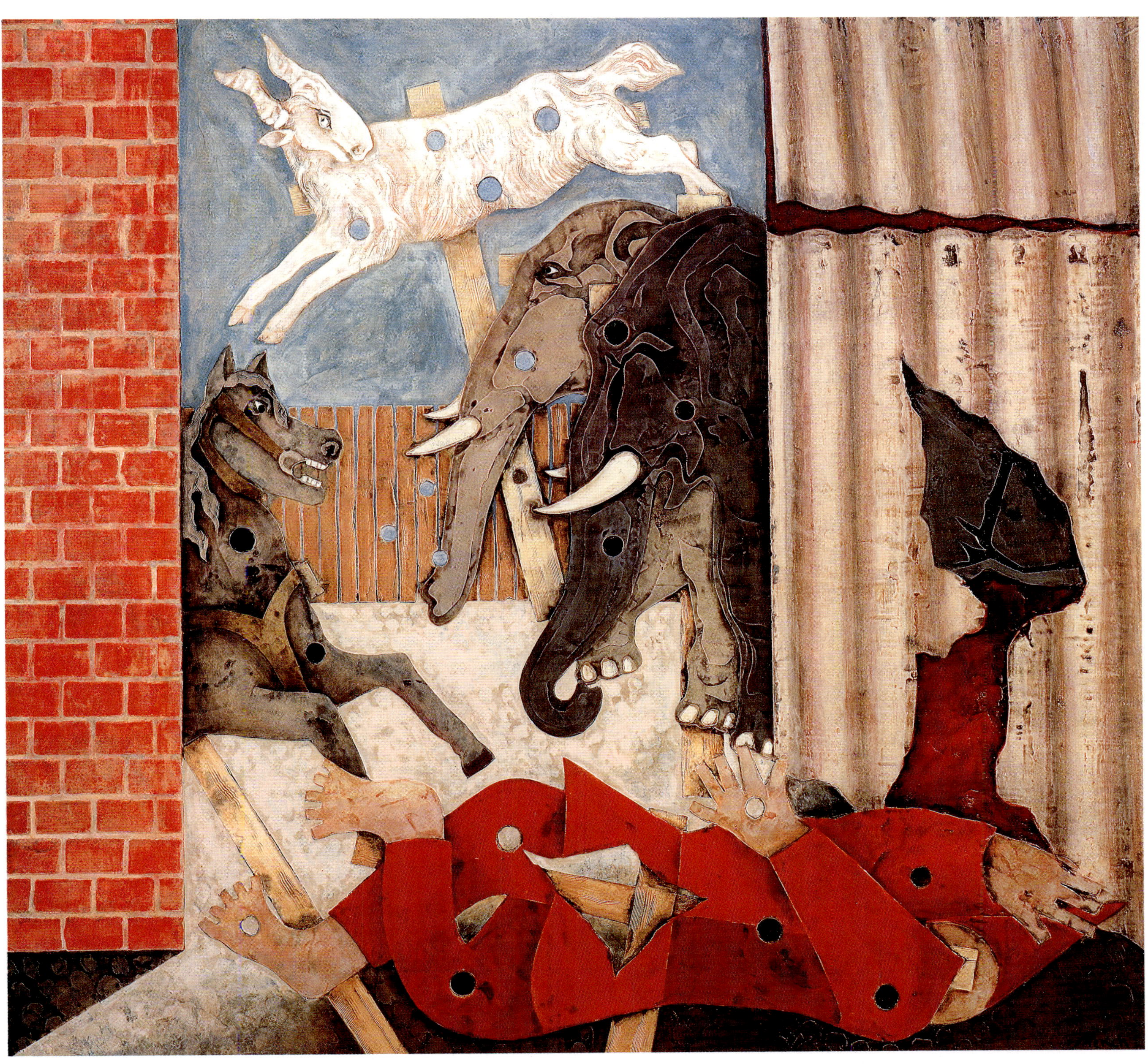

58 *Shooting Place*

DAVIDA ALLEN

Born 1951

The Death of My Father, 1981–82

Oil on canvas
165.3 × 271.9 cm
National Gallery of Victoria, Melbourne
Michell Endowment 1982

Davida Allen's father died over a period of a few weeks in 1982 when she was pregnant with her fourth child. This painting, *The Death of My Father*, together with *Death of My Father* (1983) and a series of thirty-two drawings published in a book *Death of My Father*, are Davida Allen's response to her confrontation with the loss of a parent with whom she was very close. The works are windows into another's intimate pain. They call up the crudeness and wrenchings of deaths of others we have loved; they remind us of the inevitability of our own.

The Death of My Father is dominated by the diagonal figure of the father, staring, like the priest, directly at the viewer. The horizontal figure this time is the unborn child. Both are white. Both are under attack from predatory birds—crows who attack and steal on the farm. Yet they have none of the viciousness of the bird in Peter Booth's painting (Plate 53). The sea of blue and the immediacy of the paint strokes assure us that death is ultimately about hope and new life. A father dies, a child is born, life goes on.

DAVIDA ALLEN was born in Charleville, Queensland in 1951. While she was a school boarder at Stuartholme, Brisbane, her individuality and freedom of expression were encouraged by the creative art educationist Betty Churcher; from 1970 to 1972 she studied art under Roy Churcher at the Central Technical College, Brisbane. Between 1973 and 1987 she had seven solo exhibitions through the Ray Hughes Galleries in Brisbane and Sydney; in 1987 the Museum of Contemporary Art in Brisbane held a Davida Allen Survey Exhibition. Since 1980 she has participated in a number of important group exhibitions, including Australian Perspecta, at the Art Gallery of New South Wales in 1981; the fourth Biennale of Sydney in 1982; Recent Australian Paintings, at the Art Gallery of South Australia in 1983; Vox Pop Into the Eighties, at the National Gallery of Victoria in 1983; An International Survey of Recent Painting and Sculpture, at the Museum of Modern Art, New York in 1984; Kunst mit Eigensinn, in Vienna in 1985; Celebrity Choice: Sam Neill, at the Art Gallery of New South Wales in 1986; and Australian Art, Field to Figuration, at the National Gallery of Victoria in 1987.

Davida Allen's art has always been unashamedly figurative; she has not moved, as have others in this selection, through periods that correspond to international movements such as hard edge and minimal art. From an early enthusiasm for German expressionism, especially Die Brücke as well as Nolde, Soutine and the fauves, she has developed a style that communicates powerfully the urgency and depth of her emotional response to her everyday life. Her inspiration comes from a commitment to life as she experiences and lives it. Thus as a woman, lover, mother, daughter, farmer, she reflects and responds. Her subject matter is her life, and her paintings are often like exorcisms, ridding her of the urge to destroy and be destroyed.

[*Continued overleaf*]

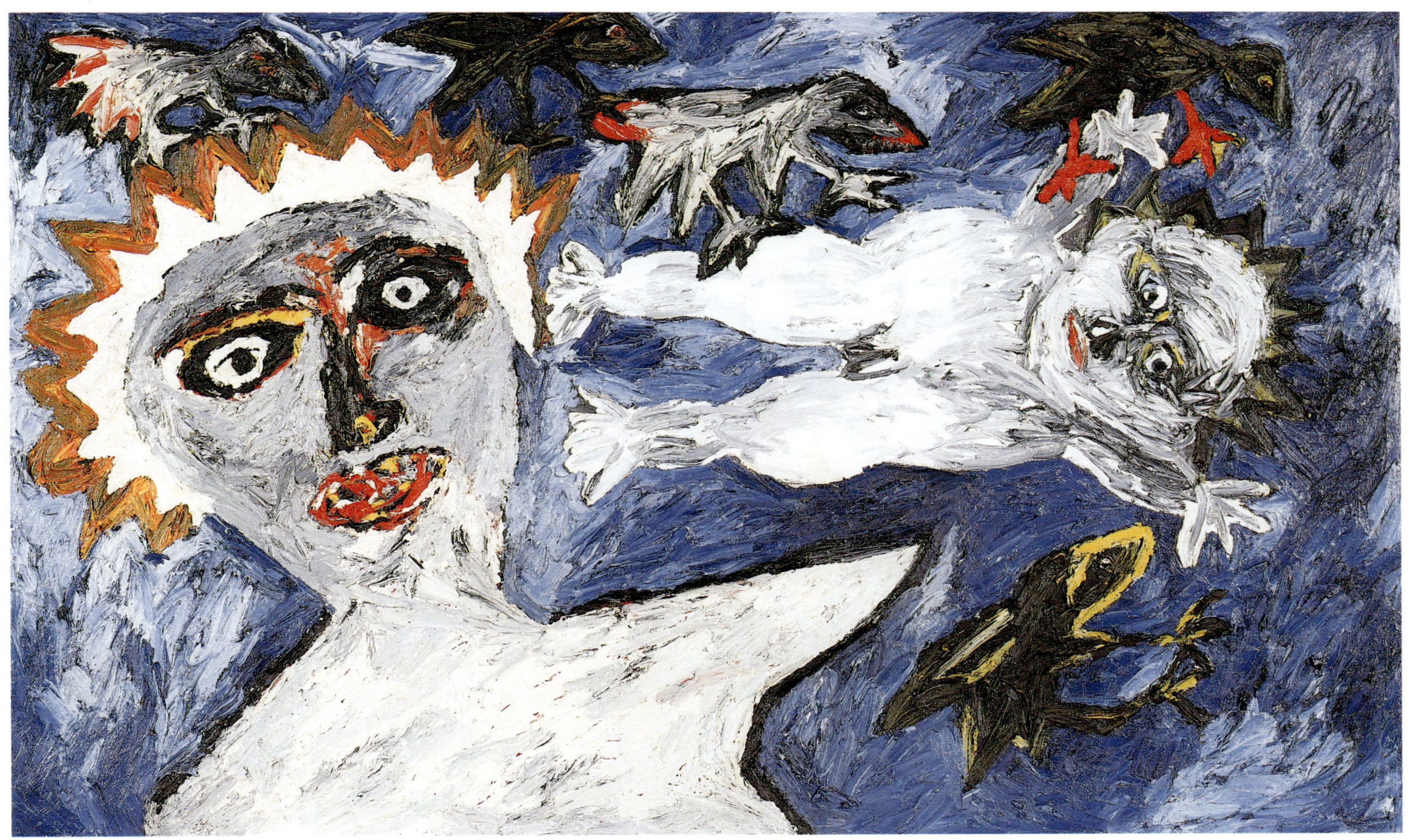

59 *The Death of My Father*

DAVIDA ALLEN

Born 1951

The Priest Painting, 1981

Oil on canvas
169 × 221 cm
Museum of Contemporary Art, Brisbane
James Baker Collection

The Priest Painting, The Priest and *Priest* are paintings in which Davida Allen explores her relationship with the Catholic Church and, in particular, with a priest who had become a close friend. The Catholic Church, its teachings and its ethos have always been a part of her life, at first a taken-for-granted part as so much of her childhood was spent in the privileged and educationally enlightened atmosphere of the Sacre Coeur boarding school. The priest who is the subject of these paintings she had met as a teacher of theology. He was young, handsome, intelligent and articulate about his personal relationship with God. The paintings are her response to the questions his life and commitment pose for her.

In *The Priest Painting*, the priest occurs twice on the right. He is clearly a symbol of authority and respect as he stands upright staring out of the frontal plane. He is sacred, for he wears the sign of the chosen over his head; and he is male. But to Davida Allen, as she explained in a letter to the author, he is two different persons. She has painted herself on the left in horizontal subservience, 'her outstretched arms reaching for the MAN-PRIEST but he is PRIEST FIRST'; the solemn, celibate, central figure separates her from the man 'who has been painted like a Rag Doll. The colour is grey—washed out compared with the respect of the deep black of the PRIEST.' As her life is intimately involved with her husband, children and home, the priest's is with God, the tabernacle and the Church. He is out of her reach.

Some of the power of this painting lies in the immediacy of its expression: paint is laid on directly and rhythmically, figures are drawn with primitive urgency and frontally. There is an inevitability about the total picture which commands attention and involvement.

In all of this she is unique in the history of Australian painting. Never before has a woman who is also a powerful communicator laid open her inner life with such directness and brutality. Her art is a record of the dreams, fantasies and reality of a woman absorbed by loving, pregnancy and caring. The titles of her paintings document a life—*Davida Allen Was Born a Catholic* (1973); *House* (1973); *Pig Dog* (1974); *Floating Nude* (1975); *Chook Painting* (1978); *Man and Dog* (1980); *Dog Woman* (1980); *I Don't Want to Go Mad* (1981); *Priest* (1981); *With Knowledge of My Fourth Pregnancy* (1981); *Death of My Father* (1982); and *My Father-in-law Hosing His Celtus Trees* (1986).

No Australian artist since Arthur Boyd has allowed the viewer such an intimate insight, and while Davida Allen's life experience may be more restricted than Boyd's, her response is usually as intense and, at times, as revelatory. She is insider in a woman's world. She delights in mothering, which strengthens but limits her; as she wrote across the painting *The Domestic and the Dream* (1986), 'To attempt to dream images not domestic but Josephine whinges about something or other.' As woman, and as young woman, she has before her a life of subject matter rarely explored before.

Davida Allen lives in the country north of Brisbane with her husband and four children.

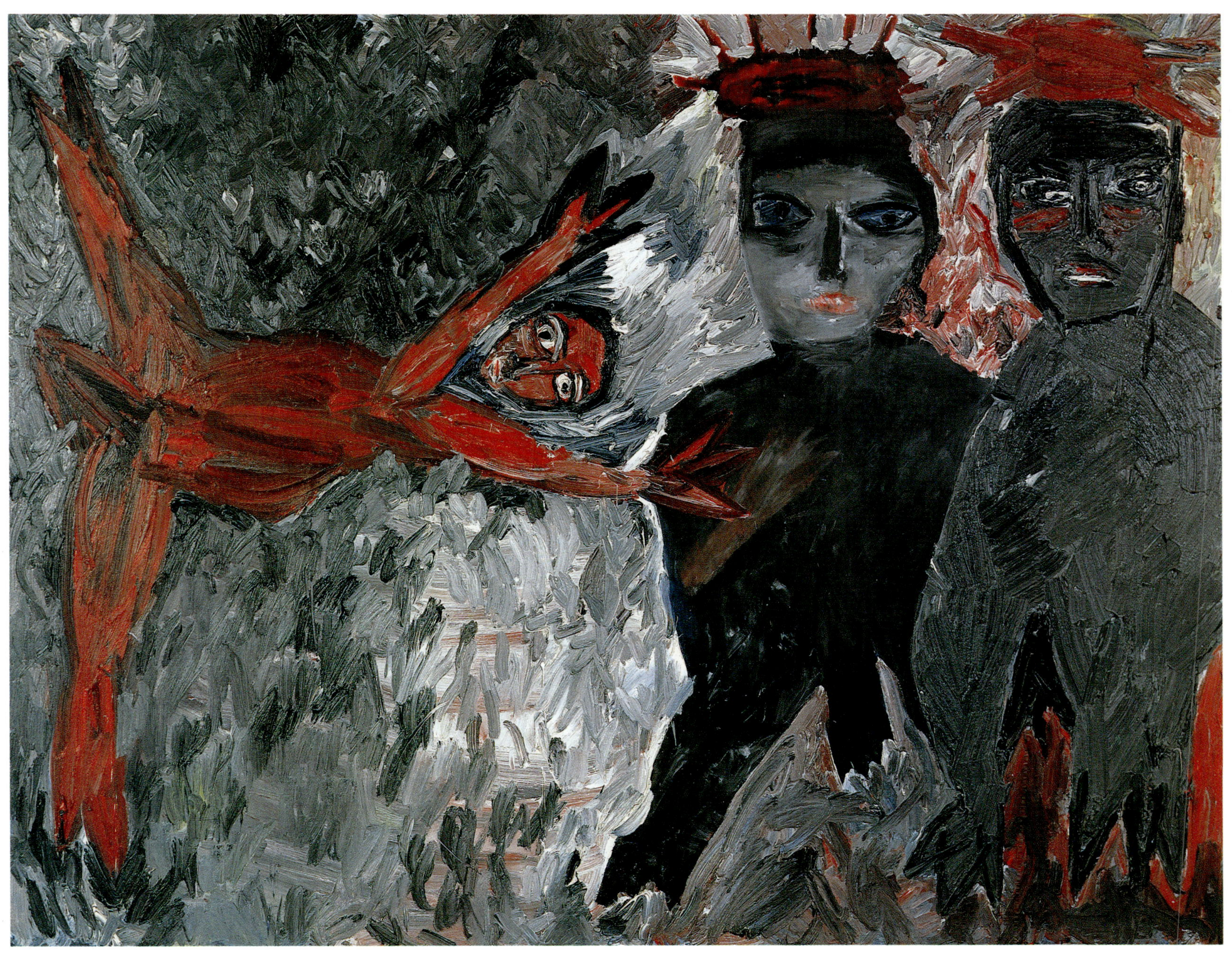

60 *The Priest Painting*

Lawrence Daws

Born 1927

Cain and the Promised Land, 1983

Oil on canvas
Two panels: 173 × 305 cm overall
Collection of the artist

Cain and the Promised Land is the second of two large versions in this series, completed by Lawrence Daws in 1983 and located in part in the Queensland canefields and the Glasshouse Mountains. Daws's preparatory drawings indicate that this series owes much to Piero della Francesca (the egg, the pearly blue sky, the perspective patchwork Piero floor of the blackened fields) and, in the visionary nature of the landscape, to John Glover's 1837 painting, *Mount Wellington with Orphan Asylum*. But the quality of the craftsmanship, the understanding of landforms and not just their surface appearance, and the vocabulary of individual symbols are the culmination of a lifetime dedicated to the pursuit of meaning through visual form.

In a letter to the author in January 1988, Lawrence Daws explained his intentions in this painting:

> *Cain and the Promised Land* is based loosely on the scriptural story of Cain, who murdered his brother, Abel, in the open fields. But it also deals with the present dilemma of mass killings—brother against brother, race against race.
>
> The location is somewhere between Israel and India; various religous groups are implicated. There are swirling spirals around the focal point of Mecca; the egg is symbolic of the Hebrews as the chosen race; the overwhelming mass of India is also present.
>
> In the left panel, all the masses of figures are making their way down ladders on the escarpment, through a system of decorative red cages (suggesting our hedonistic progression) out onto the killing fields of the right panel. There they stand, like sugarcane awaiting the canecutter. In the middle distance are red cane cages being loaded by small trains which zigzag up the hill. On the right is a womb-shaped black tunnel signalling our return to mother earth and to a rebirth. In the middle foreground is a tunnel with bars, and in the far end can be seen the silhouette of Cain.
>
> On the left is a symbol of evil—the Peruvian bat flicking out a laser-beam of green across the whole drama. The ladders down the escarpment represent 'the fall'. The water in the centre of the killing fields is reminiscent of the water in Arnold Bocklin's 1880 painting, *The Isle of the Dead*. The strange eyes that are sweeping above, observing it all, have nothing to do with the events. Perhaps they suggest the possibility of some intelligence or life existing somewhere—despite the apocalypse here on earth.

Lawrence Daws was born in Adelaide in 1927 and studied engineering and architecture before attending the Melbourne National Gallery Art School from 1950 to 1953. In 1955 his *Golgotha* won third prize in the Blake Prize for Religious Art. Daws went to Rome in 1958 on an Italian government scholarship and then lived in London for the next ten years. He travelled extensively in Europe, Asia and the Americas before returning to Australia in 1970. He has exhibited widely and is represented in important collections in Australia and the United States as well as in the Tate Gallery and the Victoria and Albert Museum in London and the Scottish National Gallery of Modern Art in Edinburgh.

Daws has always been obsessed with content in his paintings. Subject matter for him is the web with which he spins the images and myths of his search. His paintings are meant to be 'read', if not like a book, then at least in the same way as medieval mosaics and those Renaissance frescoes where each unit is often the carrier of multiple meanings for the initiated. For Daws, these meanings have been about larger life concerns—suffering, redemption, global conflict, and freedom and our inability to handle it. He has built a vocabulary of visual symbols (sometimes Jungian)—cages, mandalas, staircases, fires, tunnels, desert landscapes, even his wonderfully deep space and highly finished surfaces—with which to explore life. There is a safety for the viewer in Daws's recent work; the drama is being played out beyond real life, and the viewer is invited as spectator and philosopher rather than as participant.

Much of Daws's work has centred on themes—Scriptural (1954–59), Mandala (1960–63), Faces of Violence (1963–66), The Dolly Pond Church of God (1968–70), Mining Disaster (1969–70), Anatomy of a Relationship (1971–74), Cain and the Promised Land (1981–83), Mountains (1986–).

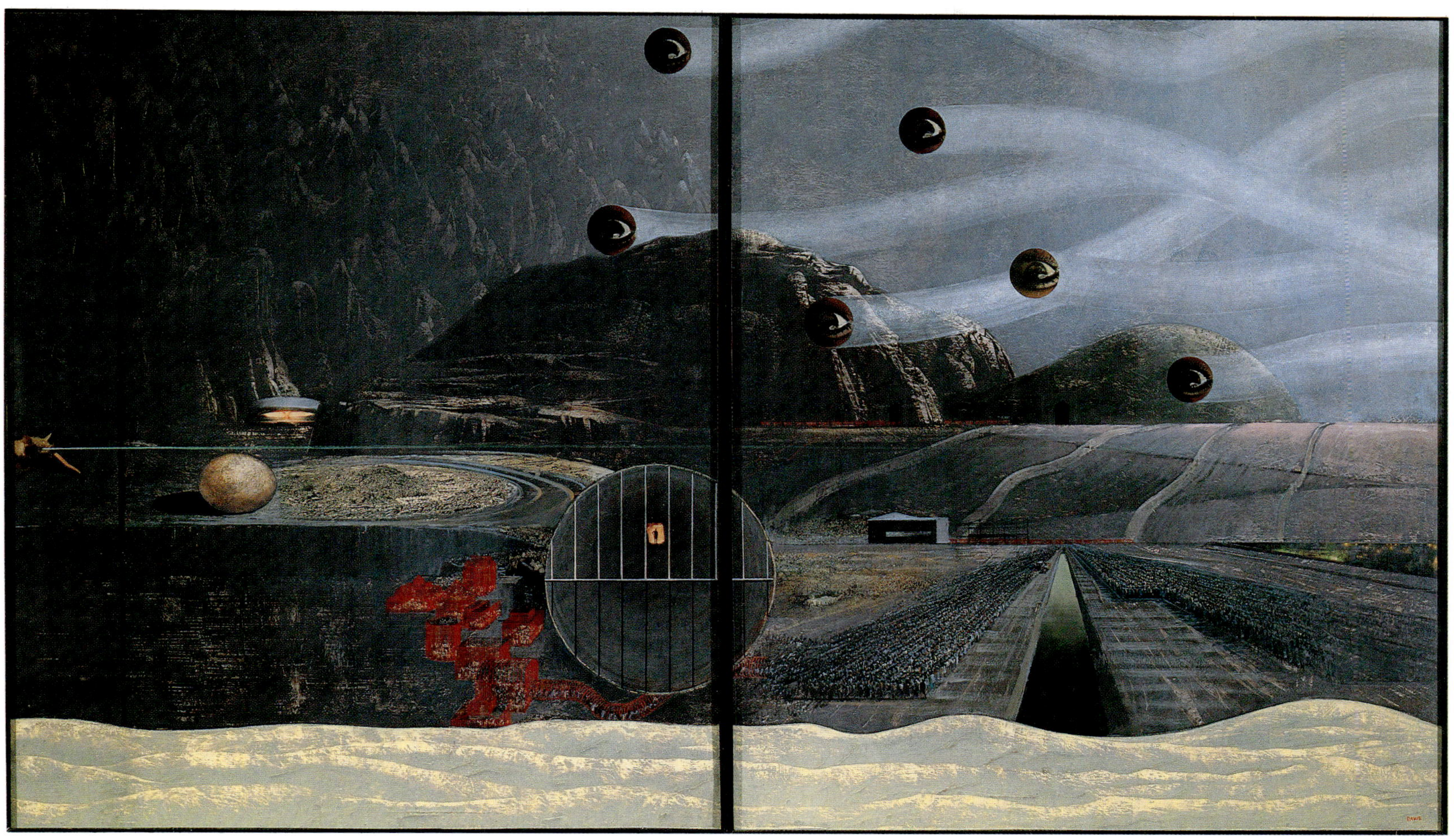

61 *Cain and the Promised Land*

JOHN NIXON — IMANTS TILLERS

Born 1949 — Born 1950

Honour and Glory, 1982

Oil and synthetic polymer paint on canvas
194.5 × 138.5 cm
Art Gallery of South Australia, Adelaide
South Australian Government Grant 1984

In 1979 Imants Tillers, while on a visit to the Basilica of St Francis at Assisi, purchased a postcard containing an aerial view of the Basilica. The image looked strangely flattened through the two-dimensional camera lens; the space was ambiguous because there was no horizon line, and the landscape seemed to shake because there was a fault in the colour registration in the printing of the postcard. Some months later in Australia, Tillers began working on a series of paintings which record, re-present and present for re-experience the event of this Assisi 'rendezvous point' (4 p.m., 12 April 1979).

The postcard became his starting point and prescribed, to some extent, the limits of the paintings. Tillers described the process in 1982: 'The postcard (10.4 × 14.9 cm) was gridded up and the image transferred to a large canvas (185.5 × 263.9 cm). This movement (flow) from postcard to painting was not only a shift in scale and surface, but also, more importantly, a shift in "point of view". As we rise higher above the earth we see *more* sky and earth.' But the sky is not 'seen' in the ordinary way, for there is no meeting place along a horizon line; here the sky exists as an invisible 'presence' between the viewer and the images. Enlarging the photograph has also emphasized the faulty colour registration with its strong warm/cool juxtaposition reminding Tillers of Cézanne's *Mont Sainte Victoire*. So Tillers named the first version of the postcard *The Modern Picture*.

The painting illustrated here, *Honour and Glory*, is one of at least sixteen other versions that followed. This time Tillers invited John Nixon, his fellow exhibitor at the Documenta 7 exhibition in Kassel, to 'sign' the painting with his 'cross'. The addition of the red Malevitch-type cross sets up further ambiguity. On the one hand it appears as a great sign in the sky and governs the way the painting can be interpreted; because of its historical and symbolic associations, it seems to identify the painting as 'religious' in some special way. On the other hand, when understood within the context of Nixon's other painting of this time—that is, as self-portrait and the appropriation of an already established symbol to question established meaning—the red cross and the entire painting raise questions about the nature of the art object and the frustration that arises if it is expected to carry any one set of meanings. *Honour and Glory* deliberately subverts established ways of approaching and understanding paintings.

John Nixon was born in Sydney in 1949, studied at the Preston Institute of Technology in 1967–68, the National Gallery School of Victoria in 1969–70 and the State College of Victoria in 1973 and, with the help of grants from the Visual Arts Board, went to the United States in 1975 and 1976 and to Britain and Europe in 1978 and 1979. Since 1970 Nixon has worked consistently within the minimalist tradition, which draws inspiration from the Russian constructivist Kazimir Malevitch. Many of his made-objects recur in different contexts with other names and as parts of other complexes. In this way Nixon pursues his goal of the deconstruction of established meaning systems.

John Nixon lives in Brisbane.

Imants Tillers lives in Sydney, where he was born in 1950 of Latvian parents. In 1972 he graduated in architecture from Sydney University with the University Medal for a thesis on environmental design. These factors, together with a long-standing reverence for the French dadaist Marcel Duchamp and the Italian metaphysical painter Giorgio de Chirico, continue to be strong formative influences in his work. Tillers has built an awesome reputation within Australia as a conceptual and minimalist artist and has been part of such important overseas group exhibitions as the Biennale São Paulo, in Brazil in 1975 (with George Baldessin), Documenta 7, in Kassel, West Germany, in 1982 (with John Nixon) and An Australian Accent, in New York in 1984. More recently he has been constructing large, multi-panelled works which present for re-experience the works of other artists and photographers (e.g., *Spirit of the Place*, 1983; *The Field*, 1982).

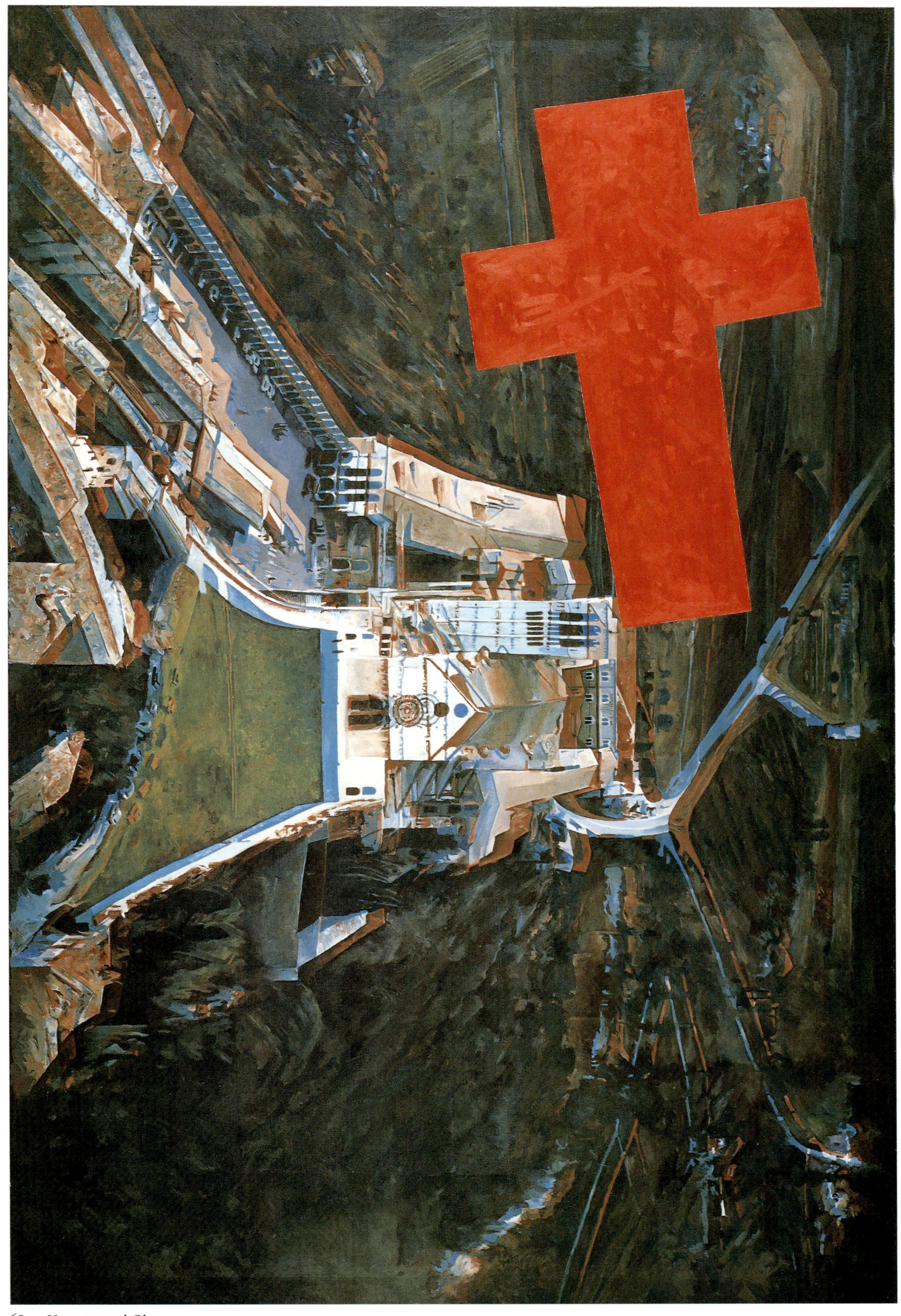

62 *Honour and Glory*

JAN MURRAY

Born 1957

The Three Graces, 1983

Oil on canvas
166.5 × 198 cm
National Gallery of Victoria, Melbourne
Michell Endowment 1984

The Three Graces is one of three works painted by Jan Murray in the wake of the disastrous Ash Wednesday bushfires in Victoria. *Three Fishes of the Sea, Descent* and this painting are about that tragedy, about a seared landscape and trees with roots laid bare and the questions the fires raised about the future of a civilization that could destroy itself. The three paintings also take the great Christian themes of Crucifixion *(Three Fishes by the Sea)*, Death *(The Descent)* and Resurrection *(The Three Graces)* and mingle these with pagan myths and classical symbols.

The Three Graces is a metaphorical painting about new life, regeneration and resurrection. The crosses stand like tree trunks at a place where earth, sea and sky meet. For Jan Murray, 'the space between earth and sea is the place of centring, of healing'. The crosses are without number, but the three in the foreground are draped in white cloth; below, and nurturing the earth, are pink crescent shapes. 'I wanted it to be very female, giving, sustaining', Murray said. The draped crosses are Botticelli's *Three Graces*, personifications in the fifteenth century of chastity, beauty and love but here meant to be faith, hope and charity—necessary virtues if life is to be renewed and the earth to have a future.

In spite of the complexity of the metaphorical language in *The Three Graces*, the painting has an immediacy that is quite physical. The action is set within a shallow stage; the trees, cloth, sea and sky push close to the viewer, their textures inviting touch. There is a sense of expectancy; the curtain has gone up and the drama is to start.

Jan Murray was twenty-six when she painted *The Three Graces*. It holds her questions—of grace and beginnings, faith and endings.

JAN MURRAY was born in Ballarat in 1957. She studied art at the Ballarat College of Advanced Education between 1976 and 1978 and then at the Victorian College of the Arts in 1980 and 1981. In 1983 she received a Visual Arts Board Grant and spent 1984–85 in Berlin at the Bethanien Artists' Studios, in sight of the Berlin Wall. As she was already impressed with Max Beckman's handling of symbol, colour and form, Murray's time in Germany was productive. Her Berlin pictures, exhibited at the Melbourne University Gallery in 1985, evoke the sense of myth and history within powerful, complex structuring. Spires, tank traps, domes and sections of classical sculpture evoke a sense of desolation and personal loneliness.

Jan Murray has been included in a number of important group shows, including Australian Perspecta, at the Art Gallery of New South Wales in 1983; Vox Pop, at the National Gallery of Victoria in 1983–84; From Another Continent, at the Museum of Modern Art in Paris in 1983; Australian Visions, at the Guggenheim Museum in New York in 1984; and Triad, at the Adelaide Festival of the Arts in 1986.

Jan Murray lives in Melbourne.

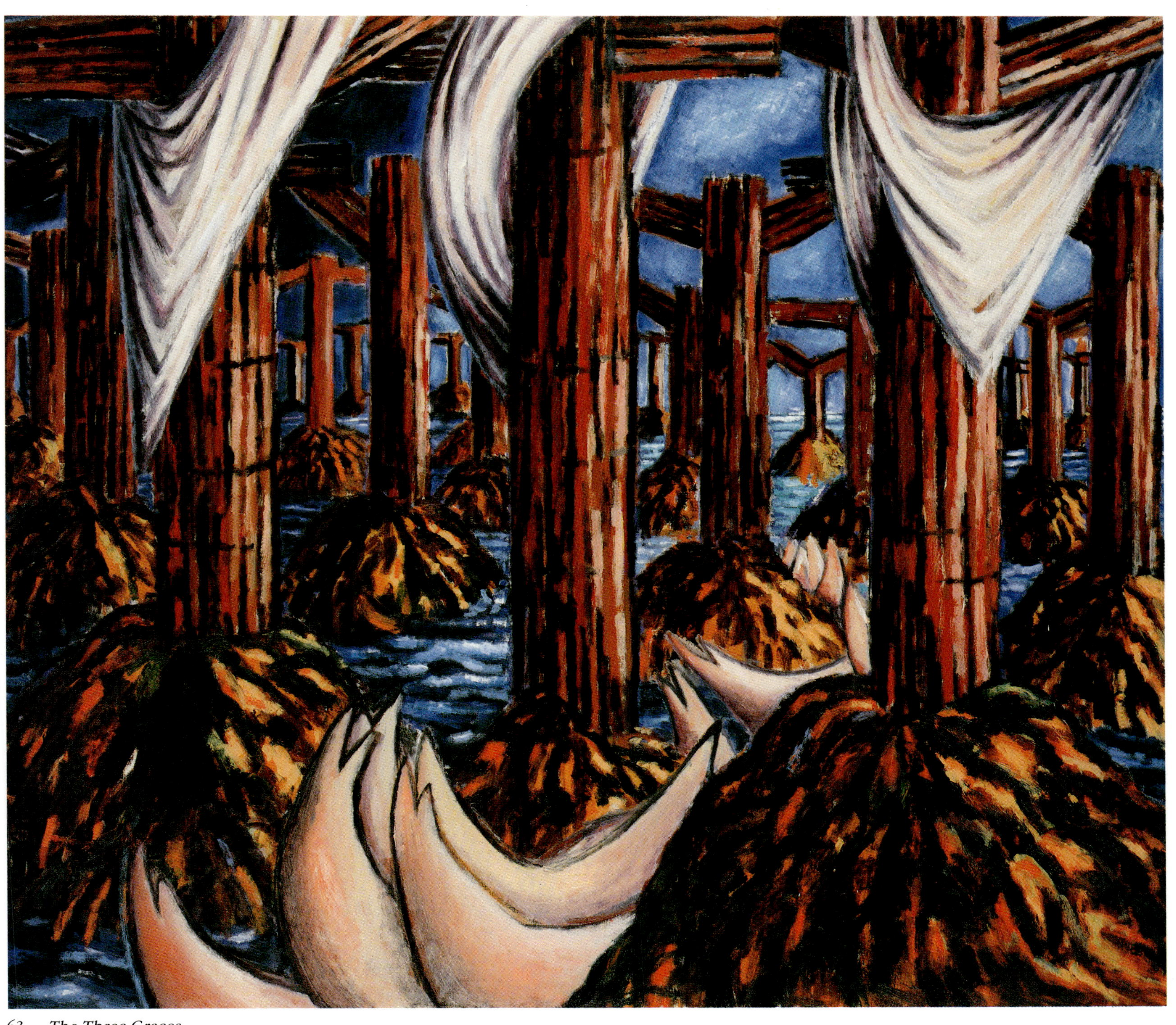

63 *The Three Graces*

JOHN R. WALKER

Born 1957

Mary, 1985

Oil on canvas
244 × 304.5 cm
National Gallery of Victoria, Melbourne
Michell Endowment 1985

John R. Walker finished this painting, *Mary*, as one of a series in 1985–86. The inspiration had come from a newspaper account of the trial of an Aboriginal woman, Mary, charged with causing grievous bodily harm to a man who had molested her with violence. As he painted, Walker came to identify himself with the woman. She came from the land at Maralinga, a member of a tribe dispossessed by atomic experiments; as a black woman in white society she easily became an object to be used by men. Alcoholic, she was at first passive to this second rape. Walker came to think of her action as understandable, even rational; she was Medea from the Greek myth, Judith from the scriptures who slayed Holofernes; she was all women who have been used as objects and possessions throughout history. Her body, like her land, was regarded as open to easy conquest by white intruders; she retaliated—and was brought before an Australian court.

The painting is dominated by the figure of Mary on the left, holding in her hand the knife of castration. Her attacker crouches, waiting. What distinguishes this painting, and others in the series, is Walker's handling of space. He has rejected the traditional notion in Western art that pictorial space is objective and impersonal and should be used to locate objects. For him, space should pulsate and be active, so that no one area is pictorially more important than another. In *Mary*, the space is shallow but alive, reminiscent more of Hokusai than of Piero della Francesca. Colour, although rich and dense, is subservient to the same sense of oneness, so that the painting communicates a spiritual depth and calm that belies the violence of its subject matter.

JOHN R. WALKER was born in Sydney in 1957. He studied art at St George College of TAFE in 1974–75 and at Alexander Mackie College, Sydney, in 1976–77. During these formative years he was influenced by Peter Upward at St George and, through him, by Bill Rose, Tony Tuckson, John Passmore and Ian Fairweather among Australian artists and by Piero della Francesca, Titian, Goya and Cézanne among the Europeans. Since then he has studied Indian sculpture and the prints and paintings of Japanese and Chinese artists. From Hokusai and, more recently, Ike No Taiga, he has learnt to order space in ways that activate the entire surface of the canvas.

After a number of successful solo exhibitions between 1979 and 1986 in Sydney and Melbourne, Walker returned to the privacy of his studio to concentrate and recharge his energies through direct study of the human figure, predominantly the female nude, drawn and painted directly from life in his studio. He also completed a number of landscapes as seen through his inner city suburban window in Parramatta Road. Some of these are nearly abstract; all of them attempt to break down the traditional barrier between drawing and painting. They are larger than life in size, painted on paper and usually completed on the floor, rather than upright. Walker works freely with sweeps of colour which vividly communicate a sense of quietness that is born of energy rather than tranquillity.

Walker sees his work as having a strong spiritual dimension reflective of his belief in some supreme being who is the focus and reason for the whole of life—plant, animal and human.

John R. Walker lives in Sydney.

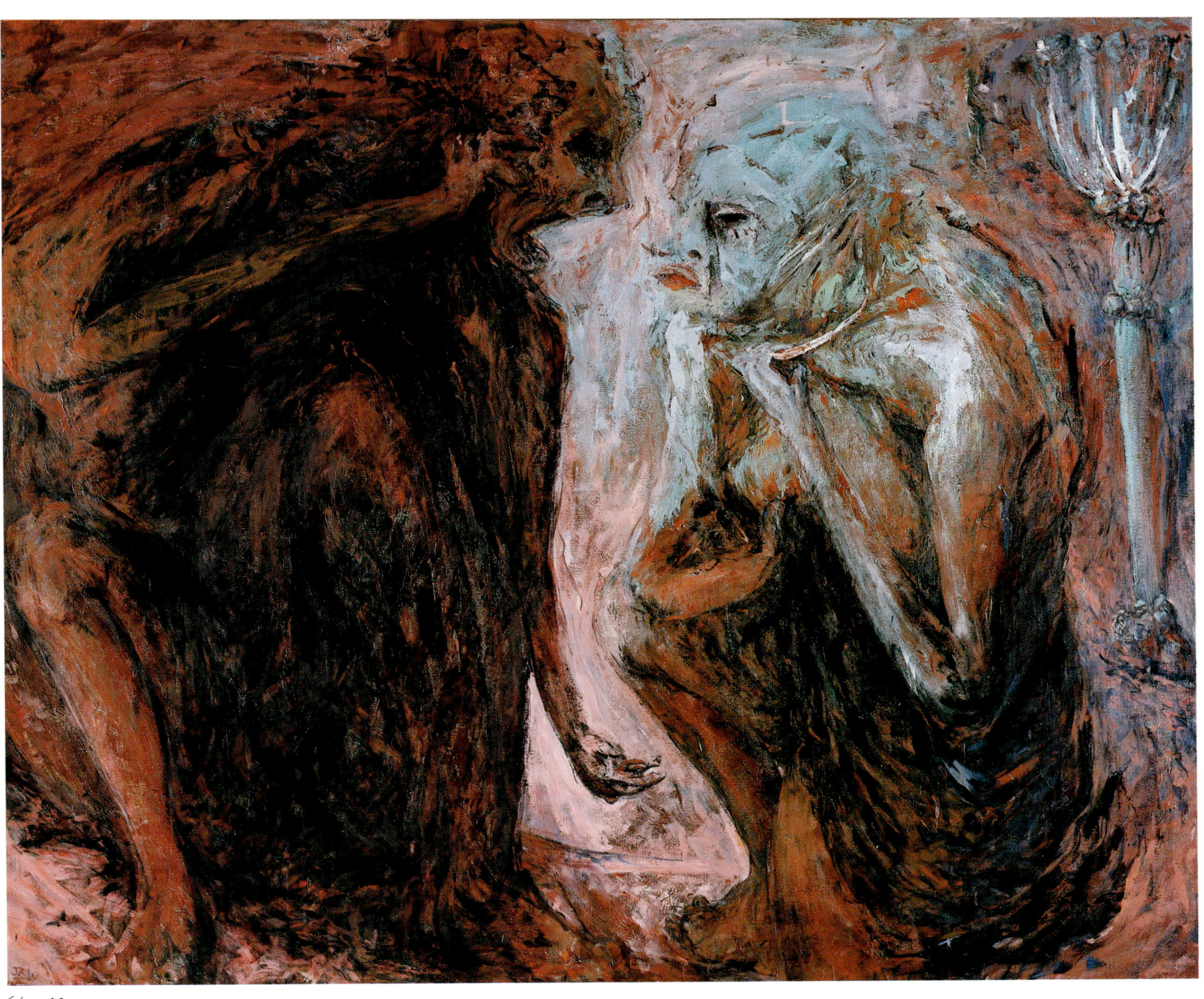

64 *Mary*

JAMES GLEESON

Born 1915

Preparations at Patmos, 1986

Oil on canvas
183 × 325 cm
Collection of Robert Holmes à Court

In the Revelation of Saint John the Divine, the writer begins the account of the vision of the apocalypse: 'My name is John . . . I was on the island of Patmos . . . and the Spirit possessed me and I heard a voice behind me shouting like a trumpet.'[1] Then follows the dramatic and mysterious vision of the apocalypse. James Gleeson has set his *Preparations at Patmos* on the island just before the time of the revelation. The island—earth, sea and sky—are making themselves ready to receive the terrible word of God that the end of an era is at hand and a new one beginning. Gleeson has them in travail, heaving and moving rhythmically in expectation.

But this apocalypse is not about past history. For Gleeson the time is now. In speaking about the painting, Gleeson recalled that he was born during one world war, spent his young manhood in another, and has lived since with the ever-present threat of nuclear disaster—the worst possible apocalypse. The sky is his reminder that destruction, when and if it comes, will be from the air. The painting is rich in deliberate allusion. The calm morning light on the left is the alpha, the purple darkness on the right is the omega. In between, the drama plays itself out on an island inspired by Shakespeare's *Tempest*. The standing figure with upraised arms is Prospero as well as Saint John. Land and sky are crowded with organic forms at different moments of evolution and metamorphosis. Rocks become shells, claws and crustaceans; clouds suggest human and animal forms in sinuous movement. Bosch, Brueghel and Grünewald are never far away; nor is Dali. But the real birthplace of many of the forms is in photographs of organic forms seen with a neutron microscope.

Preparations at Patmos is a superb example of Gleeson's mastery of draughtsmanship and complex colour orchestration. The underdrawing in charcoal was enlarged from a carefully worked black-and-white tonal drawing. Each square was then almost completely painted with a very extensive palette of perhaps sixty colours, beginning in the top left corner and working to the right, then to the lower parts. Each colour was laid on separately and then sometimes blended with a fine brush. The finished painting glows with a baroque splendour and a resignation which belies its terrible message.

1. Revelation, 1 : 9–10.

JAMES GLEESON was born in Hornsby, New South Wales, and studied art at the East Sydney Technical College from 1934 to 1936 and, in 1937–38, at the Sydney Teachers' College under the creative art educator May Marsden, who encouraged individual research and freedom of expression. Gleeson became involved, both as a writer and a painter, in the theories of psychoanalysis and surrealism. His *Attitude of Lady Lightning to a Lady Mountain* (1939) and *Massive Journey to a Nocturnal Object* (1939), in the first exhibition of the Contemporary Art Society in Melbourne, established him in the forefront of Australian surrealism and made clear his debt to Salvador Dali. In 1940 his essay 'What Is Surrealism?'[1] promoted surrealism as a weapon against totalitarian dictatorship.

Gleeson has remained resolutely a surrealist, although he no longer believes it to be able to effect change in society. In 1948 he shared an exhibition at London Gallery with Lucien Freud and Robert Klippel. A second extended period in Europe and the United States in 1958–59 broadened his critical appreciation of Jackson Pollock and the abstractionists but confirmed his personal preference in his own work.

Gleeson has held important national and state art administrative positions. He has published six books on aspects of Australian art history, and between 1949 and 1972 he was art critic for the Sydney papers the *Sun* and the *Sun-Herald*. Since his retirement in 1983, he has held six successful one-man exhibitions.

James Gleeson lives in Sydney.

> I think I was born a surrealist. From my first encounter with it—even earlier, through reproductions of Bosch, early Brueghel, Grünewald and Altdorfer, I recognized the language. They spoke that way I thought. I was resolutely at home with such paintings.[2]

1. James Gleeson, 'What Is Surrealism?' *Art in Australia*, November 1940.
2. James Gleeson, *Landscape out of Nature* (Sydney: Beagle Press, 1987), p. 12.

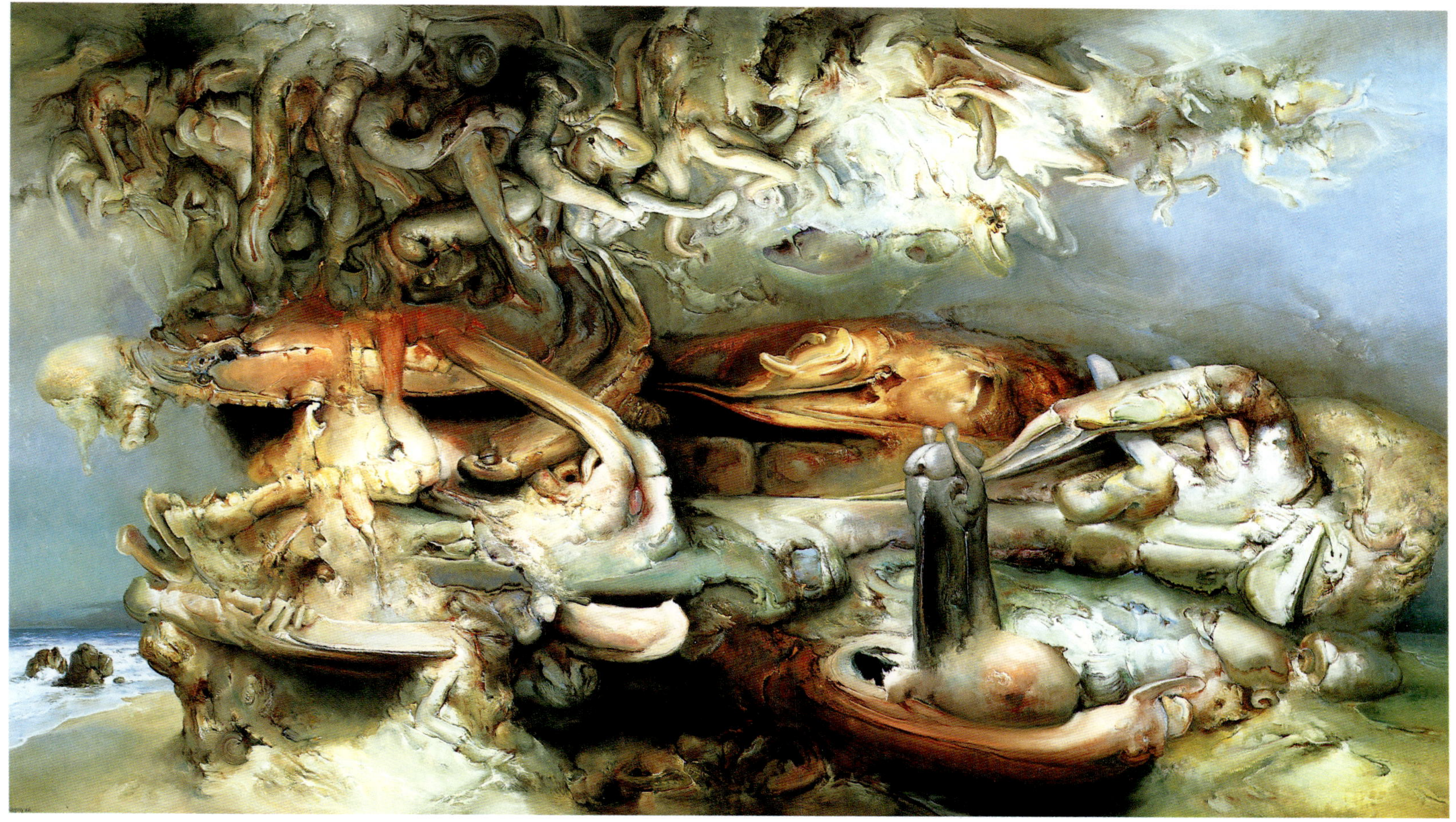

65 *Preparations at Patmos*

Irene Barberis

Born 1953

Cherubim, 1987–88

Acrylic on wood
244 × 488 cm
Collection of the artist

When Irene Barberis completed *Cherubim* in March 1988, she said that at last she had managed to wed her life's beliefs harmoniously yet explicitly into her painting. *Cherubim* is a painting of revelation, of a life that finds within its daily routine the hand of God in the way the scriptures speak of the intervention of God in the life of the Jewish people. *Cherubim* moves between sacred and secular without making such distinctions; everything in this painting reveals, for those who can see it, the working of God.

Cherubim is a large, four-panel work. On the left is an eagle, spirit of God, with wings outstretched over the world below reflected in a mirror; at the bottom an empty milk carton and an ashtray, 'a beautiful butterfly shape filled with ashes' as Barberis has described it. Near the eagle she has painted herself: 'a rough grey drawing of me, crying black tears of paint; I believe in revelation.'[1] The second panel is dominated by the figure of John the Evangelist holding the Book of Revelation. Near him a huge broken breakfast cup spills out objects from Barberis's everyday life—eggcup, paper goat, a box of Greek custard, a Vegemite jar (her paper zebra has his nose in the Vegemite), a bowling ball, a picture of the sea and ships, a sandshoe, a pencil sharpener. The right panel contains the vision of Ezekiel:

> I saw a storm wind coming from the north, a vast cloud with flashes of fire and brilliant light about it; and within was a radiance like brass, glowing in the heart of the flames. In the fire was the semblance of four living creatures in human form . . . their faces were like this: all four had the face of a man and the face of a lion on the right . . . the appearance of the creatures was as if fire from burning coals or torches were darting to and fro among them; the fire was radiant . . . I saw wheels on the ground . . . the wheels sparkled like topaz . . . a wheel within a wheel . . . and the rims of the wheels were full of eyes all round. When the living creatures moved, the wheels moved. [Ezek 1:4–19]

Cherubim is emphatically not an illustration of Ezekiel. Barberis has built an extremely complex painting over a long period of time without losing spontaneity or verve of expression. The colours retain immediacy and strength, their rhythms dense but without confusion. The compositional excitement in the painting is due partly to the diagonal axis which cuts through from left to right and then changes direction, and partly to the contrast created between the objects that spill out of the lower half of the painting and the serenity and calm of the top half, which clearly focuses on the figure of John. Only the eyes are disconcerting as they directly engage the viewer, coercing involvement that is at once visual, emotional and intellectual in the drama that is the painting.

1. Interview with author, 7 March 1988.

Irene Barberis was born in London in 1953. She studied for her diploma in fine arts at Prahran College of Advanced Education in 1972–73 and Preston Institute of Technology in 1975–76 and completed a postgraduate diploma in painting at the Victoria College of the Arts in 1977–78. In 1979 she was awarded the Keith and Elisabeth Murdoch Travelling Fellowship, in 1980 the Power Institute award for residence at the Cité Internationale des Arts, Paris, and the Visual Arts Board award for residence at the International Village at Vence, France.

Like Peter Booth, Jan Murray and many Melbourne younger-generation painters in the seventies, Irene Barberis is influenced by twentieth-century figurative expressionist painting, although her work is generally optimistic and not overtly emotional, closer in spirit to the fauves and Bonnard than it is to Die Brücke and Beckmann. Many of her large works are composed of smaller panels which have been added in the process of the painting, analogous to the steps in a classical dance. Her work since 1980 often gives visible credence to her deep Christian commitment, although it rarely uses traditional themes from scripture or is overtly and recognizably 'religious'. Her painting is usually an exuberant celebration of everyday life, and her religion is within it—flowers, figures, cups, teapots, fruit and Vegemite jars along with angels, a cross and haloes. She has participated in a number of community art projects, including the completion, in 1984, of a six-panel billboard for the Victorian Ministry of the Arts.

Irene Barberis lives in Melbourne.

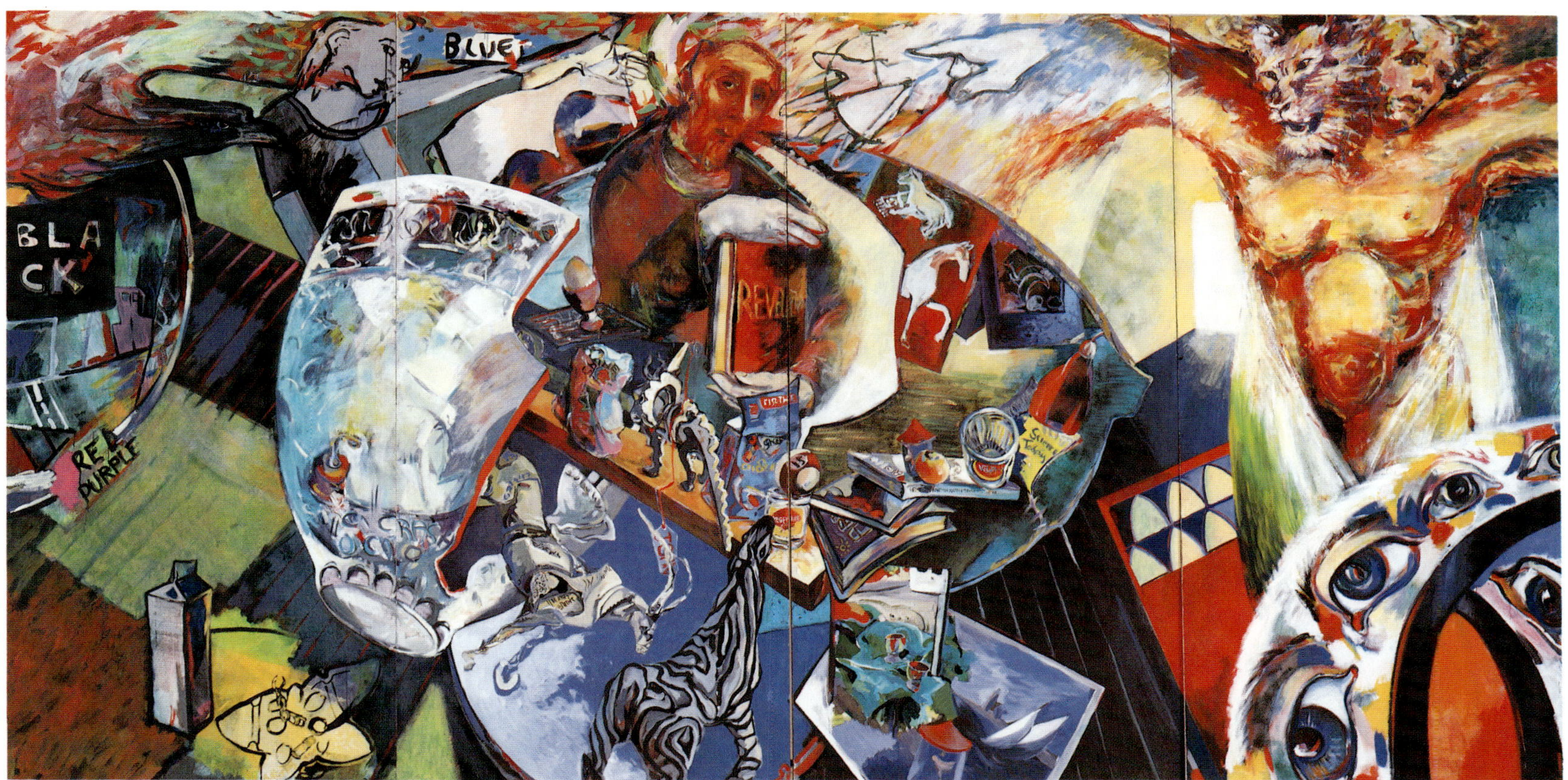

66 *Cherubim*

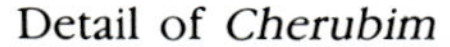

Detail of *Cherubim*

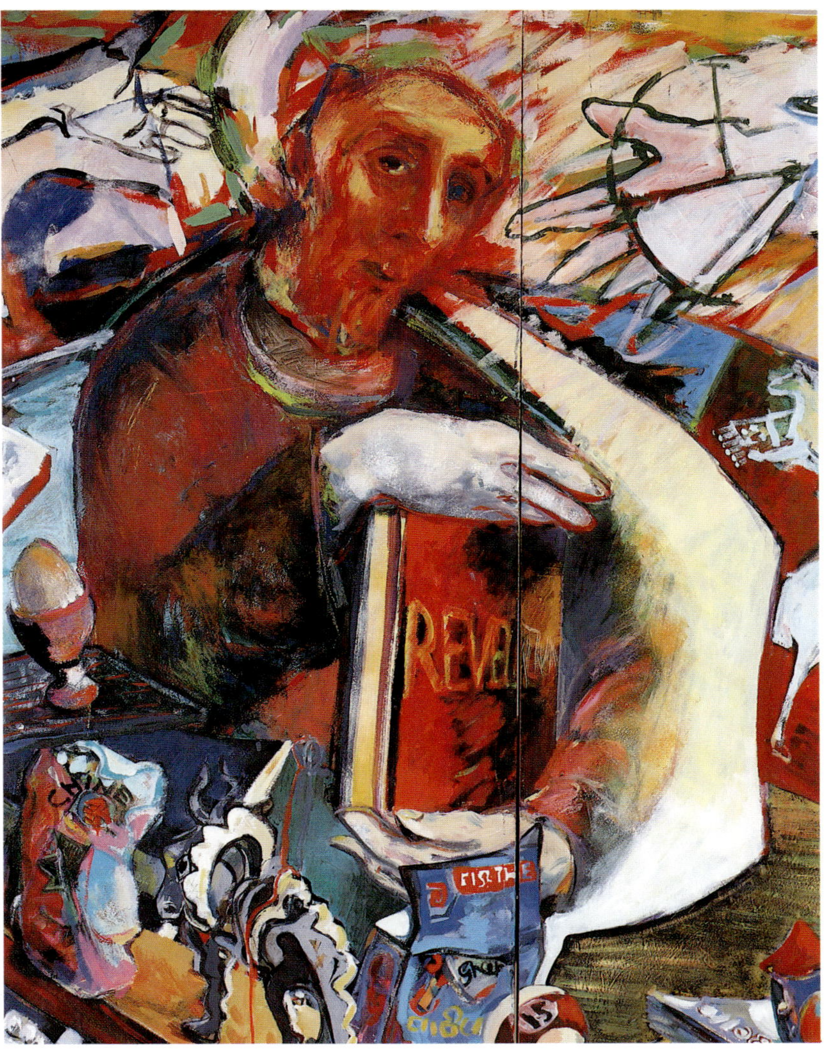

ALAN OLDFIELD

Born 1943

The Theophany, 1985–87

Oil and acrylic on canvas
137 × 137 cm
Collection of the artist

The Theophany is one of nine major paintings in a series, The Revelations of Divine Love of Julian of Norwich, completed by Alan Oldfield between 1985 and 1987 and exhibited first in Sydney, then at Norwich Cathedral, England, as part of the 1988 Norwich Festival of the Arts. Each of the paintings encloses more than one vision but has references to the other paintings; together the paintings build into a series with overlapping and repetitive themes, deliberately akin to the rhythms of medieval chant. Oldfield intends the paintings to be genuinely narrative, that is, to encapsulate as much as possible of the truth of the experiences the fourteenth-century anchoress Julian of Norwich has recorded and to express as little as possible of his own emotional response to them. Yet Oldfield is not a detached onlooker; he is a Christian believer who has made a deep study of the visions and finds their theology of compassion and optimism very convincing.

Because these are narrative paintings, an understanding of their content is important; it is not sufficient simply to appreciate their formal qualities and composition or the superb craftsmanship so typical of all of Oldfield's works. Artistic meaning in these paintings is in the interrelationships of many layers. One of these is subject matter. In *The Theophany*, Oldfield has in mind the vision as described by Julian:

> He [God] showed me something else, a tiny thing, no bigger than a hazelnut lying in the palm of the hand, and as round as a ball. I looked at it, puzzled and thought, 'What is it?' The answer came, 'It is everything that is made.' I wondered how it could survive. It was so small that I expected it to shrivel up and disappear. Then I was answered, 'It exists now and always because God loves it . . . in this small thing—three truths—first God made it, second God loves it, and third God looks after it.'[1]

Oldfield has clothed Julian, a lay woman, in a nun's habit. In her hand is the tiny ball, no bigger than a hazelnut. Behind her is a blue drape symbolizing the unveiling; in front is the wall, curtain and cross, fourteenth-century devices to signal the separation of this world and the next. Julian is in this world, Christ in the next. He is bathed in golden light and is clothed in the blue of heaven; she is in the brown of the earth. Everything is clear and ordered; as Julian has written, 'All shall be well, all manner of thing shall be well.'

1. H. Backhouse, and R. Pipe, eds, *Revelations of the Divine Love of Julian of Norwich* (London: Hodder & Stoughton, 1987), p. 68.

Born in Sydney in 1943, ALAN OLDFIELD studied painting at the National Art School, Sydney, between 1962 and 1966 and in Italy in 1974 and 1975 on a Visual Arts Board Grant. Although associated for a time with the Central Street Gallery, Oldfield never succumbed totally to abstraction or to colour-field painting. As early as August 1969 he identified the move to a new realism and outlined his own goals and directions. 'Realism now cultivates a stance that is new and different,' he wrote in the Contemporary Art Society's broadsheet, 'it attracts painters motivated by social comment, wit, referential environmental relationships, erotica and biography. Technically, its strength lies in draughtsmanship, line and closed composition, its success in allusiveness and anonymity.'

Oldfield's mature paintings, drawings and theatre designs carry out this brief and incorporate the insights of colour field and hard edge. Often his paintings include explicit reference to paintings and to painters he admires, such as Piero della Francesca, Fra Angelico, Verrocchio, Caravaggio, David Hockney and Balthus. Like Balthus, he often places a frame around a moment of time (e.g., *Two Figures and an Abstract Device*, 1978), correcting reality, so that the picture space becomes like the theatre stage and the figures become like actors frozen in time and isolated often from each other.

Oldfield's homage to other artists is always overt, sometimes ironical and usually acknowledged. His is an articulate and self-aware pursuit of objectivity.

Alan Oldfield lives in Sydney.

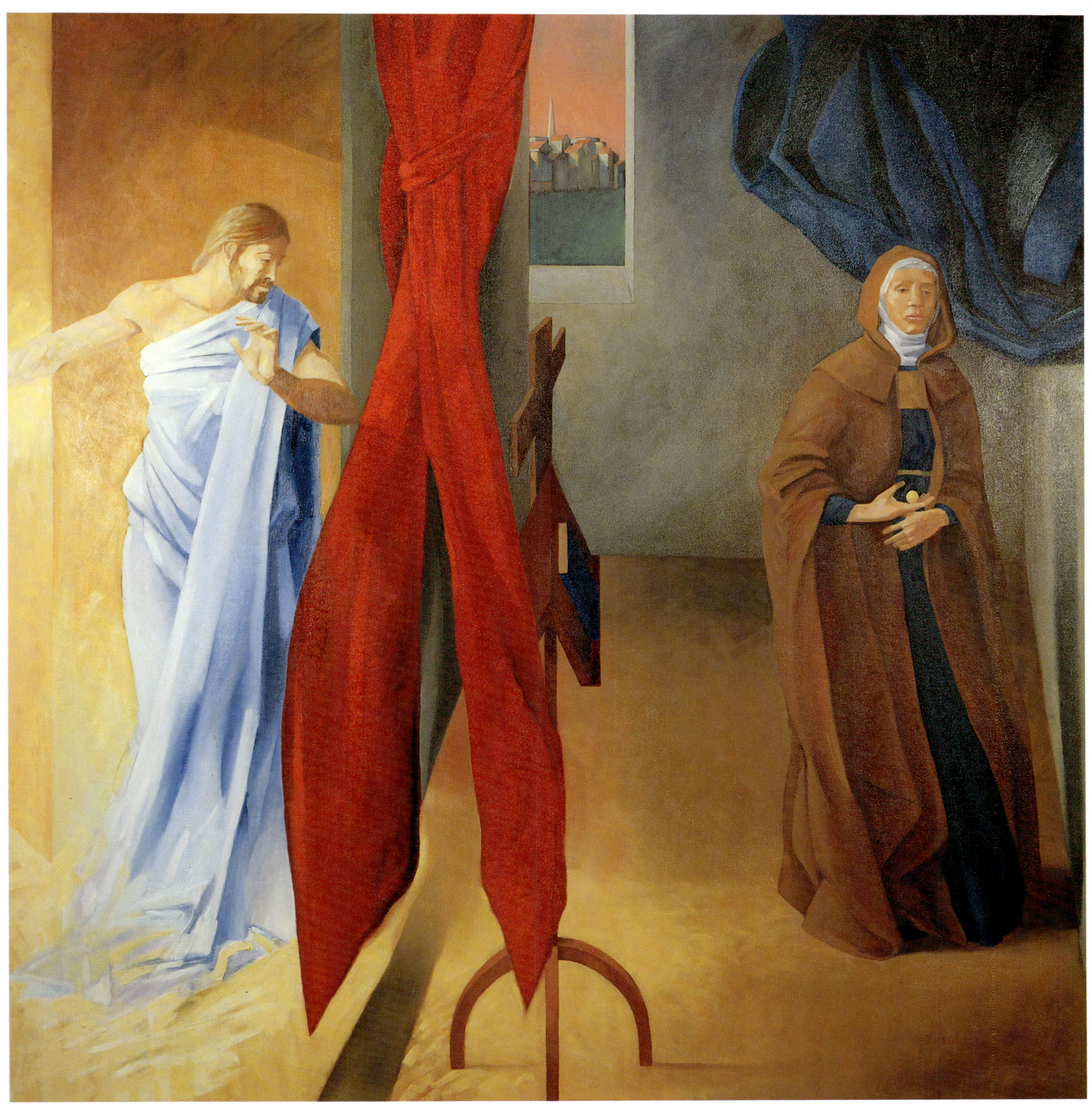

67 *The Theophany*

PART II

Islands of Reflection

ARTHUR BOYD

Born 1920

The mining town, 1946–47

Oil and tempera on composition board
87.2 × 109.2 cm
Australian National Gallery, Canberra

When Arthur Boyd completed *The mining town (Casting the Money Changers from the Temple),* he was living at Open Country, in pottery partnership with John Perceval and Peter Herbst and happily married with a small child. Some of the rollicking contentment of those days is reflected in the painting. He and Perceval were studying Pieter Brueghel's paintings and experimenting with large compositions teaming with crowds of figures in local settings. Many of these took inspiration and subject matter from biblical narratives, and techniques such as the use of oil with tempera were taken from the old masters.

This is a painting to enjoy. Below Boyd (and the viewer) is the chaos and drama of suburban Melbourne as well as the gospel event. Port Phillip Bay twinkles on the right, the jetties, the tiny white lighthouse (since demolished) and the long Station Pier identify the suburb as South Melbourne. Other suburbs and fields stretch up to the very high horizon line. The foreground teems with life and activity, with more than seventy-two people, thirteen pigs and numerous birds, cats, and horses as well as carts, a funeral procession, bikes, gardens and trees. On the left is the temple, now a church (sprouting weeds and greenery) from which Christ drives out the money lenders. In the Scripture narrative (Matthew 21: 12–14), the temple dealers were trading in money and doves for the sacrifice. Here the Christ sweeps the men and their tables down the steps, setting up a chain reaction: a truck spills its load as it hits a tree; the escaping pigs cause panic; a cripple runs away; a kite flier grabs a pig; muzzled dogs drag their owner along. Eventually everybody will be affected by the action which has already halted a funeral procession. Only the lovers in the garden are unaffected, but Boyd has wound a serpent around some trees to watch these two.

Many of the elements in the painting are familiar from earlier Boyd works. The cripples, the man in the wheelchair, the kite flier, the factory with the pulley on top, the tranquil fields and ponds are parts of his pictorial language which occur also in many of his later works, often metamorphosed and given new symbolic meanings. In another painting done at this time, *Melbourne Burning,* Boyd has taken the fire from the middle of this work and exploded it into a frightening apocalyptic vision of war and retribution.

ARTHUR BOYD rarely speaks of himself in egocentric ways. He easily speaks of his family, of events that reveal society as rampant with materialism and a destructive patriotism, and of art as the expression of the conscience of the community and so of belonging to it. In 1975 he gave more than two hundred paintings and a thousand drawings to the Australian people through the Australian National Gallery, Canberra, and in 1982 he offered his home in Tuscany to the Australia Council's Visual Arts Board.

Arthur Boyd was born in Murrumbeena, Victoria, the second of five children to Doris Gough, a painter, and her husband, Merric Boyd, a painter and potter. His paternal grandparents were the artists Emma Minnie à Beckett and Arthur Merric Boyd, and his maternal grandmother, Evelyn Gough, was a feminist, intellectual and writer. The Boyd family home, Open Country, was a gathering place for artists and writers and their friends. It was also a deeply religious household. Arthur Boyd recalls sitting on his grandmother's knee as she read him stories from a large, illustrated family Bible and he peered with fascination at the illustrations. He remembers the intensity of his father's religiosity and his burning desire to be ordained. Albert Tucker, who was a frequent visitor to the house in the 1940s, tells of prayer gatherings initiated by Merric Boyd at which visitors were expected to participate. Open Country was a place of hospitality, compassion and artistic and literary stimulus. It was within such a familial climate that Arthur Boyd was nurtured.

[*Continued overleaf*]

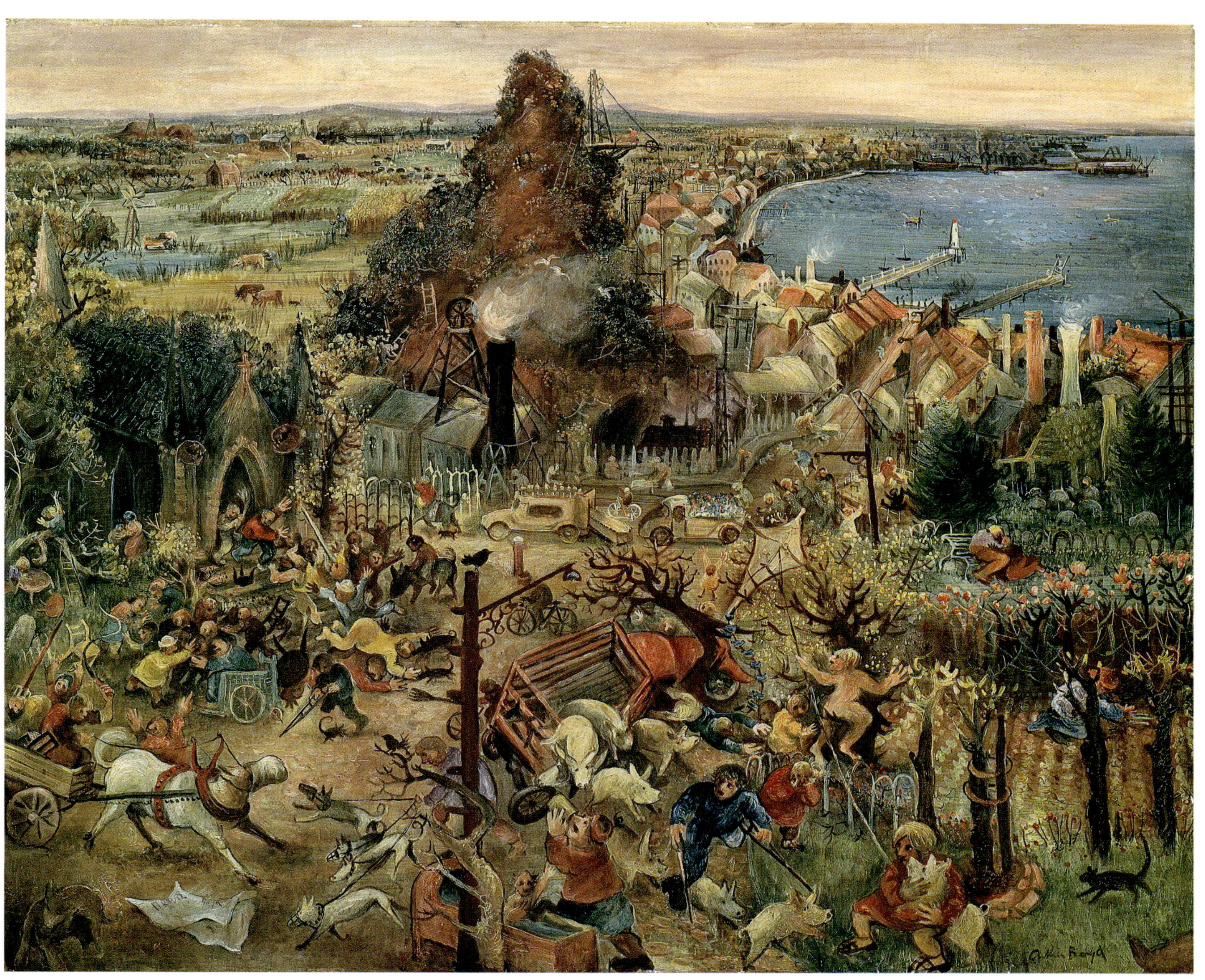

68 *The mining town*

ARTHUR BOYD

Born 1920

Angel Spying on Adam and Eve, 1947–48

Oil and tempera on board
86.4 × 122 cm
Collection of Helen and Maurice Alther, Melbourne

In *The mining town (Casting the Money Changers from the Temple)* Boyd's view is detached; he is the witness, laconically recording events which delight rather than frighten him. In *Angel Spying on Adam and Eve* the artist is again a witness, but this time Boyd has created a scene so intimate and real that the viewer is caught into visual participation and identification with one or another of the three participants. Adam and Eve embrace in a moment of great intimacy and privacy. The angel, a male with a hooked nose and bulging eyes, gazes greedily at them. They, the innocents, are naked. He, the knowing, is clothed in red. At their feet rests a ram, often in Boyd's paintings a symbol of rampant sexual desire. But here the ram is white, the colour of light. This ram may as easily evoke the Christian symbol 'Lamb of God' or Christ, the 'new Adam'.

Again Boyd has transcended the limitations of time and place in his narrative. His Adam and Eve are credible persons, as is his angel; they engage in fundamental human action that transcends a particular time or geography. Boyd's Garden of Eden is the feathery Australian bush around Melbourne, his light is the distinctive soft light of the southern part of this continent (as opposed to the harsh, white light of the Shoalhaven [Plates 75, 76]). Everything in this painting bespeaks great sensuality and yet reverence for all that is most human and of the earth.

In a companion painting, *The Expulsion* (1947–48), Adam and Eve are driven out of paradise by a screaming, avenging angel. Their nakedness has lost its innocence, and the bush, so idyllic here, has become rocky and threatening. Pain replaces serenity as exile becomes a reality.

Boyd left school during the Great Depression when he was fourteen to work in his maternal uncle's paint factory in Fitzroy. For some months he attended drawing classes at night at the National Gallery School. When Minnie Boyd died, he went to live with his grandfather at Rosebud and was encouraged by him to paint full time. Some of the landscapes he produced at this time, along with portraits and interiors, were included in his first solo exhibition at the Westminster Gallery, Little Collins Street, Melbourne, when he was seventeen. Even then it was clear in paintings such as *She-oak Reflected in Tidal Creek* (1937) and *Rosebud Landscape with Haystacks* (1939) that Boyd understood and valued the Australian landscape tradition exemplified in the paintings of Charles Conder and Arthur Streeton and that he had a youthful enthusiasm for van Gogh. Boyd's second exhibition, held with Josl Bergner, a Jewish refugee and social realist painter, was organized by Max Nicholson; both were frequent visitors to Open Country. Nicholson had introduced the Boyds to the writings of Dostoevsky, Kafka and T. S. Eliot. In Arthur Boyd's painting *Three Heads* (1938), the portrait heads of the Boyd brothers are the Brothers Karamazov, and the more sombre mood of many of the other works reflects the influence of Bergner.

[*Continued overleaf*]

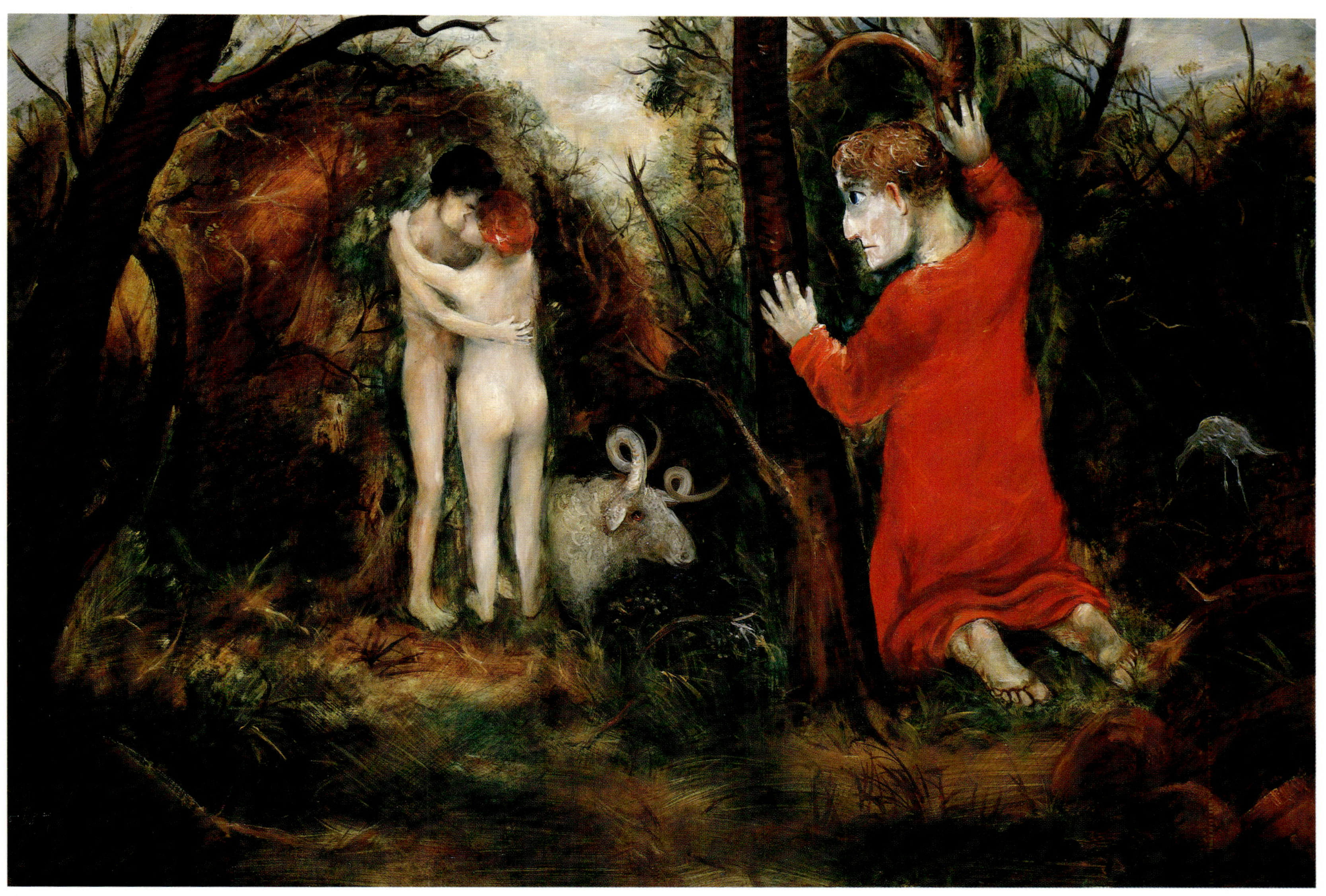

69 *Angel Spying on Adam and Eve*

ARTHUR BOYD

Born 1920

Moses Leading the People, 1947

Oil and tempera on board
104 × 122 cm
Collection of Helen and Maurice Alther, Melbourne

The classical compositional device of a large figure in the foreground which directs attention to the central action that takes place in the middle picture plane, such as Boyd used in *Angel Spying on Adam and Eve,* is here, in *Moses Leading the People,* replaced by the more mannerist invention of using a large figure which pushes out of the frontal plane towards the viewer. The background remains a curtain of activity to support the central character.

Boyd's Moses is a great patriarch who strides, grim-faced at the head of his people. Like the spying angel he wears a red tunic, but his passion is for rescue. Behind him, in a funnel of light in the Australian bush, the chosen people struggle to follow. They are more particularized than the figures in *The mining town (Casting the Money Changers from the Temple).* A woman clutches her child, a man grabs a tree for support while another claws himself up the bank. In the background a horse and cart cause chaos. But the focus of the painting is the huge figure of Moses, saviour of his people, heedless of the dangers of the Australian bush.

Moses Leading the People is unusual in that Boyd has included no overtly religious symbolism. The figures and the landscape carry the meaning alone. The year before, 1946, Boyd had completed two other paintings of the Moses epic, *The Golden Calf* and *Moses Throwing Down the Tablets of the Law,* both of which contain many explicitly religious symbols. They are Brueghelian compositions in which the golden calf, Adam and Eve type figures, the rampant ram, dogs, birds and figures clutching each other vie for attention and demand to be understood. *Moses Leading the People* is a simpler painting, but just as powerful.

From 1941 to 1944 Boyd was in the army, much of the time in a cartographic warehouse in South Melbourne. Open Country remained home to Boyd and a place to bring his friends and to discuss art; among those who came were Sidney Nolan, Albert Tucker and John Perceval. These years saw little painting but many drawings, especially of the people he encountered in the depressed areas of South Melbourne. By 1944 most of the images that constantly recur in his later work had been developed. Grazia Gunn has identified seven such 'persistent images',[1] foundation stones of Boyd's personal iconography. All come from his life experience at home (pottery chimney and smoke; outstretched figure of his father, who was epileptic; Peter, the family dog; figures on crutches or in wheelchairs) or around South Melbourne (woman walking a crippled dog; man with a trumpet and handkerchief [kite]; fountain and lovers).

In 1944 Boyd's sister Mary married John Perceval, and in 1945 Boyd married fellow artist Yvonne Lennie. Boyd, Perceval and Peter Herbst formed a partnership to make utilitarian pottery as a way of providing enough security to continue painting. Boyd turned to the Bible of his childhood for inspiration, subject matter and a means to express some of the horror of the past war as well as some of the idyllic calm and idealism that was Open Country.

[*Continued overleaf*]

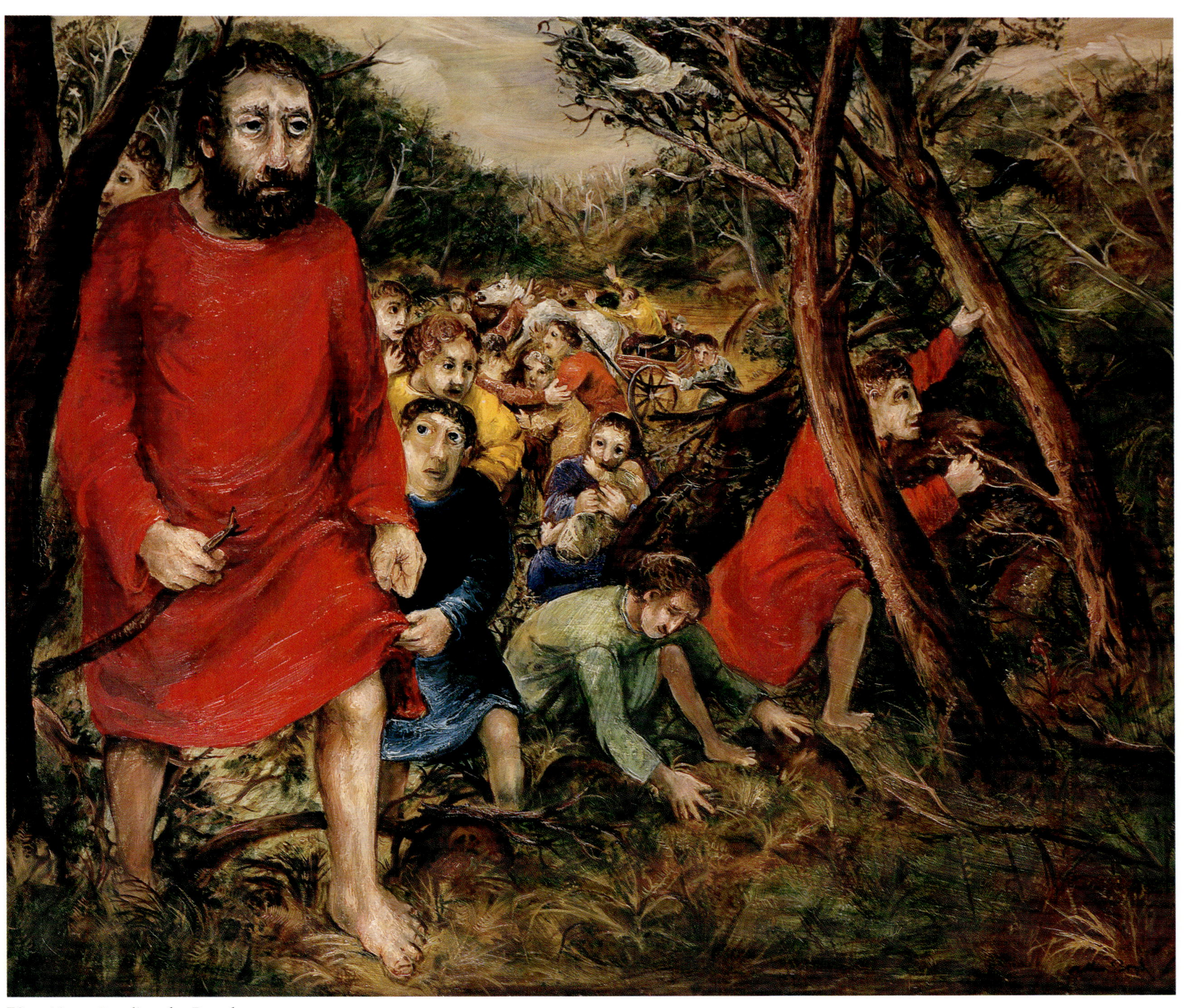

70 *Moses Leading the People*

ARTHUR BOYD

Born 1920

The Whale Putting Jonah into Its Mouth, 1950

Ceramic painting
33 × 40.7 cm
National Gallery of Victoria, Melbourne

As a child at Open Country, Arthur Boyd would often be sent to warn the neighbours to take their washing off the line as his potter father was about to fire the kiln. Clay, like paint, was a material he came to understand early. Technical competence as a tool of visual expression was highly valued in this family, many of whom excelled in visual communication.

The Whale Putting Jonah into Its Mouth is one of more than ninety ceramic paintings which Boyd completed between 1944 and 1953. The process of making a clay tile of this size is quite demanding; painting it demands sureness of hand and clarity of vision, as mistakes are hard to rectify if the colours are to stay brilliant. Each tile is shaped from a putty-like clay that is heavily 'grogged' (mixed with crushed fired clay). Colours are made from oxides mixed with liquid clay to the consistency of thin oil paint. The painting is completed while the tile is wet; the tile is dried slowly and then sprinkled with a powdered lead glaze before firing very slowly to about one thousand degrees Centigrade.

The Whale Putting Jonah into Its Mouth belongs with *The Airman* (1952–53) and *Child Being Fed* (1952–53) in that it reveals Boyd's growing interest in the simplified curvilinear forms of Picasso's cubism. The huge whale, orange against the brilliant green-blue sea, is in the very act of pushing a very reluctant, wide-eyed Jonah into its mouth. Boyd delights in the myth of Jonah; in 1973 he completed a series of drawings and etchings to accompany Peter Porter's poems published under the title *Jonah*.

Many of the ceramic paintings from this time have biblical themes from both the Old and the New Testaments. Some, like this one and a large, nine-panel *Temptation of St Anthony* (1951), are quite humorous; others, such as *The Kiss of Judas* (1951), *The Thirty Pieces of Silver* (*c.*1950) and *The Disrobement* (1950–51) are deeply moving expressions of great power.

Between 1963 and 1965 in London, Boyd turned again to ceramic painting, making and firing his own tiles. Again he turned for inspiration to his earlier drawings and subjects, many of them biblical. One of the most important works from this time is the *Romeo and Juliet* polyptych commissioned for the 1964 Shakespeare Exhibition at Stratford-upon-Avon and now in the National Gallery of Victoria.

In 1948 Boyd's uncle, Martin Boyd, returned to Australia after living in England and Europe for many years and commissioned him to decorate the walls of his grandfather's house, The Grange, at Harkaway, near Berwick. He turned to the Scriptures and the old masters for these murals, now destroyed. From these years also come landscapes of Berwick, Wimmera and the Grampians. In 1951, influenced by Russell Drysdale's paintings of dignified Aborigines and by Nolan's accounts of his travels in the outback, Boyd visited Alice Springs and Arltunga. He was so appalled by the plight of the people that it was not until 1956 that he began working on the series from that visit. Love, Marriage and Death of a Half-Caste (the Bride) series portray in myth and symbol something of the alienation and degradation of the Australian Aboriginal people.

In August 1959 Boyd participated in the Antipodean Exhibition and signed the manifesto of the participants, although he made no written suggestions to Bernard Smith, organizer of the manifesto, about its content, as did many of the other signatories. In September Merric Boyd died, and in November Arthur and Yvonne left Australia for a brief visit to England. 'I had a feeling of dead-endedness about what I would do next,' he explained, 'a need to seek new experience, not within myself, but from the outside. For a long period I had taken stuff out of myself, there was not time to put it back.'[2] They have lived there ever since.

[*Continued overleaf*]

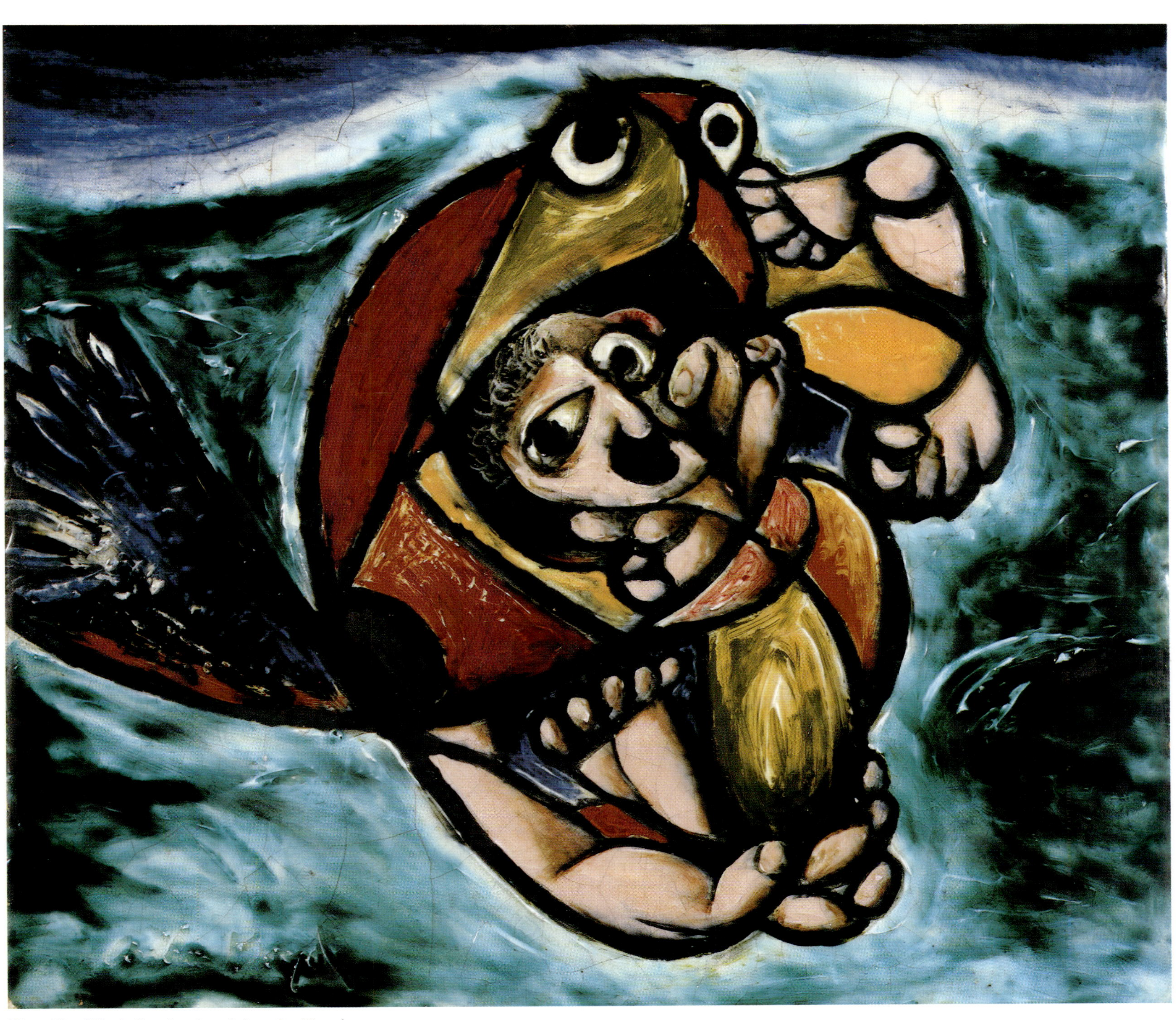

71 *The Whale Putting Jonah into Its Mouth*

ARTHUR BOYD

Born 1920

Susanna and the Elders, c.1962

Oil on perspex
Four paintings: each 108 × 113 cm
Collection of Helen and Maurice Alther, Melbourne

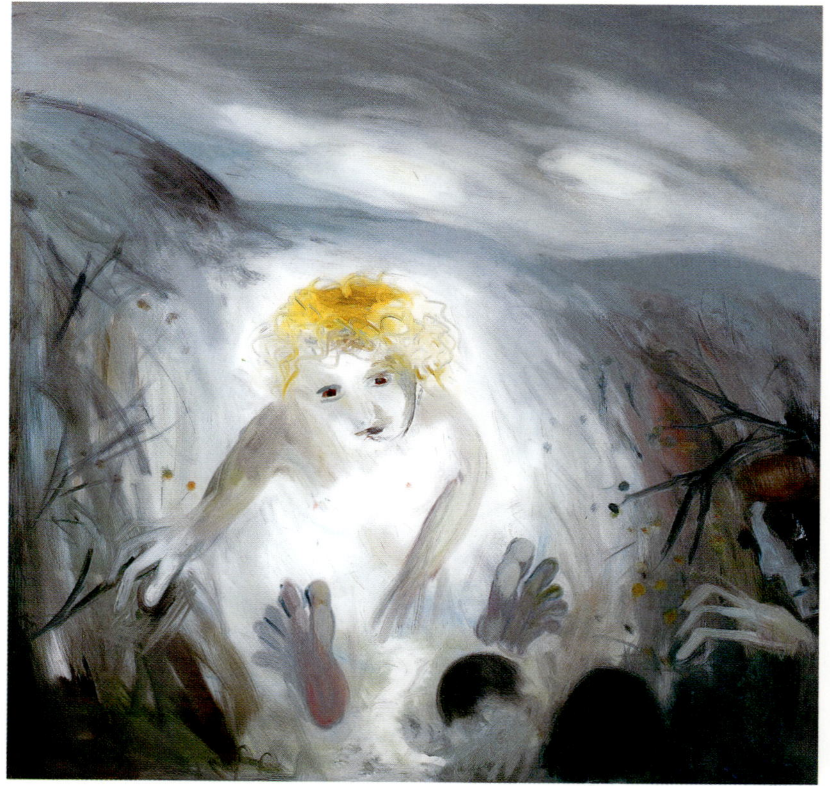

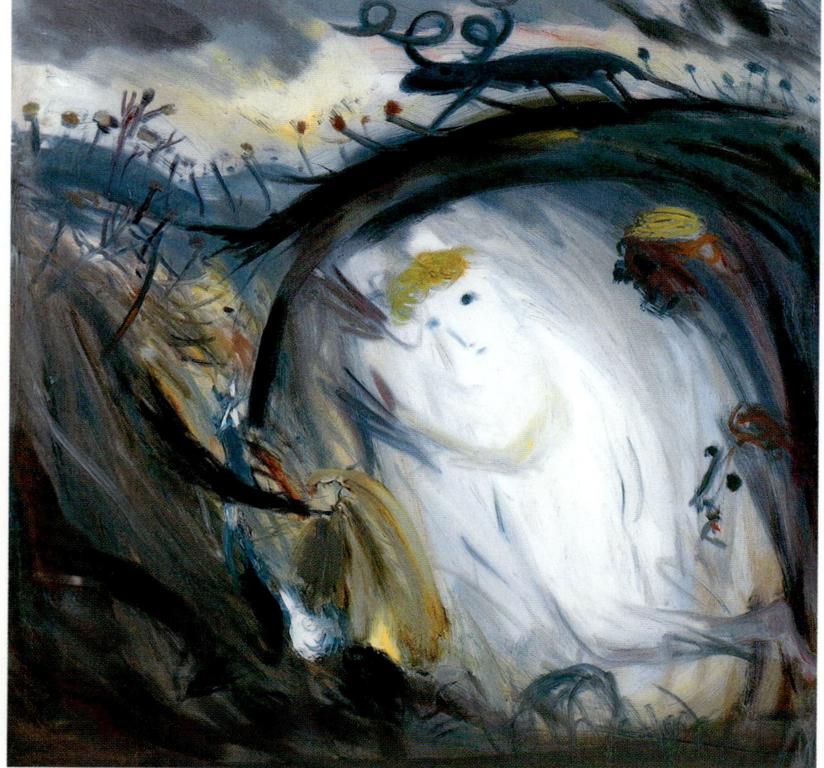

72 *Susanna and the Elders*

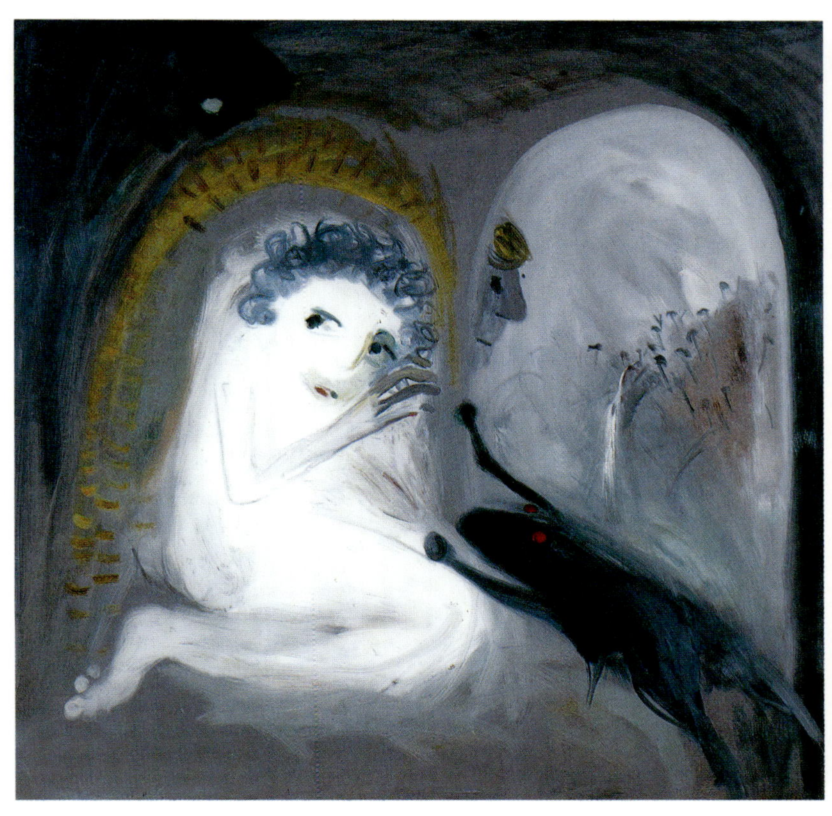

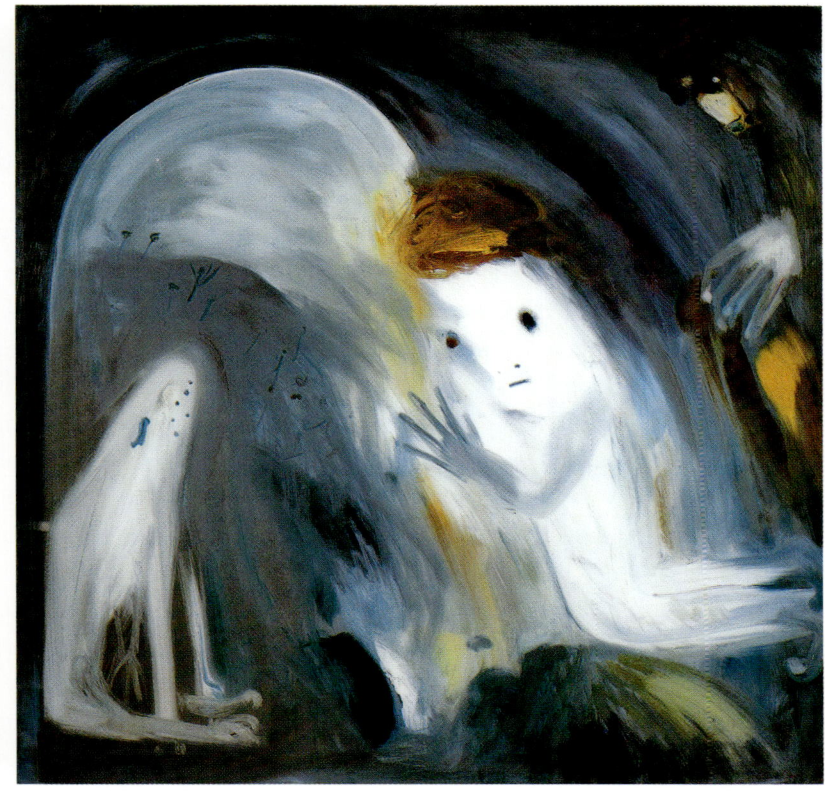

ARTHUR BOYD

Born 1920

Susanna with the Elders, 1945

Oil on canvas
66.8 × 97 cm
Australian National Gallery, Canberra

Susanna and the Elders was completed in London sometime in the early 1960s. In it Boyd experimented with perspex as a new surface on which to paint. The painting is on the reverse side of the perspex; his signature is scratched on the front. To paint in this way requires 'reverse thinking', as details and highlights must be put in first, the final layer of paint becoming the areas furthest from the viewer.

In London, Boyd was greatly influenced by Piero di Cosimo's *Death of Procris* in the National Gallery. Piero's Procris lies dead and is watched over by a faun and by the dog she had given to her husband, Cephalus, as symbol of her fidelity. The Procris and Cephalus legend has its echo in the biblical story of Susanna, 'a woman of great beauty and delicate feeling', who enters her husband's garden to bathe and is spied upon by two elders who plan to seduce her. 'If you refuse, they said to her, we shall give evidence against you that there was a young man with you and that was why you sent your maids away. Susanna groaned and said, I see no way out. If I do this thing, the penalty is death; if I do not, you will have me at your mercy. My choice is made. I will not do it. It is better to be at your mercy than to sin against the Lord' (Daniel and Susanna 21–23, 30).

Boyd's four panels are set in the garden in this part of the narrative. In two of the panels Susanna is bathing, unaware of the watching elders. She, like Adam and Eve in Plate 69, is innocence observed. In the second panel a ram, symbol here of illicit sexual desire, stalks the branch that frames her; the garden is the Australian landscape through which Moses moved in Plate 70. In the third panel Susanna shrinks in fear as Evil claws at her; one elder waits. In the last panel, a white dog, reminiscent of Procris's watcher, sits guard with Susanna as she opts for fidelity, regardless of the consequences.

In 1945 Boyd had painted *Susanna with the Elders* depicting the moment when the servants and others in the household, hearing her cries, rush into the garden. In this version Susanna covers her nakedness with her arms, the garden is a cave in the Australian landscape, and the ram again stalks the horizon.

In England in the 1960s, Boyd experienced a great surge of creative activity. From his first exhibition in Anton Zwemmer's Gallery in London it was clear that the international art world recognized and valued his genius, not only as a painter but also as a draughtsman, ceramicist and print-maker. Although he arrived at a time when England was rediscovering Australia, his acceptance was not built on any colonial loyalty. Boyd's mastery of myth and symbol, the magic of his craftsmanship and the sharpness of his perception assured his success. For him, Europe and England became home, even while he continued to draw on his Australian pictorial vocabulary with which to respond to the present. His paintings from these years include the Diana and Actaeon series (1962), the Nebuchadnezzar series (1966–69) and the Potter series (1967–69), which are a tribute to his father, and some fine portraits, including *Four Portraits of Joseph Brown* (1969). Among the stage designs from these years are *Renard* for the 1961 Edinburgh Festival and *Electra* for Covent Garden in 1963. In 1964–65 Boyd completed twenty-one pastels and sixteen lithographs to illustrate T. S. R. Boase's book on St Francis.

[*Continued overleaf*]

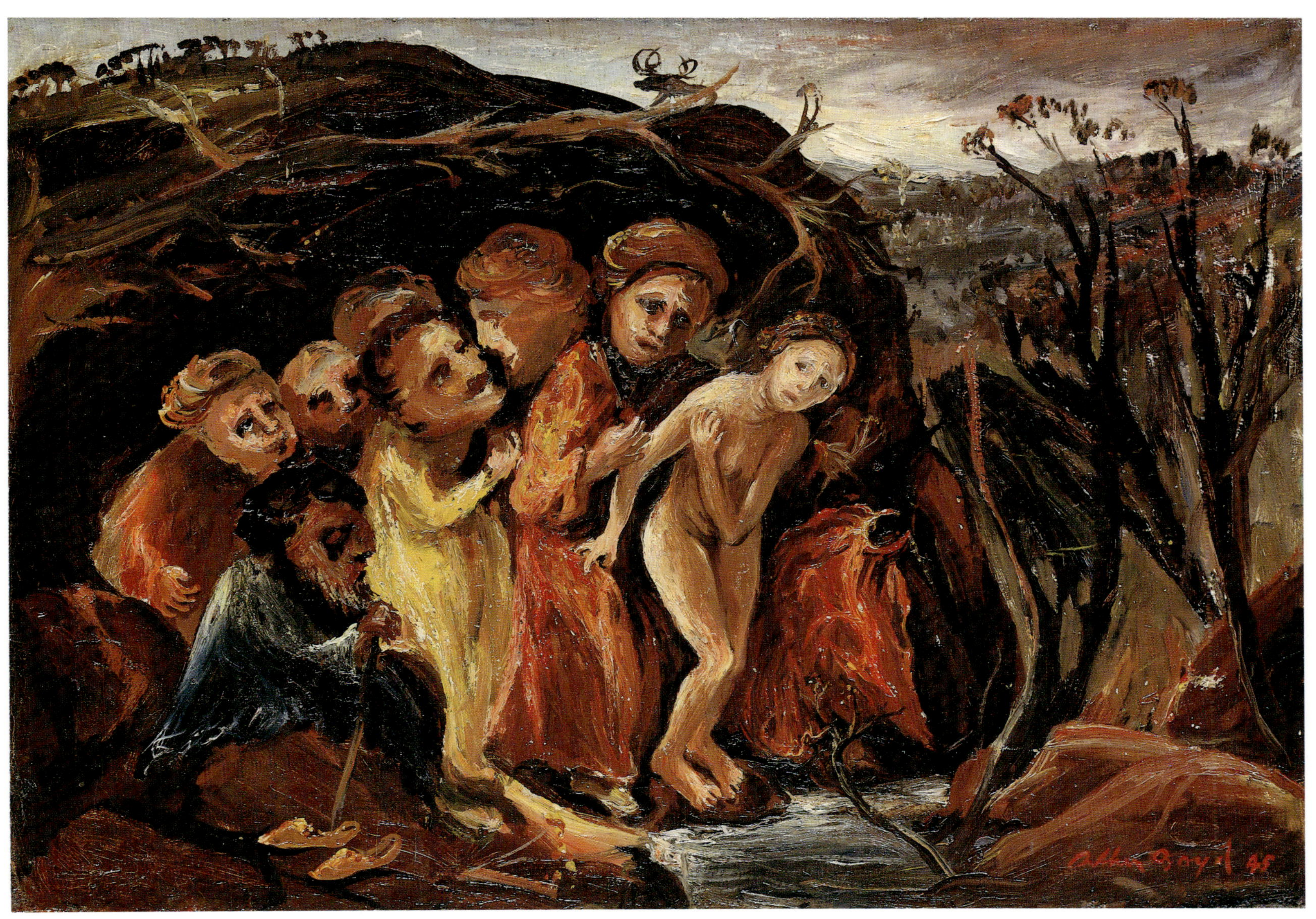

73 *Susanna with the Elders*

ARTHUR BOYD

Born 1920

Nebuchadnezzar Running in the Rain, 1968–71

Oil on canvas
174.5 × 183 cm
Australian National Gallery, Canberra
The Arthur Boyd Gift 1975

In 1966 Boyd began a series of more than thirty-five paintings and seventeen drawings on the theme of Nebuchadnezzar, the Babylonian king of the Book of Daniel, who becomes so consumed by power, wealth and greed that he is condemned to madness and for seven years wanders in the wilderness, where he was driven from men 'and began eating grass like cattle, and his body was drenched with the dew of heaven, until his hair had grown like eagles' feathers, and his nails like birds' claws . . . his heart was made like that of beasts, and his dwelling place was with the wild donkeys'. (Daniel 4:33, 5:21)

Boyd's paintings take this biblical text as his starting point. He makes no attempt to tell the whole story, nor even to translate the narrative into a contemporary setting in the same way as he had done with many of his other religious paintings. The series follows Nebuchadnezzar in his frenzy of madness through desert and Australian bushland as he is metamorphosed into a wild animal, runs on all fours, eats grass, grows feathers, is attacked by crows, goes blind and meets a lion. All the time he is consumed by lust, his genitals on fire. Eventually, a rainbow heralds hope, but Boyd does not allow Nebuchadnezzar to be saved.

These paintings are perhaps the most uncompromising of Boyd's statements. Lust and greed for gold are shown as the greatest evils, capable of driving even the wise leader beyond rationality and basic humanity into personal, psychological and physical dissolution. The intensity of Boyd's personal involvement in the paintings is reflected in the urgency of the surfaces, where paint has been squeezed directly from the tube, laid on with the palms of the hands or with fingers. There are no 'watchers' in these paintings; the artist has become the subject. T. S. R. Boase, the biblical scholar for whom Boyd began the series, sees Boyd as 'a second Daniel come to judgment of our contemporary obscure and secret impulses.'[1]

No precedent exists in Western art history for such immense concentration on Nebuchadnezzar. The prodigious quality of Boyd's imagination is unsurpassed, his debt to William Blake's coloured print of Nebuchadnezzar on hands and knees eating grass is more than cancelled out by the power of this series. In *Nebuchadnezzar Running in the Rain*, the king, like an animal, runs through thick white rain, his body filled with the gold coins that symbolize crass materialism.

1. T. S. R. Boase, Arthur Boyd: *Nebuchadnezzar* (London: Thames and Hudson, 1972), p. 42.

In 1971 Boyd returned to Australia to take up a Creative Art Fellowship at the Australian National University. Shortly after, he began paintings of landscape around Nowra. These, the Shoalhaven River paintings, together with the Narcissus series, are the major paintings of the seventies, a decade that saw Boyd more frequently in Australia, especially after he bought the properties Riversdale and Bundanong on the banks of the Shoalhaven. But his major base continued to be in Suffolk, England.

In the eighties Boyd has continued to paint series on the Shoalhaven and to work in etching and aquatints on the Narcissus theme. In 1984 he was commissioned to create the tapestry for the new Parliament House, Canberra, and to paint sixteen canvases for the foyer of the State Theatre, Victorian Arts Centre, Melbourne. He was the Australian artist chosen to be extensively represented at the Venice Biennale in 1988.

[*Continued overleaf*]

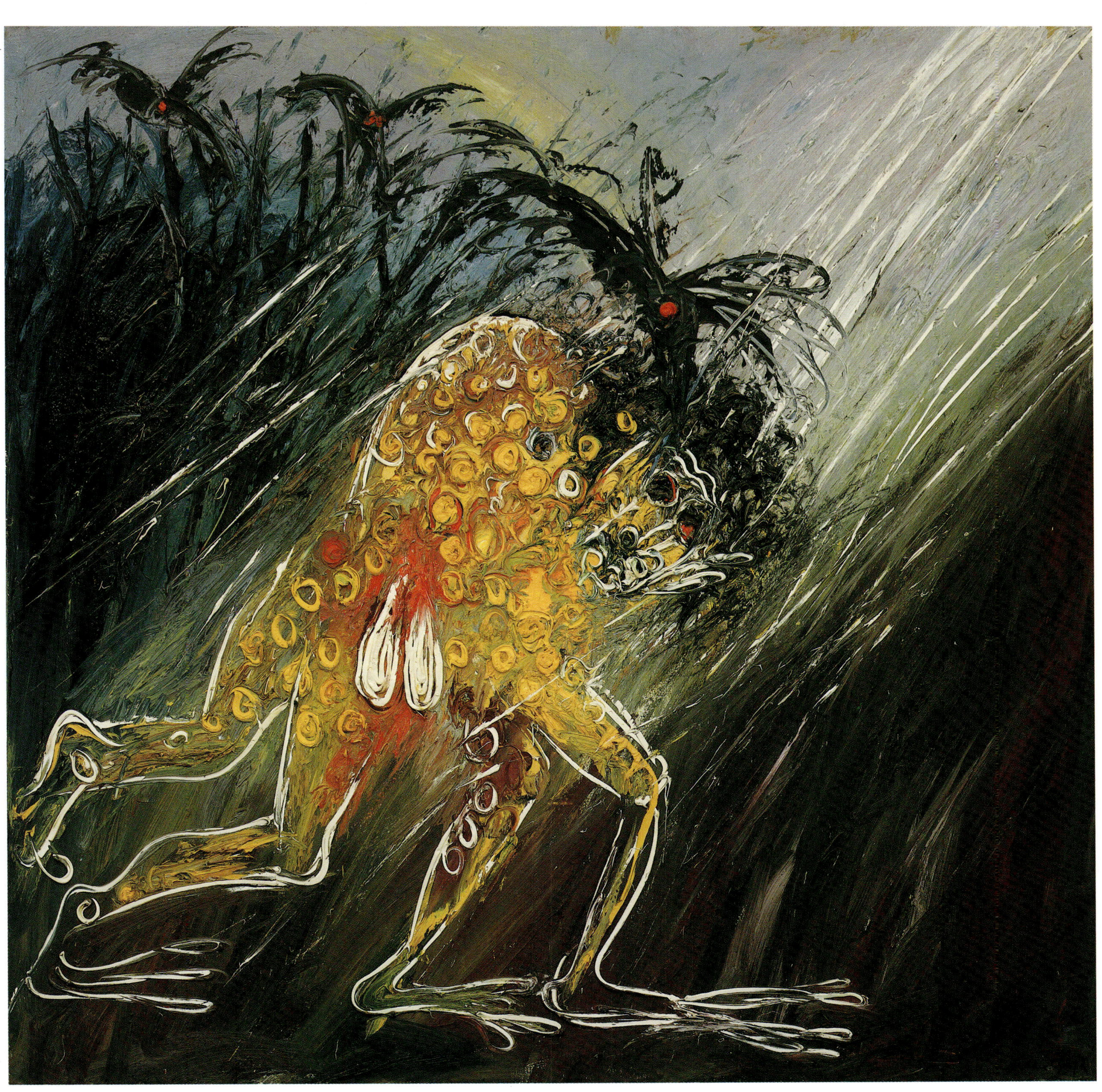

74 *Nebuchadnezzar Running in the Rain*

ARTHUR BOYD

Born 1920

Crucifixion, Shoalhaven, 1979–80

Oil on canvas
185 × 177 cm
Collection of the artist

Just as London provided Boyd with a new creative stimulus in the 1960s, the countryside around the Shoalhaven stimulated a surge of painting in the 1970s. After a decade of intense work in England on allegorical series such as Nebuchadnezzar, Boyd drenched himself in the heat and the floods of this new landscape. Its drama captured him. 'It has a knife-edged clarity,' he said. 'Impressionism could never have been born here, but Wagner could easily have composed here. He could not have composed at Port Phillip Bay. In fact, I think Wagner lived in the Shoalhaven.'[1] Most, but not all of the paintings of this area are without allegorical content and complex symbolism. It is as though the wilderness here bewitched Boyd's eyes and energy and fed his lyricism.

Crucifixion, Shoalhaven and *Crucifixion and Rose* are exceptions. They startle so much because of the juxtaposition of the crucifix, Christianity's most powerful symbol, against the Australian landscape. The crosses stand, not on the hill of Golgotha, but in the still waters of the Shoalhaven River. Unlike the crucifixes in Boyd's earlier paintings such as *The Mockers* and *The Mourners,* where the figures writhe in the midst of surging crowds, these stand starkly, without visual relief. In each painting the image is frontal, nude, uncompromising but without overt drama. They stand inert and neutral in a landscape which is realistically recreated.

In *Crucifixion, Shoalhaven,* Boyd has broken with a two-thousand-year tradition by placing a woman on the cross. 'I do not believe it is enough to say *he* represented all of us,' Boyd said in 1987. 'I do not wish to separate the idea of suffering by allowing just the male to be seen. There has been an awakening consciousness of the potential and force of women in our time.'[2] The picture is startlingly simple in its composition. Three horizontal bands divide the picture surface: sky, hillside and water. Each is a straightforward statement of visual reality, acutely rendered. The vertical of the cross is repeated in the trees on the hill. All is still. It is up to the viewer to cope with the dislocation and confrontation of tradition.

1. Quoted in *The Artist and the River,* by Sandra McGrath (Sydney: Bay Books, 1982), p. 62.
2. Interview with author, Suffolk, 3 September 1987.

Arthur Boyd's achievements have been acclaimed in articles, monographs and film. His world status is recognized internationally, yet he remains a person who is outside any mainstream of contemporary painting. His works pay obvious homage to past masters, particularly to Bosch, Brueghel, Leonardo, Rembrandt and Picasso, and his basic symbols are those devised before 1940. Yet he remains an artist with a clear sense of himself and the contribution he can make within society. Herein lies some of his genius. His images and symbols continue to exploit the limitations of both time and space. They rarely delineate. Even when they occur in paintings that are quite descriptive, they move beyond the particular moment. Boyd's art reaches beyond the merely transitory to celebrate, capture or comment on what life is and can mean. His is an art consistently on the side of the deeply human, the oppressed and the forgotten. In this sense Arthur Boyd is one of the great religious painters of our time.

1. See Grazia Gunn, *Arthur Boyd: Seven Persistent Images* (Australian National Gallery, 1985).
2. Ibid, p. 59.

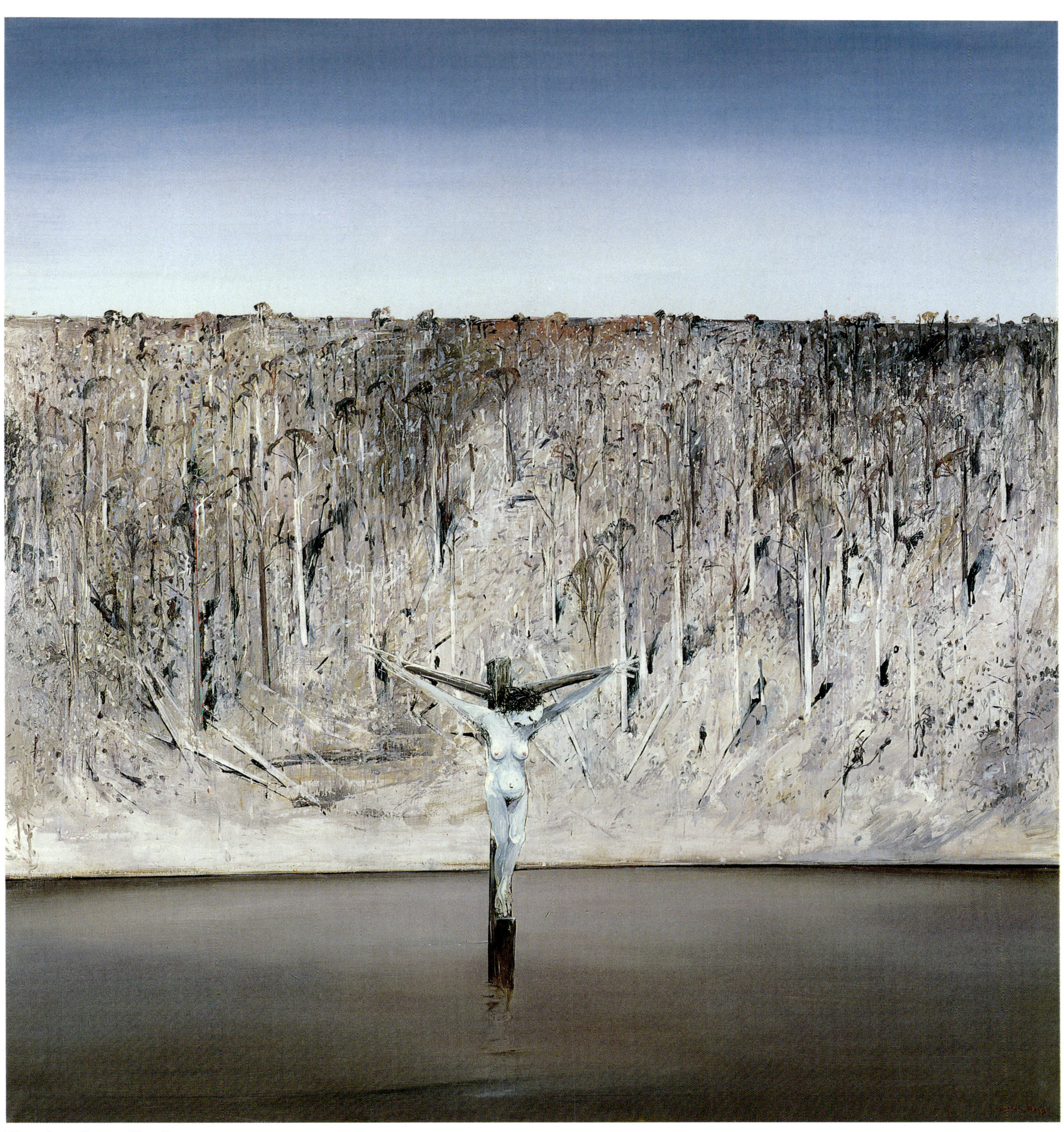

75 *Crucifixion, Shoalhaven*

ARTHUR BOYD

Born 1920

Crucifixion and Rose, 1979–80

Oil on canvas
155 × 123 cm
Collection of the artist

In *Crucifixion and Rose* Boyd has used horizontal bands to reflect the warmth of a changing sky. In the river a single rose floats by the crucified one. In Christian iconology the rose symbolizes the Virgin Mary—Rosa Mystica, of the Litany of Loreto. By association it can indicate purity, virginity or even celestial happiness. But in the Shoalhaven paintings Boyd has given it another meaning; it is the English rose, symbol of an English culture which cannot take root in the ruggedness of the Australian climate. The inclusion of the rose is meant as a warning. As he said in 1982, 'The rose represents the desperate attempts of the Europeans to impose their culture on an essentially primitive landscape. It floats because it cannot take root. If it does, it destroys, like lantana.'[1]

> I'd like to feel that through my work there is a possibility of making a contribution to a social progression or enlightenment. It would be nice if the creative effort or impulse was connected with a conscious contribution to society, a sort of duty or service. I think you have to be able to make something which does involve concepts and ideas.[2]

1. McGrath, *Artist and the River* p. 272.
2. Grazia Gunn, *Arthur Boyd: Seven Persistent Images* (Australian National Gallery, 1985).

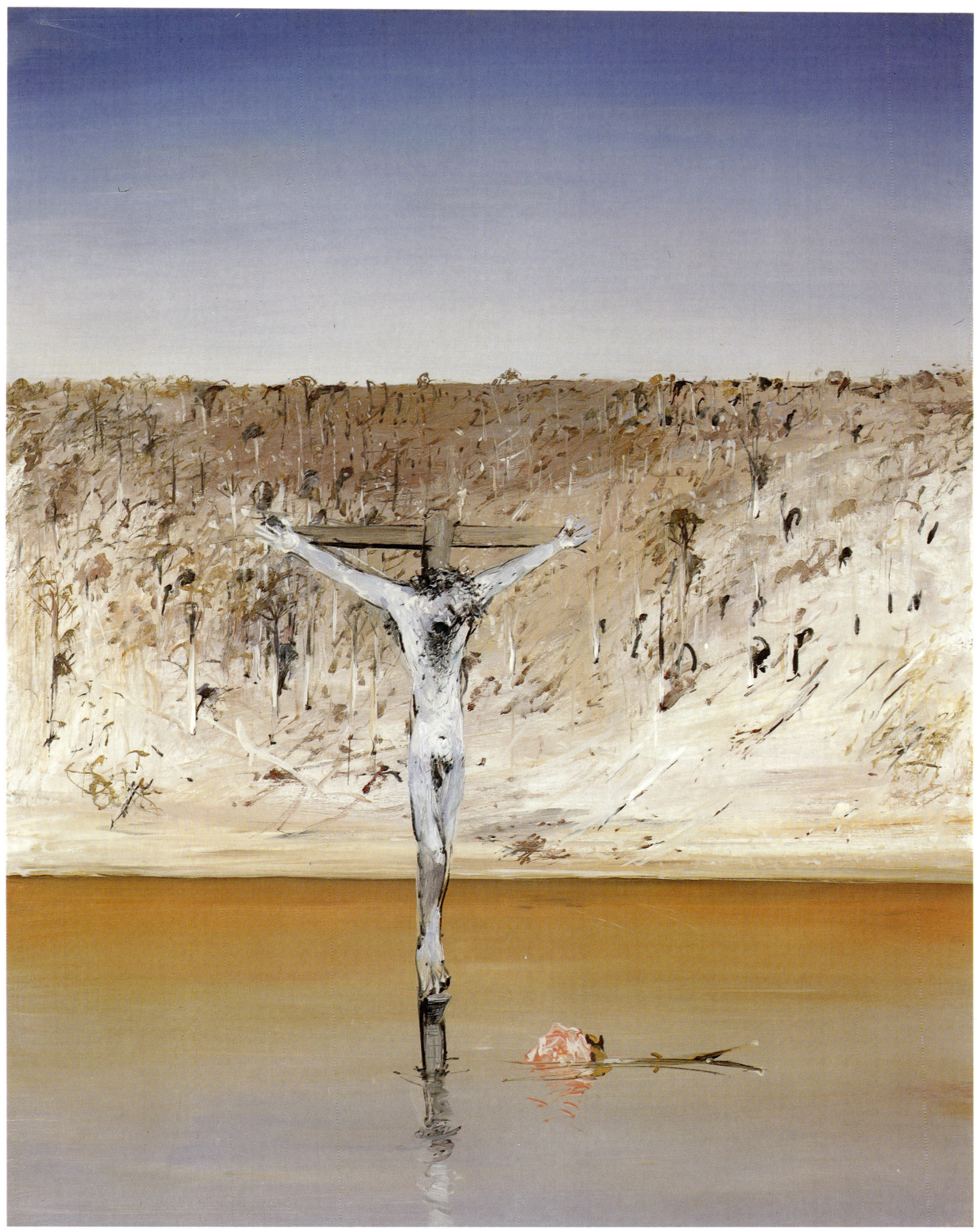

76 *Crucifixion and Rose*

LEONARD FRENCH

Born 1928

The Seven Days, 1964–65 — *The First Day*

Enamel on hessian-covered hardboard
183 × 160 cm
Australian National University, Canberra

The Seven Days series was completed in 1964–65 and shown in Sydney in 1965. The paintings were purchased anonymously as a gift for the Australian National University and were then exhibited in London at the Commonwealth Institute. As a series they relate closely to the six Genesis paintings which Leonard French submitted for the Helena Rubinstein Scholarship in 1961 as well as to the Campion paintings of 1962. They employ many of the same basic symbols—cross, square, fish, circle—and the same technique of building up a rich surface pattern through many layers of enamel and glaze combined with the use of pure gold leaf. Although they evoke in themselves a strong sense of procession, of beginning and of new life, they also signal the end of French's preoccupation with explicitly religious themes. His interest in the hero, the heraldic, and the big symbolic statement were to remain.

> In the beginning of creation, when God made heaven and earth, the earth was without form and void, with a darkness over the face of the abyss, and a mighty wind that swept over the surface of the waters. God said, 'Let there be light', and there was light, and God saw that the light was good, and he separated light from darkness. He called the light day, and the darkness night. So evening came, and morning came, the first day. [Genesis 1: 1–5]

In *The First Day* Leonard French has created a painting of calm and order. Light and darkness are separated, and the light is filled with embryonic forms and basic symbols; the darkness hides its life. French remembers how these paintings came to be: 'On the Greek island of Samos in the summer of 1962, my son swam out through the clear water and on reaching me asked, 'How did it all begin?' 'It began here in all this clear whiteness.' These paintings grew out of my attempt to answer his question.[1]

1. *Daily Telegraph* (Sydney), 16 November 1965.

LEONARD FRENCH was born in Brunswick, Melbourne, in 1928. He left school aged fourteen, was apprenticed to a signwriter the following year and attended evening art classes at Melbourne Technical College between 1944 and 1947. At the age of nineteen, and on his own initiative, he completed two large frescoes on the walls of the local Congregational church in Brunswick in the style of the Mexican social realist painter José Orozco. (He supplied his own powder paint for the colour and plaster for coating the surface of the wall and was paid five pounds by a somewhat disgruntled congregation.) He spent 1949–51 in Europe, searching, as he said, 'for the place where real artists lived'. By the time he arrived back in Melbourne he had a working knowledge of, and great admiration for, Celtic forms, the Belgians Marcel Gromaire and Constant Permeke, the big, mechanized forms of Fernand Léger and the colour theories of orphic cubism and Robert Delaunay. But the event that stands out most for him now from that time is viewing Paolo Uccello's *Battle of San Romano*.

[*Continued overleaf*]

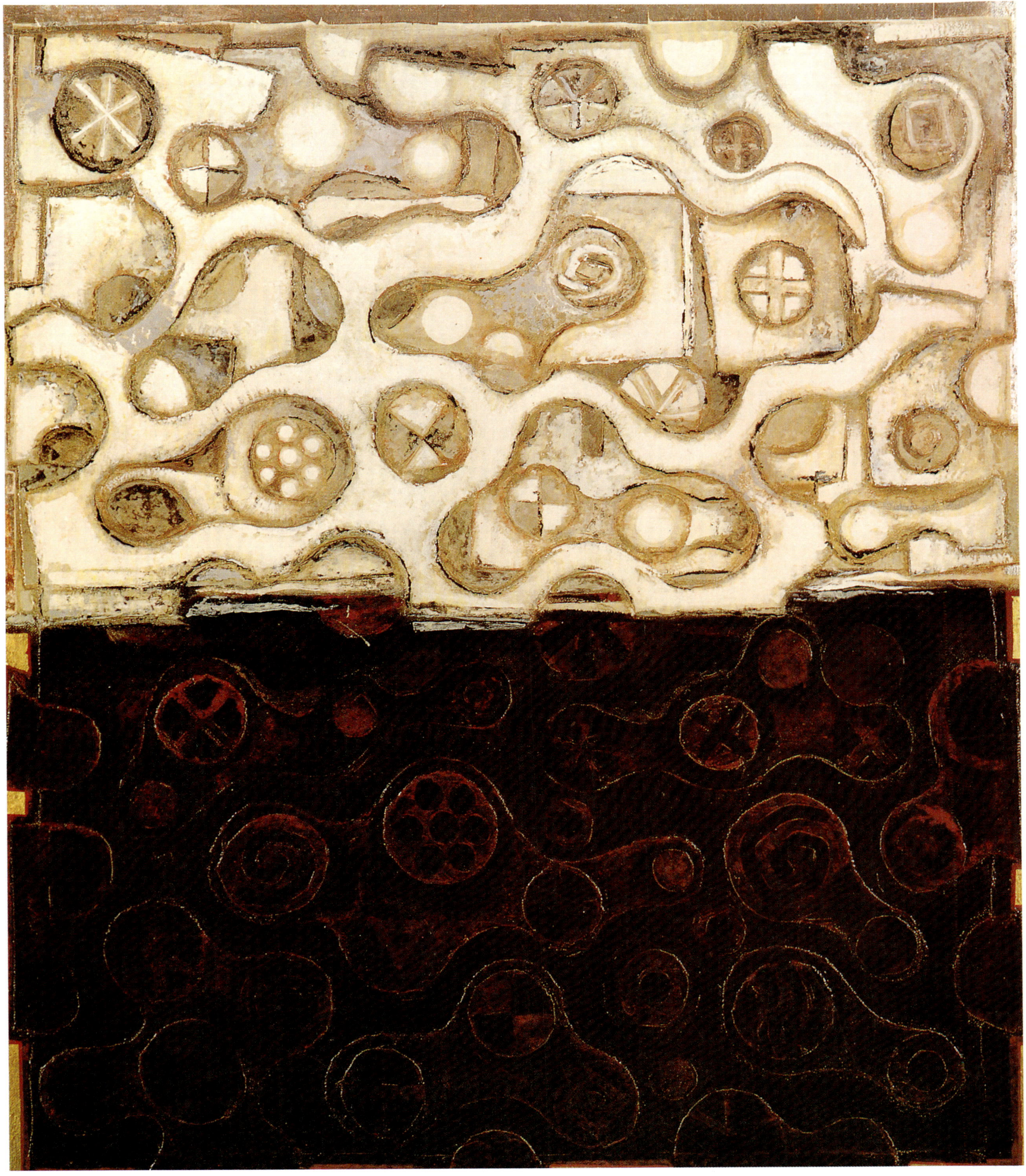

77 *The First Day*

LEONARD FRENCH

Born 1928

The Second Day

Enamel on hessian-covered hardboard
183 × 160 cm
Australian National University, Canberra

> God said, 'Let there be a vault between the waters, to separate water from water.' So God made the vault, and separated the water under the vault from the water above it, and so it was; and God called the vault heaven. Evening came, and morning came, a second day. [Genesis 1: 6–8]

In *The Second Day* the dividing line of *The First Day* has become a horizon. French has added rich and glowing ribbons of rainbow colours and called it 'sea'. Within the sea, life is already forming in the shape of a great fish with circle head and eye. The static symbols of *The First Day*—circle, cross and square—are no longer obvious. On this day the dark red earth struggles for breath and the sky is crowded with flapping bird forms. *The Second Day* is a painting of the birthing of earth, sea and sky.

From 1952 until the present, most of French's work has been concerned with heroic themes, especially the theme of the journey or battle against great odds, the mythical struggle of good over evil. His early series, the Iliad and Odyssey (1952–55), used strong, angular forms in semi-abstract cubist compositions, but by 1961, when his Book of Genesis paintings were exhibited for the Helena Rubinstein Scholarship, it was clear that he had evolved a powerful basic set of symbols and colours and a technique that set him apart from other Australian painters of his generation. Rudy Komon, the Sydney gallery director, offered him security and patronage and thus secured French's immediate future. At this time he won the Sulman, Crouch and Perth prizes.

[*Continued overleaf*]

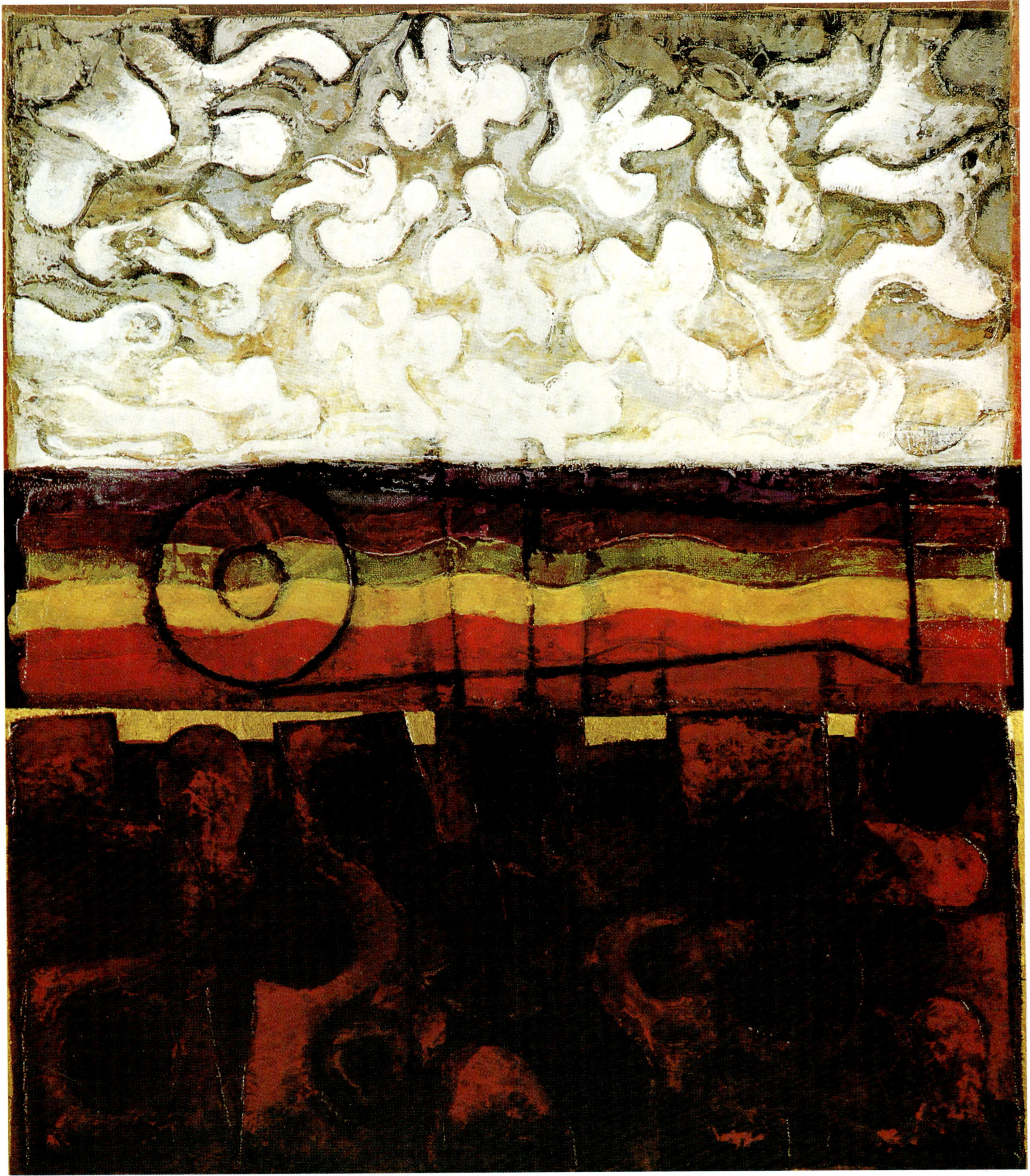

78 *The Second Day*

LEONARD FRENCH

Born 1928

The Third Day

Enamel on hessian-covered hardboard
183 × 160 cm
Australian National University, Canberra

God said, 'Let the waters under heaven be gathered into one place, so that dry land may appear'; and so it was. God called the dry land earth, and the gathering of the waters he called seas; and God saw that it was good. Then God said, 'Let the earth produce fresh growth, let there be on the earth plants bearing seed, fruit-trees bearing fruit each with fruit according to its kind.' So it was; the earth yielded fresh growth, plants bearing seed according to their kind and trees bearing fruit each with seed according to its kind; and God saw that it was good. Evening came, and morning came, a third day. [Genesis 1: 9–13]

The rainbow sea of *The Second Day* has disappeared. The sea in *The Third Day* has become the underworld, a mysterious deep green band filled with fish. The earth has taken its place in the red centre and holds three great circles crossed through and separated by a ribbon of white. The circles are replete with meaning—perfection, ideal motion, wheel of life, head, sun, shield, machinery cogs. At different times in his painting, French has used the circle to suggest all of these. Here he is thinking of the circle especially as the turtle, creature of sea and land, symbolic of protected life.[1] The ribbon of white is the serpent. The third horizontal band is the heavens. It is cool white and filled with celestial beings in aureoles of white light. For French, they are the birds that fill the air.

1. In many mythologies the turtle is a creator god or a saviour on whose back the world was formed. The 'voice of the turtle' is the echo on earth of the deity's voice, and in Christianity it is the voice of the Holy Spirit. French was aware of the richness of this symbol.

In 1962, in his Campion series, French again picked up the theme of the hero and used it to build a series of images rich in symbolism and stunning in their use of thin glazes over enamels and pure gold leaf. They were not meant to be biographical, although Evelyn Waugh's *Edmund Campion* was the original inspiration. 'It is the symbol I painted, not the man,' French said.[1]

French then left for Greece, his avowed intention to study Greek art, particularly icons, at their source. Secretly, he was escaping from the 'metaphysical impasse' to which the Genesis and Campion paintings had brought him. Instead, his new work was to retain his distinctive formal language, themes and technique but to incorporate a new use of whites and creams reminiscent of the light and the architecture of the Greek islands. One of the new paintings, *Ancient Fragments*, won the Blake Prize for Religious Art in 1963.

[*Continued overleaf*]

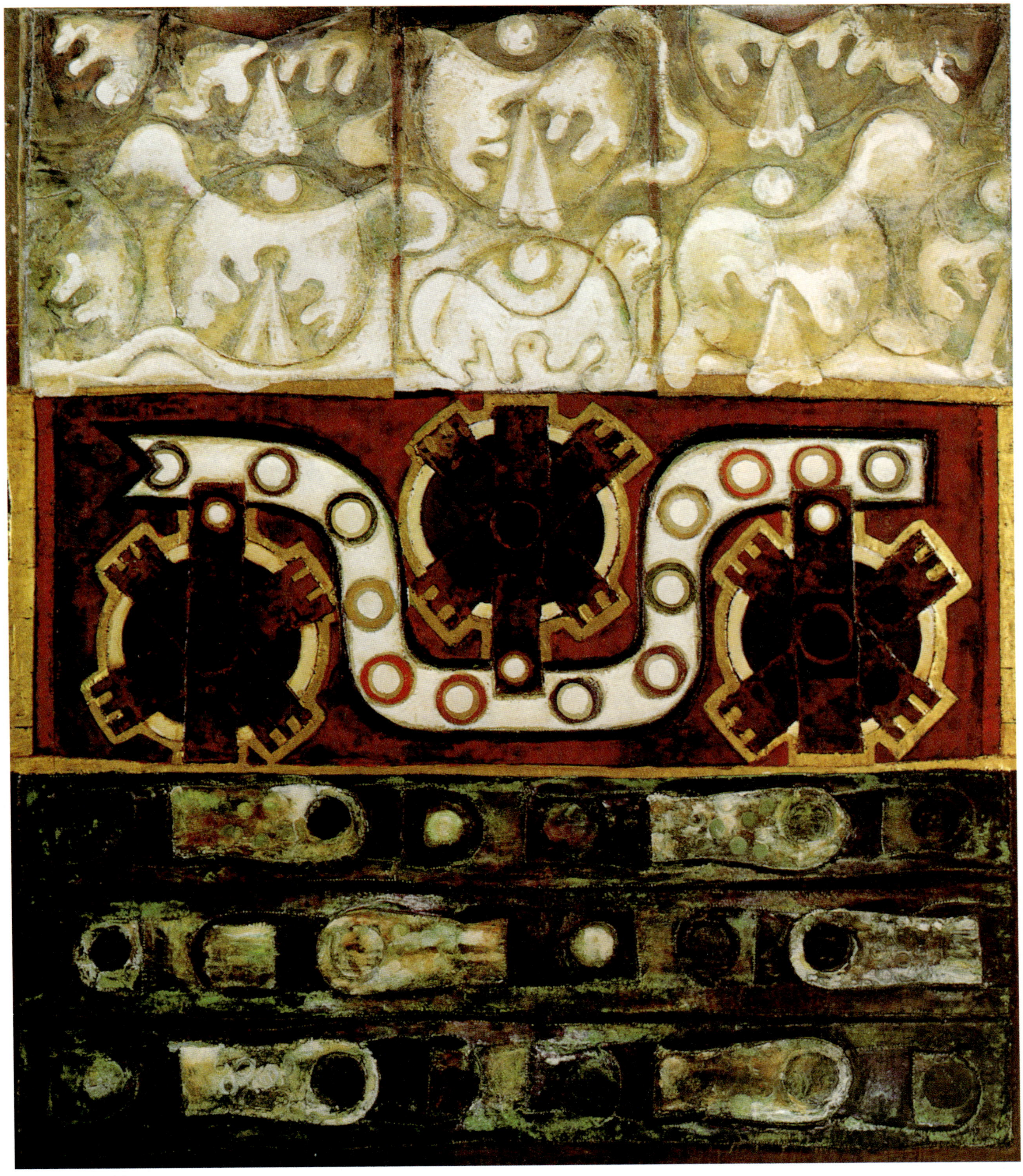

79 *The Third Day*

LEONARD FRENCH

Born 1928

The Fourth Day

Enamel on hessian-covered hardboard
183 × 160 cm
Australian National University, Canberra

> God said, 'Let there be light in the vault of heaven to separate day from night, and let them serve as signs both for festivals and for seasons and years. Let them also shine in the vault of heaven to give light on earth.' So it was; God made the two great lights, the greater to govern the day and the lesser to govern the night; and with them he made the stars. God put these lights in the vault of heaven to give light on earth, to govern day and night, and to separate light from darkness; and God saw that it was good. Evening came, and morning came, a fourth day. [Genesis 1: 14–19]

In *The Fourth Day* French ritualizes and solemnizes the separation of night and day and of sky and earth. Three gold banners hang in the Greek-white sky. The two small banners hold circles. Within one is the white bird of light, of peace, of Pentecost; within the other, the cross of night, of suffering, of redemption. Between them is the fish. In the Campion paintings, the fish was often Campion the Jesuit martyr, alive, suffering, transcendent; in Christian iconography it is Christ, who by his death brought new life. Here the giant fish becomes a phallic symbol penetrating the solid earth to give life to what is there. Deep in the earth a man is asleep, entwined by the serpent. There is no movement, just heraldic splendour and the silence before dawn.

About 1963 he began work on two important projects—the Seven Days, a new creation series, and the stained-glass ceiling (50 by 14.6 metres) for the Great Hall of the new building of the National Gallery of Victoria. Both used many of the same symbols: circle, mandala, leaf, turtle, cross, serpent. French constructed the ceiling in segments in his studio at Heathcote; it was transported on trucks and lifted into frameworks prepared by the architect, Roy Grounds.

French's paintings after the mid-1960s often reflect a newer mood of pessimism, although always within his already established style. The Raft series (1968–71) has as hero a solitary man, adrift against the elements. A visit to North America on a Harkness Fellowship produced the epic Journey paintings of 1970. A powerful anti-war statement, the Death of a Revolution series, followed after he returned from South America in 1976. In these paintings, the hero figure is the paradoxical anti-hero of a general, symbolized by a red jacket, shot through with bullet holes. 'I saw [in South America and elsewhere] that nothing would change', he said. 'It would always be the same for the oppressor as for the oppressed, waiting to be knocked over by the next group.'[2]

[*Continued overleaf*]

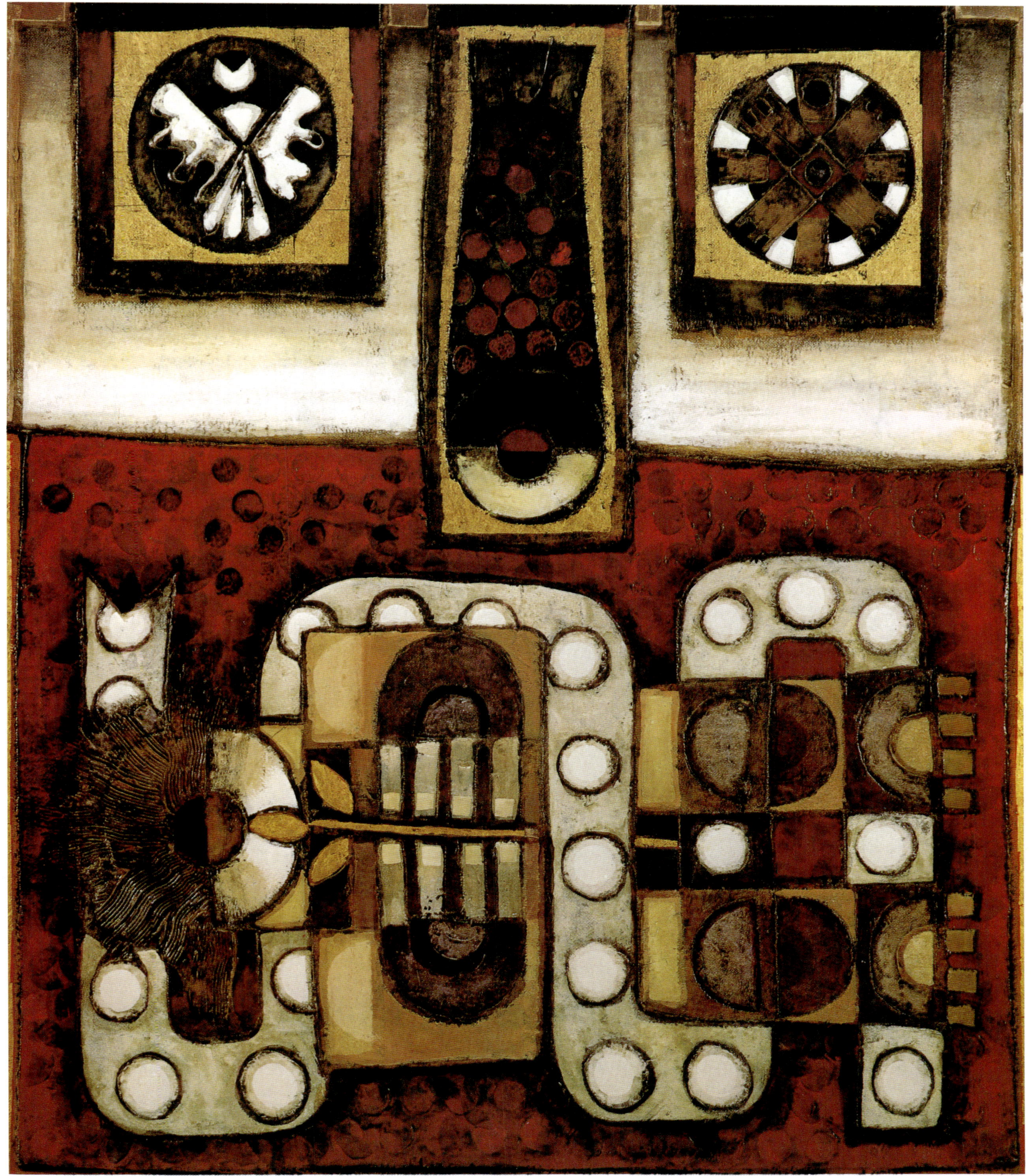

80 *The Fourth Day*

LEONARD FRENCH

Born 1928

The Fifth Day

Enamel on hessian-covered hardboard
183 × 160 cm
Australian National University, Canberra

> God said, 'Let the waters teem with countless living creatures, and let birds fly above the earth across the vault of heaven . . . and God saw that it was good. So He blessed them and said, 'Be fruitful and increase, fill the waters of the seas; and let the birds increase on land.' Evening came, and morning came, a fifth day. God said, 'Let the earth bring forth living creatures, according to their kind: cattle, reptiles, and wild animals, all according to their kind' . . . Then he said, 'Let us make man in our image and likeness to rule the fish in the sea, the birds of heaven, the cattle, all wild animals on earth and all reptiles that crawl upon the earth.' So God created man in his own image; in the image of God he created him. [Genesis 1: 20–26]

Man, asleep and entwined by the serpent in *The Fourth Day*, breaks free; he pushes up through the earth, which heaves to allow him to stand upright for the first time, his hand thrust into the sky. Now he is clothed in the banners of the first days. He is, French has said, 'garbed in the rituals that his life will bring'. A chasuble shape carries familiar emblems and symbols—fish, bird, circle, sun, square, diamond, turtle, leaf. In the centre of the cross is the ancient chi-rho, the monograph of Christ seen by Constantine on the eve of his battle with Maxentius. The power of the serpent has been broken at this new birth.

His Fire and Rain series of 1978 provided a brief respite, but in 1981 he exhibited a group of paintings, A Dark Circus (see Plate 58) which attack specifically the violence in Latin America through images of a child's circus. The optimism of the Seven Days was replaced by a brooding pessimism, not always obvious because of the rich surface of the enamels and the gold leaf. 'The dark image behind the bright image,' French said in 1981, 'I've been brooding about that for a long time.'[3]

[*Continued overleaf*]

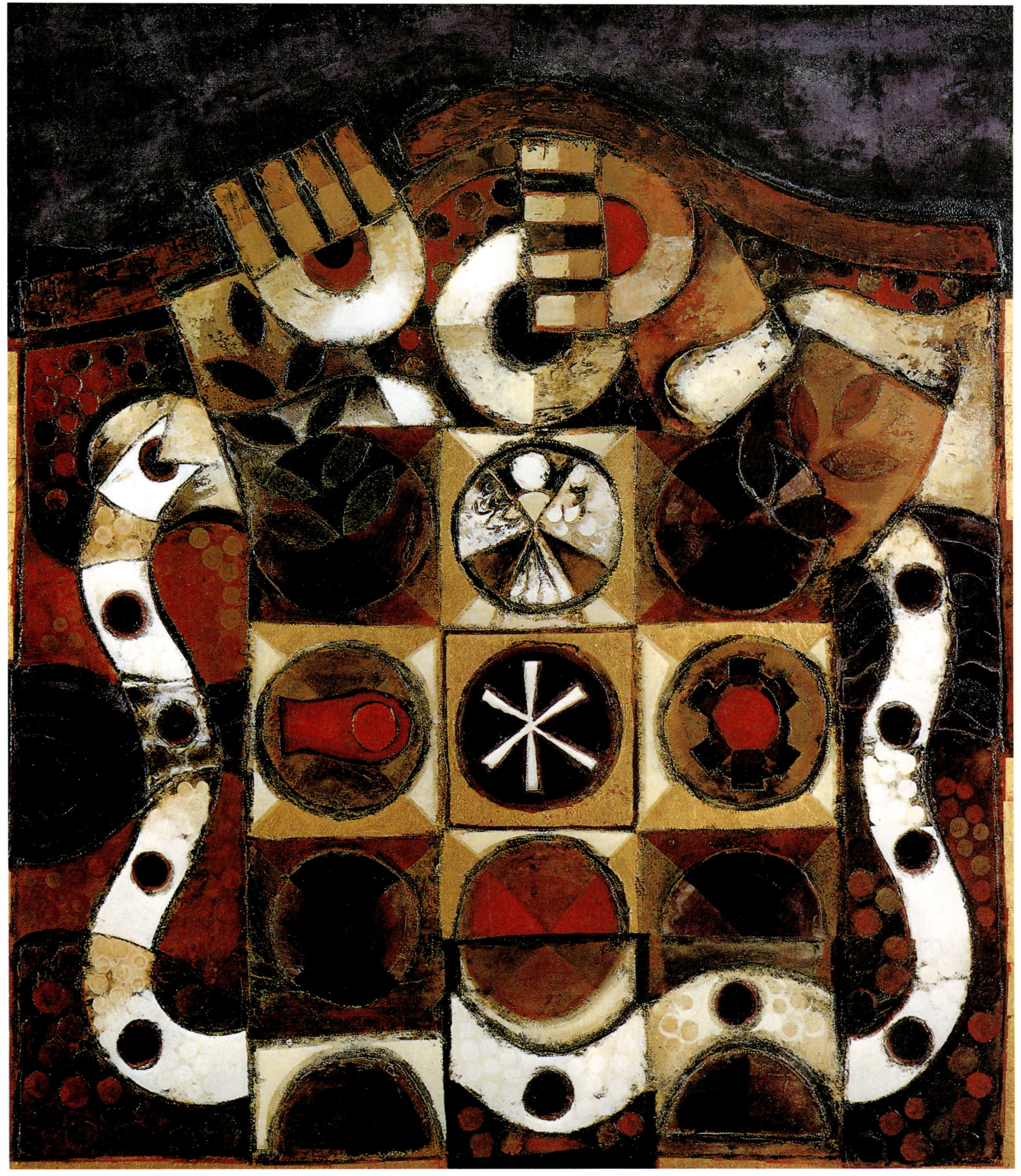

81 *The Fifth Day*

Leonard French

Born 1928

The Sixth Day

Enamel on hessian-covered hardboard
183 × 160 cm
Australian National University, Canberra

> So God created man in his own image; in the image of God he created him; male and female he created them. He blessed them and said to them, 'Be fruitful and increase, fill the earth and subdue it, rule over the fish in the sea, the birds of heaven, and every living thing that moves on the earth.' God also said, 'I give you all plants that bear seed everywhere on earth, and every tree bearing fruit which yields seed: they shall be yours for food. All green plants I give for food to the wild animals, to all the birds of heaven, and to all reptiles on earth, every living creature.' So it was; and God saw all that he had made, and it was very good. Evening came, and morning came, a sixth day. [Genesis 1: 27–31]

The garden has become lush and beautiful. Leaves have become branches, and branches trees which frame the central action. The serpent, once harmless and decorative, is now sinister and black. Man and woman embrace in the presence of evil.

The Sixth Day is a celebration of what has gone on in the other five paintings. All creation is assembled to welcome the first man and the first woman. They are the life principle and will care for the earth; they have been told to nurture creation and not to dominate it. Leonard French understands this. *The Sixth Day* is a liturgy of life respected.

In 1982 French began what he considers is his most important work—a huge anti-apartheid mural for the Brenthurst Library in the South African home of Harry Oppenheimer, chairman of De Beers. Unable to portray political brutality directly, French clothed his anger in the metaphor of a medieval battle which takes place on a bridge. People are caught and destroyed as the bridge collapses and burns at the height of the bloody battle. The symbolism of a war waged in the name of God was transparent enough. The mural, and Leonard French's visit, were totally ignored by art critics and the South African press. Back in Australia, French worked out his anger and shock at the situation in Pretoria in a powerful series, The Bridge, shown in the Powell Street Gallery, Melbourne, in 1985.

[*Continued overleaf*]

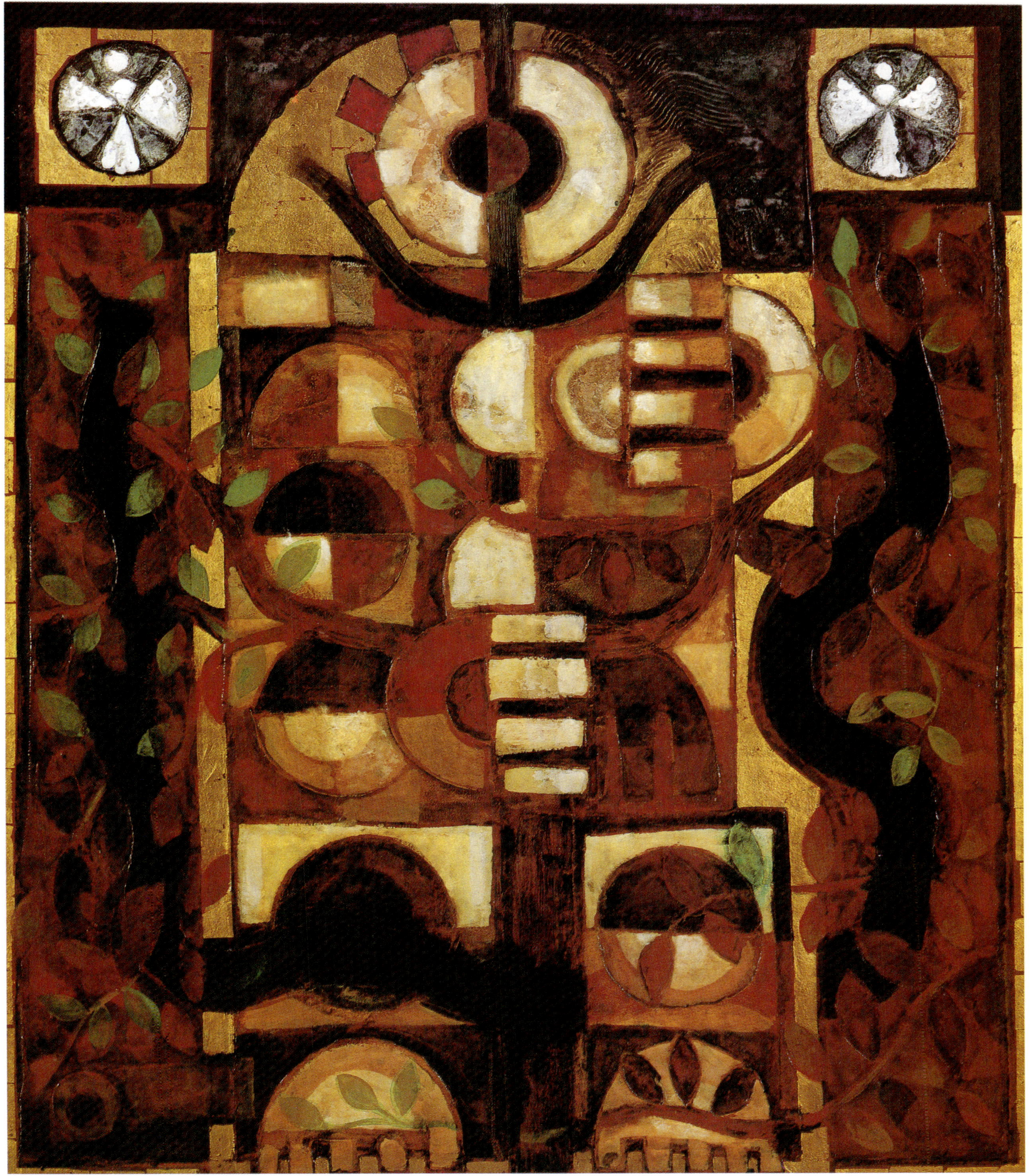

82 *The Sixth Day*

LEONARD FRENCH

Born 1928

The Seventh Day

Enamel on hessian-covered hardboard
Circular, diameter 430 cm
Australian National University, Canberra

> Thus heaven and earth were completed with all their mighty throng. On the sixth day God completed all the work he had been doing, and on the seventh day he ceased from all his work. God blessed the seventh day and made it holy, because on that day he ceased from all the work he had set himself to do. [Genesis 2: 1–3]

From the time when he conceived the idea for the series, French planned the 4.3-metre circle of *The Seventh Day* to be a culmination and a climax. As he said, 'All the days became one and everything was alive on the earth.' *The Seventh Day* is like a huge garden of concentric circles.[1] Cross and circle, two most powerful symbols, interplay for visual attention in a way reminiscent of, but different from, the art of Victor Vasareley. The innermost circle is a tiled garden, a 'sacred geometry'. It is also the centre of a large cross. The upright of the cross holds the sun at its head and the moon and stars at its feet; on the horizontal beam are hands extended in open blessing or crucifixion. In the next circle are two serpents, fish and the rainbow of earlier days. In the outer circle, two horizontal figures rest in the darkness; gardens and sea teem with life, and banners again proclaim that this is a ritual celebration, not a literary narrative. *The Seventh Day* is dance, symphony, a hymn of praise, an Easter *Exultet*.

1. French had seen such a garden on a visit to Peking: 'It had a circular wall. You'd come out of this and there was another circle and another garden . . . a sort of celestial garden' (quoted in the *Australian*, 6 May 1967).

Leonard French has never stood easily within any of the mainstream movements of contemporary art. When the Melbourne figurative painters such as Nolan, Boyd, Tucker, and Perceval were friends and colleagues in the 1940s, French was an apprentice in an industrial suburb and did not even know of their existence. By 1959, when his success was acknowledged and his paintings easily recognized, he opposed the Antipodean Exhibition on the grounds that it was too provincial a manifesto.[4] But beside the painterly abstract expressionism of Sydney painters such as Olsen and Rapotec, or even his Melbourne mentor and friend Roger Kemp, his symbols and his technique looked studied and even traditional.

French's stature as artist and architectural craftsman in stained glass was publicly recognized with a doctorate of laws (*honoris causa*) at Monash University in 1972; his work is held in major galleries and private collections in Australia and overseas. Among his other stained-glass commissions are windows in the Australian National Library, Canberra, and windows at La Trobe and Monash universities in Melbourne. At the time of writing (1988), he was completing forty-seven windows and an altar painting for the chapel in Haileybury College in Springvale, Victoria.

Leonard French lives in Heathcote, outside Melbourne.

1. Vincent Buckley and Leonard French, *The Campion Paintings* (Melbourne: Grayflower Publications, 1962), p. 15.
2. *Age*, 25 February 1977.
3. *Weekend Australian*, 8–9 August 1981.
4. In a conversation with the author on 11 March 1988, French differed from Bernard Smith's account in *The Death of the Artist as Hero* (Melbourne: Oxford University Press, 1988), pp. 201, 208.

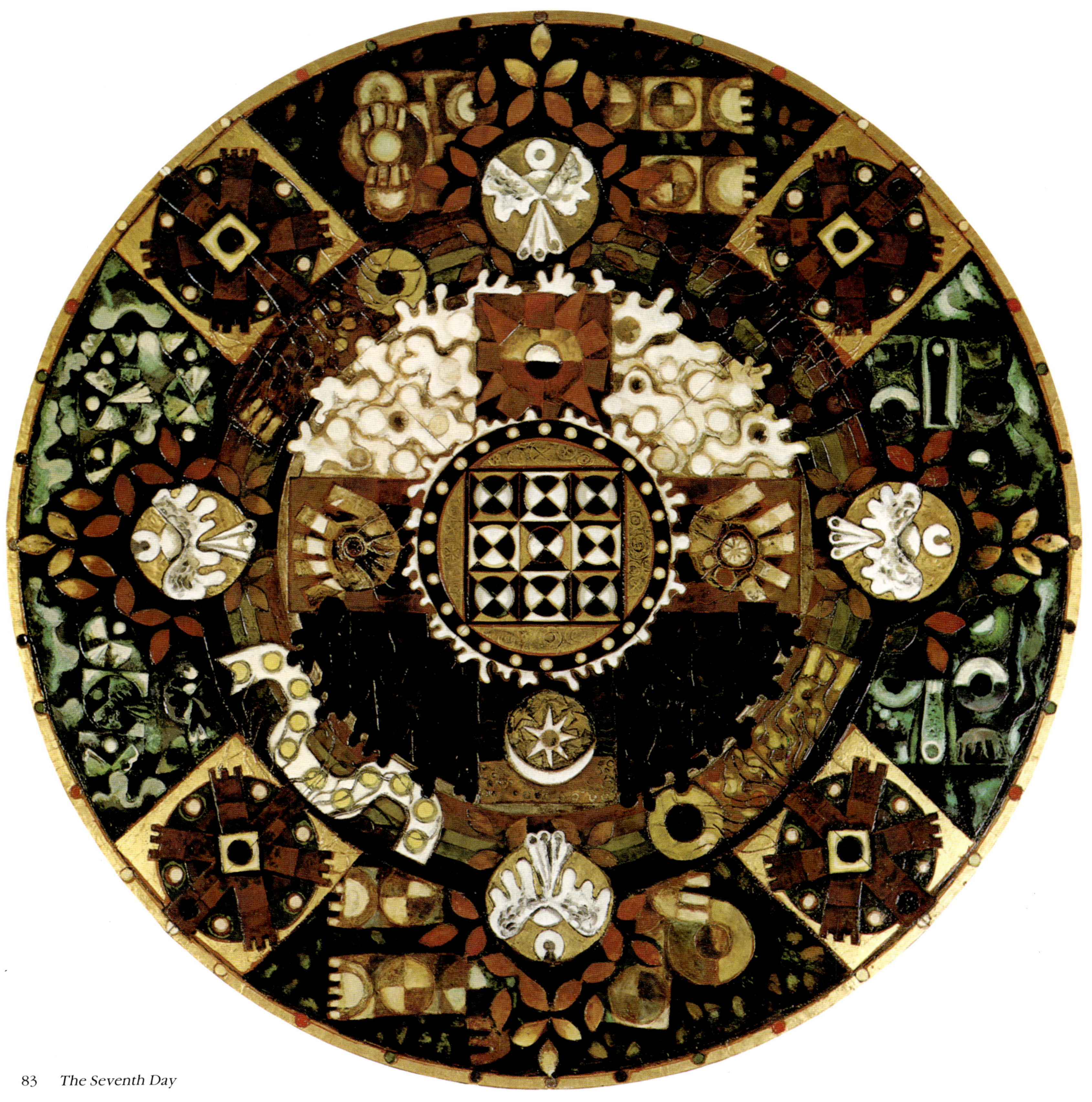

83 *The Seventh Day*

MITINARI (Attributed)

1929–76

Galbu clan, Dua moiety

Yirrkala, north-east Arnhem Land

The Thunderman, Djambuwal, 1951

Earth pigments on bark

94 × 45 cm

Collection of Gabrielle Pizzi, Melbourne

The Thunderman is depicted here as a forked thunderbolt, whose power emanates from his sacred site—a red disc in the lower left of the painting. The black spikes suspended from his scarecrow-like arms are his spears which are used for snaring rock cod. The cod are outlined in yellow to his right. On the Thunderman's head is the double-ended club or bolt which he wields to make lightning and also to break up the cliff-face into fragments. The short dashes represent rain with which he covers the country by urinating, the stain of his urine eating grooves into the cliff-face. The radiating lines are the waves he creates as he moves through the water. A small Macassan prau, dwarfed by the Thunderman's overriding presence, wavers in the lower right. This image represents the Macassan traders who passed Thunderman's sacred site on their way home to Port Bradshaw. Angered by their approach, Djambuwal hurled down his thunderbolts, creating a fierce storm at sea.

This representation of the Thunderman is unusual because it is both simple and intense. The bold use of black in loud, spiky rhythms dramatizes Djambuwal's role in creating thunder, lightning and tropical storms, all integral to the continuance of life. Thunderman is more commonly depicted with elongated penis, urinating and surrounded by images of clouds and nature's abundance.

DJAMBUWAL (or Bodngu) is an important mythical being for members of the Dua moiety.[1] The Thunderman song cycle is part of Dua moiety *nara* rituals which re-enact incidents in the journey of the *Djanggawul* (procreative ancestral beings). The Thunderman's songs and dances are also performed during circumcision rites.

Ceremonial objects associated with Djambuwal include his bush tucker, the long yam; his club which is used to strike the cliff-face; his spear for catching fish (and which today, can sometimes be seen as a shooting star) and his curving stick which suggests the clouds where he lived in The Dreaming.

1. Moiety: a division of society into two groups on the basis of generation, sex or descent.

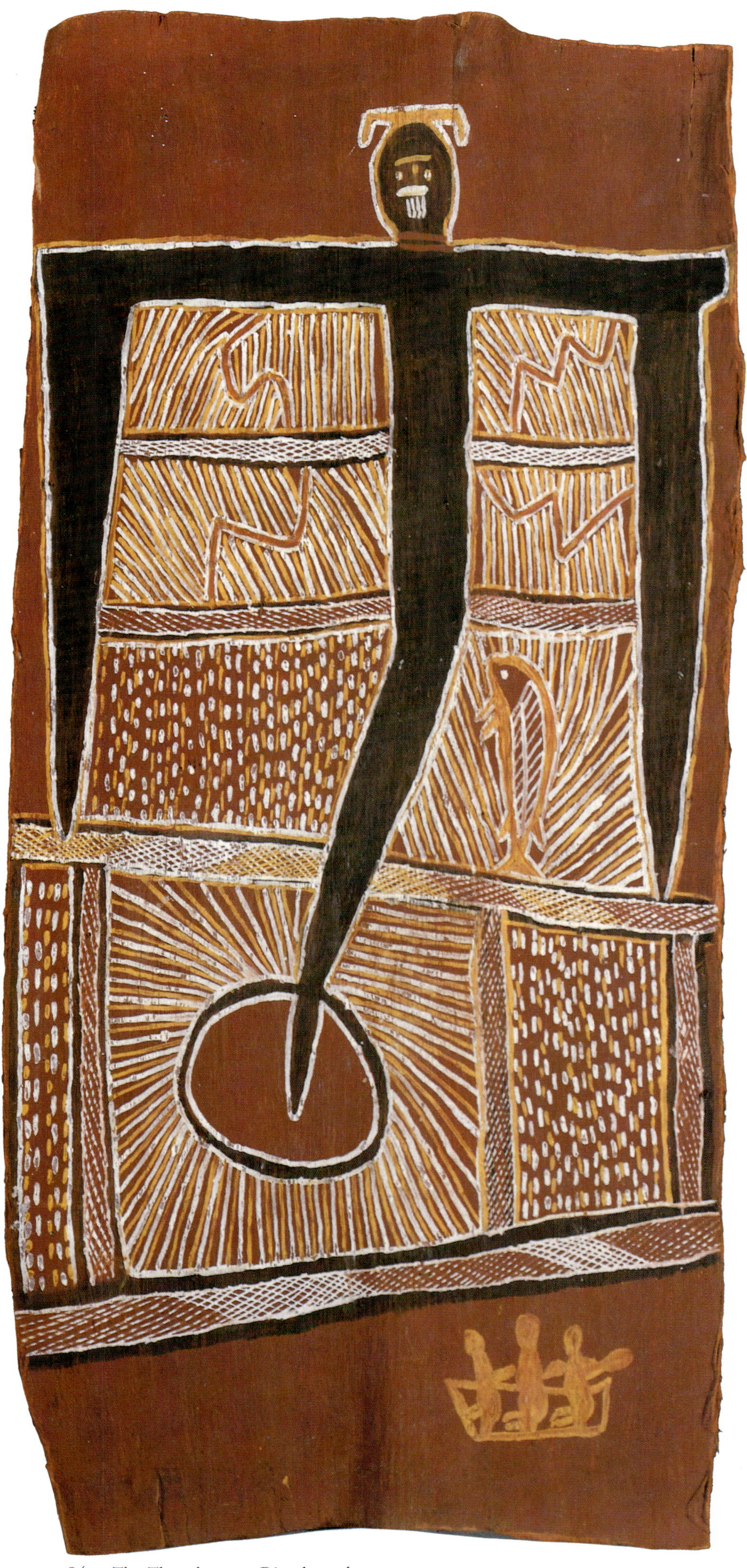

84 *The Thunderman, Djambuwal*

MATHAMAN

*c.*1916–70
Riradjingu clan, Dua moiety
Yirrkala, north-east Arnhem Land

Wagilag Ceremony, 1963

Earth pigments on bark
157.5 × 62.8 cm
National Gallery of Victoria, Melbourne
Presented by Mr J. A. Davidson 1967

Mathaman's painting depicts part of the Wagilag myth cycle (a great metaphor of the spirit of life) and the chant which invests the epic with vitality and many nuances of meaning. The Wagilag myth is the story of two sisters who travelled from south-central Arnhem Land to its north-east. On their journey they touched and named (but did not create) flora and fauna. These became Dua moiety totems and specific localities. At last the Wagilag sisters came to a sacred waterhole, home of the Rock Python, Julunggul. There, they stopped, and built a small bark shelter. But when giving birth to a child one sister allowed afterbirth blood (in some versions menstrual blood) to fall into the sacred waterhole. This enraged the imperious Python who arose in a fierce electrical storm and approached the Wagilag sisters. In a vain attempt to ward him off they performed their ceremonies, but the Python swallowed them, regurgitated them, and swallowed them again, as monsoonal rains were flooding the land. Julunggul then stood erect and told the other pythons that he had swallowed the Wagilag sisters.

In this painting Mathaman depicts one of the ceremonies associated with the Wagilag myth. The stemmed circles represent pandanus palms, proliferating near the Arafura Lagoon. The curving black lines indicate water flowing into the lagoon. Below the wavering line of palms are headbands to the left and right, with dilly bags, woomeras and spears in the centre. Beneath them are ceremonial dancers, some with spears. Their bodies are ritually decorated with lines of dashes that are also found on the headbands and on the bodies of the spirit beings in the central panel. These may be symbolic of rain. The central image shows descendants of the Wagilag sisters beneath the surface of the Arafura Lagoon, flanked by four ceremonial leaders. The black footprints leading into and out from the sacred centre of the composition represent the Wagilag sisters' journey. The rhythm of the lowest section, devoid of ceremonial participants, is less frenzied than the upper third. The pandanus motifs loom larger and the watercourses curve more lazily. The rhythmic repetition of densely interwoven motifs throughout the painting creates a visual equivalent of the sacred chant of the Wagilag song cycle.

MATHAMAN, the head of the Riradjingu clan and leader of the Dua Moiety, died in 1970. Both positions were of the greatest honour in his society. Mathaman lived most of his life on the shores of the Arafura Sea, his hereditary country. In the past this area was often visited by Macassan traders from the South Celebes but their visits were banned by the Commonwealth Government in 1908.

In 1930 the life of the Riradjingu clan was again interrupted, this time by Japanese pearlers, who were reported to have violated the Aboriginal women. A reprisal action known as the Caledon Bay massacre followed and in 1932, for his part in this, Mathaman was gaoled for two years. By the time he returned to his country a Methodist mission had been established at Yirrkala. Gradually the economy of Yirrkala became increasingly dependent on the marketing of art and Mathaman was important in this movement.

Mathaman also played a central role in the Gove Land Case, in which the Yulngor of north-east Arnhem Land claimed legal title to the bauxite-rich Gove Peninsula. The Yulngor challenged the combined might of the Commonwealth Government and the mining consortium, Nabalco Pty Ltd. For the first time, a bark painting was tabled in court as evidence of mythologically sanctioned rights in land. Mathaman died, at peace with The Dreaming, before the case was finished. The case was eventually defeated.

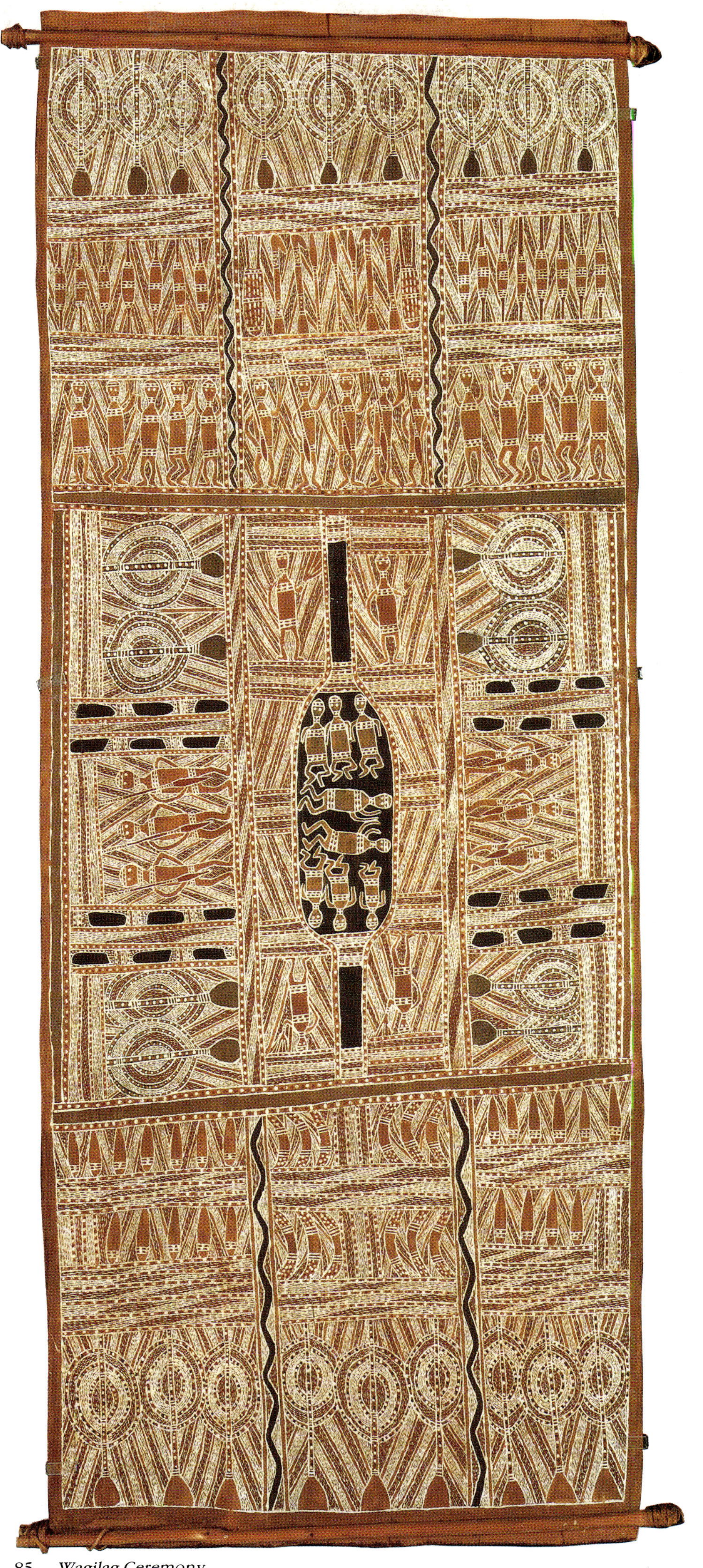

85 *Wagilag Ceremony*

OLD MICK TJAKAMARA

Born *c.*1910
Luritja/Warlpiri
Papunya, central Australia

Old Man's Dreaming on Death or Destiny, 1971

Synthetic polymer on composition board
61.5 × 46 cm
National Gallery of Victoria, Melbourne
Purchased through the Art Foundation of Victoria 1987

An old man facing death is the theme of Tjakamara's painting. When the old men became frail and were unable to keep up with the rest of the group, they would be left behind with food, shelter and water. They very rarely used the food and water but would lie down, practise a form of self-hypnosis, and die. They welcomed their destiny, their return to the ancestors of their totem, from which they had originally sprung to life at their particular conception site or Dreaming.

In contemplating his own death, Old Mick Tjakamara has painted a profoundly simple image of man's destiny. The large half-circles represent an old man lying on the ground; the smaller black arcs are the same old man sitting by the fire. At the bottom of the painting is a windbreak, traditionally built of witchetty bush, mulga and twine made from human hair. The striated area at the top of the painting represents the root structure of the bush tucker, the dots throughout the painting are other forms of vegetation. The black *tjurunga*, or sacred carved board, is the spirit of Tjakamara, alive and strong and the red ochre *tjurunga* on the right is the eternal symbol of the totemic ancestor.

The work has a raw concentrated power. The design elements expose what is sacred and abiding in the artist's world.

PAPUNYA. Papunya, an expression of government assimilationist policy, was officially declared a settlement in 1960. An agglomeration of tribal groups were brought into this confined area, where they existed in considerable tension and degradation, cut off from lands that they understood to be their own. Against this grim backdrop, the growth of the Papunya art movement reads like a fable.

In 1971, a young art teacher, Geoff Bardon, encouraged the senior men of the settlement to paint their traditional designs on to board. Formerly, these sacred designs were only found on cave walls, on *tjurungas* or in ephemeral sand paintings. The artists created works of remarkable purity and truth on this seemingly incongruous European material.

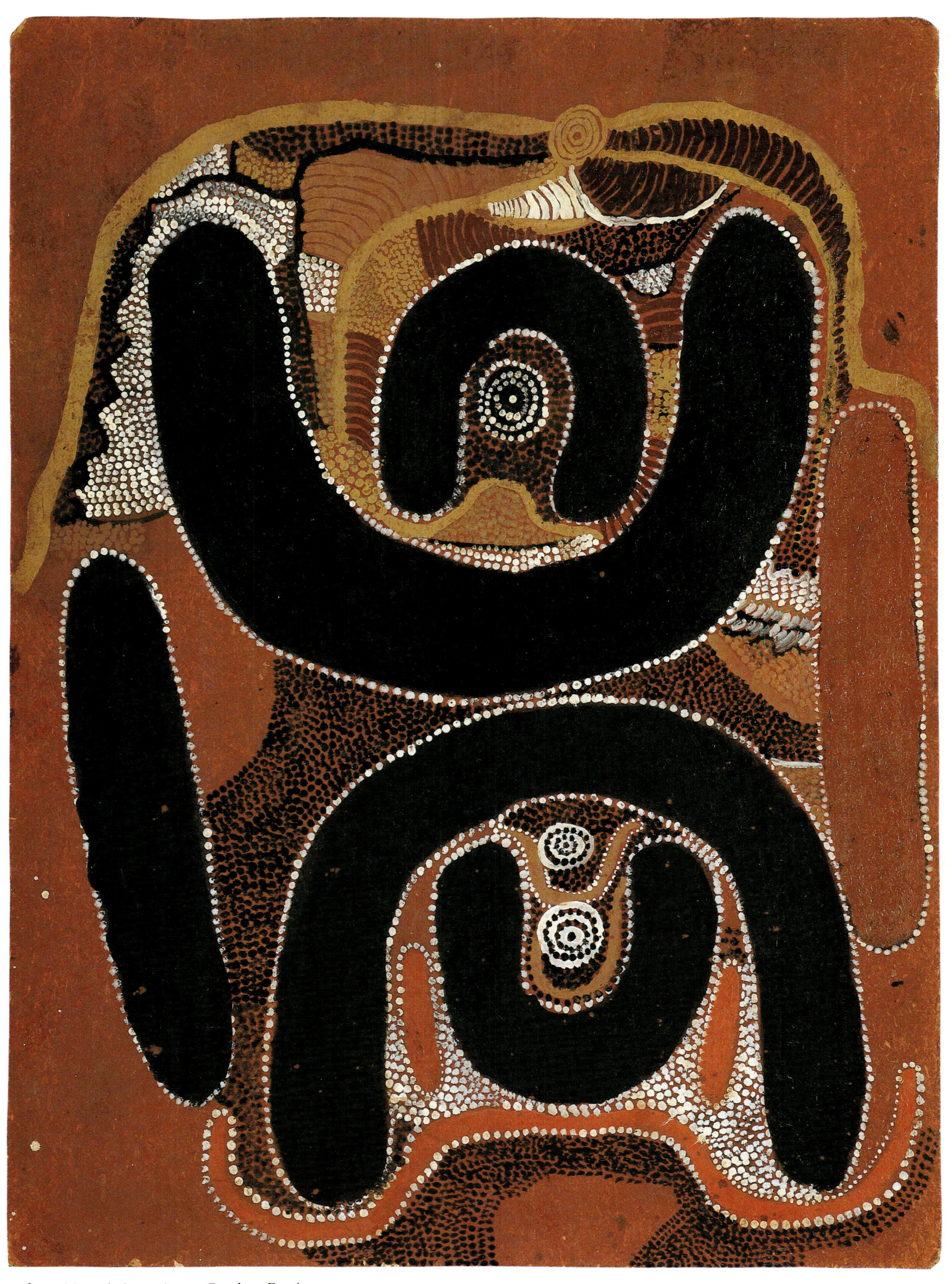

86 *Old Man's Dreaming on Death or Destiny*

JOHNNY WARRANGULA TJUPURRULA

Born 1918

Luritja

Papunya, central Australia

A Bush Tucker Story, 1973

Synthetic polymer on composition board
91.5 × 66 cm
National Gallery of Victoria, Melbourne
Purchased through the Art Foundation of Victoria 1987

A Bush Tucker Story was painted on board primed with red ochre in three distinct stages. For the first two stages a camel hair brush was used, for the last, grass stems, sometimes chewed at the end to give a softer edge. The artist first painted all the dry rivers and creeks in black, and painted concentric circles for the sites of soaks and naturally occurring wells. Striated oblongs depict the sites, flattened by the women's feet, where men of the water totem would dance the increase rites. The painting was then put aside for two months.

The second stage was painted when the rains came. Tjupurrula dotted in the soaks and rivers, still using the camel hair brush.

At the third stage, when the rains came again, he changed his brush for grass stems. He worked on the painting every day for three weeks, applying tiny brush strokes in thin layers of colour. These strokes mirror the wondrous transformation of the desert, alive with new seeds, flowers and grasses. The black specks represent the black seeds the women grind into damper, while the white flecks represent another type of seed that proliferate in the area after rain.

Pat Hogan, who purchased the painting from the artist, was the owner of the Stuart Art Centre in Alice Springs. She recalls flying into Papunya after the rains and seeing 'the wild flowers, the rain still in pools, the colour like a beautiful mosaic'.[1] She visited the paint shed and saw this same vision of desert renewal on Johnny Warrangula's board. Many of the other artists there recognized in the painting the eternal things of their culture. While Pat Hogan was there they went down to the creek together where 'the wild potato men chanted the wild potatoes, sang about the tomatoes and the little plant whose black seeds they put in their damper.' Old Walter Tjampitjinpa, custodian of the Water Dreaming, 'chanted the rain, Old Tutuma Tjapangati sang about the feathers that would have been used in the original ground mosaic'.[2] Mick Mamerari Tjapaltjarri intoned the music of the roots' growth, seen in the straight lines on the right hand side of the painting. Such ritual chanting often accompanies an artist's application of pigment and also joyously affirms the sacred or eternal truths inherent in the painting.

1. Pat Hogan, background notes on the painting, 1987, now in gallery archives.
2. ibid.

JOHNNY WARRANGULA TJUPURRULA was born at Tjikari, an important cave site north-west of the Ehrenburg Range in traditional Luritja country.

His art is marked by a magical sense of light and colour. He has always mixed his own pigments, experimenting with broken hues and tonal nuances which counteract the harsh acrylic medium. He gradually evolved a unique style in which calligraphic line and spontaneous blotches of colour are overlaid by masses of tiny dots. By 1972 Tjupurrula had introduced a technique of over-dotting in feather-like layers. His intuitive dotting technique was to be copied by fellow Papunya painters and soon became fashionable. In Tjupurrula's work dotting is a powerful visual metaphor, not a mechanical infilling device.

From 1974 Tjupurrula chose to work on a much larger scale. His recent canvases show Dreaming paths through huge sections of his native country, seen as a patchwork studded with sacred sites.

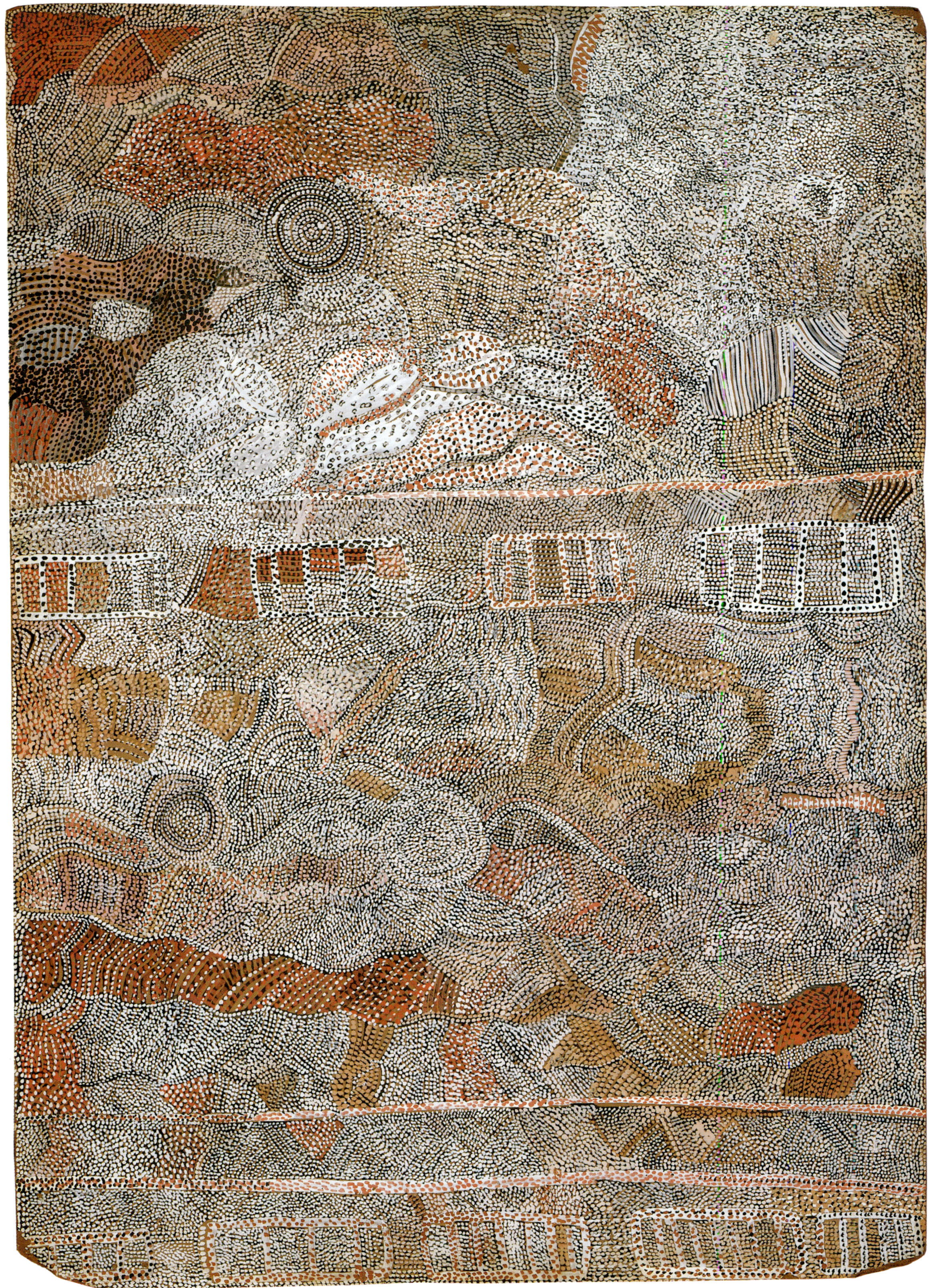

87 *A Bush Tucker Story*

Tim Leura Tjapaltjarri

c.1930–84

Anmatjera/Aranda

Papunya, central Australia

Rock Wallaby Dreaming, 1982

Synthetic polymer on canvas
120 × 179 cm
National Gallery of Victoria, Melbourne
Purchased from Admission Funds 1987

Rock Wallaby Dreaming reflects Tim Leura's empathy with his desert environment. The violet shadows cast across the red earth and stone by the desert light are reflected in an opalescent section on the right hand side of the painting. This contrasts with the olive-green plant life along the watercourses. The sparing use of intense red ochre lends depth to the restrained palette.

The artist has depicted Ngunyunpa, a water soak and Rock Wallaby Dreaming site north-east of Napperby Station. This site is the large roundel towards the centre of the painting. Other concentric circles represent campsites and the adjoining 'U' shapes depict the ceremonial participants. Four of the camps are protected by windbreaks. A group of men decorated for a corroboree are depicted with unusual realism in the centre left. They are engulfed by the land which is central to their spiritual identity. A pubic belt (traditionally made from spun human hair and wallaby fur), larger in scale than the figures, is a reminder of the hunter-gatherer lifestyle. Above the figures are an emu and a goanna, indicating that the Emu and Goanna Dreaming trails both pass through this particular site. The tracks of the wallaby and the emu can be seen, as can the footprints of the hunters, moving in search of game. The weapons of the hunters—boomerang, hooked boomerang, woomera, club, hafted stone axe—thrust at right angles in the central triangle are outlined by a diagonal spear. The shield, decorated for ceremonial use, is adjacent to the corroboree performers and suggests a separate layer of meaning.

In *Rock Wallaby Dreaming,* Tim Leura sees his hereditary country through a veiled prism of soft light. It is a world in which Dreamtime past, present and future are held in balance.

An artist of rare sensibility, Tim Leura Tjapaltjarri died of a brain tumour in 1984. His birthplace, Kooralia, is a creek on Napperby Station in traditional Anmatjera country north-east of Papunya.

His art is marked by a sombre, clouded palette, muted dotting and the use of smoky washes for spatial effects. In common with other Anmatjera artists, Tjapaltjarri often intersperses figurative images amongst abstract symbols, and reveals some familiarity with the landscapes of the Aranda watercolourists at Hermannsburg.

Between 1970 and 1975 he painted a series of separate Dreamings, including the Honey Ant, Possum, Yam Spirit, Wild Plum, Sun and Moon, and Fire. These small works of graceful symmetry dramatize important segments of the artist's tribal religious knowledge: a knowledge which is conveyed communally in song and dance, and in sand designs.

In his later works on large canvases Tjapaltjarri attempts to place many Dreaming trails, or story lines, in geographical relationship to each other. In them he is mapping the mythological journeys of different ancestors. His natural world is empowered by the presence of creator beings, often transformed into geographical features.

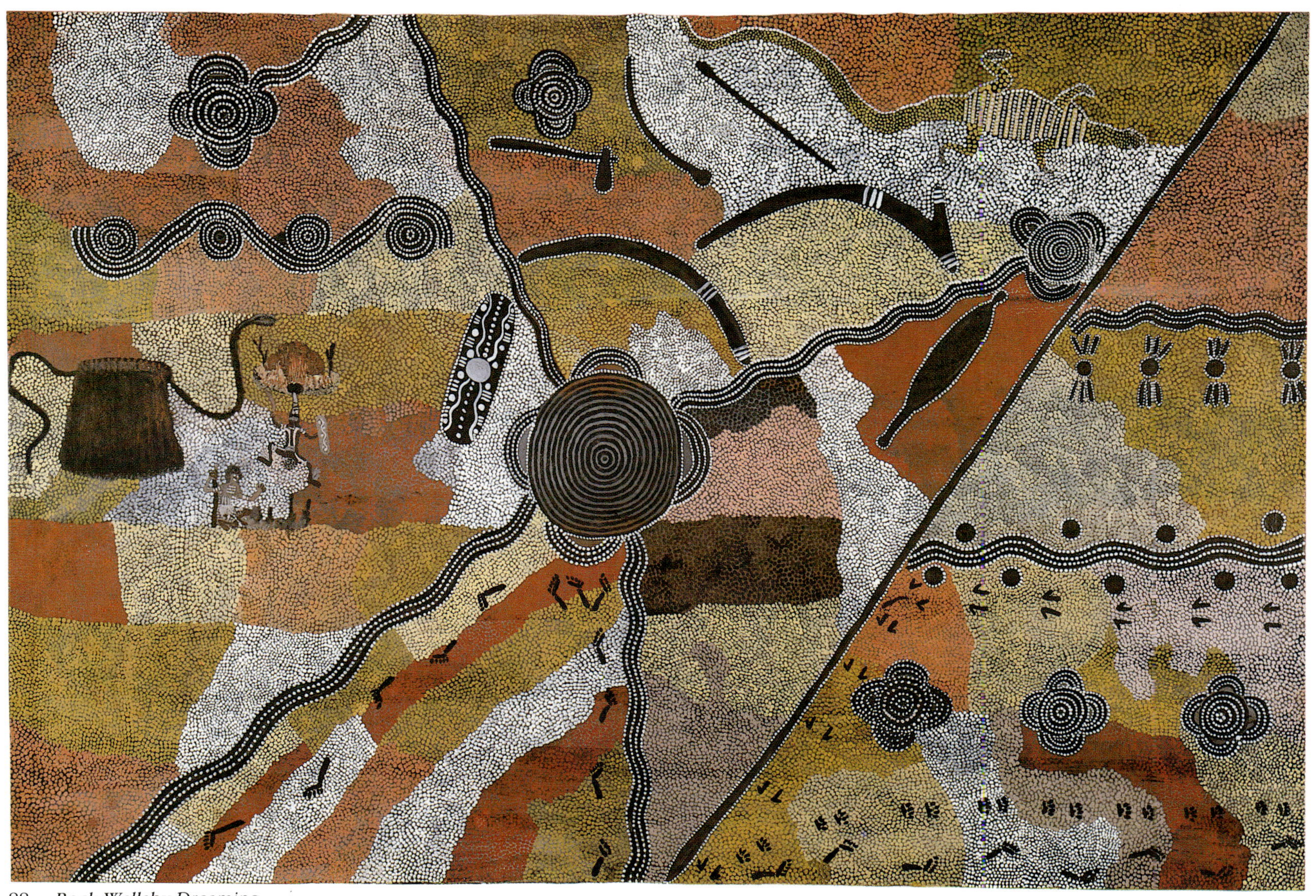

88 *Rock Wallaby Dreaming*

TOMMY LOWRY TJAPALTJARRI

*c.*1940–87

Pintubi

Kintore, central Australia

Moon Dreaming, 1987

Synthetic polymer on canvas
182.5 × 182.7 cm
Collection of Gabrielle Pizzi, Melbourne

Tommy Lowry Tjapaltjarri's *Moon Dreaming* is a representation of the site of Tjunpaninga to the south of Kintore, where most of the Pintubi now reside.

An old woman ancestor of the Nangala subsection was sleeping at this site. The circle is her camp and the arcs show where she slept, seen as shadows or indentations left in the sand. The straight lines represent the passage of the voice of the moon ancestor who was imparting tribal knowledge to the old woman. The wavering concentric lines enclosing the old woman's camp represent speech patterns invading the stillness of the site with the spirit essence of the moon ancestor. After camping there for some time, the old woman flew to a site further south, to again implant in the ground traces of her sacred presence.

THE DREAMING. The sacred chord of The Dreaming unites and sustains Aboriginal people. This inviolate metaphor of the natural order encodes a multiplicity of meanings which elude scientific rationalism.

The Dreaming refers to a creative epoch in which men and women and all of nature have come to be as they are. Persons, customs, geographical features, languages and the bases of Aboriginal law all derive from the actions of powerful totemic figures whose lives of travel or Dreamings criss-cross the country. An Aborigine might call the place from where his Spirit came Dreaming, or refer to his totem as his Dreaming. The Dreaming also explains the existence of a social or moral imperative. T. G. H. Strehlow, in his *Central Australian Religion,* (1978), notes that among desert groups a person's Dreaming is located, and the totem determined, by the place where the mother experiences her first symptoms of pregnancy.

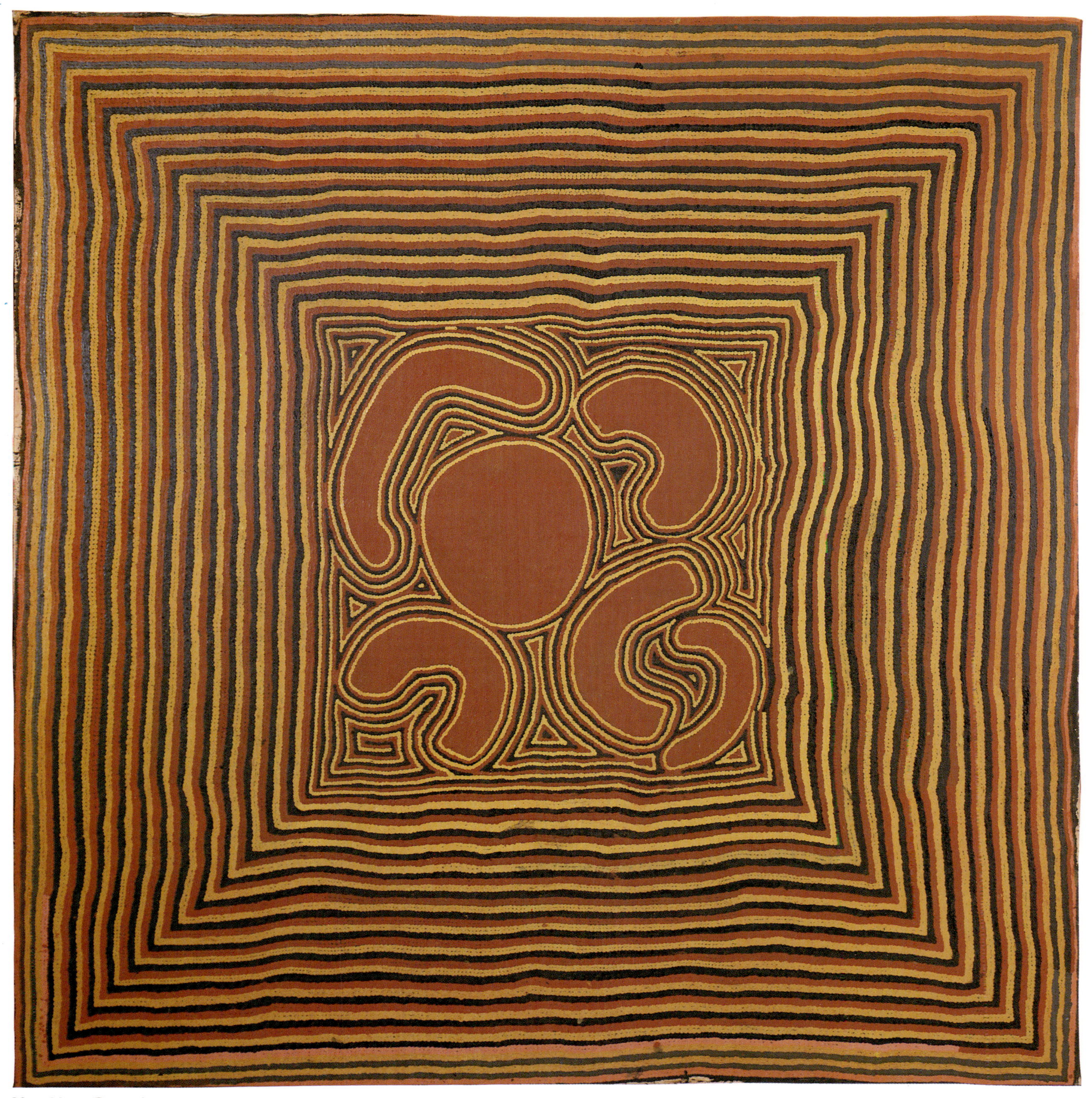

89 *Moon Dreaming*

ANATJARI TJAMPITJINPA

Born *c.*1925
Pintubi
Kintore, central Australia

Tingari Dreaming at Wilkinkarra, 1986

Synthetic polymer on canvas
164 × 46 cm
Collection of Anthony and Beverly Waldegrave-Knight, Melbourne

Tjampitjinpa has, in this painting, represented Wilkinkarra (Lake McKay), an important *Tingari* ceremonical site. Large groups of ancestral beings passed through sites of Kiwikurra, Walla Walla and Utti before arriving at Wilkinkarra. The artist suggests, through undulating meanders of colour, the many lines of travel of the *Tingari* through sandhill country. In this painting the lines and colours ripple and undulate like cadences in a sacred song. The same lines can also be seen in ritual body painting.

TINGARI CYCLE. The Pintubi find common identity and purpose in the *Tingari*, a long Dreaming story about mythological travelling groups of senior men and circumcised novices.

Three main geographical lines of named places are described as *Tingari*, meaning that they were visited and created in the Dreaming by three large bands of travelling ancestral beings. Secluded from women and the uninitiated, these bands hunted, argued, fought and performed and witnessed ceremonies of revelation, thus providing a mythological blueprint for desert living. Their patterns of continual travel and resting through the territories of disparate tribal groups serve to link specific localities so that Pintubi country is one unbounded, continuous entity.

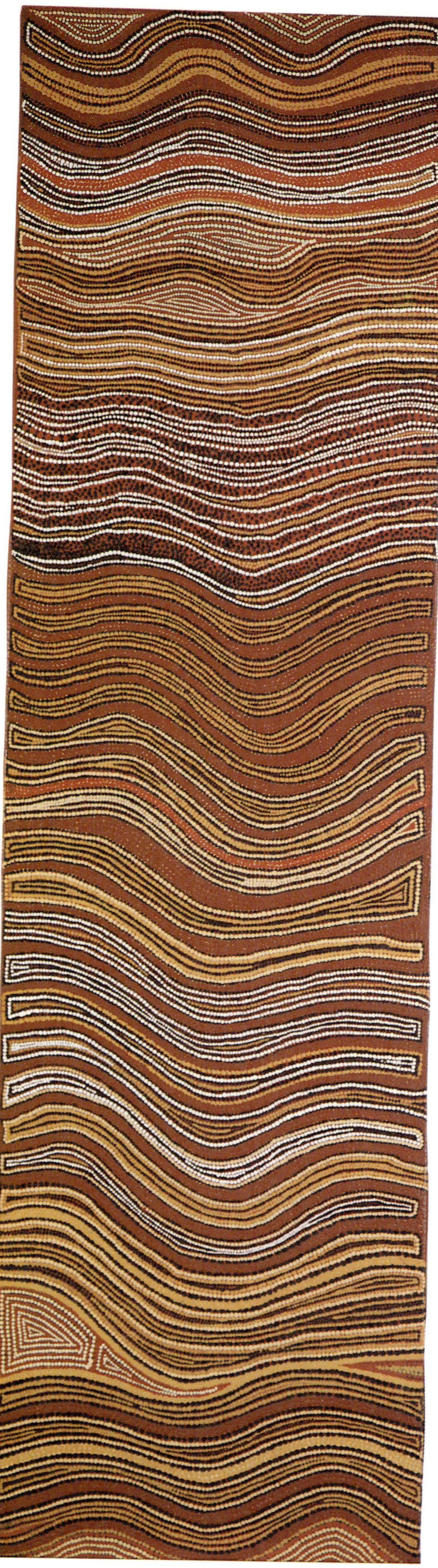

90 *Tingari Dreaming at Wilkinkarra*

Yala Yala Gibbs Tjungurrayi

Born *c.*1928

Pintubi

Kintore, central Australia

Tingari Dreaming at Marra-pintinya, 1982

Synthetic polymer on canvas
153.8 × 186 cm
Collection of Gabrielle Pizzi, Melbourne

Yala Yala Gibbs Tjungurrayi provides a window to the sacred ceremonial life of the men of his tribe. He celebrates what is enduring in their world.

Tjungurrayi depicts Marra-pintinya, a major water supply in the far western territory of the Pintubi, and a *Tingari* site of special significance to the artist. Since this area is rich in water and, therefore, sustenance, many story lines criss-cross the site. The artist provides a visual equivalent of the lengthy song cycles which are a part of the secret, post-initiatory form of the education of all Pintubi men. There are many layers of meaning in this painting and the inner layers are not revealed to the uninitiated. At one level the tessellated currents of concentric lines represent the surrounding country and plant foods eaten by the *Tingaris*, as well as their ritual body decoration and ceremonial objects. The large concentric circles represent sites, and the squares are the ritual participants, the size indicating their importance. Sexual activities are indicated by the jostling line of small circles. A number of angular lines linking large circles probably indicate poles erected during ceremonies.

The whole canvas can be read as a vast textured sand painting or a topographical map with sites receding or advancing through subtle variations in tone.

The Pintubi. Shielded by the harshness of their terrain, the sandhills and spinifex country of the Gibson Desert, the Pintubi were the last of the desert groups to encounter Europeans. Some, including Yala Yala Gibbs Tjungurrayi, drifted into the government settlement of Haasts Bluff in the mid 1950s, but many did not leave the desert until the mid 1960s, when they came to Papunya in response to offers of food, water and schooling. As a result of this relative seclusion, Pintubi art is free of European inspired motifs. Its dominant rhythm of myriad circles and travelling paths is an intense expression of Pintubi pride in the mythological geography of their own country.

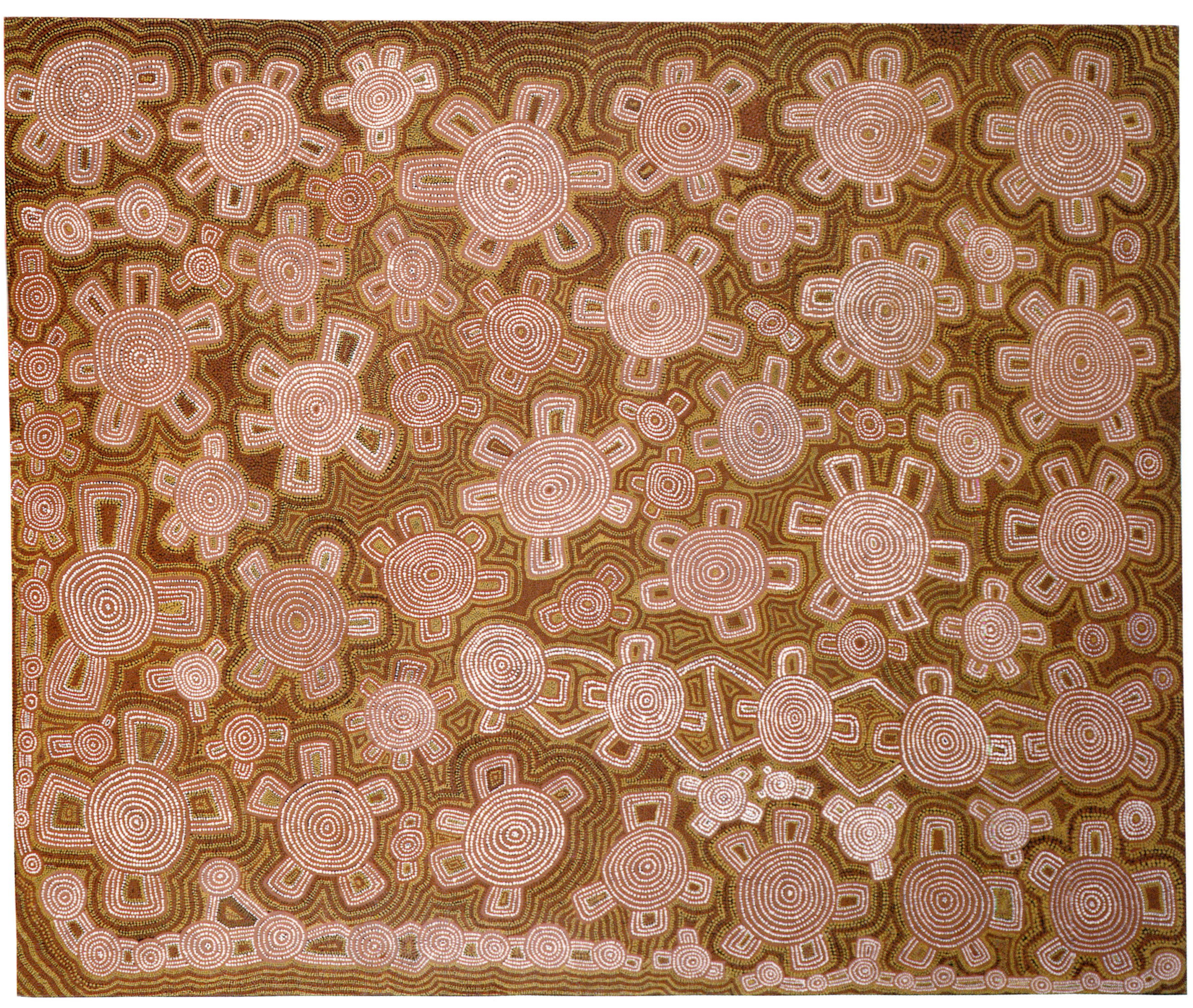

91 *Tingari Dreaming at Marra-pintinya*

Paddy Jupurrula Nelson

Born *c.*1919

Warlpiri

Yuendumu, central Australia

Larry Jungarrayi Spencer

Born 1919

Yarla Jukurrpa (Bush Potato Dreaming), 1986

Synthetic polymer on canvas
196 × 170.5 cm
Collection of Gabrielle Pizzi, Melbourne

Paddy Jupurrula Nelson and Larry Jungarrayi Spencer are two of the senior men who worked on the Yuendumu Doors. Their *Bush Potato Dreaming* is uninhibited in its use of dappled, luminescent colour. Yumurrpa, the country of the yarla plant, is painted in intimate detail. Its geographical undulations and variations in vegetation are perceived from above through a spectrum of shifting hues. The concentric circles represent the yarla plant; the spiralling lines, its roots—which are a constant source of food in the desert. On another level of meaning, the circles are significant sites or resting places and the driving lines signify the nomadic travelling principle—celebrating an eternal idea in Warlpiri culture.

In *Bush Potato Dreaming* the artists sing of the abundance of the yarla plant in a tapestry of vibrant colours.

Yuendumu Artists. Yuendumu, a large community 300 kilometres north-west of Alice Springs, is home to many members of the Warlpiri group. The outburst of painting now evident in the community began with the painting of the local school doors with traditional designs. The Yuendumu senior men recorded their major Dreamings on thirty doors as a visible source of instruction for the children, thereby ensuring the continuation of their culture.

This co-operative venture was suggested by headmaster Terry Davis in 1983. In contrast to Papunya, where senior men were painting on small boards in a locked art room, women and children were an integral part of this revelation of tribal law. An unrestricted use of singing colour is evident in the painting of the doors, which remains strongly characteristic of Warlpiri art.

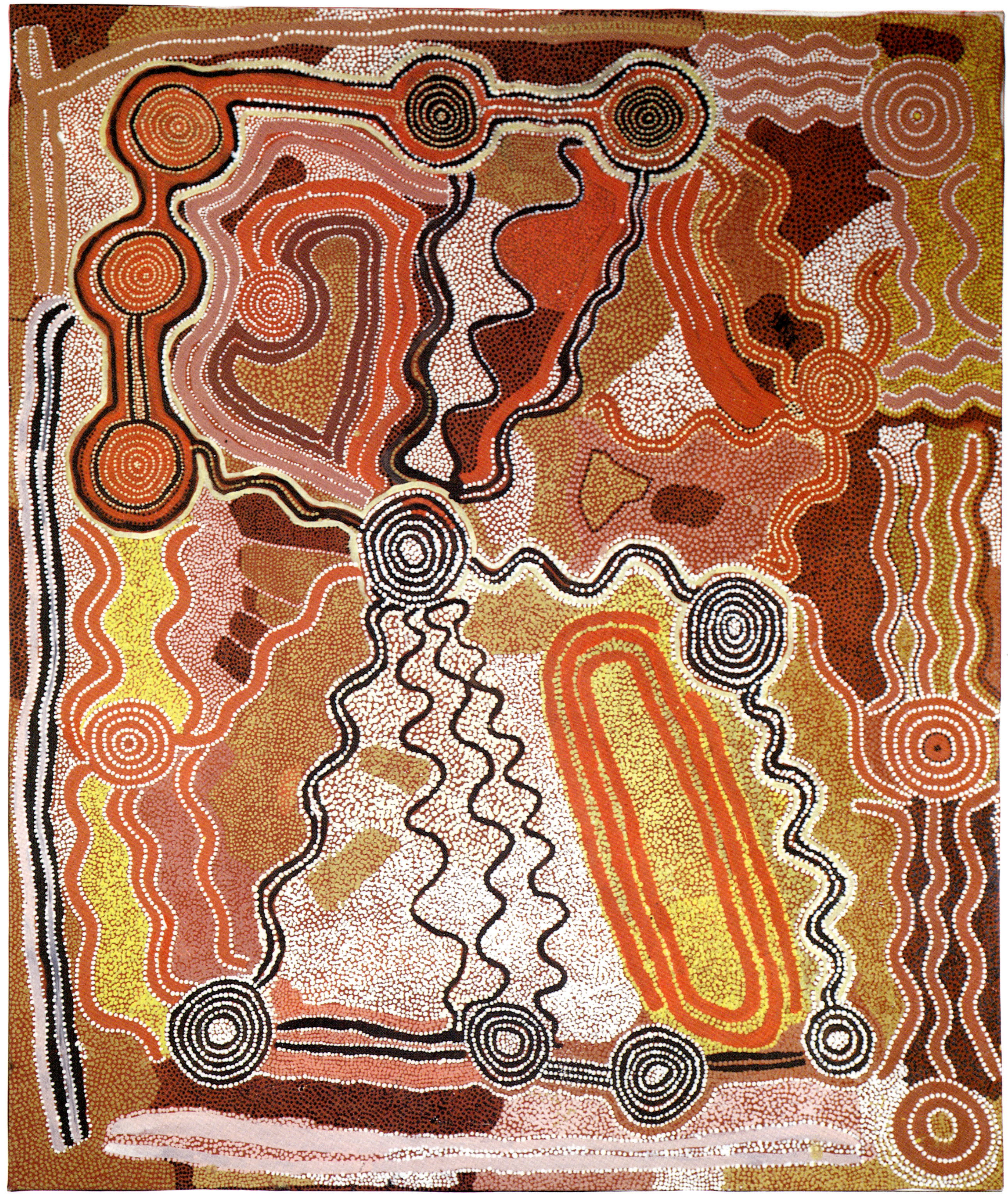

92 *Yarla Jukurrpa (Bush Potato Dreaming)*

Jeannie Nungarrayi Egan

Born 1947

Warlpiri

Yuendumu, central Australia

Yarumayi Jukurrpa, 1987

Synthetic polymer on canvas
122 × 91 cm
National Gallery of Victoria, Melbourne

Jeannie Nungarrayi Egan won the Rothman's Foundation Award for Introduced Media at the Fourth National Aboriginal Art Award in 1987. Her graphic narrative style echoes from the unbroken lines of *yawulyu* designs. These designs are painted with red ochre, charcoal and a white paste on the bodies of women for their land-based ceremonies, and on the chests and shoulders of children to aid in their growth.

Yarumayi, or Sixteen-Mile Bore, is an ochre pit east of Yuendumu where a Goanna ancestor and his wife were living in the Dreaming. The male goanna is seen travelling north towards Mount Allen, eating worms that proliferate near mulga scrub. The mulga can be seen sprouting from concentric circles which suggest vegetable foods, breasts or mother-daughter enclosures: the vital domain of the women. The male totemic ancestor is seen as growing so fat that he burst in half and thus created Yarnkimali, a site with two large rocks. This dramatic expression of the dynamic male travelling principle complements the actions of the female goanna. She remained at Yarumayi, made a hole in the red sand and laid her eggs. The eggs are transformed into a white ochre deposit, which ensured a constant source of the white pigment, integral to the *yawulyu* ceremonies of the Walpiri women. *Yarumayi Jukurrpa* is a remarkable narrative painting in which mythical ancestors are seen to metamorphose into the geographical features of the land.

Women's Art and Religion. In defiance of the common pattern in Aboriginal society, more than half of the practising artists at Yuendumu are women. In 1964 the practice of painting in acrylic on canvas was initiated by the women.

Those who consider Aboriginal art and religion to be the preserve of the men have excluded Aboriginal women from discussion of sacred and artistic spheres, and underplayed their autonomous role. However, Aboriginal religion embraces the whole of life—woman and man, plant and animal—all of which would wither without the land. Each Warlpiri woman has a strong, practical understanding of *Jukurrpa* (Dreaming Law) and identifies intimately with her own conception site and totem. This religious knowledge is clearly manifest in women's art.

Warlpiri women manage their own affairs and their secret ceremonies, which are sanctioned by their Dreamtime ancestors. Women's rituals enshrine 'their role as nurturers of people, land and relationships'.[1] Within this principle of nurturing are the biological acts of giving birth and lactation, evidence of the women's procreative power and 'otherness'.

Women's paintings reflect their role as nurturers and the responsibility they have to care for and maintain country and kin.

1. See Diane Bell, 'Aboriginal Women and the Religious Experience', in *Traditonal Aboriginal Society: A Reader*, ed. W. H. Edwards (Melbourne: Macmillan, 1987), pp. 237–56.

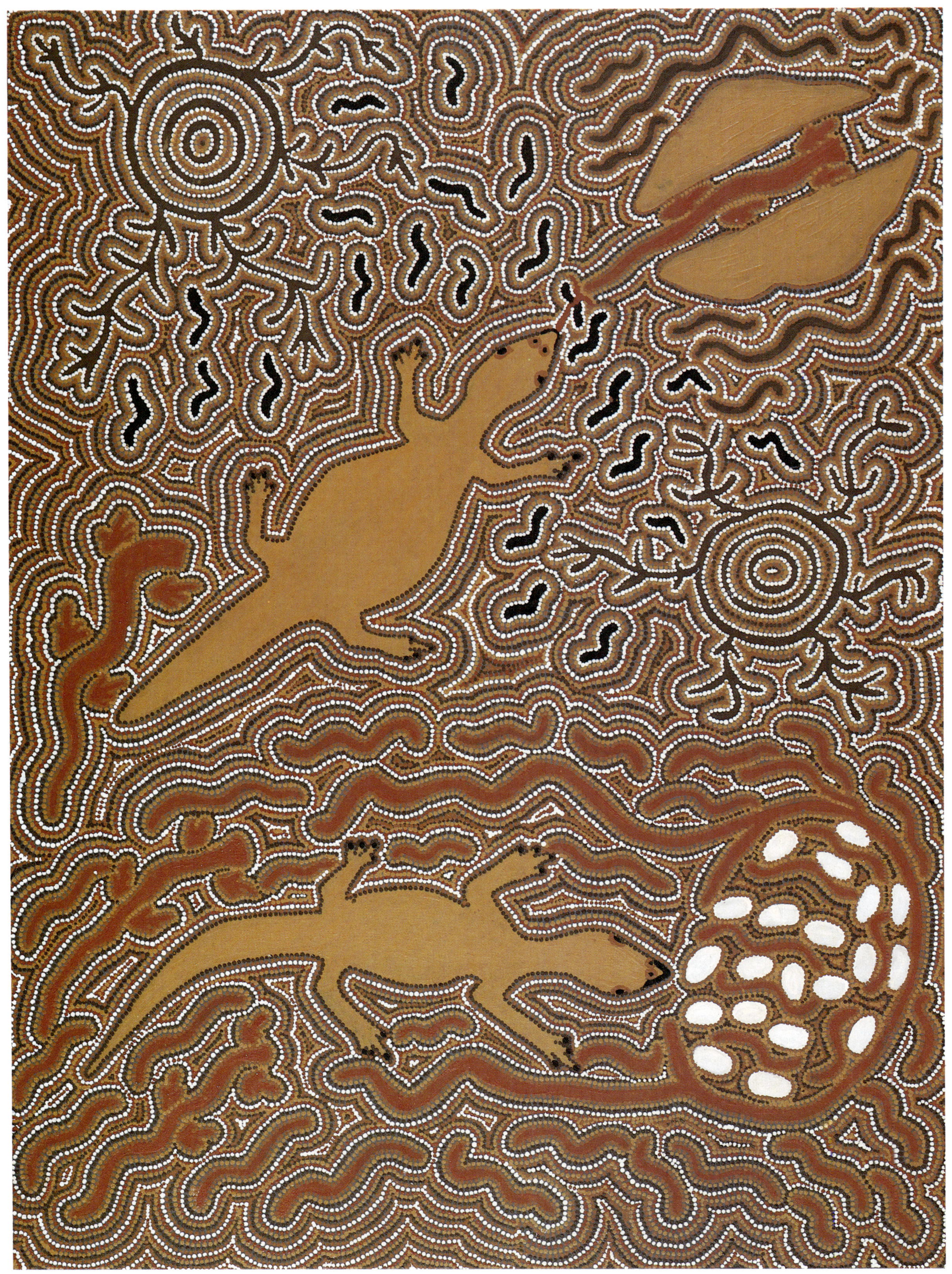

93 *Yarumayi Jukurrpa*

List of Plates

25 Albert Tucker (b.1914)
Ascension, 1962
Acrylic on hardboard 130.2 × 96.2 cm
National Gallery of Victoria, Melbourne

26 Eric Smith (b.1919)
The Scourged Christ, 1956
Oil on composition board 116 × 85 cm
Penrith Regional Art Gallery, NSW
Lewers Bequest

27 Eric Smith (b.1919)
Christ is Risen, 1959
Oil on composition board 220 × 115 cm
Canisius College, Pymble, NSW

28 Elwyn Lynn (b.1917)
Betrayal, 1957
Oil on composition board
90.8 × 121.3 cm
National Gallery of Victoria, Melbourne
Purchased 1957

29 Thomas Gleghorn (b.1925)
Head of Christ, 1958
Oil on composition board 88 × 60 cm
Blake Society for Religious Art, Sydney

30 Roger Kemp (1908–87)
*Ascension, c.*1960
Acrylic on board 120 × 183 cm
National Gallery of Victoria, Melbourne
Purchased 1983

31 Roger Kemp (1908–87)
The Cross, 1968
Oil on composition board
181.5 × 116.5 cm
Monash University, Melbourne

32 Roger Kemp (1908–87)
Movement 5, 1980–81
Acrylic on canvas 204 × 272 cm
National Gallery of Victoria, Melbourne

33 Ian Fairweather (1891–1974)
Hallelujah, 1959
PVC on paper on board 146.8 × 157.5 cm
National Gallery of Victoria, Melbourne
Purchased 1983

34 John Coburn (b.1925)
Triptych of the Passion, 1960
Enamel paint on composition board
Three panels: 106 × 182 cm overall
Courtesy St Patrick's College, Manly, NSW

35 Fred Williams (1927–82)
Adam and Eve, 1960–61
Oil and tempera on composition
board 122 × 70.5 cm
Private collection, Melbourne

36 Godfrey Miller (1893–1964)
Madonna No. 1, 1960–64
Oil on canvas 33 × 22 cm
Private collection, Melbourne

37 Constance Stokes (b.1906)
Sorrowing Mother, 1960
Oil on composition board 61 × 50.5 cm
Geelong Art Gallery
Gift of Ford Motor Company Australia Pty
Ltd 1963

38 Stanislaus Rapotec (b.1913)
Meditating on Good Friday, 1961
Oil on composition board
164.1 × 411.5 cm
Collection of P. J. Pacquola, Melbourne

39 Michael Kitching (b.1940)
Last Supper—Premonition, 1964
Wood, metal, plastic paint on board
188.5 × 223 cm overall
Private collection, Sydney

40 Rodney Milgate (b.1934)
Ascension, 1966
Encaustic, oil on composition board
Two panels: 243.8 × 182.9 cm overall
City of Hamilton Art Gallery, Victoria

41 Clifton Pugh (b.1924)
The Penitents, No. 9, 1967
Oil on composition board
121.9 × 91.4 cm
Collection of the artist

42 George Baldessin (1939–78)
First View over the City, 1967
Mixed media on composition board
380 × 430 cm
Private collection, Melbourne

43 Desiderius Orban (1884–1986)
Transition to Christianity, 1971
Oil and felt-tipped pen on pineboard
Two panels: 153.7 × 276.8 cm overall
Art Gallery of New South Wales, Sydney
Gift of the artist 1972

44 Noel Counihan (1913–86)
Laughing Christ, No. 10, 1972
Oil on canvas 122 × 106.5 cm
National Gallery of Victoria, Melbourne
Purchased 1985

45 Noel Counihan (1913–86)
Homage to Goya (Requiem for El Salvador), 1985
Oil and tempera on canvas 97 × 122 cm
Private collection, Melbourne

46 Keith Looby (b.1940)
Knock, Knock, Is God Home? 1972
Oil and pencil on composition board
Six panels: 275.4 × 367.4 cm overall
Australian National Gallery, Canberra

47 Keith Looby (b.1940)
Your Motel Calvary Still Life Flowers, 1973
Oil on canvas with mirrored glass
Two panels: 259.1 × 289.6 cm overall
Griffith University, Brisbane

48 Alun Leach-Jones (b.1937)
Time and Silence, 1972
Synthetic polymer on canvas
244 × 198.3 cm
Brisbane College of Advanced Education
Purchased 1979

49 Warren Breninger (b.1948)
Tomb of Eve Opened, 1978–79
Mixed media (silver bromide etching, gum arabic prints and photo silk-screen drawing and painting media)
Three panels: 215.9 × 299.7 cm overall
Collection of the artist

50 Warren Breninger (b.1948)
Expulsion of Eve, Series 111, No. 4, 1980–87
Mixed media on C-type colour paper
75 × 50 cm
Collection of the artist

51 Warren Breninger (b.1948)
Expulsion of Eve, Series 111, No. 22, 1980–87
Mixed media on C-type colour paper
75 × 50 cm
Collection of the artist

52 Peter Booth (b.1940)
Painting 1977, 1977
Oil on canvas 182.5 × 304.5 cm
National Gallery of Victoria, Melbourne
Presented by the artist in memory of Les Hawkins 1978

53 Peter Booth (b.1940)
Painting 1982, 1982
Oil on canvas 197.7 × 274 cm
Art Gallery of South Australia, Adelaide
A. M. Ragless Bequest Fund 1983

54 Asher Bilu (b.1936)
Spill-out, 1979
Mixed media on plywood
274(H) × 488(W) × 122 (D) cm
Collection of the artist

56 Brett Whiteley (b.1939)
The three crucifixions
Left: *'Father, forgive them . . .',* 1979
Charcoal on paper 246 × 131 cm
Collection of the artist

55 Brett Whiteley (b.1939)
'My God, my God . . . why . . .', 1979–80
Oil, gold leaf and steel on board
259 × 134 cm
Collection of the artist

57 Brett Whiteley (b.1939)
The Giving Up, 1979–80
Oil on steel 256 × 114 cm
Collection of the artist

58 Leonard French (b.1928)
Shooting Place, c.1980
Enamel, oil and gold leaf on hardboard 122 × 137 cm
Collection of the artist

59 Davida Allen (b.1951)
The Death of My Father, 1981–82
Oil on canvas 165.3 × 271.9 cm
National Gallery of Victoria, Melbourne
Michell Endowment 1982

60 Davida Allen (b.1951)
The Priest Painting, 1981
Oil on canvas 169 × 221 cm
Museum of Contemporary Art, Brisbane, James Baker Collection

61 Lawrence Daws (b.1927)
Cain and the Promised Land, 1983
Oil on canvas
Two panels: 173 × 305 cm overall
Collection of the artist

62 John Nixon (b.1949) and Imants Tillers (b.1950)
Honour and Glory, 1982
Oil and synthetic polymer paint on canvas 194.5 × 138.5 cm
Art Gallery of South Australia, Adelaide
South Australian Government Grant 1984

63 Jan Murray (b.1957)
The Three Graces, 1983
Oil on canvas 166.5 × 198 cm
National Gallery of Victoria, Melbourne
Michell Endowment 1984

64 John R. Walker (b.1957)
Mary, 1985
Oil on canvas 244 × 304.5 cm
National Gallery of Victoria, Melbourne
Michell Endowment 1985

65 James Gleeson (b.1915)
Preparations at Patmos, 1986
Oil on canvas 183 × 325 cm
Collection of Robert Holmes à Court

66 Irene Barberis (b.1953)
Cherubim, 1987–88
Acrylic on wood 244 × 488 cm
Collection of the artist

67 Alan Oldfield (b.1943)
The Theophany, 1985–87
Oil and acrylic on canvas 137 × 137 cm
Collection of the artist

68 Arthur Boyd (b.1920)
The mining town, 1946–47
Oil and tempera on composition board
87.2 × 109.2 cm
Australian National Gallery, Canberra

69 Arthur Boyd (b.1920)
Angel Spying on Adam and Eve, 1947–48
Oil and tempera on board 86.4 × 122 cm
Private collection, Melbourne

70 Arthur Boyd (b.1920)
Moses Leading the People, 1947
Oil and tempera on board 104 × 122 cm
Private collection, Melbourne

71 Arthur Boyd (b.1920)
The Whale Putting Jonah into Its Mouth, 1950
Ceramic painting 33 × 40.7 cm
National Gallery of Victoria, Melbourne

72 Arthur Boyd (b.1920)
Susanna and the Elders, c.1962
Oil on perspex
Four paintings: each 108 × 113 cm
Private collection, Melbourne

73 Arthur Boyd (b.1920)
Susanna with the Elders, 1945
Oil on canvas 66.8 × 97 cm
Australian National Gallery, Canberra

74 Arthur Boyd (b.1920)
Nebuchadnezzar Running in the Rain, 1968–71
Oil on canvas 174.5 × 183 cm
Australian National Gallery, Canberra
The Arthur Boyd Gift 1975

75 ARTHUR BOYD (b.1920)
Crucifixion, Shoalhaven, 1979–80
Oil on canvas 185 × 177 cm
Collection of the artist

76 ARTHUR BOYD (b.1920)
Crucifixion and Rose, 1979–80
Oil on canvas 155 × 123 cm
Collection of the artist

77 LEONARD FRENCH (b.1928)
The Seven Days, 1964–65
The First Day
Enamel on hessian-covered hardboard
183 × 160 cm
Australian National University, Canberra

78 LEONARD FRENCH (b.1928)
The Second Day
Enamel on hessian-covered hardboard
183 × 160 cm
Australian National University, Canberra

79 LEONARD FRENCH (b.1928)
The Third Day
Enamel on hessian-covered hardboard
183 × 160 cm
Australian National University, Canberra

80 LEONARD FRENCH (b.1928)
The Fourth Day
Enamel on hessian-covered hardboard
183 × 160 cm
Australian National University, Canberra

81 LEONARD FRENCH (b.1928)
The Fifth Day
Enamel on hessian-covered hardboard
183 × 160 cm
Australian National University, Canberra

82 LEONARD FRENCH (b.1928)
The Sixth Day
Enamel on hessian-covered hardboard
183 × 160 cm
Australian National University, Canberra

83 LEONARD FRENCH (b.1928)
The Seventh Day
Enamel on hessian-covered hardboard
Circular, diameter 430 cm
Australian National University, Canberra

84 MITINARI (attrib.) (1929–76)
Galbu clan, Dua moiety
Yirrkala, north-east Arnhem Land
The Thunderman, Djambuwal, 1951
Earth pigments on bark 94 × 45 cm
Collection of Gabrielle Pizzi, Melbourne

85 MATHAMAN (c.1920–70)
Riradjingu clan, Dua moiety
Yirrkala, north-east Arnhem Land
Wagilag Ceremony, 1963
Earth pigments on bark 157.5 × 62.8 cm
National Gallery of Victoria, Melbourne
Presented by Mr J. A. Davidson 1967

86 OLD MICK TJAKAMARA (b.c.1910)
Luritja/Warlpiri
Papunya, central Australia
Old Man's Dreaming on Death or Destiny, 1971
Synthetic polymer on composition board 61.5 × 46 cm
National Gallery of Victoria, Melbourne
Purchased through the Art Foundation of Victoria 1987

87 JOHNNY WARRANGULA TJUPURRULA (b.1918)
Luritja
Papunya, central Australia
A Bush Tucker Story, 1973
Synthetic polymer on composition board
91.5 × 66 cm
National Gallery of Victoria, Melbourne
Purchased through the Art Foundation of Victoria 1987

88 TIM LEURA TJAPALTJARRI (c.1930–84)
Anmatjera/Aranda
Papunya, central Australia
Rock Wallaby Dreaming, 1982
Synthetic polymer on canvas
120 × 179 cm
National Gallery of Victoria, Melbourne
Purchased from Admission Funds 1987

89 TOMMY LOWRY TJAPALTJARRI (c.1940–87)
Pintubi
Kintore, central Australia
Moon Dreaming, 1987
Synthetic polymer on canvas
182.5 × 182.7 cm
Collection of Gabrielle Pizzi, Melbourne

90 ANATJARI TJAMPITJINPA (b.c.1925)
Pintubi
Kintore, central Australia
Tingari Dreaming at Wilkinkarra, 1985
Synthetic polymer on canvas
164 × 46 cm
Collection of Anthony and Beverly Waldegrave-Knight, Melbourne

91 YALA YALA GIBBS TJUNGURRAYI (b.c.1928)
Pintubi
Kintore, central Australia
Tingari Dreaming at Marra-pintinya, 1982
Synthetic polymer on canvas
153.8 × 186 cm
Collection of Gabrielle Pizzi, Melbourne

92 PADDY JUPURRULA NELSON (b.c.1919) and LARRY JUNGARRAYI SPENCER (b.1919)
Warlpiri
Yuendumu, central Australia
Yarla Jukurrpa (Bush Potato Dreaming), 1986
Synthetic polymer on canvas
198 × 170.5 cm
Collection of Gabrielle Pizzi, Melbourne

93 JEANNIE NUNGARRAYI EGAN (b.1947)
Warlpiri
Yuendumu, central Australia
Yarumayi Jukurrpa, 1987
Synthetic polymer on canvas
122 × 91 cm
National Gallery of Victoria, Melbourne
Purchased from Admission Funds 1988

BIBLIOGRAPHY

Books and Articles — Australian

ABBOTT-SMITH, N., *Ian Fairweather*, Queensland University Press, 1978.

ARNOTT, FELIX, *The Church and the Arts*, Transcript Broadcast, 2BL, 13 October 1957.

BAIL, MURRAY, *Ian Fairweather*, Bay Books, Sydney, 1981.

BOASE, T. S. R., *Arthur Boyd: Nebuchadnezzar*, Thames and Hudson, London, 1972.

BUCKLEY, VINCENT, *Leonard French, The Campion Paintings*, Grayflower Publications, Melbourne, 1961.

BUTEL, ELIZABETH, *Margaret Preston*, Penguin Books, 1951.

CLARK, JANE, *Sidney Nolan, Landscapes and Legends*, International Cultural Corporation, Sydney, 1987.

CLARK, KENNETH, MACINNES, COLIN AND ROBERTSON, BRYAN, *Sidney Nolan: The Search for Australian Myth in Painting*, Thames and Hudson, London, 1961.

DIMMACK, MAX, *Noel Counihan*, Melbourne University Press, Melbourne, 1974.

EDWARDS, W. H. (ED.) *Traditional Aboriginal Society: A Reader*, Macmillan, Melbourne, 1987.

FENNESSY, P. M. 'Dodo or Phoenix? The Blake Prize and Australian Religious Art', *Quadrant*, Spring, 1963, pp. 11–20.

FULLER, PETER *The Australian Scapegoat*, University of Western Australia Press, 1986.

GERMAINE, MAX, *Artists and Galleries of Australia*, Boolarong Publications, Brisbane, 1984.

GLEESON, JAMES, *Landscape out of Nature*, The Beagle Press, Sydney, 1987.

HETHERINGTON, JOHN, *Australian Painters: Forty Profiles*, F. M. Cheshire, Melbourne, 1963.

HOFF, URSULA, *The Art of Arthur Boyd*, Andre Deutsch, London, 1986.

HOOD, KENNETH, 'Justin O'Brien', *Art and Australia*, December, 1969, p. 224.

HORTON, M. *Australian Painters of the 70's*, Ure Smith, Sydney, 1976.

HUGHES, ANNETTE, (ED.), *Davida Allen*, M.O.C.A., Brisbane, 1987.

HUGHES, ROBERT, *The Art of Australia*, Penguin Books, England, 1966.

HUGHES, ROBERT, 'The Responsible Blake', *Nation*, 25 March, 1961, p. 20.

LINDSAY, ROBERT, *Vox Pop, Into the Eighties*, National Gallery of Victoria, 1983.

LYNN, ELWYN, 'Avant Garde Painting in Sydney', *Meanjin*, September, 1961, pp. 302–306.

LYNN, ELWYN, *Sidney Nolan: Myth and Imagery*, Macmillan, London, 1967.

MACKIE, ALWYNNE, 'Roger Kemp and meaning in Art', *Art and Australia*, Summer, 1981, pp. 195–200.

MCCAUGHEY, PATRICK, 'Roger Kemp', *Art and Australia*, September, 1970, pp. 143–156.

MCCAUGHEY, PATRICK, *Fred Williams*, Bay Books, 1980.

MCGRATH, SANDRA, *The Artist and the River: Arthur Boyd and the Soalhaven*, Bay Books, Sydney, 1982.

MCGRATH, SANDRA, 'James Gleeson', *Art and Australia*, December 1967, pp. 519–523.

MCGRATH, SANDRA, *Brett Whiteley*, Bay Books, Sydney, 1979.

MCKENZIE, JANET, *Noel Counihan*, Kangaroo Press, N.S.W., 1986.

MCMULLEN, TERENCE, 'Keith Looby: the Artist as Idealist', *Art and Australia*, April–June, 1975, pp. 362–367.

MCQUEEN, HUMPHREY, *Suburbs of the Sacred*, Penguin Books, Australia, 1988.

MAUGHAN, J., ZIMMER, J., *Dot and Circle*, RMIT, Melbourne, 1986.

MENDHAM, DAWN, *The Refining Fire*, Albatross Books, N.S.W., 1987.

MISSINGHAM, HAL, 'Margaret Preston', *Art and Australia*, August, 1963.

MOL, HANS, *Religion in Australia*, Nelson Ltd., Australia, 1971.

MOORE, FELICITY ST JOHN, *Vassilieff*, Oxford University Press, Melbourne, 1982.

OGBURN, JOHN, 'Desiderius Orban', *Art and Australia*, June, 1965, pp. 14–22.

ORBAN, DESIDERIUS, *What is Art All About?* Hicks Smith and Sons, Sydney, 1975.

PHILIPP, FRANZ, *Arthur Boyd*, Thames and Hudson, London, 1967.

PLANT, MARGARET, *John Perceval*, Lansdowne Press, Melbourne, 1971.

RADFORD, RON, *Recent Australian Painting: A Survey 1970–1983*, Art Gallery of South Australia, 1983.

Reed, John, *New Painting*, Longmans, 1963.
Rozen, Alan, *The Art of John Coburn*, Ure Smith, Sydney, 1979.
Scott, Michael, 'Modern Religious Art', *Twentieth Century*, Summer, 1953, pp. 16–22.
Smith, Bernard, *Australian Painting, 1788–1970*, Oxford University Press, Melbourne, 2nd ed., 1971.
Smith, Bernard, *The Death of the Artist as Hero*, Oxford University Press, Melbourne, 1988.
Smith, Terry, 'Colour-Form Painting: Sydney 1965–70'. *Other Voices*, June/July, 1970, pp. 8–17.
Taylor, Paul (ed.), *Anything Goes, Art in Australia 1970–1980*, Art and Text, Melbourne, 1984.
Thomas, Daniel, 'Grace Cossington Smith', *Art and Australia*, March 1967.
Thomas, Laurie, 'Stanislaus Rapotec', *Art and Australia*, September 1970, pp. 126–131.
Uhl, Christopher, *Albert Tucker*, Lansdowne Press, Melbourne, 1969.
Waldman, Diane, *Australian Visions: 1984 EXXON International Exhibition*, Solomon R. Guggenheim Foundation, New York, 1984.
Wurum, Helen Groger, *Australian Aboriginal Bark Paintings and Their Mythological Interpretation*, Vol 1, Institute of Aboriginal Studies, Canberra, 1973.

General

Davies, Hugh, *Sacred Art in a Secular Century*, Liturgical Press, Minnesota, 1978.
Dillenberger, Jane, *Style and Content in Christian Art*, Abingdon Press, New York, 1965.
Dillenberger, John, *A Theology of Artistic Sensibilities*, SCM Press, London, 1986.
Egenter, Richard, *The Desecration of Christ*, Compass, London, 1967.
Focault, Michael, *The Archaeology of Knowledge*, Harper and Row, New York, 1972.
Fuller, Peter, *Images of God*, Chatto and Windus, London, 1985.
Grinten, F. J. van der, Mennekes, Friedhelm, *Menschenbild-Christusbild*, Katholisches Bibelwerk GmbH, Stuttgart, 1984.
Grinten, F. J. van der, Mennekes, Friedhelm, *Mythos und Bibel*, Katholisches Bibelwerk GmbH, Stuttgart, 1985.
Hughes, Robert, *The Shock of the New*, British Broadcasting Corporation, London, 1981.
Kleinbauer, W. E., *Modern Perspectives in Art History*, Holt, Rinehart and Winston, New York, 1971.
Male, Emile, *Religious Art,* Noonday Press, U.S.A., 1972.
Male, Emile, *The Gothic Image*, Fontana, London, 1961.
Maritain, Jacques, *Art and Faith,* Philosophical Library, New York, 1948.
Mathews, Thomas F., 'Tillich on Religious Content in Modern Art', *Art Journal*, XXVII, no. 1, pp. 16–19.
Nairne, Sandy, *State of the Art*, Chatto and Windus, London, 1987.
Rahner, K. (ed.), *Encyclopedia of Theology, the Concise Sacramentum Mundi*, Seabury Press, New York, 1975.
Read, Herbert, *Art and Society*, Schocken, New York, 1966 (first published 1936).
Regamy, P. R., *Religious Art in the Twentieth Century*, Herder, London, 1963.
Rookmaaker, H. R., *Modern Art and the Death of a Culture*, Intervarsity Fellowship, London, 1970.
Rubin, William S., *Modern Sacred Art and the Church at Assy,* Columbia University Press, New York, 1961.
Ruhrberg, Karl, *Twentieth Century Art*, Museum Ludwig, Cologne, 1986.
Rombold, Gunter, Schweebel, Horst, *Christus in der Kunst des 20 Jahrhunderts,* Herder Freiburg, 1983.
Schoonbaert, Lydia, *La Thematique Religieuse, Dans L'Art Belge 1875–1985*, Galerie CGER, Brussels, 1986.
Tuchman, Maurice, *The Spiritual in Art: Abstract Painting* 1890–1985, Abbeville Press, New York, 1986.
Wollheim, Richard, *Painting as an Art*, Princeton University Press, 1987.

INDEX OF ARTISTS

INDEX